ANECDOTES OF
PUBLIC MEN

VOLUME I

ANECDOTES OF
PUBLIC MEN

BY JOHN W. FORNEY

VOLUME I

DA CAPO PRESS • NEW YORK • 1970

A Da Capo Press Reprint Edition

This Da Capo Press edition of *Anecdotes of Public Men* by John W. Forney is an unabridged republication of the first edition published in New York in 1873 and 1881. Volume I is reprinted from a copy owned by The Columbia University Libraries. Volume II is reprinted from a copy owned by the Library of The University of North Carolina in Chapel Hill.

Library of Congress Catalog Card Number 70-87540
SBN 306-71456-6

Published by Da Capo Press
A Division of Plenum Publishing Corporation
227 West 17th Street
New York, N. Y. 10011
All rights reserved

Manufactured in the United States of America

ANECDOTES

OF

PUBLIC MEN

BY

JOHN W. FORNEY

WHILE HE WAS

CLERK OF THE HOUSE OF REPRESENTATIVES
SECRETARY OF THE SENATE OF THE UNITED STATES
EDITOR OF THE ORGAN OF THE DEMOCRATIC PARTY (THE WASHINGTON DAILY UNION)
FROM 1851 TO 1855
AND EDITOR OF THE ORGAN OF THE REPUBLICAN PARTY
(THE WASHINGTON DAILY CHRONICLE)
FROM 1862 TO 1868

Volume I.

NEW YORK

HARPER & BROTHERS, FRANKLIN SQUARE

TO

DANIEL DOUGHERTY:

UNFORGOTTEN AND UNFORGETTING.

———

I HAVE known you, my dear Dougherty, for nearly thirty years; when your hair, now turning gray, was glossy black; when both of us were struggling young men. You have met most of the characters I have attempted to describe in these plain and unpretending " Anecdotes," and I feel that I take no liberty in dedicating this volume to you. From Franklin Pierce to Ulysses S. Grant, including most of the intermediate actors, whether statesmen or lawyers, soldiers or politicians, men of work or men of leisure, the artist or the artisan, the priest or the player, you can at least do justice to the motive that has led me to speak of all of them impartially and generously. Instead of One Hundred Anecdotes of Public Men, as originally intended, you will find interwoven into these pages four times as many references to the characters who figured in the past and will be remembered in the future. One lesson I have tried to inculcate: that while none of us are indispensable, the good we do in our life is sure to be kindly, even if briefly, remembered after that life ends. And still another lesson, so well taught in your own career—the lesson of self-reliance, of sincere friendship, of personal independence and integrity, of toleration and forbearance. It is a maxim, that when men begin to write their recollections they are getting old; but you have taught me in our long and unbroken devotion to each other that nothing keeps the heart so young and so fresh as the habit of reviving the best deeds of our fellow-creatures and forgetting the worst. As I glance through these chapters, written hastily, often in the rush of editorial work, I am surprised to realize how much one man can condense into a letter repeated every week for over two years; and if those who read this book will enjoy as much pleasure in perusing it as I did in writing it, and will sympathize with me in the spirit with which it was composed, I shall be abundantly compensated.

J. W. FORNEY.

PHILADELPHIA, *June* 2, 1873.

ANECDOTES OF PUBLIC MEN.

I.

In 1850, after the triumph of the Compromise Measures, Henry Clay visited Philadelphia, and stayed at the American House, on Chestnut Street, opposite Independence Hall. As I had supported these Measures in opposition to the extreme followers of the Southern Democrats, in the columns of *The Pennsylvanian*, I felt anxious to call on Mr. Clay, the leader of that his last great work. Ex-Mayor John Swift, who is still living in Philadelphia, in the 84th year of his age, dropped in at my editorial rooms the morning after Mr. Clay's arrival, in company with my esteemed friend, Edwin Forrest, the tragedian. Mr. Swift, who had been one of Mr. Clay's active and unselfish champions, gladly acceded to my request to be presented to Mr. Clay, whom I had never met, and had firmly opposed when he was the Whig candidate for the Presidency in 1844. Forrest expressed the wish to accompany us; so we three walked over to the hotel and sent up our cards, and were quickly admitted to the great man's parlor. He looked feeble and worn —he was then over seventy-three years old—but he soon brightened. Anxious to rouse him, I quietly ventured to suggest that I had heard the speech of Pierre Soulé, Senator in Congress from Louisiana—an extremist especially distasteful to Mr. Clay—and that I thought it a very thorough and able presentation of the side adverse to the Compromise Measures. I saw the old man's eye flash as I spoke, and was not surprised when, with much vehemence, he proceeded to denounce Soulé. After denying that he was a statesman, and insisting that there were others far more effective in the opposition, he wound up by saying: " He is nothing but an actor, sir—a mere actor." Then suddenly recollecting the presence of our favorite trage- dian, he dropped his tone, and waved his hand, as he turned to Mr. Forrest—"*I mean, my dear sir, a mere French actor !*" We soon after took our leave, and as we descended the stairs, For- rest turned to Mr. Swift and myself, and said: " Mr. Clay has proved, by the skill with which he can change his manner, and the grace with which he can make an apology, that he is a better actor than Soulé !"

I never met Daniel Webster, as was natural on account of my connection with the Democratic party, but I often recall two incidents in connection with him. It was, I think, about the time Robert J. Walker's tariff of 1846 was passed that he came to Philadelphia, and stopped at Hartwell's Washington House, on Chestnut Street, above Seventh, the guest of the Whigs, whom he addressed at a splendid banquet in the cele- brated Chinese Museum, on Ninth Street. Extensive prepara- tions had been made for the occasion. The company was nu- merous, including hundreds of ladies in the galleries, the feast superb, the wines delicious, and Mr. Webster did not rise to re- spond to the toast in his honor till late in the evening. Short- hand reporting was not then what it is now, a swift, accurate, and magical science ; and I knew the Whig papers, which re- solved to print the great man's speech entire, would be delayed till long past their usual hour next morning. The town was hungry to see it, and its surprise may be readily conceived when at dawn of the succeeding day *The Pennsylvanian*, the Demo- cratic organ, then under my direction, appeared with Mr. "Web- ster's Great Speech on the Tariff." I had taken his old speech on free trade, delivered in 1824, when he was a member of the House, and converted it into a Supplement, of which many thousands were printed and sold before the joke was discovered. The Democrats were delighted—the Whigs furious, especially Mr. Greeley, of *The Tribune*, who had come over to hear Mr. Webster, and who bought several copies of the old speech, thinking it the new one. But Mr. Webster enjoyed it hugely; and when his friend, George Ashmun, handed him my Extra, he laughed heartily, and said, " I think Forney has printed a much better speech than the one I made last night." Was not that genuine manliness? The other incident happened after his defeat for the Whig nomination for President in 1852. I was then Clerk of the House of Representatives of the United States, and one of the editors of the *Washington Union*, published by that fine specimen of manhood, General Robert Armstrong, of Tennessee. Every body knew that Mr. Webster keenly felt his rejection by the party he had so honored and served. The brilliant effort of Rufus Choate to make him the candidate in the Baltimore Whig National Convention, though ineffectual to prevent the foreordained selection of the brave but vain-glorious Scott, had gone to the hearts of the people, adding not only to the grief of Mr. Webster's friends, but, as the result proved, to the forces of the Democrats, who were largely assisted by their old opponents in the ensuing election which made Franklin Pierce President. Indifferent to or ignorant of this fact, a large concourse of the Whigs of Washington City concluded to serenade Mr. Webster at his residence on Louisiana Avenue. I followed the procession. It was an exquisite moonlight summer evening. The crowd was dense ; the music delicious; the cheers inspiring. A long time elapsed before the statesman appeared, and when he did he looked like another Coriolanus. Robed in his dressing-gown, he spoke a few minutes, but in a manner I shall never forget. His voice, always clear and sonorous, rolled with deeper volume over the crowd. There was no bitterness, but an inexpressible sadness in his words, and when he bade them good-night, and said he should sleep well and rise with the lark at the purpling of the dawn—dropping no syllable in favor of General Scott—the serenaders retired as if they had heard a funeral sermon. I walked to my editorial den and wrote a leader on the scene, so full of the emptiness of human ambition and the ingratitude of political parties. The following verse from Byron closed the article :

> "As the struck eagle, stretched upon the plain,
> No more through rolling clouds to soar again,
> Viewed his own feather on the fatal dart,
> And winged the shaft that quivered in his heart,
> Keen were his pangs, but keener far to feel
> He nursed the pinion which impell'd the steel ;
> While the same plumage that had warmed his nest,
> Drank the last life-blood of his bleeding breast."

Franklin Pierce succeeded to the Presidency in 1853, aided by many Old-line Whigs and by most of the Anti-slavery Democrats now in the Republican ranks. The political events of his administration are historical. Let me say a word about the man. He was at once the kindest, most courteous, and most considerate public officer I ever knew. As President he was a model of high breeding. Receptive, cordial, hospitable to his political friends, he delighted to welcome his political adversaries, and to make them at home. Let me give one specimen of his liberality. It was my misfortune to differ from the Southern leaders at an early day, and they resolved to defeat my reelection as Clerk of the House. My mistaken " Forrest Letter " was made their pretext. I say mistaken, for, though I wrote it with the most honest purpose, I did not venture to defend the unjust but plausible construction that I had written it to obtain false testimony against a woman. My friends, and none more than Mr. Forrest himself, knew the motive that prompted me ; but I have never stopped to explain it. That letter was seized upon by the Southern leaders, who knew my settled determination to resist the further encroachments of slavery ; and they used it with so much effect that my defeat was believed to be sure.

On the night of the caucus, President Pierce sent for me and told me that he believed I could not be renominated, but that he was resolved, if I was not, to send my name into the Senate for an important mission to one of the South American States. I got through the struggle triumphantly, but I can never forget the act of the man who, in the darkest hour, extended his helping hand. Nor did his magnanimity stop here. Many of his adherents believed I ought to have supported him for President in 1856, when his name was used as a candidate for re-election; but he said: "I do not complain of you, my friend, for going with your State for Mr. Buchanan, whom you have known so long, though I fear you will be disappointed if he is President." I could not approve the removal of Governor Reeder, of Kansas, for his refusal to help to make Kansas a slave State, in 1854, '5, any more than I could the removal by Mr. Buchanan of Governor Walker, in 1858, for his refusal to sanction the Lecompton frauds; but how different the toleration of Pierce from the persecution of his successor. While the whole Democratic press was denouncing Reeder and applauding his removal, President Pierce did not ask me to join in the crusade against my friend, and the *Washington Union*, of which I was then the editor, contained no line from my pen against him. Five years later I was proscribed and hunted down, simply because I would not sanction a proceeding far more despotic and unjust. While I was in the midst of this struggle with the Administration of Mr. Buchanan, I visited New England to see ex-President Pierce. He was, as usual, in earnest sympathy with the extreme South; but he received me and treated me like a brother, and the day I spent with him lives in my memory like a picture painted by angel hands.

As I find leisure I will try to give you a few more anecdotes of the public men I have met or known, or heard others speak of. These recollections will be free from personal or partisan prejudice. I propose to show that many of those who have served the State, however abused and misrepresented, were not without the elements of a true humanity.

[January 15, 1871.]

II.

THERE is no habit of modern education so happy as that of keeping a regular diary of events. It provides the choicest of all historical material. Pleasant to cultivate, it constitutes the most profitable and pleasant of all our reading. From Pepys, in 1669, to Crabb Robinson, in 1869, with the intermediate works of Barrington, Boswell's Johnson, and Walpole's Letters—nothing survives so entirely the wreck and waste of time as these daily and delightful records of human experience. It is said that the journal of John Quincy Adams is the best monument of his stupendous industry. He kept it during all the working years of his working life. Reared to scholarship, diplomacy, and statecraft, he began it with his youth, and to the final hour, when he exclaimed, "This is the last of earth," ob‧ served the custom. The rare summary of the second President of a really great family, covering nearly two generations, has not yet seen the light, and will not, I understand, till most of the actors of whom it treats, doubtless with caustic freedom, have been gathered to their fathers. Other Presidents and statesmen were not so industrious, with perhaps the possible exception of Mr. Buchanan, whose biography has not appeared, owing to unexpected events. When it is published, we have his own pledge that it will be unstained by the use of any private correspondence, as we have the assurance from the high abilities of Hon. W. B. Reed, the gentleman selected to prepare it, that it will be a production of consummate interest. The diary of Mr. Buchanan will be a treasure to his historian.

One realizes the broad distinction between memory and memoranda, in the attempt to make the one a substitute for the other. The written record of a Life, which is a photograph of every day's doings, is incomparably superior to the faded and fading images of the mind. Hence the failure of those who give dates and names from their unaided recollections. If I do not fall into this error in these familiar sketches, it will be because I shall adventure nothing calculated to give offense, nothing not susceptible of easy vindication and general credence.

But I must emphasize the suggestion that our young men and young women can employ one or two hours every day no more agreeably and usefully than by keeping a journal. Begun after school-time while they are boys and girls, and continued as they advance in life, it will be at once monitor and guide to themselves, and may be of incalculable value in the crystallization of history.

I remember a dinner-party at the time I lived in Washington during the administration of General Pierce, which requires no diary to keep fresh in my heart. It took place at my residence, and in the house now known as the Waverley, on Eighth Street, back of *The Chronicle* office, where I resided up to 1856, when I left Washington to help make Mr. Buchanan President, and never returned, save to join in the work of overthrowing him after he broke the promise of justice to Kansas, which alone elected him. There were present some twenty of the leaders of the Democratic party, North and South, among them Mr. Slidell, Mr. Breckinridge, and I think Mr. Douglas. One of my guests was Dr. William Elder, my friend at that day, though we differed widely about slavery, just as he is to-day, when we closely agree in opposing it. I had met him on a former visit to Philadelphia, and invited him to come to Washington and sojourn under my roof. He came on the evening before the

party in question, somewhat to the consternation of those of
my family who knew his pronounced abolitionism, and the
equally pronounced pro-slavery views of those who were to
dine with me next day. But there was no help for it; indeed,
I was glad to meet the gifted and polished Doctor. My own
mind was far from clear as to the justice of the course of my
party in regard to Kansas, and I made no concealment of my
doubts. The angry protests of the North against that contemplated villainy were being heard in the elections. The Democracy had just been unhorsed, right and left, North and South,
by the Know-Nothing storm, and the old leaders knew that
meant something more than hostility to foreigners and Catholics, and was in fact the first mutterings of a far greater tempest. The Southern leaders of the day were not yet ready to
hazard a rebellion. They were eager to conciliate Northern
anti-slavery men ; and those I knew were always gentlemen in
social life. This was especially so with Slidell, Benjamin,
Breckinridge, Cobb, etc. And so, when the restraint of the
first course or two was thawed by a generous draught of champagne, those who sat at my board were quickly attracted by the
agreeable manners and dazzling wit of my abolition friend. He
gradually monopolized their whole attention by his comments
on books and men, and his full knowledge of the resources of
their own section.

At last one of them said, " Pray, Doctor Elder, how is it that
one of your tastes and learning should be so opposed to Southern rights and institutions?" That opened the ball, and, nothing loth, he answered with a story I can never forget; a story
which I believe has never been forgotten by any one who heard
it: "When I lived in Pittsburgh, gentlemen," said the Doctor,
"where I had the honor to vote for James G. Birney for President in 1844, being one of a very, very small party, which will
soon control Pennsylvania by an Andrew Jackson majority, we
had a strange character among us who occasionally made

speeches against slavery, and whose peculiarities were that when he became excited he gave way to uncontrollable tears and oaths. I always went to hear him, for there was an odd fascination about him. One night he was advertised to speak against the fugitive-slave law—a measure which roused him almost to madness—and I was among the audience. He closed his harangue with a passage something like this: 'Let us apply this law to ourselves, brethren and sisters. I live about a mile out of town, and rarely get back to my quiet home till evening; and the first to welcome me at the garden-gate are my little girl Mary and my bright-eyed son Willie—the joy of my heart, the stars of my life. Suppose, when I get home to-morrow, I meet my wife, instead of my children, at the door, and on asking for my darlings, she tells me that a man called John C. Calhoun, of South Carolina, and another man called Henry Clay, of Kentucky, had come, in my absence, and carried them down South into slavery? How would you feel in such a case? How do you think I would feel? What would I do? you ask. Well, I will tell you. I would follow the aforesaid John C. Calhoun and Henry Clay; follow them to the South; follow them to the gates of death and hell; yes, into hell, and there cram the red-hot coals down their d—d, infernal throats!'

"And this outburst," added Dr. Elder, "was punctuated with alternate sobs and swearing. I have given you one of the many causes, gentlemen, that have confirmed me in my abolitionism."

It is impossible to convey an idea of the manner in which Dr. Elder told this incident, or the effect produced upon the Southern men around him. They listened with profound and breathless interest, and more than one with a pale cheek and moistened eye; and though they did not say they agreed with the eloquent Doctor, I saw that they respected him for the candor and warmth with which he had replied to their equally candid question.

[January 22, 1871.]

III.

In Theodore Parker's frank and sympathetic analysis of the character of George Washington, he speaks of his skill and good fortune in the selection and purchase of real estate, and his fine forecast of the destiny of Virginia and the West. In this respect Stephen A. Douglas resembled the Father of his Country. He had an inspiration for land, and he delighted to tell his friends what his country must be in the course of years, if our wilderness were opened up by wise and generous legislation. He had none of the small arts that would dwarf great enterprises by counting the profits of those who led in them. He justly believed that where there are large risks there should be large recompense. I remember—who of middle age does not?—when the proposition made to tax the people of Philadelphia and the State for the construction of the Pennsylvania Central roused a hurricane of opposition. We were overwhelmed by sinister prophecies; and yet the seed sown by the success of that proposition has already produced a work which in another generation will carry the trade of the Orient through Philadelphia, and open to it a commerce with Europe infinitely greater than any ever dreamed of in our wildest aspirations. The Pennsylvania Central, like the Mississippi River, is fed by many branches, which it feeds in turn, and with its manifold tributaries capable of extending itself to all the nations of the South, giving wealth to them in bounteous supply, and receiving in exchange other riches and bounties. Had the bold, brave men who first pushed it failed, their reputations would have rotted in the category of the projectors who began other magnificent schemes in other centuries, and broke only because they were ahead of their time.

Stephen A. Douglas died too soon, for many reasons, and chiefly because, had he lived, he would have enjoyed the ripe fulfillment of many of his predictions and labors. But I began this sketch rather to relate an incident illustrative of his kindness to his friends than of his extraordinary prescience in the matter of the development of the public domain.

He had, as I have said, the inspiration of the soil. To him I am indebted for my first and only speculation—the better to be recollected because it was successful. And the incident is the more interesting because, just now, the region where I made my money is the point whence one of those empire lines is going forth to penetrate the wilderness and to convert it into a garden—I mean the North Pacific Railroad. I suspect that the Civilizer and Christianizer Jay Cooke, who pioneers this mighty work, was nearly as poor a man as I was when Stephen A. Douglas came to me one day in 1853, and said, looking up at the map, "How would you like to buy a share in Superior City, at Fond du Lac, the head of Lake Superior?" and, before I could answer, he got on a chair and told me that from that point, or near it, would start the greatest railroad in the world, except the one on the thirty-second parallel, just surveyed by Captains George B. McClellan, John Pope, and others, which was to open up the South. "But," I said, "old fellow, I have no money, and to buy a share in the proposed location will require much." "No," he replied, "I can secure you one for $2500, and you can divide it with ——," naming one of the best of the future Confederates, "and he will be greatly obliged." I knew nothing of the location, had never been there, had no money of my own, but I saw Judge Douglas was in earnest and wanted to serve me, and when he left, I borrowed the $2500, bought a share, divided it with the Southern gentleman referred to, who honorably paid his $1250; and after cutting my share into five parts, sold and gave three fifths to other friends, and with my two fifths bought the Waverley House, in Washington. The proceeds of my moiety of the one share of Superior City realized $21,000. For that I was indebted to Stephen A. Douglas—God bless him! I believe my Confederate friend has held on to his interest, and I shall be glad if he is as fortunate as I was. Duluth is now the fashion, and I wish it all success, because it can not grow rich without reflecting some of its wealth upon Superior City, its near neighbor.

In 1868, the Republicans of Pennsylvania, by a unanimous vote, put me at the head of their delegation to the Republican National Convention, to vote for General Grant as their candidate for President. The first thing I did, after getting to Chicago, was to go out to look on the monument to Stephen A. Douglas, on the shore of Lake Michigan ; the next to visit the massive buildings of the Illinois Central Railroad Company, the enterprise which he alone carried through Congress. The monument was not complete, but the palatial edifices of the railroad were. I could not help it, but when I remembered how in Paris and London, just the year before, I had seen Illinois Central securities quoted among the consols of the oldest governments, and that that road was enriching all connected with it—I say I could not help, as I thought of these things, drawing the contrast between the vital and vigorous championship of Douglas of this stupendous work and the studied neglect of his memory by those who have profited by it. After passing through the magnificent dépôt and the adjacent buildings, I said to an employé, "Who owns the most stock in the Illinois Central ?" " Indeed, I do not know, sir," was his reply. " Well, my friend, I think the man who ought to own the most of it, and whose children should be most benefited by it, was Stephen A. Douglas." I think the man may have heard of Douglas, but it was clear to me, from his look, that he thought I was a lunatic.

[January 29, 1871.]

IV.

MANY of our public men are capital amateur editors. Thomas H. Benton was a valuable and vigorous contributor to *The Globe* in the war upon the United States Bank. His style was trenchant and elevated, and his facts generally impregnable. James Buchanan was a frequent writer in my old paper, *The Lancaster Intelligencer & Journal,* and in *The Pennsylvanian.* His diction was cold and unsympathetic, but exact, clear, and condensed. His precise and elegant chirography was the delight of the compositors. Judge Douglas wrote little, but suggested much. His mind teemed with "points." I never spent an hour with him which did not furnish me with new ideas. He grasped and understood most questions thoroughly. When he read was always a mystery. Social to a degree, dining out almost daily when not entertaining his friends at his own hospitable home, visiting strangers at their hotels, leading in debate or counseling in committee, he was rarely at fault for a date or a fact. He was a treasure to an editor, because he possessed the rare faculty of throwing new light upon every subject in the shortest possible time. Ex-Attorney-General J. S. Black would have made a superb journalist, and was a ready and useful contributor. His style was terse, fresh, and scholarly. Caleb Cushing is another statesman who once delighted in editorial writing, and still occasionally varies his heavy professional toil by the same agreeable relaxation. I have known him to stand up to his tall desk and dash off column after column on foreign and domestic politics, on art, on finance, with astonishing rapidity and ease. Unlike his aggressive successor, General Cushing is anxious to end his career at peace with all the world. It is said that he is now receiving more money for legal services than any man in his profession. Of course his labors are heavy, but he lightens them by his calm and cheerful philosophy, his cultivated literary tastes, and his love of the society of the tolerant and refined.

Writing of Thomas H. Benton recalls an incident that happened during the Presidency of James K. Polk, when Mr. Buchanan was Secretary of State. Colonel Benton was a sharp thorn in the side of the Administration on the Oregon question. His criticism was merciless, and stung the President and his premier to the quick. Accordingly *The Pennsylvanian* was called upon to review his positions, which was done in three articles that bore, he thought, distinct official ear-marks. Indignant at my temerity, he addressed me a curt note, demanding the name of the author of the articles and threatening a Senatorial investigation. I responded by assuming the whole responsibility, and took the train for Washington to anticipate and watch events. I quartered, as usual, with Mr. Buchanan, and there waited for the summons. None came, however. Just before returning to my post in Philadelphia I was invited to a reception at the British Minister's, and in one of the currents of the throng was carried into a corner where they were serving out the seductive compound known as Roman punch. I had hardly got a glass of it in my hand when I found myself in the presence of Colonel Benton. He greeted me kindly, and as we enjoyed our punch he quietly remarked, " I got your letter, but I did not proceed because I know you assumed the responsibility that belonged to another." It is needless to add that the Secretary of State was as much relieved as I was by the majestical Missouri Senator.

Although Buchanan and Benton never were intimate friends, the latter went to Cincinnati in 1856 to advocate Buchanan as the Democratic candidate for President, and supported him when nominated against his own son-in-law, General John C. Fremont. Nobody was more surprised than Buchanan himself. He knew that Benton disliked him as sincerely as he esteemed General Fremont. But the matter was easily explained. The

Missouri statesman believed that the Pennsylvanian candidate would, if elected, be true to the great work of justice to Kansas; that he would check the design of forcing slavery into that Territory; and that he would tranquilize the country by arresting the sectional tendencies of the times. He lived, like hundreds of thousands of others, to realize his mistake; but he passed off before the war that resulted from the absence of a little courage to maintain the most solemn pledge ever made to a confiding people. Thomas Hart Benton died the 10th of April, 1858.

[February 4, 1871.]

V.

DAVID C. BRODERICK, of California, was in some respects a remarkable character. Born in the District of Columbia in 1818, and killed in a duel in September of 1859, his short career was a succession of strange events. Twenty-five years of it were spent in New York in the rudest scenes, and more than ten among the turbulent men who then, as now, dominated over that great city. Of these he became the early and imperious leader—a leader blindly followed and blindly obeyed. But he never fell into their habits of dissipation, and perhaps his unbroken command over them resulted from his silent and sober nature. The foreman of a fire-company and the keeper of a saloon, he never lost his dignity, but would retire to his books whenever he had a moment of leisure. Removing to California in 1849, he quickly secured the confidence of the people, and was elected by them to high and honorable positions. He was a useful member of the convention that adopted the first California constitution, and was two years in the State Senate, and president of that body. In 1856 he was elected a Senator

in Congress for six years from the 4th of March, 1857. I had
seen him but once before, in 1848, when Mr. Edwin Croswell,
the well-known editor of the *Albany Argus,* who is still living
in New York, greatly esteemed for his amiability and learning,
visited my office in his company ; but when I met him a second time in Philadelphia, after his triumph and that of Mr. Buchanan, to whose Presidential aspirations he had given such
effective aid, I felt as if I had known him intimately from boyhood. We were nearly the same age, and had supported Mr.
Buchanan from the same motive—that of settling the slavery
question, at least for the time, by even-handed justice to the
people of Kansas. California had been a secession rendezvous from the day it became a part of the Union, but the
Southern leaders there soon found in Broderick a stubborn and
a dangerous enemy. His rough New York schooling had made
him especially abhorrent of obedience to such tyrants, and so
he grappled with them promptly. In a little more than six
years he mounted over their heads into the most important
offices, and when he elected himself to the United States Senate he also magnanimously elected his adversary, Dr. W. M.
Gwin, for the short term. But he was not long in Washington
before he realized that the new President was his foe, and that
the solemn pledge of justice to Kansas was not to be maintained. The national patronage on the Pacific slope was con-
centrated in the hands of his colleague, and the young Senator
began his career by finding his friends stripped of the power
they had fairly won.

The disappointment was grievous, but it called out all his better nature. He devoted himself to his studies and his duties
with renewed assiduity. He always lived like a gentleman.
Generous to a fault, he delighted to have his friends around
him. His bearing, his dress, his language, indicated none of
the hard experience of his youth. He was fond of books, and
was a rare judge of men. I have his picture before me as I

write, and as I look into his dark eyes and watch his firm-set mouth I almost see the flash of the one and hear the good sense that often came from the other.

There were not many of us in the Democratic ranks to stand up for fair play to Kansas. We started with a goodly array, but the offices of the Executive were too much for most of our associates, and when the final struggle came we were a corporal's guard indeed. Broderick was the soul of our little party. I understood how he managed men in New York and California as I watched his intercourse with Senators and Representatives in that trying crisis. Some he would persuade, others he would denounce. He seemed to know the especial weakness to address; but nothing was more potent than his appeal to the constituency of the hesitating member. "I tell you," he used to say to such as doubted, "you can make more reputation by being an honest man instead of a rascal."

Broderick was one of the few "self-made" men who did not boast of having been a mechanic. He was not like a famous ex-President who delighted to speak of his rise from the tailor's bench. He did not think a man any worse for having worked for his living at a trade, nor did he believe him any better. And this theory sprang from the belief that the laboring men of America are seldom true to the bright minds so often reared among them. His memorable words in reply to the haughty Hammond of South Carolina, on the 22d of March, 1858, after the latter had spoken of the producing class of the North as the "mudsills" of society, illustrate this theory. Mr. Broderick said:

"I, sir, am glad that the Senator has spoken thus. It may have the effect of arousing in the working men that spirit that has been lying dormant for centuries. It may also have the effect of arousing the two hundred thousand men with pure skins in South Carolina, who are now degraded and despised by thirty thousand aristocratic slaveholders. It may teach them to demand what is the power—

> "'Link'd with success, assumed and kept with skill,
> That moulds another's weakness to its will;
> Wields with their hands, but still to them unknown,
> Makes even their mightiest deeds appear his own.'

"I suppose, sir, the Senator from South Carolina did not intend to be personal in his remarks to any of his peers upon
this floor.   If I had thought so I would have noticed them at
the time.   I am, sir, with one exception, the youngest in years
of the Senators upon this floor.   It is not long since I served
an apprenticeship of five years at one of the most laborious mechanical trades pursued by man—a trade that from its nature
devotes its follower to thought, but debars him from conversation.   I would not have alluded to this if it were not for the remarks of the Senator from South Carolina; and the thousands
who know that I am the son of an artisan and have been a mechanic, would feel disappointed in me if I did not reply to him.
I am not proud of this.   I am sorry it is true.   I would that I
could have enjoyed the pleasures of life in my boyhood days;
but they were denied to me.   I say this with pain.   I have not
the admiration for the men of the class from which I sprang
that might be expected; they submit too tamely to oppression,
and are prone to neglect their rights and duties as citizens.
But, sir, the class of society to whose toil I was born, under our
form of government, will control the destinies of this nation.
If I were inclined to forget my connection with them, or to deny
that I sprang from them, this chamber would not be the place
in which I could do either.   While I hold a seat I have but to
look at the beautiful capitals adorning the pilasters that support this roof, to be reminded of my father's talent and to see
his handiwork.

"I left the scenes of my youth and manhood for the 'Far
West' because I was tired of the struggles and jealousies of
men of my class, who could not understand why one of their
fellows should seek to elevate his condition upon the common

level. I made my new abode among strangers, where labor is honored. I had left without regret; there remained no tie of blood to bind me to any being in existence. *If I fell in the struggle for reputation and fortune, there was no relative on earth to mourn my fall.* The people of California elevated me to the highest office within their gift. My election was not the result of an accident. For years I had to struggle, often seeing the goal of ambition within my reach; it was again and again taken from me by the aid of men of my own class. I had not only them to contend with, but almost the entire partisan press of my state was subsidized by Government money and patronage to oppose my election. I sincerely hope, sir, the time will come when such speeches as that from the Senator from South Carolina will be considered a lesson to the laborers of the nation."

Prophetic words indeed!

The last time I saw Broderick was one night in April, 1859, at the corner of Sixth and Chestnut Streets, Philadelphia, where he took the omnibus to the New York dépôt, intending to sail in a few days for San Francisco. The shadow of his fate was upon him. He was much depressed. We had broken the Administration party to pieces in most of the Northern States, obliterated the pro-slavery majority in the House, and had given prospective and substantial freedom to Kansas. Our little phalanx had made a breach in the columns of the Democracy that was to widen into a chasm never to be closed. California was to vote on the 7th of September, and Broderick was going back to meet his people. His magnificent campaign against the Southern policy of forcing slavery into Kansas had aroused the bitterest resentment, and the worst elements were organized against him in his own State. "I feel, my dear friend, that we shall never meet again. I go home to die. I shall abate no jot of my faith. I shall be challenged, I shall fight, and I shall be killed." These were his words. I tried to rally him on these forebodings; told him he was young and brave, and would live to be even more honored in the years to come. "No," he said, with a sad smile I shall never forget; "no, it is best; I am doomed. You will live to write of me and to keep my memory green; and now good-by forever." On the 7th of September, the very day of the election, I predicted the duel which took place on the 13th of the same month, and on the 16th my poor friend died from a wound received at the hands of the pro-slavery Democrat leader, David S. Terry, who was living at the last accounts in the State of Nevada. The Democrats carried the election on the 7th, and the heroic Broderick died on the 16th. But the blood of the martyr was the seed of the redemption of California. The people rose at the sight of a tragedy so deliberate, fore-planned, and anticipated. Had Broderick fallen before the election of 1859 California would have repudiated the Buchanan Administration. He himself postponed the duel till the ballots were cast, and then he passed to his death. But that death saved California to the Union. The traitors who tried to hand her over to the rebellion were baffled by the uprising that followed his sacrifice. The Broderick Democrats joined the Republicans and held California fast to her allegiance, and so proved at once their love of their great country and their gratitude to their unselfish leader.

[February 12, 1871.]

VI.

It is one of the penalties, if penalty it be, of those who abstain from national affairs, that they are rarely heard of outside their own vicinage. Many a mediocrity becomes a celebrity when his name figures in the Congressional yeas and nays, just as many a nobler intellect remains rooted to the spot of its birth, full of knowledge of a world that knows it not. There is hardly a county in the United States of which this statement is not true, more or less. There is not a reader of these sketches who can not point out eminent men of his own acquaintance who would suffer for want of national reputation if they had not studiously disregarded it, and honestly preferred the comforts of home and the golden opinions of their own neighbors.

Two men lived in Pennsylvania a little more than twenty years ago who came partly within this category. They were, indeed, known far beyond their vicinity; but as they did not seek for notoriety, they are not as well remembered as if they had been aspirants for Congressional honors. I refer to Robert T. Conrad, of Philadelphia, and George Washington Barton, of Lancaster, Pennsylvania. They differed in almost every thing. Conrad, in his prime, was a model of manly beauty. His auburn hair, his delicate complexion, his musical voice, made a strong contrast with the tall, somewhat ungainly figure, swarthy skin, black hair, and discordant tones of Barton. Conrad was a Whig, Barton was a Democrat; and though frequently in conflict, they were, the best part of their lives, devoted friends. I knew them and loved them both, and as I never shared in their temporary differences, I was always a sort of peacemaker between them. Their very incongruities seemed to attract them to each other. Barton and myself were born in the same town, and for many years his star shone unrivaled as a consummate orator. Conrad came along from Philadelphia as a lecturer and Whig speaker. He was as much the idol of his party as Barton was of ours. They seemed to "take to" each other from the first, and when Barton moved to Philadelphia and was associated with Conrad in the local judiciary, they became almost constant companions. They were born in the same year, 1810, and died all too early, for their gifts were precious indeed, and deserved to be enjoyed for a long time alike by themselves and their country. Conrad lived until 1858, when he was forty-eight years old; and Barton is supposed to have been drowned in the Bay of San Francisco, on the 25th of January, 1851, when he was only forty-one. Yet, short as their experiences were, they are remembered by thousands as among the most brilliant in the records of human genius.

As my sketches are not biographies in any sense, but rather glances at public men, I will not, therefore, follow these experiences in detail, but confine myself to a few instances of marked individuality, more to show how much real merit is found outside of the National Councils than to do justice to extraordinary talents. *That* is a duty I should conceive it a special honor to discharge if I had at once the material and the ability.

Barton was an orator I have never heard surpassed in either House of Congress, and I may safely say this, as I never heard Henry Clay. He lived, unhappily, in the days when shorthand reporting was in its infancy. His utterance was so rapid, his retorts so quick, his humor so eccentric, that it would have required a rare adept to follow him.

He was the favorite of every social circle—was sought after for his wit, his scholarship, and his memory. Mr. Buchanan delighted to have him at his frequent dinner-parties, and to introduce him to his distinguished guests as a prodigy. He read much and recollected every thing, and thus acquired a style all his own. His declamation was peculiar to himself, but his English was exact and pure. Rich and figurative to a degree, it was always classic and correct. Some of his similes and outbursts, if reported at the time, would survive like the best of Curran, Phillips, or Webster. He resembled Rufus Choate in astonishing rapidity of speech and in splendor of diction. How often I have regretted that his memorable passages were not preserved. The courts of Pennsylvania and the Democratic conventions resounded with his unparalleled eloquence, and when he reached San Francisco he leaped into a practice that promised to lead all others. His last speech in that city is still spoken of as one never equaled and never forgotten. I will

not attempt to give an idea of one of the many I recollect, for
fear of doing injustice to his very great talents. His respected
widow, living in Philadelphia, has some of his MSS. in her possession, and will, I hope, soon present a memoir of her gifted
husband. Conrad was more fortunate. He printed much that he spoke
and wrote. He was the editor of the *Philadelphia North American* for a time, while I was editor of the *Philadelphia Pennsylvanian*, and we had many exciting controversies. The Whigs
were sure that he had the best of me during the Mexican war,
and the Democrats were as sure I had the best of him: but
neither side knew that more than once the severest things we
said of each other were written when we were dining together
at the same table, and in the midst of mutual discussion and
good nature. There were not many days of that heated and
angry period that we did not meet as bosom friends; and
when his last remains were borne to their repose, I followed
among those who mourned the loss of one of the richest intellects and warmest hearts in the ranks of men. Few did more
varied labor in life. He was a splendid journalist, orator, and
dramatist, and alternated from one practical post to the other;
was a good judge, a brave mayor of Philadelphia, and a vigorous railroad president. He lives in some of the finest lyrics of
the language, and in his great play of "Jack Cade," which holds
the stage with tenacious popularity. Had he figured in Congress he would be classed among the Wirts, the Prentisses, the
Benjamins, and the Prestons, masters, as they were, of the
school of graceful eloquence, precisely as Barton would have
figured among the original Randolphs, the sarcastic McDuffies,
the imperious Marshalls, and the fiery Poindexters.

[February 19, 1871.]

VII.

THE 3d of February, 1860, was one of the coldest days I ever knew in Washington, and the night was especially severe. The effort to elect a Speaker of the House of Representatives of the United States, though not so long as that of 1855–56, when General Banks was chosen, was equally exciting; and when ex-Governor William Pennington, of New Jersey, was declared presiding officer of that body on the 1st, the next point of interest was the choice of a Clerk. It was a period of anxious solicitude to patriotic men. The possibilities of secession began to multiply. The North was determined, the South defiant; Douglas had been re-elected Senator from Illinois in spite of "my Lord Cardinal;" Broderick had been killed in the previous September; Reeder, who had been removed by President Pierce from the governorship of Kansas, had been chosen delegate from that territory, and was on the floor contesting the seat of J. W. Whitfield, who had got the certificate. John Schwartz had defeated the Presidential favorite, J. Glancy Jones, in Berks County; Hickman had been returned by an enormously increased majority; Haskin, of the Yonkers district, New York, had triumphed in his open record of open hostility to the Administration. Instead of getting at least fifty Democrats in Congress from the three States of New Jersey, New York, and Pennsylvania, they got but two from the first, but five from the second, and but two from the third. John W. Geary and Robert J. Walker had followed the example of Andrew H. Reeder, and had given their experience as governors of Kansas in fearless scorn of the frauds of the slaveholder.

On the cold Friday referred to, February 3, 1860, I was elected Clerk of the House, by a single vote, over all others. It was the last drop in the bitter bowl of Democratic disappointment, and it created an overflow of anger on the one side and of satisfaction on the other. The event was naturally most distasteful to President Buchanan, crowning as it did a long and gloomy procession of disasters. On the evening of that Friday a large number of my personal friends met at Mr. John F. Coyle's, whose guest I was, on Missouri Avenue, to celebrate the event. Among these were many Southerners, and some who had voted against me only a few hours before. As I count over their names, I find that not a few have since been entered on the books of death. Schwartz, Burlingame, Pennington, Eliot, Stevens, have passed away. They were all present. The usual speeches common to such occasions were fired off; the old songs were sung—"John Brown" had not yet become popular—the old jokes repeated. When my time came, I spoke some grateful words to the large crowd in the streets and the hilarious company in the rooms. It was fair poetical justice to remind the Administration of their persecution of the men who had resisted Lecompton, and of the vindication of these men by the people in the elections; and as I stood out on the balcony I thought of the famous lines of Lord Byron in "Mazeppa:"

> "They little thought, that day of pain,
> When launched, as on the lightning's flash,
> They bade me to destruction dash,
> That one day I should come again,
> With twice five thousand horse, to thank
> The Count for his uncourteous ride.
> They played me then a bitter prank,
> When, with the wild horse for my guide,
> They bound me to his foaming flank.
> At length I played them one as frank,
> For time at last sets all things even;
> And if we do but watch the hour,
> There never yet was human power
> Which could evade, if unforgiven,
> The patient watch and vigil long
> Of him who treasures up a wrong."

But, like many an unfortunate in a similar situation, the whole stanza escaped my memory, and I could only refer to it. James S. Jackson, of Kentucky, one of the bravest and best men I ever knew, stood at my side, and I asked him, *sotto voce*, to help me out. "Remember it yourself, you infernal Black Republican," was his quick reply, and I finished my remarks as best I could. Jackson was elected to Congress from his State as a Union man in 1861, and before the expiration of his term raised a regiment of Kentucky volunteers, and was killed in the battle of Perryville in 1862. Mr. Lincoln had just made him a brigadier-general. He died too soon. Nature had been prodigal of her gifts to Jackson. To a face of singular, almost feminine beauty, was added the graceful form of an athlete and the manners of a Chesterfield. He took the right side in a community tainted with wrong views. It would have been far easier for him to have followed his intimate friends Breckinridge, Hawkins, and Preston into the Confederate service, and it was a hard struggle to differ with them, but he did it bravely, preserving their love in life, and calling out their manly sorrow over his gallant death.

At the risk of talking a little more about myself than I care to do, I venture to reproduce the following from the speech of Hon. John B. Haskin, of New York, on that memorable evening:

"A short time ago the *New York Herald* had, at the instigation of Mr. Buchanan, as he knew, revived the Forrest letter, and had suggested that it be read from the Clerk's desk when Forney was nominated. Singularly enough, this had not been done, but, expecting that it would be, Colonel Forney had addressed him a letter in relation to this famous Forrest letter, so much misconstrued. He would have read this letter in the House, but there was no necessity for it. He would now read it, however, as he knew those present would like to hear it. The following is the letter·

"'WASHINGTON, Feb. 1, 1860.

"'MY DEAR SIR,—I need not repeat to you that my name has been associated with the position of Clerk of the House, rather through the partiality of kind friends like yourself than because of any efforts of my own to become a candidate. I have importuned no single Representative for his vote. In the present condition of politics I have preferred to let events take their course, so far as I am concerned, maintaining the position I have held for the last two years of uncompromising hostility to the proscriptive and shameless policy of the present Administration of the General Government, and of hearty co-operation with all men who look to the overthrow of that Administration, its advocates and its indorsers. I have been informed, however, that, if my name should be presented to the House, an issue is to be made on account of a letter which I wrote nearly ten years ago, in connection with the case of Mr. Edwin Forrest. I had hoped that no one would be found willing to make this act of devotion to a cherished, and, as I believed, deeply injured friend, the pretext of an assault upon my reputation. If in writing this letter I committed an error, I only became conscious of it when I saw how it could be misconstrued ; and, if I needed any assurances that this error had been overlooked, I had it in my re-election to the Clerkship of the House in 1853, in the unanimous indorsement of my conduct by members of all parties of that body after I had presided over the deliberations of the House in the stormy struggle of 1855 and 1856, in my nomination, by the Democrats of the Pennsylvania Legislature, as their candidate for United States Senator in 1857, and in the repeated voluntary tenders of distinguished official position by the present President of the United States, who has not permitted the recollection of my many years of championship of his aspirations to outweigh the fact that I could not conscientiously follow him in his abandonment and violation of the pledges and principles upon which alone he was chosen Chief Magistrate. I will not imitate the example set by his personal organ, the *New York Herald*, in making the revelation of a private letter a matter of public discussion. If I could sink so low, I might find additional evidence of the fact, over his own name, that my connection with the Forrest case never deprived me of a particle of his confidence and affection, which up to a certain period he so freely and so flatteringly bestowed upon me.

"'You can make any use of this note you see proper. Should the House elect me Clerk, I will accept the office and discharge the duties in the spirit in which it is conferred. Should the result be otherwise, my position will remain unchanged. I have tried the experiment of conducting an independent journal against all the office-holding power of the Federal Government, and I will not surrender my relation to that enterprise whether I gain or lose the position with which my name has been once more associated.

        "'Yours, very truly,   J. W. FORNEY.

    "'Hon. JOHN B. HASKIN.'"

A curious sequel to this same evening happened while I was in London in May of 1867. I was invited to a club of young Englishmen who had been the pronounced friends of our Union during the war. Mr. Benjamin Moran, the accomplished Secretary of the American Legation, kindly accompanied me, and introduced me to most of those present. One gentleman was especially cordial, Lord Frederick Cavendish, second son of the Duke of Devonshire. I found him an advanced Liberal, and very pleasant and intelligent. As we sat smoking together on the sofa, he turned to me and said : " By-the-way, I heard you make a very fiery speech on a very cold night in Washington, in the early winter of 1860. It was from the window or balcony of a house on Missouri Avenue." I looked at him with surprise, when he laughingly said : " I lived in Washington for some time as a member of the British embassy, and felt an interest in the Democratic dissensions. When you were elected Clerk, myself and two friends took a carriage, and, expecting a speech, rode to your lodgings, and we were well rewarded even for the cold we endured among the outside audience." It was a pleasant and a curious reminiscence, and as such I record it in these hasty sketches.

[February 26, 1870.]

VIII.

THE public man with a reputation for wit is apt to become responsible for all the best jokes, old and new. Many a Joe Miller was and is still credited to Thaddeus Stevens and Abraham Lincoln. Things they never said, now that both are gone, are boldly laid upon their memories. But no two men, perhaps, so entirely different in character, ever threw off more spontaneous jokes. Mr. Stevens rarely told a story. He was strong in repartee, in retort, in quiet interrogatory. He must have been terrible at the cross-examination of a witness. There is nothing finer, as I think, in the annals of humor than his quaint questions to David Reese and John Chauncey, the two officers of the House who in his last days used to carry him in a large arm-chair from his lodgings across the public grounds up the broad stairs of the noble Capitol—"Who will be so good to me and take me up in their strong arms when you two mighty men are gone?" Here was not only uncommon wit, but a sense of intellectual immortality. A consciousness of superiority of another sort was his answer to John Hickman, who called as Stevens laid on his bed, when he felt the grip of the grim messenger fastening on him. Hickman told the old man he was looking well. "Ah, John!" was his quick reply, "it is not my appearance, but my disappearance, that troubles me." A member of the House who was known for his uncertain course on all questions, and who often confessed that he never fully investigated a mooted point without finding himself a neutral, asked for leave of absence. "Mr. Speaker," said Stevens, "I do not rise to object, but to suggest that the honorable member need not ask this favor, for he can easily pair off with himself." He was charitable, but never ostentatiously so. "Oh, sir!" said a beggar woman to him one cold morning as he was limping to the House, "Oh, sir! I have just lost all the money I had in the world." "And how much was that?" "Oh, sir! it was seventy-five cents." "You don't say so," was the old man's answer, as he put a five-dollar bill into her hands; "and how wonderful it is that I should have just found what you had lost!"

Shortly after I was elected Clerk of the House, in 1860, a

lady friend, since deceased, called my attention to the fact that the wife of one of her best servants, Sam, was about to be sent away from him to Georgia, and that unless over eight hundred dollars could be raised for her in forty-eight hours, her master, a man living at Georgetown, D. C., would be sure to sell her to strangers. The case was a terrible one. Sam was a fine fellow, and his distress was grievous. I sat down and wrote out the facts, headed the subscription, and in a few hours raised the money, paying over three hundred dollars myself. The papers were made out to me, and I set the woman free. "Well," said Mr. Stevens, as he paid his fifty dollars, "this is the first time I ever heard of a Democrat buying a negro and then giving her her liberty!"

He affected much indignation when President Lincoln consigned Roger A. Pryor to me as a sort of prisoner-guest in 1865, and regularly every morning would greet me with the grim remark: "How is your Democratic friend, General Pryor? I hope you are both well." I was a little annoyed by his sarcasm, and when an appeal was made to me by an old citizen to assist in pardoning another Confederate, I referred him to Mr. Stevens. He happened to know the Great Commoner, and went over to him with my message. Judge of my surprise when he returned with the proposition that whatever I wrote he [Stevens] would sign. I dictated the strongest appeal to the President, and Mr. Stevens put his name to it. Of course, I indorsed the petition; but I did not fail to remind my neighbor that very day of his inconsistency. "Oh! you need not be riled about it," was the retort; "I saw you were going heavily into the Pardon business, and thought I would take a hand in it myself."

Mr. Lincoln was a humorist of another school. He delighted in parables and stories. His treasures of memory were inexhaustible. He never failed for an illustration. He liked the short farce better than the five-act tragedy. He would shout

with laughtei over a French, German, or negro anecdote, and
he was always ready to match the best with a better. More
than once, when I bore a message to him from the Senate, he
detained me with some amusing sketch of Western life. He
seemed to have read the character, and to know the peculiarities
of every leading man in Congress and the country, and would
play off many an innocent joke upon them. I will not attempt
to repeat what has been so often described. There was also a
sacred confidence around many of those scenes which could
not be violated without offense to many living good men ; and
as I do not write to wound the feelings, I will not profane an
illustrious memory by reviving what would only give unnecessary pain.

His two inaugurations were accompanied by apprehensions
of his assassination, and the second was followed in a little
more than a month by his murder. At the inauguration of
March 4, 1861, I was present as Clerk of the House. At the
inauguration of March 4, 1865, I was present as Secretary of
the Senate. James Buchanan, as ex-President, heard the remarkable first message of the man who succeeded him, just as
Andrew Johnson heard the still more remarkable inauguration
of the man he succeeded. War followed the one, peace and
assassination the other. The scene in the Senate of the United
States on the 4th of March 1865, when Andrew Johnson was
sworn in as Vice-President, has too often been painted to be
set out into daylight again. Let it rest. I refer to it now
only to relate one incident. After we reached the eastern and
middle portion of the Capitol, where Mr. Lincoln took the oath,
Johnson was under a state of great excitement, and was in my
immediate charge. I was confident, however, that he would be
subdued before the President finished his inaugural. To the
surprise of every body however, except, perhaps, the Cabinet,
Mr. Lincoln did not consume five minutes in repeating it. As
soon as the people outside saw that he was done, loud cries

were raised for Johnson, upon which we hastily retreated to the
Senate chamber, and closed the unhappy and inauspicious day.
On the 14th of the succeeding month of April, the murder
planned four years before, and baffled by superior foresight, was
executed, and Abraham Lincoln was dying from the pistol-shot
of Booth.

[March 5, 1871.]

IX.

CIRCUMSTANCE often controls men as inexorably as conscience.   Many a Confederate would have been a Radical if
he had lived in the North, just as many a Radical would have
been a Confederate if he had lived in the South.   Howell Cobb
was one of the best types of this idea.   There was an under-
current of anti-slavery, or rather a profound devotion to the
Union, in his nature.   Take his campaign against the Nullifiers
of the South in 1850, when he ran as an independent candidate for governor of Georgia, and was elected over Charles J.
McDonald, the leader of the Calhounites.   At the close of his
first eight years in Congress, and at the end of his Speakership
of the House, I sat with him in his official room at the Capitol,
and heard his eloquent declaration that he would make war
upon these men, cost him what it might.   The contest was exciting to a degree.   Personal vituperation and personal threats
were as common against Cobb as they were twenty years after
against Bullock, the Republican governor of Georgia.   In 1855
Governor Cobb was again sent to Congress, and there took
early and patriotic ground against the extremists.   He was so
anxious to make Mr. Buchanan President, that in 1856, on my
invitation, he came into Pennsylvania, and traversed Chester
County with John Hickman, pledging the Democracy to justice

to the people of Kansas. His argument was exceedingly effective, and thousands voted for the "favorite son" because they believed the impassioned Georgian.

Yet as the controversy deepened Governor Cobb yielded to the exactions of his section, and when the rebellion burst upon us he was one of the foremost and most resolute of the secession chiefs. He died in New York in 1869, in his 54th year, greatly mourned in Georgia, where he leaves large family connections. Before we revive the censure of his conduct as James Buchanan's Secretary of the Treasury, and as one of the members of the government of Jefferson Davis, let us "put ourselves in his place."

Another illustration of the force of circumstances is that of John Cabell Breckinridge, of Kentucky. I have always believed that he espoused the Confederacy, if not reluctantly, at least in the conviction that it would forever end his political career. He inherited hostility to slavery. When he came to Washington in 1851 as a Representative from the old Henry Clay Lexington district, in Kentucky, he was in no sense an extremist. At that early day, when he had just attained his 30th year, and I was in my 34th, we conferred freely and frequently on the future of our country. He used to relate how Sam Houston, for whom he had great respect, would expatiate upon the dangers and evils of slavery; and it was not difficult to trace the operation of the same idea in his own mind. But he was too interesting a character to be neglected by the able ultras of the South. They saw in his winning manners, attractive appearance, and rare talent for public affairs, exactly the elements they needed in their concealed designs against the country. If they were successful in arousing his ambition and finally making him one of themselves, we must not forget that few men similarly placed would have been proof against such blandishments. Let this be said of him. He was never prominent in the small persecutions of the Democrats who refused to indorse the course of the Administration of which he was Vice-President. No doubt that lost him the confidence of the President and his immediate followers.

He was made a Senator in Congress from Kentucky when the Buchanan *régime* expired, taking his seat on the very day that his venerable chief retired to Wheatland ; and he remained a Senator in Congress till the close of the called session, which opened on the 14th of July, and closed on the 6th of August, 1861. He was the leader of the Democracy in that exciting month, and though he gave no sign of his intention to join the rebel army, nobody was surprised when he was reported at Richmond, Virginia.

Perhaps the most dramatic scene that ever took place in the Senate Chamber—old or new—was that between Breckinridge and Colonel E. D. Baker, of Oregon, on the 1st of August, 1861, five days before the adjournment *sine die*, in the darkest period of the war, when the rebellion was most defiant and hopeful. The last week of that July was full of excitement in Congress and the country, and I know how much labor and patience it required to keep alive the hopes of our people. The course of Powell and Breckinridge, of Kentucky, and Bright, of Indiana, in opposing the Government, had nearly obliterated party feeling in the Senate. McDougall, of California, Rice, of Minnesota, Thompson, of New Jersey, all Democrats, had declared for force to crush the rebellion. These men were especially emphatic, though closely endeared to Breckinridge. Thompson, of New Jersey, spoke loud and firm from his seat—" I shall vote for the bill as a war measure—I am in favor of carrying on the war to crush out the rebellion." The same day McDougall questioned the right of Powell, of Kentucky, to his seat in the Senate. Andrew Johnson reiterated his determination to stand by the flag to the last. Carlile, of West Virginia, would vote for force to put down the rebel foe.

It was in the midst of this feeling that Breckinridge rose to make his last formal indictment against the Government. Never shall I forget the scene. Baker was a Senator and a soldier. He alternated between his seat in the Capitol and his tent in the field. He came in at the eastern door (while Breckinridge was speaking) in his blue coat and fatigue cap, riding-whip in hand. He paused and listened to the "polished treason," as he afterward called it, of the Senator from Kentucky, and, when he sat down, he replied with a fervor never to be forgotten. One or two of his passages deserve to be repeated :

"To talk to us about stopping is idle; we will never stop. Will the Senator yield to rebellion? Will he shrink from armed insurrection? Will his State justify it? Will its better public opinion allow it? Shall we send a flag of truce? What would he have? Or would he conduct this war so feebly that the whole world would smile at us in derision? What would he have? These speeches of his, sown broadcast over the land—what clear, distinct meaning have they? Are they not intended for disorganization in our very midst? Are they not intended to dull our weapons? Are they not intended to destroy our zeal? Are they not intended to animate our enemies? Sir, are they not words of brilliant, polished treason, even in the very Capitol of the Confederacy?" [Manifestations of applause in the galleries.]

The presiding officer (Mr. Anthony in the chair).—"Order!"

MR. BAKER. "What would have been thought if, in another Capitol, in another Republic, in a yet more martial age, a Senator as grave, not more eloquent or dignified than the Senator from Kentucky, yet with the Roman purple flowing over his shoulders, had risen in his place, surrounded by all the illustrations of Roman glory, and declared that advancing Hannibal was just, and that Carthage ought to be dealt with in terms of peace? What would have been thought if, after the battle of Cannæ, a Senator there had risen in his place and denounced every levy of the Roman people, every expenditure of its treas-

ure, and every appeal to the old recollections and the old glories? Sir, a Senator, himself learned far more than myself in
such lore [Mr. Fessenden], tells me in a voice that I am glad
is audible, that he would have been hurled from the Tarpeian
Rock. It is a grand commentary upon the American Constitution that we permit these words to be uttered. I ask the Senator to recollect, too, what, save to send aid and comfort to the
enemy, do these predictions amount to? Every word thus uttered falls as a note of inspiration upon every Confederate ear.
Every sound thus uttered is a word (and, falling from his lips,
a mighty word) of kindling and triumph to a foe that deter-
mines to advance. For me, I have no such word as a Senator
to utter. For me, amid temporary defeat, disaster, disgrace, it
seems that my duty calls me to utter another word, and that
word is bold, sudden, forward, determined war, according to
the laws of war, by armies, by military commanders, clothed
with full power, advancing with all the past glories of the Republic urging them on to conquest."

Breckinridge had made the following prediction :

"'War is separation,' is the language of an eminent gentleman now no more ; it is disunion, eternal and final disunion.
We have separation now; it is only made worse by war, and
an utter extinction of all those sentiments of common interest
and feeling which might lead to a political reunion founded
upon consent and upon a conviction of its advantages. Let
the war go on, however, and soon, in addition to the moans of
widows and orphans all over this land, you will hear the cry
of distress from those who want food and the comforts of life.
The people will be unable to pay the grinding taxes which a
fanatical spirit will attempt to impose upon them. Nay more,
sir ; you will see further separation. I hope it is not 'the sunset of life gives me mystical lore,' but in my mind's eye I
plainly see 'coming events cast their shadows before.' The
Pacific slope now, doubtless, is devoted to the union of States.

Let this war go on till they find the burdens of taxation greater than the burdens of a separate condition, and they will assent to it. Let the war go on until they see the beautiful features of the old Confederacy beaten out of shape and comeliness by the brutalizing hand of war, and they will turn aside in disgust from the sickening spectacle, and become a separate nation. Fight twelve months longer, and the already opening differences that you see between New England and the great Northwest will develop themselves. You have two confederacies now. Fight twelve months, and you will have three; twelve months longer, and you will have four."

Baker, in reply, made the following prediction, which he did not live to see fulfilled — having died in battle at Ball's Bluff, Va., on the 21st of October, 1861 — less than three months after:

"I tell the Senator that his predictions—sometimes for the South, sometimes for the Middle States, sometimes for the Northeast, and then wandering away in airy visions out to the far Pacific, about the dread of our people as to the loss of blood and treasure, provoking them to disloyalty—are false in sentiment, false in fact, and false in loyalty. The Senator from Kentucky is mistaken in them all. Five hundred million dollars! What then? Great Britain gave more than two thousand millions in the great battle for constitutional liberty which she led at one time, almost single-handed, against the world. Five hundred thousand men! What then? We have them; they are ours; they are children of the country; they belong to the whole country; they are our sons—our kinsmen, and there are many of us who will give them all up before we will abate one word of our just demand, or will retreat one inch from the line which divides right from wrong.

"Sir, it is not a question of men or of money in that sense. All the money, all the men, are, in our judgment, well bestowed in such a cause. When we give them we know their value.

Knowing their value well, we give them with the more pride and the more joy. Sir, how can we retreat? Sir, how can we make peace? Who shall treat? What commissioners? Who would go? Upon what terms? Where is to be your boundary-line? Where the end of principles we shall have to give up? What will become of constitutional government? What will become of public liberty? What of the past glories? What of future hopes? Shall we sink into the insignificance of the grave — a degraded, defeated, emasculated people, frightened by the results of one battle, and scared by the visions raised by the imagination of the Senator from Kentucky upon this floor? No, sir! a thousand times, no, sir! We will rally—if, indeed, our words be necessary—we will rally the people, the loyal people of the whole country. They will pour forth their treasure, their money, their men, without stint, without measure. The most peaceable man in this body may stamp his foot upon this Senate-chamber floor, as of old a warrior and a Senator did, and from that single tramp there will spring forth armed legions. Shall one battle determine the fate of empire or a dozen? The loss of one thousand men or twenty thousand, of one hundred million dollars or five hundred million? In a year, in ten years at most, of peaceful progress we can restore them all. There will be some graves reeking with blood, watered by the tears of affection. There will be some privation; there will be some loss of luxury; there will be somewhat more need for labor to procure the necessaries of life. When that is said, all is said. If we have the country, the whole country, the Union, the Constitution, free government—with these there will return all the blessings of well-ordered civilization; the path of the country will be a career of greatness and of glory such as, in the olden time, our fathers saw in the dim vision of years yet to come, and such as would have been ours now, to-day, if it had not been for the treason for which the Senator too often seeks to apologize."

An amusing episode followed the debate. Breckinridge thought it was Sumner who answered Baker's interrogatory, "What would have been done with a Roman Senator guilty of such treason?" by exclaiming that "He would have been hurled from the Tarpeian Rock." And he denounced the Massachusetts Senator in severe and angry Saxon. When Breckinridge discovered it was Fessenden and not Sumner who had given this response, he did not complain of the first nor apologize to the second. The Senator from Massachusetts has a sort of vicarious office to this day, and suffers a great deal from the sins of others.

The contrast between the prophets, living and dead, is useful, and does not seem to have been lost upon the survivor, Mr. Breckinridge, if we may judge by his deportment since the close of the war, and by the following words spoken by him at Louisville, Kentucky, on the 13th of October last, at a meeting called to do honor to the memory of Robert E. Lee, the Confederate military leader. It was a meeting of men of all parties, and he said: "If the spirit which animates the assembly before me to-night shall become general and extend over the whole country, then indeed may we say that the wounds of the late war are truly healed. We ask only for him what we concede to the manly qualities of others. Among the more eminent of the Federal generals who fell during the war, or have since died, may be mentioned Thomas and McPherson. What Confederate would refuse to raise his cap as their funeral train passed by, or grudge to drop a flower upon their soldier-graves?"

And doubtless if he had thought of it he would have included in the list of "Federal soldiers" the gallant Baker of Oregon, whose prediction of the collapse of the rebellion he has lived to realize, and, I hope, not to regret.

[March 12, 1871.]

X.

JOHN QUINCY ADAMS was a Representative in Congress from 1831—three years after he left the Presidency—to the 23d of February, 1848, when he fell from his seat in the House, and died literally in harness. The lives of the Adamses have been unusually busy and brilliant. John, the second President, was a patriot of the impulsive school, honest and self-willed. John Quincy, his son, was in some respects a larger and a riper mind; Charles Francis, his living grandson, is a more cautious and conservative personage, while his great-grandsons are spoken of as men of learning and culture. This family is one of the few evidences of the transmission of genius in the same blood. There is really no representative left of Washington, Jefferson, Clay, Webster, Calhoun, or Jackson. It seems to have been ordained that each was to be the last of his race, and that none should be left to eclipse his fame. The first time I ever saw John Quincy Adams was also the first time I ever saw Stephen A. Douglas. This was in May of 1846, while Polk was President, and James Buchanan Secretary of State. The annexation of Texas was the reigning issue. Parties were divided upon it, and John Quincy Adams led the opposition. He was in his seventy-ninth year. Douglas was in his thirty-third. The contrast was marked between the feeble and bald-headed statesman and the boyish face and figure of the black-eyed and black-haired partisan. The one was closing out his eventful career—the other was beginning his, not so varied, but crowded with almost as many trials. As I sat in the gallery that sweet May morning, and looked down upon the men who led and dominated the deliberations, I little thought of the terrible future before us, and that I should outlive many who were then in the prime of a vigorous manhood. Young as I was, I was editor enough to know the leaders, either personally or by name.

There were Hannibal Hamlin, of Maine, Adams and Winthrop, of Massachusetts, Collamer and Foot, of Vermont (both afterward in the Senate and since dead), Preston King, of New York (afterward a Senator and since dead), Brodhead, Charles J. Ingersoll, Joseph R. Ingersoll, Lewis C. Levin, and David Wilmot, of Pennsylvania, the first and last afterward in the Senate, and the whole number now in their graves ; Thomas H. Bayley and George C. Dromgoole, of Virginia, both since dead. There also were McKay, of North Carolina, Linn Boyd, of Kentucky, Cave Johnson, of Tennessee, S. F. Vinton and Joshua Giddings, of Ohio, all gathered to their fathers. And there also were many yet living, like Andrew Johnson, of Tennessee, Stevens and Toombs, of Georgia—these two last among the most active of the moderate men of that period ; Whigs as earnest as young Delano and Schenck, of Ohio, who were in the same House, one of them now General Grant's Secretary of the Interior, and the other his Minister to England.

In this same Congress, a Representative from Illinois, was E. D. Baker, afterward a Senator from Oregon, whose noble reply to Breckinridge, some fifteen years later, I quoted from in my last number. Born in England, and "brought to this country when a child, and left an orphan in Philadelphia," this boy of genius, this handsome, whole-hearted man, this statesman in the Senate and hero in the field, had no idea, at that early day, when he fought Douglas in the House, that they two would harmonize in love of country at last, and that they would go to meet their father-God in the same year, and only a few months apart. How bitter these Whigs and Democrats were ! How angry they got themselves, and how angry they made their respective friends ! And yet at the end of less than a generation we find Douglas and Baker, intense party foes in the year 1846, lying down together almost in the same grave, at nearly the same time, martyrs alike to the same holy cause, in the year 1861. They were strangely alike in many things. They were

familiar to a degree. Their tastes were similar. They loved
their friends without hating their foes. Neither believed in the
philosophy of revenge. They thought they did sometimes in
their impulses, but when the passion passed off they forgave
like gods. Mean men only live in the darkness of malice. It
is the great soul alone that outlives in history and memory the
mean soul, unless the latter is so infamous as to stand as
a beacon and a warning. Of this school were Baker and
Douglas. But to my story.

I sat in the gallery of the old House, now the glorious recep-
tacle which I hope decent courage in our public men will secure
from the profanation of being a sepulchre for every dead-beat
in the way of art, where Stephen A. Douglas made his magnificent speech in favor of the annexation of Texas in reply to
ex-President Adams. I shall never forget that sweet and odor-
ous 13th of May, 1846. Nowhere, as it seems to me, is there
an atmosphere like Washington in May and June. Nature
seems to revel in the supreme luxury of her own charms. That
spot, without snow in winter, prolonging its equal reign far into
the summer, and resuming its neutral sway early in September,
seems to have been chosen as the "golden mean" alike of politics and climate. I had come from my little country-city to
hear and to see, and I was gratified.

In view of the fact that Texas is now the fertile outpost of
an athletic civilization, and of the other fact that if we had not
conquered her from Mexico, she would be to-day a sort of middle ground, compounded of guerillas and knights of the free
lance, the friends of annexation may claim a sort of poetical
vindication. Mexico is still a most vexatious problem. What
would Texas be if left to the mercy of Mexico, or to the manip-
ulations of foreign powers? In this light the annexation of
1846, consummated by the treaty of Guadaloupe-Hidalgo in
1848, was a measure of consummate foresight.

I shall never forget how eagerly John Quincy Adams listened

to the young member from Illinois, Stephen A. Douglas, as he was speaking on the 13th of May, 1846. Mr. Delano, of Ohio, now Secretary of the Interior, had made a decided argument against annexation, which gave great satisfaction to the venerable ex-President.

Mr. Douglas said, with the courtesy which distinguished him, looking at Mr. Adams: "I perceive the venerable gentleman from Massachusetts, before me now, nods approval of the sentiment." [The sentiment of Mr. Delano.]

MR. ADAMS. "Yes, sir. Mr. Chairman, I approve and indorse every word and syllable of it."

Thus encouraged, the wily young Illinois orator proceeded in his well-considered speech. It will be recollected that the great point in issue in 1846, so far as Texas was concerned, was the boundary between Texas and Mexico. Mr. Delano, with masterly ability, had denied that the Rio del Norte was the western boundary, and Mr. Adams had accepted the version of Mr. Delano. I can never forget the following colloquy:

MR. DOUGLAS. "Mr. Chairman, I believe I have now said all that I intended for the purpose of showing that the Rio del Norte was the western boundary of the republic of Texas. How far I have succeeded in establishing the position I leave to the House and the country to determine. If that was the boundary of the republic of Texas, it has, of course, become the boundary of the United States by virtue of the act of annexation and admission into the Union. I will not say that I have demonstrated the question as satisfactorily as the distinguished gentleman from Massachusetts did in 1819, but I will say that I think I am safe in adopting the sentiment which he then expressed, that our title to the Rio del Norte is as clear as to the island of New Orleans."

MR. ADAMS. "I never said that our title was good to the Rio del Norte from its mouth to its source."

MR. DOUGLAS. "I know nothing of the gentleman's mental

reservations. If he means, by his denial, to place the whole emphasis on the qualification that he did not claim that river as the boundary 'from its mouth to its source,' I shall not dispute with him on that point. But if he wishes to be understood as denying that he ever claimed the Rio del Norte, in general terms, as our boundary under the Louisiana treaty, I can furnish him an official document, over his own signature, which he will find very embarrassing and exceedingly difficult to explain. I allude to his famous dispatch as Secretary of State, in 1819, to Don Onis, the Spanish minister. I am not certain that I can prove his handwriting, for the copy I have in my possession I find printed in the American State Papers, published by the order of Congress. In that paper he not only claimed the Rio del Norte as our boundary, but he demonstrated the validity of the claim by a train of facts and arguments which rivet conviction on every impartial mind, and deny refutation."

MR. ADAMS. "I wrote that dispatch as Secretary of State, and endeavored to make out the best case I could for my own country, as it was my duty. But I utterly deny that I claimed the Rio del Norte as our boundary in its full extent. I only claimed it a short distance up the river, and then diverged to the northward some distance from the stream."

MR. DOUGLAS. "Will the gentleman specify the point at which his line left the river?"

MR. ADAMS. "I never designated the point."

MR. DOUGLAS. "Was it above Matamoras?"

MR. ADAMS. "I never specified any particular place."

The old man had evidently forgotten the dispatch he wrote as Secretary of State in 1819—twenty-seven years before—and the young man had had it recalled to *his* attention. It was a bombshell. It was a new thing to see John Quincy Adams retreating before anybody. He seemed to feel as if he had fallen into a trap. His solicitude to hear Douglas was perhaps a sort of explanation of his course. The House was divided between admiration for the new actor on the great stage of national affairs and reverence for the retiring chief. I recollect my own feelings as I sat in the gallery and witnessed this conflict.

Douglas was a Vermonter; Adams was a Massachusetts man. Perhaps the idea that controlled their common star was the New England idea, which has done so much and dared so much in human civilization and redemption. It is curious to note the influence of this idea upon all our future. It has never failed to vindicate itself. John Adams proclaimed it, but he did not plant it. John Quincy Adams tenderly nourished it. If the grandson of the one, and the son of the other, and the sons of the last, choose to neglect it, the followers of Stephen A. Douglas will not allow it to die for want of culture and care.

[February 19, 1871.]

XI.

NOTHING is more remarkable in history than the fact that States and statesmen often undergo entire revulsions of political sentiment and conviction. To doubt the sincerity of these changes is to question the justice of every sort of conversion. Slavery has been the most potent element; but other causes have been effective. The free-trade speech of Daniel Webster in 1824, able as it was, was not a particle more conscientious than his protection argument in Philadelphia twenty-two years later. The leading Federalist in Lancaster County from 1814 to 1827 was the same James Buchanan who, in a few years after, became the admitted Democratic chief of Pennsylvania. Henry Clay's early Democracy did not prevent him from becoming the defiant enemy of that party after Andrew Jackson took command of it. Calhoun became a free-trader after hav-

ing made some of the strongest arguments for protection, thus
exactly changing places with Daniel Webster. When, however,
slavery began to dominate the field, we had a succession of
astonishing transformations. States wheeled out of one party
into another with magical celerity. Democratic fortresses like
Maine, New Hampshire, Illinois, Iowa, Pennsylvania, New
York, and Ohio, which had stood by the Democracy in every
trial, and had routed the Whigs in repeated campaigns, joined
the Republican column, while veteran Democrats like Hamlin
of Maine, Trumbull of Illinois, Wilmot of Pennsylvania, D. K.
Cartter of Ohio, Preston King and Reuben E. Fenton, of New
York, Morton of Indiana, ranged themselves on the same side,
not as privates, but as general officers, each with an army at
his back. There was little compensation for these losses. It
is true the South consolidated to save the peculiar institution,
but little was gained by the halting support of such formerly
intense Whig States as Maryland and Kentucky. They could
not so readily forget their devotion to Clay and their hatred of
Jackson. The sectionalism born of slavery also gave rise to war,
and then came some of the strangest of revolutions. Hundreds
of thousands of Democrats became Republicans when they saw
the treatment that Reeder and Douglas, and their compatriots,
had received; but the oddest sight was to see hosts of "Old-
line Whigs," who had been denouncing slavery all their lives,
joining the Democrats! Hon. James Brooks, of New York,
and Hon. Josiah Randall, of Philadelphia, were the pioneers in
this singular diversion; and they were followed by quite a procession of men of the same school when hostilities commenced.
There is now hardly a considerable town in the United States
in which some "Old-line Whig" is not among the Democratic
leaders. Most notable of these are the grandsons of John
Quincy Adams. The living junior of that name is an accepted
authority, and one of his brothers is said to be among the best
of the numerous writers for the *New York World*, whose edito-

rial columns are frequently enriched by contributions from the finished and fertile pen of William B. Reed, for a long time the most brilliant and effective of the antagonists of the Democratic party in Pennsylvania. Mr. Reed was an earnest advocate of Mr. Buchanan for the Presidency in 1856. He did much for his election. He was eminently loyal to his new friend ; and when he was sent forth on the Chinese mission, he was true to that friend, and entered heartily into the extreme views of those who sympathized with the rebellion. Let us not forget that his very intensity in that strife was only a copy of his intensity on the other side, and that his course in both experiences is perhaps the very best proof of his sincerity. As I read his articles in *The World*, so caustic and courteous, I have but one regret, and that is that they are not in logical accord with his old anti-slavery record. Nobody in Philadelphia who knows W. B. Reed, whatever his present feelings, will deny that if he had followed this record he would have been among the dictators of the Republican party. As I study men like Mr. Reed, and notice that Hon. Isaac E. Hiester, the Whig son of a Federal father, in the county of Lancaster, Pennsylvania—both having served that great district in the Congress of the United States, and both chosen by the anti-Democratic vote, and the son dying a few weeks ago one of the captains of the Democracy—I feel that I have no right to question motives. Hiester Clymer, who ran for Governor against John W. Geary, of the same State, in 1866, is another instance. Perhaps the most thoughtful member of the Philadelphia bar was the late George M. Wharton, an " Old-line Whig," and yet his last hours were filled with sympathy with the Democratic party.

It is difficult, and often disreputable, to divine the motives of men who change religions or politics. Yet it is interesting to know how they excuse themselves. Consistency is often a species of moral cowardice. Many shelter themselves under this shadow, and lie through a life-time, publicly indorsing an idea they hate in their hearts. The brave spirits are those who welcome the truth as they see it, and fight it out. The fool often lives and dies in his own errors. The wise man investigates and rejects them. As none are perfect in life, so all should aspire to be perfect in the Christian virtue of toleration.

[March 26, 1871.]

XII.

LISTENING to Mr. Dougherty's brilliant lecture, at the Philadelphia Academy of Music, on the evening of March 13, memory carried me back many years. He was right when he said that the days of oratory were over, and that the men fittest for declamation generally prefer the plainest and most practical way of expressing their sentiments. I am disposed to think the change for the better, inasmuch as the most thoughtful men are not always the best speakers, and the best speakers are not always the most thoughtful men. A calm, conversational style necessitates logic or an attempt in that direction, and leaves reason a clearer, because less exciting, field to combat with error. High art seems to have given way to exact science. Words weigh little. Adjectives are accepted as confessions of weakness. Fact so rules the world that even the novelist can not be successful unless he weaves the very best likeness of it into his fictions. A great and wise man said to me lately, after reading one of Charles Reade's wonderful creations, "This book reminds me keenly of the singular adage, that many a romance is history without the proper names, just as many a history is romance *with* the proper names."

How well I remember some of the orators of other days— the men of the generation succeeding Andrew Jackson! The South always predominated in fascinating and plausible rhet-

oric. Winter Davis, of Maryland, was at once a logician and
a declaimer. His sharp tenor voice, his incisive sentences and
ready wit, his fine figure, were admirably re-enforced by acute
reasoning powers and admirable legal training. A rare specimen of the same qualities was Judah P. Benjamin, of Louisiana, now a practitioner in the various law-courts in London.
His handsome Jewish face, his liquid tones, and easy enunciation, contrasted well with his skill as a debater and his accuracy
as a student. Pierre Soulé, a Senator from the same State, was
a different, yet as peculiar a type. His swarthy complexion,
black, flashing eyes, and Frenchified dress and speech, made
him one of the attractions of the Senate. He is now in his
grave, after a strangely eventful and novel career. He was an
artificial man—brilliant in repartee, yet subject to fits of melancholy; impetuous, yet reserved; proud, but polite—in one
word, such a contradiction as Victor Hugo, with a vast fund of
knowledge, and a deposit of vanity which was never exhausted.
He was a ready-made Secessionist when the rebellion came,
and yet his light shone feebly in that dark conspiracy. Virginia
always had a supply of good speakers. Thomas H. Bayley,
with his gold spectacles and ambrosial locks, and his Southern
idiom, a compound of the negro and the scholar; Charles
James Faulkner, with his pleasant smile, dandy dress, and
flowing phrases; James M. Mason, with his Dombey diction
and pompous pretense; R. M. T. Hunter, with his quiet and
careful conservatism; Roger A. Pryor, with his impetuous and
dazzling temperament — these were all first-class speakers,
though as distinct as their own faces. The noisiest man in
the immediate ante-war Congress was George S. Houston, of
Alabama; the most quarrelsome was Keitt, of South Carolina;
the best-tempered, Orr, of the same State; the most acrid,
George W. Jones, of Tennessee; the jolliest, Senator Jere Clem-
ens, of Alabama; the most supercilious, Senator Slidell, of
Louisiana; the most genial, Senator Anthony Kennedy, of

Maryland; and the boldest and coarsest, Wigfall, of Texas.
Breckinridge was, in many respects, a true orator, and seemed
to copy much from Clay and Crittenden.   Jefferson Davis was
always a capital dialectician, not strong in argument, but always
stern in convictions.   Hammond, of South Carolina, had a good
presence and a persuasive tone, but was not a great man.
Toombs, of Georgia, was the stormy petrel, often grand as a
declaimer, and always intolerant, dogmatic, and extreme.   He
was as violent in 1850, when he was a Unionist, as he was in
1860, when he became a Secessionist.

Two scenes are deeply imprinted on my memory.   They exhibit the two schools of oratory, West and South.   One was the
remarkable appeal of Hon. James McDowell, of Virginia, in the
House of Representatives, on the 3d of September, 1850.   That
was the initiative period—the porch, so to speak, which introduced us to the arena of civil war; and McDowell, like other
patriots, stood upon its steps and predicted the dark future if
we did not harmonize.   He was then in his fifty-fifth year, not
in good health, but full of genuine love of liberty.   He had won
high honors as a popular speaker in Virginia.   Born in that
State, and educated at Princeton College, New Jersey, he was
profoundly attached to the Union.   He was filled with apprehensions of dismemberment in 1850.   The extremists demanded that California should not be admitted as a free State without an equivalent in the extension of slave territory—an exac-
tion indignantly resisted by the North.   The agitation was intense — the peril imminent.   At this moment Mr. McDowell
rose to address the House.   His tall form, graceful gestures,
and commanding voice revived the expectations created by his
fame as a Virginia orator, and his sustained and splendid appeal confirmed them.   When he proclaimed these noble words
the House broke forth into involuntary applause, which could
not be restrained by Speaker Cobb :

"From the empire of Nebuchadnezzar to that of Napoleon,

how immense the distance, how stupendous the revolutions that have intervened, how intense the fiery contests which have burned over continents and ages, changing their theatre and their instruments, and leaving upon the whole surface of the globe scarce a spot unstained by their desolating and bloody track ; and yet no national offspring has sprung from them all so fitted as our own United America to redeem for the world the agonies they have cost it. Whatever, in that long period, other nations may have risen up to be, and however truly and illustriously a few of them may have prolonged their day and advanced the civilization and the wisdom of themselves and the world, still none of them has ever embodied such an aggregate of rational happiness or political truth as our own Republic, and none like it has ever fulfilled the ultimate problem of all government, that, namely, of making the utmost freedom of the citizen and the utmost power of the State the co-existing and the upholding conditions of one another. With a freedom only inferior to that of Rome in the worst qualities of hers, those of aggression and conquest, and superior to that of Greece in its best, those of civilization and defense ; with nothing but this freedom, its story and its triumphs, our Republic has become confederate alike with the liberty sentiment of the world and with the majestic power of human sympathy to propagate itself, and hence its flag is destined to wave not only over an empire of illimitable means but over the illimitable empires of re-born and self-governing man. And now that this Republic of freedom, happiness, and power is a heritage of ours, who that has shared, as we have done, in the countless blessings that belong to it—who that knows it, as we do, to be the heritage of every good which human nature can enjoy or human government secure—who, so situated, could make it or could see it the sport of violent, selfish, or parricidal passions? Who of us, without putting forth every faculty of soul and body to prevent it, would see it go down, down under some monstrous

struggle of brother with brother, an external crush upon ourselves, an external example for the shuddering, the admonition,
the horror, and the curse of universal man? There have been
those who, impelled only by their own noble and generous nature, have rushed forward on the field of battle and given their
own bosom to the blow of death, that thereby some loved comrade or commander might be spared, or some patriotic purpose
vindicated and secured; there have been those who have gone
into the dungeons of misfortune and of guilt, and worn out the
days and years of their own lives that they might alleviate the
disease or the despair of their wretched inmates, and, at least,
kindle up for another world the aspirations and hopes which
were extinguished for this. And there have been others, too,
who have companioned with the pestilence, and have walked,
day by day, in its silent and horrid footsteps, that they might
learn in what way to encounter its power, and so be enabled,
reverently, to lift up from crushed and anguished communities
the too heavy pressing of the hand of the Almighty. And are
we, who hold the sublimest political trust ever committed to the
hands of any other people—are we alone to be incapable of any
and every dedication of ourselves which that trust requires?
Can we stand calmly, helplessly, and faithlessly by, and allow
it to be wrecked and lost?

"In this hour of danger—this eventful hour of the age—this
hour which is all in all to us and to millions besides, those oppressed millions of other lands who are ruled by irresponsible
power, and who, as they lie upon the earth, overwhelmed and
crushed by the weight of altars or of thrones, still look to us for
hope, and pour out their hearts in sobbings and in prayer to
Heaven that ours may be the radiant and the steady light which
shall never bewilder or betray; in this hour, so full of interest,
our mother country comes into our very midst, and taking *each
by the hand, says to each:* 'Son, give me, give me thy heart.'
And will we not, can we not do it? Can we not give it freely,

proudly give it all? keeping no part of it back for any end or
any passion of our own, though dear, it may be, as a right eye
or a right arm.   If any of us can not—if there is any lingering,
denying, clinging feeling which the heart will not or can not deliver over at such a moment, let us tear that heart from our bosom if we can, and lift up our supplications to the Father above
that he would send us another in its place, better fitted for the
sight of Heaven and for the service and fellowship of man.

"Give us in our duties here but something of the spirit of
the Roman father, who delivered up his son to the axe of justice because he loved his country better than his blood, or that
of the gallant young officer of the Revolution, who was detected
and executed while performing under the orders of his immortal chief the service of a spy. [Lieutenant Hale.]   When led
to the spot of execution, as he stood upon it and looked forth,
for the last time, upon the smile of day, and upon the bright and
benignant sun of Heaven as it beamed upon him, and felt the
agony that all—all was gone, his young and hopeful and joyous
nature involuntarily shrank, and he is said to have cried out
with impassioned exclamations : 'Oh, it is a bitter, bitter thing
to die, and how *bitter*, too, to know that I have but one life
which I can give to my country!'   Give us only this spirit for
our work here ; doubt not but that it will be approved of by our
land, and be crowned with a long futurity of thankfulness and
rejoicing."

The other scene was when, some ten years later, Owen Lovejoy, of Illinois, startled the House by one of those terrific explosions of eloquence so uncommon in these now formal times.
It will be recollected that his brother had been killed by a pro-
slavery mob at Alton, Illinois, some years before, simply for
publishing an anti-slavery paper.   He made this the text of his
argument, and never was there a more thrilling or effective one.
He was much affected, and his emotions affected others on both
sides of the House.   I regret I can not fix the exact date of

this memorable display, to complete the parallel with the Virginia statesman and patriot.

They were eminently representative men. As orators they
were most dissimilar. McDowell was tall and dignified; Lovejoy short, quick, and impetuous. McDowell's complexion was
light; Lovejoy's dark as a Spaniard's, save in moments of excitement, when it fairly glowed. Had McDowell lived during
the war he would undoubtedly have been a Secessionist, like all
of his school; but his words are not less applicable to-day than
they were in 1850. Lovejoy lived to see three years of war,
and to enjoy the abolition of slavery, for which he had prayed
and toiled. He preceded his friend, Abraham Lincoln, a little
more than a twelvemonth. I knew him well. He was as generous as he was brave; as gentle as he was sincere. A devoted friend, a chivalric foe, he has left a record honorable to
himself, his posterity, and his country.

McDowell died in August of 1851, in less than a year after
his noble speech from which I quote, aged fifty-five. Lovejoy
died March 25, 1864, aged fifty-three. They should have lived
longer, but they lived long enough to leave thousands to mourn
their loss and to revere their memory.

[March 2, 1871.]

XIII.

JAMES BUCHANAN had, like most men, a few favorite anecdotes, which he was sure to reproduce to every new visitor who
ate his excellent dinners and drank his nutty old Madeira.
One of these related to President Jackson. It was a custom
of Mr. Buchanan's enemies to say that he never had the entire
confidence of Old Hickory. Certain it is he never had the support of Amos Kendall, Francis P. Blair, or Andrew J. Donel-

son, Jackson's immediate friends, or Kitchen Cabinet; yet not less true is it that, when James K. Polk was chosen President in 1844, the venerable Jackson, then at the Hermitage, near Nashville, wrote a strong letter to his friend and neighbor, the new Chief Magistrate, recommending Mr. Buchanan for Secretary of State. George M. Dallas, of Pennsylvania, was chosen Vice-President on the same ticket with Mr. Polk. He, like Buchanan, was a standing candidate for the first office in the nation, and it may well be conceived that there was no love lost between the rivals and their friends. What reader of these sketches who lives in Pennsylvania does not remember those days? Colonel James Page, Benjamin Harris Brewster, George W. Barton, Horn R. Kneass, Henry M. Phillips, Henry Simpson, William Badger, Ellis B. Schnable, and last, not least, Henry Horn, were among the leaders who fought under the respective banners of Dallas and Buchanan. The city of Philadelphia was the theatre of their bitter contests for many years. But the great field of strife was Harrisburg. Simon Cameron, of Dauphin; Reah Frazer and Benjamin Champneys, of Lancaster; Arnold Plumer, of Venango; Wilson McCandless, H. S. Magraw, and S. W. Black, of Alleghany; Henry D. Foster, of Westmoreland; Henry Welsh, of York; Morrow B. Lowry, of Erie; John Hickman and Wilmer Worthington, of Chester; John B. Sterigere, of Montgomery; Richard Brodhead and A. H. Reeder, of Northampton; C. L. Ward, David Wilmot, and Victor E. Piollet, of Bradford; W. F. Packer, of Lycoming; Asa Packer, of Carbon—these and a host more, many since dead, stood forth to fight for these two men in the Democratic State Conventions with a devotion not usual in these more selfish times. The election of Dallas was a hard blow at our Buchanan side of the house; but J. B. was not easily baffled; and so, when we got Old Hickory to indorse him for Secretary of State, we felt that we had checkmated the Philadelphia favorite. And we were right, for no Vice-President was ever more ignored

than George M. Dallas—not even John C. Breckinridge, who
fell under the suspicion of President Buchanan the moment he
was nominated, and never fully recovered from it. Notwithstanding this, James Buchanan retained George M. Dallas as
minister to England all through his rule, and thereby proved
that if he could forget a friend he could also forgive a foe.

But to my anecdote. I heard Mr. Buchanan repeat it the
last time at the Sunday dinner-table of John T. Sullivan, of
Washington, one of the most interesting and genial of men,
known and beloved alike at the nation's capital and in Philadelphia. He was a Democrat of the old school—a Jackson
Democrat ; was a Government director in the Bank of the
United States with Peter Wager and Henry D. Gilpin; and yet
he was so còsmopolitan and catholic that every man of distinction was glad to receive and prompt to accept his invitations.
Clay, Webster, Calhoun, Crittenden, Clayton, Silas Wright, Doctor Linn, Colonel Benton, Sam Houston, William C. Rives,
Charles Jared Ingersoll, Edward Everett, Rufus Choate, frequently discussed public affairs over his roast beef, baked po-
tatoes, and iced wines. I was a boy when first asked into this
select circle, with its feast of reason and its flow of soul—its generous inaugural of soup, re-enforced by good wines, and supple-
mented, after dinner, by unforgotten punch, brewed by the hand
of the good old man now in his grave. At one of these dinners I heard Old Buck repeat his story of General Jackson,
probably for the hundredth time.

Shortly after Mr. Buchanan's return from Russia in 1834, to
which he had been sent by President Jackson in 1832, and immediately following his election to the Senate of the United
States by the Legislature of Pennsylvania, to fill the unexpired
term of William Wilkins, resigned, who, in his turn, was sent to
succeed Buchanan in the same foreign mission, Buchanan called
upon Old Hickory with a fair English lady, whom he desired to
present to the head of the American nation. Leaving her in the

reception-room down stairs, he ascended to the President's private quarters and found General Jackson unshaved, unkempt, in his dressing-gown, with his slippered feet on the fender before a blazing wood fire, smoking a corn-cob pipe of the old Southern school. He stated his object, when the General said he would be very glad to meet the handsome acquaintance of the new bachelor Senator. Mr. Buchanan was always careful of his personal appearance, and, in some respects, was a sort of masculine Miss Fribble, addicted to spotless cravats and huge collars; rather proud of a small foot for a man of his large stature, and to the last of his life what the ladies would call "a very good figure." Having just returned from a visit to the fashionable continental circles, after two years of thorough intercourse with the etiquette of one of the stateliest courts in Europe, he was somewhat shocked at the idea of the President meeting the eminent English lady in such a guise, and ventured to ask if he did not intend to change his attire, whereupon the old warrior rose, with his long pipe in his hand, and, deliberately knocking the ashes out of the bowl, said to his friend : "Buchanan, I want to give you a little piece of advice, which I hope you will remember. I knew a man once who made his fortune by attending to his own business. Tell the lady I will see her presently."

The man who became President in 1856 was fond of saying that this remark of Andrew Jackson humiliated him more than any rebuke he had ever received. He walked down stairs to meet his fair charge, and in a very short time President Jackson entered the room, dressed in a full suit of black, cleanly shaved, with his stubborn white hair forced back from his remarkable face, and, advancing to the beautiful Britisher, saluted her with almost kingly grace. As she left the White House she exclaimed to her escort, "Your republican President is the royal model of a gentleman."

[April 9, 1871.]

XIV.

SHORTLY after the return of Henry E. Muhlenberg from the court of Austria, to which he had been appointed minister by President Van Buren in 1838, I was invited by General Cameron to take a ride with him from Middletown to Reading, *via* Pottsville. It was in May of 1841 or '42, the loveliest spring month of the year. We took it leisurely, had a fine pair of horses and a comfortable carriage, and enjoyed the scenery, the weather, and the conversation of the people, with whom General Cameron was, even at that early day, on the most familiar terms. It was very pleasant to notice how intimately he understood the habits and history of the people of the whole country-side through which we passed—how, at intervals, he would stop the carriage, hail the passer-by, ask about his health, joke with him on politics, inquire after his wife, sons, and daughters by name, and enter into a familiar speculation as to the coming crops. I can not recall all the incidents of this delightful drive. There was no railroad in those days from Harrisburg to Lebanon and Reading, and none from Pottsville to Reading, so that after free and cordial intercourse with the politicians at John W. Weaver's old-fashioned hotel in Pottsville, we proceeded to the county seat of Berks, where the carriage was dismissed, as we had determined to go to Philadelphia by the Reading Railroad, which then terminated at that place. Calling upon Mr. Muhlenberg, we found him full of anecdotes of his over two years' residence at Vienna. His son and namesake Henry (who was elected a member of the Thirty-third Congress, in which body he only appeared a single day, having sickened with typhoid fever, from the effects of which he died on the 9th of January, 1854) had accompanied his father as Secretary of Legation, and was present on the occasion of our visit. General Cameron was an ardent partisan of Mr. Muhlenberg, who was then a prominent candidate for Governor. As my relations to Mr. Buchanan were close and intimate, and my preferences rather for Francis R. Shunk—the great rival of Mr. Muhlenberg—it was thought that my visit to the Berks County statesman would do much to control the delegates from my native county. I think I preserved a proper neutrality for so young a man—six years younger than Mr. Muhlenberg's son. We conversed freely about Europe and about his father's prospects. It will be recollected that James Buchanan was a candidate for President for more than twenty years before he attained that high position. He could not afford, therefore, to take part between the competitors for State offices, and it was primarily necessary that the delegates from his own county of Lancaster to the State convention should be divided between the two great men who were then contesting for the gubernatorial prize. I was particularly struck with the affable and cordial manners of Mr. Muhlenberg, and with the foreign graces imported into good old Berks by his brilliant and self-assured son. We talked very little politics, but as the object was to make a good impression upon us, Mr. Muhlenberg directed the servant to open a bottle of Johannisberger (the wine celebrated for centuries, yet as utterly unknown to me as if it had been the nectar of the gods), and as he opened the cork he said: "This is the genuine article," the only wine of the kind that had ever come to America up to that period, "and was presented to me by the Emperor himself"—of whom it is historical justice to say that Mr. Muhlenberg, who was a thorough German scholar and a gentleman, was always a confidant and friend. When the cork was drawn, the aroma of the wine seemed to fill the room, and the first bottle was soon dispatched, when General Cameron, with his own peculiar manner, insisted on another, upon which Mr. Muhlenberg gayly remarked, "You shall have it, although it costs a great deal of money." The contest between Muhlenberg and Shunk will be remembered

by all the Pennsylvania politicians.   Muhlenberg won the nomination, and Buchanan lost Muhlenberg's confidence.

He died before the election, on the 12th of August, 1844, and
the flag of the party was placed in the hands of his defeated
competitor, Francis R. Shunk, who was elected in October of
the same year.   Had Muhlenberg lived, with his large wealth,
fine acquirements, and winning manners, he would have been
the most formidable enemy of Buchanan's Presidential aspirations.   As it was, his successor, Governor Shunk, soon got into
collision with Buchanan, not because he deserved that fate, but
because of his inability or the inability of any aspirant for the
Presidency to steer by devious courses between rival candidates
for other and inferior places.   Mr. Buchanan at last secured
the nomination for the Presidential bauble, and there was, I
think, no living Muhlenberg who supported him, except the
venerable Dr. Muhlenberg at Lancaster.

[April 16, 1871.]

XV.

THE wit and sentiment of the dinner-table, encircled by intelligent men and women, if they could have been recorded,
say for the last thirty years, would be a treasure above price.
Flashed out under the influences of generous fare and refined
familiarity, they startle or delight, like so many meteors, and
are as speedily forgotten, or, if remembered at all, never repeated with their original brilliancy.   The only man alive that
I know, for instance, who can tell us about Daniel Webster at
the dinner-table, is the world-known host of the Astor House,
New York, Charles Stetson.   I saw him a few weeks since, and
found him as genial and as full of incident as he was when I
first met, under his storied roof, the leading characters of the

period—between 1846 and 1851—when John Van Buren, Henry J. Raymond, George Law, Horace Greeley, James T. Brady, E. B. Hart, John Brougham, Daniel E. Sickles, Edwin Forrest, Thurlow Weed, Dean Richmond, Henry G. Stebbins, Peter Cagger, congregated there in social intercourse, to discuss politics and poetry, science and art, steam-ships and railroads, candidates and creeds. This goodly company is now widely scattered. Some have been introduced to the mysteries beyond the grave. Webster, John Van Buren, James T. Brady, Dean Richmond, Peter Cagger, Henry J. Raymond, are entered upon the endless roll of death. Thurlow Weed is writing his memories in honored and philosophical retirement; George Law is living respected upon his immense fortune, the product of a career of unmatched energy; Marshall O. Roberts, after an experience of even greater daring and progress, emerges from his repose to lend his large wealth and ripe judgment to the grandest of all the Pacific railroads; Horace Greeley vibrates between his editorial room and his farm, happy in his perfect independence and in the consciousness that he has secured the golden opinions of all sorts of people; Daniel E. Sickles crowns a stormy and brilliant life as his country's representative at one of the oldest European courts; John Brougham is as fertile, alike as actor and author, as he was in 1851; Forrest, after fifty years' service on the stage, is slowly withdrawing from an arena in which he has all this long period figured as the uncontested monarch, living on the rich harvest of his brain in his noble mansion in Philadelphia, surrounded by his books, which he enjoys with a student's zest, and by his engravings, his photographs, his pictures, and his statuary; Colonel Stebbins is the beloved centre of a circle of devoted friends, the patron of art, the philosopher, the statesman, the advanced Democrat who was chosen to Congress without solicitation, and resigned because if he voted with the men who elected him he would dishonor himself, and if he voted against them he would betray them—the Republican who dines at the Democratic Manhattan Club, and still associates with those who know he differs from them from honest convictions; E. B. Hart, the leading representative and the best type of the Hebrews of New York, watching the vast charities of his race as their trustee and counselor. The Astor House, once the chosen rendezvous of these men and their contemporaries, sees them rarely within its honored walls. The wave of fashion and of wealth has carried them up town. Business holds them only a few hours in its vicinity; the afternoon and night find them in their distant homes, or in the more convenient clubs and hotels that have risen like so many palaces along and near the magnificent avenues stretching toward the Central Park.

Ah! that I could recall and describe the happy hours I have spent with most of these men—the humor, the sentiment, the learning, the information, that made our meetings so pleasant and profitable. They are gone, like many who mingled in our delightful symposia.

One of these I specially cherish. It was a night spent with Forrest, George W. Barton, James T. Brady, E. B. Hart, Elliott (the matchless portrait-painter), William A. Seaver, one of the choice writers for *Harper's Magazine* and *Weekly*, Lewis Gaylord Clark, of *The Knickerbocker*, Captain Hunter, of the navy, and one or two more I can not recollect. The speech of Barton, the anecdotes and imitations of Forrest, the jokes of Clark, the repartees of Brady, the art-history of Elliott, the sea-legends of Hunter—I bear them all in memory, and almost see their faces, though more than twenty years have gone, and the flowers and verdure of this early spring are blossoming and growing above the graves of Brady, Elliott, and Hunter.

John Van Buren was the despot of the dinner-table. He had a way of assuming the command that made him resistless, and he had the bearing, the voice, and the domination that

seemed to give equity to the title of " Prince," bestowed by his
enemies and adopted by his friends.

James T. Brady's massive head, with its coronal of curls, his
graceful form, electric wit, ready rhetoric, and Irish enthusiasm—how I see and hear and feel them all, now that he, too,
like Van Buren, has been gathered by the great Shepherd to
the eternal fold.

The best dinner-table orator, the sharpest wit when the cloth
is removed, the most genial of public hosts, is my dear friend,
Morton McMichael, of Philadelphia. Time has not withered
him, either in humor or digestion, judging by my last two experiences : that when he spoke to the trustees of the Peabody
fund, some weeks ago, at the Continental Hotel, in Philadelphia, and that when he presided over the dinner given by the
journalists of Philadelphia to Colonel Charles J. Biddle, the
editor of *The Age*, the Democratic organ of Pennsylvania.

Probably no man ever lived in this country who made, at
least in his short career, more impression upon society generally than John T. S. Sullivan, a Boston-born gentleman, the
college-mate of Charles Sumner, who removed to Philadelphia,
and died there on the 31st of December, 1848, aged thirty-five.
He was singularly, perhaps dangerously, gifted. Lawyer, orator, scholar, and man of society, loved alike by men and women,
he passed away too early, but left behind him a name never to
be forgotten by his friends.

Nobody I know excels Daniel Dougherty, of Philadelphia,
in ready wit at the dinner-table, in powers of imitation, in graceful conversation, and apt response. He is our James T. Brady.
Gray hairs are gathering over you, dear friend, but you have
preserved an unspoiled name, and are growing in wisdom and
caution with increasing greenbacks and years.

[April 23, 1871.]

XVI.

A GREAT many people who read the proceedings of Congress puzzle themselves with the question what is meant by the executive session of the Senate of the United States. This session is, in fact, the Masonry of American legislation. There is perhaps nothing like it in civilized government, although the theory of it pervades the administration of all nations. This theory is that there are certain things in public affairs which can not be intrusted to the public. Among these are treaties with foreign powers, and important official nominations. To discuss these in the presence of an inquisitive newspaper world would be to reveal to outside rivals much that ought to be concealed, and to expose private character to universal criticism. The executive session of the Senate is in many respects like the confidential meetings of the Odd Fellows, the Knights of Pythias, and the Masons, without partaking of any of the peculiar traits of these honored and honorable orders. When the Senate resolves to go into executive session the galleries are cleared of spectators, and the newspaper and *Globe* reporters retire, frequently with a gladsome smile, because, in many cases, they have become fatigued with the "damnable (rhetorical) iteration." Our friend Murphy, the pleasant successor of the venerable Mr. Sutton, with his official corps of rapid and ravenous short-handers — who transcribe the oratorical volume poured out day after day by the Senate, and poured into the columns of *The Globe*—recedes to his little room when the president announces that the Senate will go into executive session, unutterably relieved. Sometimes a motion to go into executive session is carried before a word has been spoken in public debate, and that is the welcome exception to Murphy. I wish I could tell you all that transpires when the doors of the Senate are shut, and the spectators and newspaper men are driven out;

but as my obligations to keep this secret did not terminate with my resignation as Secretary of the Senate, I can only talk to you of the manners of that highly respectable conclave. The first thing is the utter *abandon* of the Senators. They have no audiences to look down upon and listen to them. They have no gentlemen with the lightning pen to telegraph them to distant points. They are not called upon to face and to fear their constituency. Bound together by a solemn covenant not to reveal what transpires, they do exactly what pleases them most. I must say, with my frequent opportunities of observation, I have seen few who ever overpassed the courtesies and the proprieties of the place. All are easier and more familiar than when under the universal eye of a suspicious People. Those who smoke, smoke ; those who like to be comfortable, take off their coats—but there is no such thing as dissipation, at least inside the chamber. Debate is made free because there is nobody to take it down, and the altercations, common in the open Senate, are not uncommon between those walls ; and yet the perfect familiarity of the Senators, and the absence of all restraint, contribute to the adjustment of every dispute, however violent.

Talking about these executive sessions reminds me of the difficulty of keeping an official secret. The Senators are all oath-bound not to disclose executive business, and they rarely do so, unless as regards nominations and confirmations for political offices ; but as these involve nothing of important political concern, there is a common courtesy that when a man is rejected or confirmed the circumstance may be freely spoken of ; and it deserves to be said of the Senators generally that they keep what is intrusted to them with unusual fidelity. To exercise ordinary discretion and care requires extraordinary tact. The doors of the Senate are scarcely opened after executive session, when the whole newspaper tribe besiege the Senators with inquiries, and he must be a rare man who can refuse to drop a word to an editorial or reportorial friend.

Cabinet Ministers have many secrets confided to them, and great ingenuity is required to rescue them from dangerous revelations. The safest depositary of an official secret I ever knew was James Buchanan. This may have resulted from his cold and unimpassioned nature. Certain it is, he never betrayed what took place either in the Senate or in the Cabinet. The manner in which he preserved and kept from public view the fact of his nomination as Secretary of State under President Polk, twenty-nine years ago, is a good illustration. He was regarded as the probable successor of Daniel Webster, who held that great portfolio under most of the administration of John Tyler, but there were many doubters. I remember being present at a dinner given at the National Hotel by Commodore Stockton, of New Jersey, a few days before the inauguration of President Polk, in February of 1845. Among the guests were General William O. Butler, of Kentucky; George Bancroft, of New York; Robert J. Walker, of Mississippi; and John R. Thompson, of New Jersey—all since dead, except Bancroft, now at Berlin. Commodore Stockton was exceedingly anxious to discover the material of the incoming Cabinet, and he offered a wager that he could name a majority of the men who were to compose it. That wager was taken by Mr. Buchanan, without an allusion to his contingent connection with the new Administration. He was so careful and cautious that, up to the time of his nomination by President Polk, no friend—not even the one nearest to him—could positively assert that he would be associated with it in any way.

I observe that the *Lancaster Examiner*, without absolutely contradicting my statement that General Jackson recommended James Buchanan to James K. Polk for Secretary of State, questions it upon the theory that General Jackson had never previously trusted " Pennsylvania's favorite son." All I have to say in reply, is that I have no doubt this letter of General Jackson in favor of Mr. Buchanan will be found among the

private papers of the latter, and that his biographer will establish the fact as I have stated it. That General Jackson was
never a special friend of James Buchanan is most true, but that
he recommended Buchanan to James K. Polk as the first man
in his Cabinet is my sincere belief.

[April 30, 1871.]

XVII.

THE winter before the war, shortly after having been again
elected Clerk of the House of Representatives of the United
States, I rented two large chambers on the lower floor of what
is known on Capitol Hill as "The Mills House," and occupied
them, with brief intervals, until March of 1871—sometimes including the two upper parlors, and occasionally taking possession of the whole house, which was very large and commodious;
but this only happened when I called my friends around me,
about once every three months. I began these assemblies
shortly after the outbreak of the rebellion, for the purpose of
creating and cementing a patriotic public opinion. My guests
were always numerous enough to fill every room in the house,
including the basement. They were men of all ideas, professions, and callings. We had no test but devotion to our country. We met like a band of brothers—the lawyer, the clergyman, the editor, the reporter, the poet, the painter, the inventor,
the politician, the stranger, the old citizen, the Southerner and
the Northerner, the soldier and the statesman, the clerk and
the Cabinet Minister, and last, not least, President Lincoln
himself. Nothing was spared to add to the interest of these
symposia. We had speeches and recitations, vocal and instrumental music, all adding to the main objective point — the
awakening of an enthusiasm for the assailed Republic. If a

leading man reached Washington on the day of our meeting he was instantly invited. A journal of the proceedings of these hearty foregatherings would be unusually attractive reading. At one table Thaddeus Stevens would be found playing a game of whist with the Democratic Representative from Indiana, the venerable John Law; at another William Pitt Fessenden and Senator Nesmith, of Oregon. Speaker, now Vice-President Colfax, would be seen in the corner with his inevitable cigar, talking with Hon. Samuel J. Randall, the Democratic Representative from the First Pennsylvania district. In another recess George D. Prentice, of the *Louisville Journal*, would be discussing politics with Joseph Medill, of the *Chicago Tribune*. The great portrait-painter, Elliott, would be engaged in art-ethics with Brady, the photographer; and so on through all the grades of sentiment and society.

One evening in particular I shall never forget, when William H. Russell, the famous correspondent of the *London Times*, was present. While we were singing the " Star-spangled Banner" (this was before we got rid of the peculiar institution), he joined in the chorus in a loud voice, singing " America, the land of the free, and the home of *the slave*." There were argumentations and discussions, but no quarreling. Another night, when nearly all the Cabinet were present, General Cameron, Secretary of War, startled the proprieties by taking bold ground in favor of arming the negroes. He was immediately answered by Hon. Caleb N. Smith, Secretary of the Interior, and the controversy became exceedingly animated, enlisting all the company, silencing the music, and creating a deal of consternation. Robert J. Walker, George D. Prentice, and several more participated in the discussion, while Edwin M. Stanton, then a quiet practitioner of the law, stood by, a silent figure in the scene.

Edwin Forrest was always one of us whenever he visited Washington, and, as I said in a former number, was the toast and the star of the night. He gave liberally to the Union cause, without being a Republican. Though he did not unite with us when we sung "John Brown," none could have been more graceful and ready in contributing to the general pleasure. One dramatic night I shall never forget. Forrest was in royal condition. He came early and stayed late. He seemed to be prepared to make every body happy. He needed no solicitation to display his varied stores of humor and of information : sketches of foreign travel ; photographs of Southern manners, alike of the master and the slave ; his celebrated French criticism upon Shakespeare ; his imitation of the old clergyman of Charleston, South Carolina, who, deaf himself, believed every body else to be so ; his thrilling account of his meeting with Edmund Kean, at Albany, when Forrest was a boy ; his incidents of General Jackson ; his meeting with Lafayette at Richmond, in 1825. Few that heard him can ever forget that night. But nothing that he did will be remembered longer than the manner in which he recited " The Idiot Boy," a production up to that time unknown to every body in the room except Forrest and myself, and to me only because I heard him repeat it seven years before, when I lived on Eighth Street, in the house lately known as the Waverley. These lines are so beautiful and so unique that I print them for the benefit of the readers of these hasty sketches.

To add to their present value, it may be interesting to say that the verses subjoined are taken from an autograph copy, forwarded to me yesterday by my dear friend Forrest himself, accompanied by the following note. The style of Mr. Forrest's writing is as clear, correct, and careful as it was twenty years ago :

"PHILADELPHIA, May 4, 1871.

"MY DEAR FORNEY,—I could not find the book that contains the little poem. I think friend Dougherty has it, and so I have written it from memory.

"The author, who is doubtless in Heaven, will, I trust, pardon all mistakes.   Your friend,   EDWIN FORREST.

"Colonel JOHN W. FORNEY.

"'THE IDIOT BOY.

"'It had pleased God to form poor Ned
    A thing of idiot mind,
Yet, to the poor unreasoning boy,
    God had not been unkind.

"'Old Sarah loved her helpless child,
    Whom helplessness made dear;
And he was every thing to her,
    Who knew no hope or fear.

"'She knew his wants, she understood
    Each half-articulate call,
For he was every thing to her,
    And she to him was all.

"'And so for many a year they lived,
    Nor knew a wish beside;
But age at last on Sarah came,
    And she fell sick—and died.

"'He tried in vain to waken her,
    He called her o'er and o'er;
They told him she was dead!
    The words to him no import bore.

"'They closed her eyes and shrouded her,
    While he stood wondering by,
And when they bore her to the grave,
    He followed silently.

"'They laid her in the narrow house,
    They sung the funeral stave;
And when the fun'ral train dispersed,
    He lingered by that grave.

"'The rabble boys that used to jeer
    Whene'er they saw poor Ned,
Now stood and watched him by the grave,
    And not a word they said.

"'They came and went and came again,
   Till night at last came on;
Yet still he lingered by the grave,
   Till every one had gone.

"'And when he found himself alone,
   He swift removed the clay;
Then raised the coffin up in haste,
   And bore it swift away.

"'He bore it to his mother's cot,
   And laid it on the floor,
And with the eagerness of joy
   He barred the cottage door.

"'Then out he took his mother's corpse,
   And placed it in a chair;
And soon he heaped the hearth,
   And made the kindling fire with care.

"'He had put his mother in *her* chair,
   And in its wonted place,
And then he blew the fire, which shone,
   Reflected in her face.

"'And, pausing now, her hand would feel,
   And then her face behold:
"*Why*, mother, do you look so pale,
   And why are you so cold?"

"'It had pleased God from the poor wretch
   His only friend to call;
Yet God was kind to him, and soon
   In *death* restored him *all*.'"

The picture of the Idiot Boy and his widowed mother, the broken voice and sobs of the son when the poor woman died and was followed to the grave by her witless child—if this grand picture could have been presented from the stage, it would have been even greater than his *Lear* or his *Richelieu*. I had Jefferson more than once as a visitor, and Davenport, and generous, true-hearted Murdoch.

But long before I was a tenant in the old Mills House it had

a peculiar story of its own.   It is one of the institutions of
Washington.   Occupied during the last hundred years by men
of all shades of politics, there is hardly a room in it that has
not a legend by which to be remembered.   George Washington, John Marshall, and their contemporaries, have met and
counseled within its walls, and the political leaders of a later
period have successively gathered there.   When I bade farewell, nothing seemed more saddening to me than to feel that I
had probably left the old house forever, and yet, whenever business calls me back to the National Capital, I return to these
ancient rooms as a son goes back to home and fireside.   But
there are so many more reminiscences connected with these reunions that I shall venture some other allusions to them in a
future number.

[May 7, 1871.]

XVIII.

RUFUS CHOATE, of Massachusetts, must have been, in most
of his qualities, very like the lamented George W. Barton, of
Pennsylvania.   Quick and impetuous of speech, wholly original
in manner, abounding in rich and gorgeous imagery, he was
also a melancholy man, and his keen, quick intellect wore out
and wore through a nervous organization.   It will be remembered that his great heart was severely wounded when Daniel
Webster was defeated by General Scott for the Whig nomination for President at the Baltimore Convention in 1852, which
he attended as a delegate from Massachusetts, and that from
that hour his allegiance to his favorite party began to weaken,
until 1856, when he took ground in favor of James Buchanan
in his celebrated speech at Worcester—the effect of which will
be recalled by the unforgotten sentence in which he called

upon his friends to support the Democratic candidate, because he " carried the flag and kept step to the music of the Union." I heard a very pleasant incident, some evenings ago, related by a distinguished Senator in Congress from one of the Western States, who was himself the party immediately benefited. Anxious when quite young to complete the study of his profession, he visited Boston, and called upon Mr. Choate and offered himself as one of his students. Struck by the earnestness and frankness of the appeal, the great lawyer took him into his confidence, and soon realized that he could be made useful. At the end of two years, the student informed the preceptor that he intended to begin the practice of his profession in the flourishing State of Wisconsin. The answer of Mr. Choate was characteristic. He said : " I honor your determination, but I was selfish enough to hope that you might remain with me ; yet, as you have resolved upon this step, you can always rely upon my friendship;" then asked if he had any money, to which the young man replied that he had no means to purchase his law library ; whereupon Mr. Choate said, " Go to Little & Brown (the old-established law publishers), select your books, and refer them to me as your security." Elated by this renewed mark of his esteem, he laid in what he conceived to be a good assortment, and took the list back to the great man, who, glancing over it, said, " Your list is too small;" and, taking up the legal catalogue, he designated with his own hand a very much increased collection, amounting to some four or five thousand dollars, adding, " With these tools you can begin something like effective work." Our young practitioner started for the West, and opened his office, but, as bad luck would have it, was stricken down by one of the dangerous fevers of the country. Of course he could not pay the note when it fell due, but Mr. Choate kindly and carefully protected his credit. With unbroken spirit and restored health he began the practice of the law, and at the end of a comparatively short time earned enough money to liquidate his obligation; "but," he said, "as long as life lasts I shall never cease to cherish the name of Rufus Choate, and I would walk from here to Boston barefooted to serve any of his kith or kin."

Dwelling upon the devotion of Choate to Webster, and of Webster to Choate, our regret increases that these remarkable men had not, like John Quincy Adams, preserved a steady record of their busy and distinguished lives. How full of incident they must have been! They reveled in the enjoyment of literature and of all descriptions of learning. Wholly different in temperament, and yet alike in their eagerness to lead in great mental strifes, their written experience would have filled priceless volumes. Webster died in his seventieth year, and Choate in his sixty-first—the first in 1852, and the second in 1859, and the finest tribute ever paid to the Great Expounder was paid by his affectionate follower and friend at Dartmouth College, on July 27, 1853.

How faithfully the elder statesman has described the difference between the recollections of the mind and the memory of the heart will be realized in the following beautiful lines, not often published, which he contributed to a lady's album:

"If stores of dry and learned lore we gain,
  Close keep them in the memory of the brain:
  Things, dates, and facts, whate'er we knowledge call,
  There is the common ledger of them all;
  And images on this cold surface traced
  Make slight impression and are soon effaced.

"But we've a record more beautiful and bright
  On which our friendships and our loves to write:
  That these may never from the mind depart,
  We trust them to the memory of the heart.
  There is no dimming—no effacement here,
  Each new pulsation keeps the record clear;
  Warm golden letters all the tablet fill,
  Nor lose their lustre till the heart stands still."

[May 14, 1871.]

XIX.

SOMBRE manners do not always prove the statesman. The greatest men I ever knew were plain of speech and plain of dress. Even those who could not tell a good story relished one from others. The clearest logician in the days of Jackson and Van Buren was Silas Wright, who was strangely modest and unobtrusive. Henry Clay, haughty and imperious as he often was, delighted in anecdote. The unequaled Webster was too wise and sensible not to enjoy humor. John C. Calhoun was almost child-like in his ways. William Wirt was ambitious, and literally reveled in the flowers of literature. John Quincy Adams was too thorough a master of diplomacy not to know the value of wit. No man now living, either at home or abroad, more keenly enjoys music, painting, and poetry, and talks better about them, than Charles Sumner. His tastes are refined, his hospitalities generous, and his plate, pictures, and engravings rare; and he could pronounce as learned a discourse upon art as upon politics. There are not many wits in Congress at the present day. If you exclude Nye, of Nevada, in the Senate, and Proctor Knott, of Kentucky, in the House, you will perhaps sigh for such old-time men as James Thompson, of Pennsylvania, and "Jack" Ogle, of the same State; Mike Walsh, of New York; Felix Grundy McConnell, of Alabama; William H. Polk, of Tennessee, and Sergeant S. Prentiss, of Mississippi. All these are dead but Thompson, who now presides over the Supreme Court of Pennsylvania, enjoying the confidence of men of all parties. It used to be a saying that the laugh of James Thompson, of Pennsylvania, was the most infectious laugh in the House. He could not sing, but he was a capital story-teller; and to-day, when he unbends his judicial dignity, he can bring back the men of the past more vividly than any other man I know. I recollect well the pleasant evenings I spent while he was a member of Congress, with winning, magnetic Jack Ogle, from my native State. How rapidly, between the stories of the one and the songs of the other, time passed away! Ogle had two favorites, one the famous poem entitled "Jeannette and Jeannot," which ought to have been often sung during the recent war between France and Germany. I shall never forget the effect produced by his exceedingly handsome face, ringing voice, and flashing eye, as he rolled forth these simple stanzas. They deserve to be repeated in every household in the civilized world in this era of approaching peace and fraternization. Excuse me for reviving them:

"JEANNETTE AND JEANNOT.

"You are going far away, far away from poor Jeannette—
There is no one left to love me now; and you, too, may forget;
But my heart it will be with you, wherever you may go,
Can you look me in the face and say the same to me, Jeannot?
When you wear the jacket red and the beautiful cockade,
Oh! I fear that you'll forget all the promises you've made.
With your gun upon your shoulder, and your bayonet by your side,
You'll be taking some proud lady, and be making her your bride.
    You'll be taking, etc.

"Or when glory leads the way, you'll be madly rushing on,
Never thinking if they kill you that my happiness is gone.
Or if you win the day perhaps a general you'll be;
Though I am proud to think of that, love, what will become of me?
Oh! if I were Queen of France, or still better, Pope of Rome,
I'd have no fighting men abroad, no weeping maids at home:
All the world should be at peace, or, if kings must show their might,
Why let those who make the quarrels be the only men to fight.
    Yes, let those, etc."

The other was a piece of domestic poetry, known as the "Arkansas Traveler." This would have been a monotonous recitation if it had not been relieved by a violin accompaniment, which made it irresistibly comic. It was no doubt borrowed from the extreme South, whence it derived its name, yet it was always a favorite among the Scotch-Irish of Western

Pennsylvania, and is doubtless to this day recited along the Juniata, the West Branch, and in Lancaster and Chester counties, in fact, wherever the Irish Presbyterian element is to be found. Ogle had caught the idea and utilized it in his Congressional campaigns, and it was really a treat to see him, drawn up to his full height, playing the air on the violin, and then asking humorous questions, as follows:

"Stranger, how far is it to the next tavern?"

"About a mile," was the reply. Then again, resuming his bow, would play the monotonous chorus, and continue the dialogue:

"Stranger, can you give us the other part of that tune?"

"Oh, yes," and repeat precisely the same strain, in addition to the printed words of the song.

Ogle, during his performance, would introduce every person present and every joke in his recollection, and would thus run through an interminable length, tiring nobody except the chief actor himself, who would finally drop his instrument out of sheer exhaustion.

So true it is that work without amusement is a sure preparation for death; that the brain, like the body, must have rest, and that when either is overworked, it is like the taper that goes out for want of oil. There is no sight more painful than the incessant occupation of public men, whether statesmen, scholars, editors, railroad officers, divines, or mechanics, who, misled by the fatal idea that labor may be pursued without pause or repose, discard all relaxation, and end either in sudden death, or, what is worse, premature decay. There is no class of what may be called public men who live a longer average life than the actors, and why? Because, however hard they may work, they alternate work with pleasure. In fact, their work itself is pleasure. The philosophy of it consists, perhaps, in the romance of their profession, that while they are personating nature and depicting art, they are separated from the hard realism of the outer world; but whatever it may be, we are taught one lesson—that no man can enjoy real happiness without occasional recreation and freedom from care.

Abraham Lincoln was a character by himself, incomparable and unique. He was among the saddest of humanity, and yet his sense of the ridiculous was so keen that it bore him up from difficulties that would have broken down almost any other man. That he gave way to uncontrollable fits of grief in the dark hours of the war is a fact beyond question—that sometimes his countenance was clouded with sorrow, all who met him know; and yet he could, so to speak, lift himself out of his troubles, and enjoy his own repartees and the good things of others. Nothing gave me more pleasure in my frequent visits to him, as Secretary of the Senate and editor of *The Chronicle*, than to take with me men who would tell original stories in an original way; for I felt that if I could lighten his cares and brighten his gloom I would be conferring a real favor, and I never was half so welcome as when in such company. The old quirks and quips of the clown in the circus, the broad innuendoes of the low comedian, the quiet sallies of the higher walks of the drama, interested him more than the heavy cadences and profound philosophy of tragedy. Had his life not been extinguished by the assassin, his rare love of his kind, his perfect disinterestedness, his uncouth, yet entirely natural simplicity of character, and his absolute idolatry of every thing that was happy in nature and in man, would, I believe, have prolonged his life far beyond the Psalmist's age.

[May 21, 1871.]

XX.

No Pennsylvania statesman is more kindly remembered than William Wilkins, who was born at Carlisle, Pa., December 20, 1779, and died at Homewood, near Pittsburgh, June 23, 1865, in the 86th year of his age. His career may be said to have been unusually fortunate and distinguished ; and when called away he was sincerely mourned by a community in which he had lived a long period, and taken an active part in public affairs. A Senator in Congress from 1831 to 1834, successor to James Buchanan at the Court of St. Petersburg, Representative in Congress from 1843 to 1844, Secretary of War under John Tyler from 1844 to 1845, member of the State Senate in 1857, and intermediately a successful practitioner of the law and judge in the higher courts of his district, he filled all these diversified stations with signal dignity and tact. His family was closely identified with the Government in its political, judicial, military, and naval service—many of his connections to this day holding high and responsible positions. Reared to the habits and manners of good society, and well educated, he was one of the most agreeable of men ; and yet, while mingling much in fashionable life, he had confessedly few of its vices. I have seen him many an evening, when jollity, wit, and humor ruled the hour, yet he never touched a glass of wine, and was the chief attraction, by his endless flow of spirits and his peculiar magnetic amiability. When I was the Democratic candidate for United States Senator, in 1857, before the Legislature of Pennsylvania, of which Mr. Wilkins was a member, I felt that we should have exchanged places, and that the post for which I was selected ought to have been tendered to him, and called upon him to make the suggestion. His answer was characteristic : " Ah, my young friend, I have seen the elephant, and it is quite time that you should have an opportunity of making his acquaintance," a luxury, by the way, which General Cameron stepped in and reserved for himself.

I am reminded of this interesting character by a letter which I received a few days ago from my old friend, Dr. Jonas R. McClintock, of Pittsburgh, who attended the venerable statesman during his last illness, and who is devoting himself to the praiseworthy task of reviving the past history of Pittsburgh and Western Pennsylvania. His materials will run back a hundred years, and will, when embodied in book form, constitute not only a valuable depository of facts, but, if written, as they will be, in the Doctor's pleasant style, one of the most fascinating memoirs of the times. If men like Dr. McClintock would occupy a little of their leisure in the accomplishment of the same purpose, in their respective localities, they would honor themselves and enrich the literature of their country. As a specimen of the work now in course of preparation by Dr. McClintock, he inclosed to me the following striking incident of the last hours of his venerable friend, Judge Wilkins, now for the first time published :

"Judge Wilkins gloried in the unimpeachable integrity that marked the 'bench,' and jealously guarded his own status in the profession by well and carefully determined opinions. It was a treat to listen to his criticisms on the public acts of the various departments of the Government as they transpired during the recent rebellion. It was a current on which he delighted to glide, affording invigorating exercise and securing an intellectual clearness that accompanied him through life.

"On the occasion of a several days' anticipated visit, during the last few weeks of life, from his nearest neighbor, a medical friend, who was prevented making his customary unprofessional call, the Judge was found in a half-reclining position on his couch, in pleasant conversation with members of his family seated around, while the music of the little birds that had become wedded to the broad eastern portico by his punctual supplies, broke upon his ear their joyous song of thanks.

"After a pause, hesitating to mar this lovely patriarchal picture, the defaulting visitor entered the open September door, to
whom the Judge turned, and after words of sharp but playful
rebuke, closing with finding ample apology for apparent neglect
in sickness at home, he said : 'You can not guess, Doctor, how
I have passed some of the tedious hours on my cot.' Pausing
for a moment, he continued : 'I have been trying Jefferson
Davis for high-treason. I have gone through the whole formu-
la with all the solemnity of a great State trial; the court properly constituted, the jury impaneled, and the prisoner arraign-
ed, the latter answering to all counts in the indictment, "Not
guilty."

"'In opening the case for the United States, I took occasion
to assure the court that I would economize its valuable time so
far as the prosecution was concerned, and close the case of the
State in half an hour.

"'The first witness called to the stand was General Longstreet, who, having been duly sworn, stated, in answer to an interrogatory, that he had commanded the armed forces of the
Southern Confederacy who had invaded the District of Columbia, and within the limits of the city of Washington had killed
and wounded more than one hundred Union soldiers, and that
in so acting he had but obeyed the order of the chief commander, General R. E. Lee. Waiving further question the witness
was discharged, and General Lee called and duly sworn, who
testified as to his position in the Confederate service, his direc-
tions to Longstreet, and his subordination to Jefferson Davis,
president and commander-in-chief of the army and navy of the
Confederate States, from whom he had received instructions to
invade Maryland and the District for the purposes carried out
by his lieutenant-general. At this point I closed and rested
my case. After hearing the defense, and without a word of argument, I asked the jury to render a verdict of guilty. His
fate was then sealed. The defense of want of jurisdiction—too

late in presenting, and weak if entertained—left the prisoner's counsel to a silent submission, and he was duly convicted.

" 'Yet in mercy I looked at the matter in another light, and to that end constituted myself the leading advocate of the prisoner. After solemn arraignment, the calm, worn, but inflexible offender, who did not appear to shrink from the bloody consequences of his acts, or tremble at his own peril, following *my judgment and counsel* as his only hope for the future, to the question put in the ponderous tones of the clerk—"Guilty or not guilty?" said: "May it please the court, I answer *guilty! not morally, but politically guilty.* Permit me to say further, the first lessons that fell on my ears at the hearthstone of my father —the first political teachings received at the feet of the wise and learned men of the academy and the university, and vindicated by the universal sentiment of those with whom I mingled in Southern homes, comprehended the doctrines inculcated by the Virginia resolutions of 1798, teaching allegiance as first due to the sovereignty of my State, subordinating that of the General Government.

" ' "This may in your wisdom, and in the judgment of the world, be determined a high crime ; but I submit that it was done in the faith of the right, and with the belief, however misguided, of conscientious duty.

" ' "I therefore throw myself on the judgment of the court, and ask its merciful recommendation to pardon."

" 'I,' said the Judge, 'felt that this was his *only chance of escape.*

" 'Thus I have been filling up my time, dreaming myself away in the sturdy hope for an early return of fraternal feeling among the States.' "

Standing on the very verge of the grave, after an eighty years' buffet with the world, pleasantly rehearsing the line of thought that had engaged his last hours, forgetting his weariness and weakness in first grasping treason by the throat, and

then turning from the sacrifice and counseling such frank ac-
knowledgment as could not fail to reach the magnanimity of the
authorities so deeply offended—such was the loved, not fault-
less, sage of " Homewood" during the fortnight that transpired
before the "golden bowl was broken," or the flowers of his own
choice placed upon his bier.

> "Stronger by weakness, wiser men become,
> As they draw near to their eternal home ;
> Leaving the old, both worlds at once they view,
> They stand upon the threshold of the new."

[May 28, 1871.]

XXI.

CALLED to Washington on official business, I find myself this
warm and breezy morning of the 30th of May seated at the
open window of my old room in the Mills House, once more
looking over into the sacred grounds of Arlington, where twenty thousand Union soldiers sleep their last sleep, and silently
yet sternly sentinel the Capitol they saved. And this is Decoration day ! The Departments are closed in honor of the dead
heroes. From Maine to Mexico, wherever the grave of a
Union soldier is found, it will be visited by some Union man
or woman.

> "Such graves as these are pilgrim shrines,
> Shrines to no code or creed confined ;
> The Delphian vales, the Palestines—
> The Meccas of the mind."

The fervor with which Decoration day is venerated proves
the undying love of our people for their country. The sentiment is a conviction that grows with every hour, and ripens
only to be renewed in freshness and vigor. Decoration day is,

therefore, another Independence day; precisely as the abolition of human slavery in 1863 gave force to the abolition of British surveillance in 1776. But it was more than this. It was the intellectual disenthralment of four millions of blacks and thirty millions of whites. It revolutionized the wicked work of ages of misrule. It wrought in less than nine years the destruction of the evils of almost as many centuries.

Where were we all on the 30th of May, 1861? As I ask the question, Robert E. Lee's Arlington house shines out white from the dark green foliage of the southern side of the Potomac, and seems to answer: "Ten years ago this day my owner had just tendered an unstained sword, with a troubled heart, to his country's foe. Ten years ago Abraham Lincoln, Stephen A. Douglas, Stonewall Jackson, James Buchanan, Edward D. Baker, Howell Cobb, John B. Floyd, Lewis Cass, Owen Lovejoy, were living; they have since gone before the Great Judge, and have answered for all their mortal deeds. Ten years ago the thousands of slain around me, and 'three hundred thousand more,' were active and intelligent men, useful fathers, husbands, sons, and brothers. But these dead have left behind lessons and warnings that will not die."

"Ah! gentlemen," said Frederick Douglass, the really great leader of the colored race of America, yesterday afternoon, "who shall tell the story of these last ten years? I can not. To me all is changed; and what an unutterable, indescribable change! From slavery to liberty, from ostracism to equality, from ignorance to self-respect, from sin to schools, from the lash to the light, from the bludgeon to the ballot, from a country bound in chains to a nation robed in glory, from a capital that seemed to be rooted in despotism to a great city, free and wholesome and beneficent. Find your orator to tell us of these marvels. I have no speech to describe, though my heart cherishes them all."

"Blessed be this night," said another of the same race on another occasion. "Five times have I been sold into slavery in Washington—three times on the block, and twice with the ball and chain on my feet; and now I am free, and all my children, and their children's children."

And what could John M. Langston, the law professor of the Howard University, say? The son of a gentleman of Virginia by his own slave, he lives to represent the intellect of his father as his accepted offspring, and to honor and bless his mother.

But on this sacred day other memories are revived. I recall as I write the face, the form, the character, and history of James S. Jackson, of Kentucky, who sleeps with the blessed Union martyrs. The readers of these hasty anecdotes will perhaps recollect my reference to him on the night of my Mazeppa speech on Missouri Avenue, after I had been elected Clerk of the House of Representatives in December of 1859. Jackson was afterward a Whig Representative in the Thirty-seventh Congress from Kentucky, and when elected was about forty. He was chosen as a pro-slavery man, with intense attachment to Henry Clay, John J. Crittenden, and the old leaders of that school of politics, but also with intense attachment to the Union. I never met him until I met him as a Representative in the great Congress preceding the rebellion. His genial nature, his extremely handsome face and athletic form, his eloquence of speech and magnetism of manner, attracted me; and yet, although somewhat differing in politics—he as the ideal of the old Whig Party in its best days, and I as the ideal of the better days of the Democracy—we coalesced in ardent devotion to the Union. He was against me for Clerk, yet he was glad I was elected—not because he cared for me, but because he desired to rebuke the administration of Mr. Buchanan, whose course on the Kansas Question he did not hesitate to denounce as unutterably bad.

On this Decoration day, as I look out upon Arlington Heights and hear the guns thundering over the graves of those

who perished that their country might live, I think of handsome
Jackson, and of an incident related to me by one of his devoted
Kentucky friends, now holding a high and honorable position
under General Grant's administration. Jackson left his seat in
the House to offer his life to the Republic.   In doing this he
felt that he was separating from many near and dear friends
in Kentucky, all of whom, equally devoted to the Union, were
also devoted to slavery.   He had served several months in the
war when slavery was abolished in the District of Columbia.
His old associates, believing they could swerve him from his
fidelity to his country, conceived that emancipation would greatly disappoint him, and one of their number wrote him a letter,
stating now that the Yankees had shown that this was simply
an abolition war, he ought to leave the "Federal" army and
come over to his old friends, in which case a better position
awaited him.   This letter, owing to circumstances unnecessary
to relate here, fell into the hands of his brave wife, a Kentucky
woman.   She was so indignant at the attempt to debauch her
husband that she tore it up, but immediately after, believing
that he had better see it, womanlike, gathered the fragments
and sent the missive forward to her husband.   He received it
in the company of friends, laughed heartily at it, and referred
to the Confederate who had written it as a capital good fellow, but as one who had wholly misunderstood his character.
Among those who heard of the letter was the well-known Brigadier-General William Nelson, subsequently killed by General
Jefferson C. Davis in a personal rencontre at the Galt House,
in Louisville, on the 29th of September, 1862.   Nelson remarked, after the letter to Jackson had been read, that the writer
seemed to *know his man* or he never would have written it.
This observation was reported to Jackson by some convenient
friend, who belonged to the order of men who always report
unpleasant remarks, and resulted in a challenge from Jackson
to Nelson.   Nothing prevented a mortal meeting but the inter-

vention of the venerable John J. Crittenden, the friend of both, who came from Louisville to the camp and stepped between the young Hotspurs. But they never spoke until after one of the subsequent battles, in which Nelson displayed almost superhuman bravery. Jackson's cavalry regiment could not be called into the fight, and he lay chafing at a distance from the field. But when he came into camp and found that praise of his adversary was in the mouth of every soldier, he rushed up to him, and threw his arms around his neck, and said : " I never can be the enemy of a man who has fought so bravely for the old flag."

They both died in 1862—Jackson at the head of his regiment in the battle of Perryville, Kentucky, and Nelson, as I have said, by the hands of Jefferson C. Davis, a brave and noble soldier, now in New York, whom Nelson had grossly insulted. Jackson and Nelson were both men of strong convictions ; they were men of storm and tempest, but of noble hearts ; they loved Clay, Crittenden, Breckinridge, Preston, and Prentice of the *Louisville Journal.* To go into the Union cause against all their social prejudices and friends was a great struggle, but go they did. They died young, but they had lived a long experience. Nelson was a commander in the navy, and died a brevet major-general in the army. Jackson had just got into Congress when the war broke out, and died before he finished his Congressional career.

[June 4, 1871.]

XXII.

LOOKING back along more than half a century of the varied, brilliant, and useful works of Adolphe Thiers, the present virtual head of the French government, who is now seventy-four years old, the thought occurred to me what an interesting chapter

could be written of other venerable men still living. Brougham
lived to his ninetieth, and Palmerston survived to his eighty-
first year. Earl Russell is eighty. Lyndhurst died in his ninety-first year. The French historian and publicist, Guizot, is
eighty-four. The civic and martial chieftains of Germany, who
figured most prominently in the late terrific campaign, are many
of them very old.

Philadelphia has an unusual share of remarkable men still
living between seventy and eighty, and a number even beyond
that great age. The posterity of the well-known merchant,
Daniel Smith, presents a record rarely paralleled. The mother
died in 1799, leaving seven children, five of whom are now living. The oldest brother, James S., died in 1861, in his eighty-
first year. Francis Gurney Smith is still living, in his eighty-
eighth year; also Richard S. Smith, president of the Union
Mutual Insurance Company, who will be eighty-two in August;
Daniel Smith, Jr., was eighty last February; William S. Smith
is seventy-nine; and Charles S. Smith, seventy-two in April.
Mrs. Poulson, the sister, died last year, aged seventy-six. The
six brothers have lived over fifty years each with their wives.
They have lived blameless, useful, and honorable careers as
merchants and as leaders in great public works. What is most
delightful of all is that the wives of four of these gentlemen survive at nearly the same age as themselves. They have all celebrated their "golden weddings." It is not often that a single
family can present such longevity and such unstained and even
distinguished reputations. Like their ancestors, they are true-
hearted Philadelphians; and he who would gather some of the
most interesting memoirs of the city founded by William Penn,
could do nothing better than to interview the eldest of these
five brothers at his residence on Pine Street, Philadelphia. I
have several times referred to Horace Binney, in his ninety-first
year—in his day among the ripest and ablest lawyers in the
world. General Robert Patterson is the evergreen of his time

—still vigorous in his eightieth year. Prominent on every great occasion, ready of speech and wit, hospitable in his own home, patriotic and public-spirited, one of the most active cotton merchants in Philadelphia, rising with the lark, working at his counting-house without eating a morsel until his dinner at five in the afternoon, frequently closing the day as the most active and genial guest at a social gathering; he is a *rara avis*. William D. Lewis, former Collector of the Port, also in his eightieth year, is one of the same school, preserving in his old age a youthful and generous heart and an undaunted spirit. He will tell you of St. Petersburg nearly sixty years ago, which he visited as a youth, regale you with incidents of Philadelphia in the olden time, and fill your memory with anecdotes of the good and great men whose confidence he shared.

Few persons know that Thomas Sully, the eminent portrait-painter, is yet among us, on the eve of his eighty-eighth year. The visitor to his studio is impressed by the remarkable brightness and activity of the venerable man, who is still inspired with the true fire of his art.

He was born in England. Originally the family came from France. His father's name was Matthew Sully. His mother was English, and came first from England to Norfolk, Virginia, in 1794. Mr. Sully took his first lessons in Charleston, from a coach-painter. He began as a miniature-painter when only seven years old. From Charleston he came to Philadelphia, then to New York, by advice of Cooper, the actor, then back to Philadelphia about 1810, where he has ever since remained. He twice visited England, once in 1837, to paint Queen Victoria. He also took lessons at different times of West, Lawrence, and Stuart, the last named not even surpassed in certain qualities by Vandyke.

Mr. Sully is a musician of considerable proficiency. He played the flute in the orchestra of the Musical Fund Society for many years, and he is now its vice-president. His charac-

teristics, as a painter, are grace, delicacy, fancy, ideality, purity.
He is still painting—often without glasses.   Many of the great
men of his day have sat to him.   Lafayette, Jefferson, Jackson,
Adams, Monroe, Rush, Binney, Cooke, Cooper, Kemble—indeed, among his sitters will be found the distinguished of the
bar, the pulpit, the stage, medicine, etc.   No collection is complete without one or two of his works.   The parlors of Colonel
Fitzgerald, of Philadelphia, are filled with the choice works of
this master.

But none of the men of seventy-eight are so interesting in
character as Henry C. Carey, the memory of whose father, Matthew Carey, is recalled with affectionate reverence, and whose
son may well be styled the worthy son of a worthy sire.   Living in elegant ease on Walnut Street, near Eleventh, Philadelphia, surrounded by his books and his pictures, honored and
loved by troops of friends, kind, generous, and social, busy with
his pen, and always ready to converse with the intelligent of all
parties, Henry C. Carey may be said to have outlived enmity
and envy.   His life is in fact the very best vindication of his
favorite theories, especially in regard to the protection of American industry.   Upon this doctrine, so elaborately and for so
long a period enforced in this country, he may confidently rest
his fame.   It has triumphed not only here but elsewhere.   Riding the other day with our young railroad monarch, Colonel
Thomas A. Scott, between New York and Philadelphia, I listened with pleasure to his tribute to Mr. Carey, and especially
to his statement that a distinguished gentleman recently returned from Germany had told him that the works of Mr. Carey on
political economy, translated into German, were scattered
through the whole nation, and were standard books among
statesmen and text-books among the people.   They have also
been converted into the languages of other countries, so that
the days of successful ridicule of his doctrines may be said to
have passed away forever.

Mr. Carey's pleasant Sunday "vespers" at his own home have been described by others. Here he loves to meet his friends in the confidence of innocent social intercourse. Here, regularly, for years past, winter and summer, have assembled some of the ablest intellects of the nation—men of different and differing tastes meeting on the same level—the level of toleration and freedom of discussion, and unity in love of country. Long may these aged men survive—ornaments of society and examples of integrity and patriotism.

[June 11, 1871.]

XXIII.

I HAVE already told you something about the old men of Philadelphia. Now let me write familiarly and frankly of a younger citizen—one who is, perhaps, as generally discussed as any living person. There is a mystery about him which is rather increased by the fact that he is a quiet, though incessant worker —not often seen, yet as ubiquitous as if he possessed the power of repeating himself indefinitely. I mean Thomas Alexander Scott, vice-president of the Pennsylvania Central Railroad, or, as he is every where called, by high and low, from the President to the proletaire—"Tom Scott." Filling a large space in large enterprises, wielding immense resources, combining extraordinary elements, and dealing literally with empires, Colonel Scott is still comparatively young, and qualified, with ordinary care over his reserved forces, physical and mental, for a long and most distinguished life. His experience is another illustration of the elasticity of our institutions; another proof that when the offspring of the wealthy, spoiled and enervated by over-indulgence, fail to grapple with grave duties and responsibilities, we can always find fitter material in the humbler walks, and recruit the energies of the nation from the sons of those who have been hardened in the stern school of necessity and toil.

Thomas Alexander Scott was born in the village of Loudon, Franklin County, Pennsylvania, on the 28th of December, 1824, and on his next birthday will be forty-seven years old. He began as a boy in a country-store at a very low salary, after having completed his education in the one village school, with the one teacher, Robert Kirby, of Loudon ; and upon the death of his father, in 1834, went to live with his eldest sister, whose husband kept a country-store near Waynesborough, in Franklin County, where he remained eighteen months ; then he lived a short time with his brother, James D. Scott, also a merchant, at Bridgeport, in the same county; then with Metcalf & Ritchie, merchants in Mercersburg. In all these situations he exhibited the same energy, and had the confidence and respect of employers and associates for the ability and correctness now so universally awarded to the man. In all his past history his frank, honest, candid, clear, and prompt manner in business transactions has deservedly secured him the confidence and respect of the business world—above all, his goodness of heart, the measure of his favors and charities being the necessities of the friends. My first recollection of him was in Lancaster County, where he was a clerk of Major James Patton, his brother-in-law, who was collector of tolls at Columbia, on the State road, under the administration of Governor Porter, I think, in the year 1838. From this he was transferred to the extensive warehouse and commission establishment of the Leeches, at Columbia, where he remained until 1847, when he came to Philadelphia as chief clerk at Seventh and Willow Streets, on the Schuylkill front, under A. Boyd Cummings, collector of tolls at the eastern end of the Public Works. In 1850 he entered the service of the great Pennsylvania Central at Duncanville, as their general agent of the Mountain or Eastern division. On

the opening of the Western division he was put in charge of
that, and there he remained till he was called to take control
of the entire line, in consequence of the ill-health of General
H. J. Lombaert, the superintendent. In 1859, on the death of
Hon. William B. Foster, vice-president of the road, he was elected to that position, which he continues to fill.

There is no romance in this career, and yet how few now living excite so much curiosity and attract so much attention as
Thomas Alexander Scott! His rapidity and courage alike as
an administrative and executive officer have given him a prestige known wherever a railroad is operated. It was these qualities that induced the Administration to call him into the government service as Assistant Secretary of War after the outbreak of the rebellion; and those of us who studied him then
can well understand how thoroughly he deserves his present
high reputation. He was summoned to Washington early in
1861, at a period when the whole North was panic-stricken—
when the capital was cut off by the rebels lying between it and
the Susquehanna. A man of railroad genius, tact, and experience was imperatively needed. Governor Curtin wanted him
to remain in Pennsylvania, but Mr. Lincoln, the Secretary of
War, and General Scott insisted that the young vice-president
of the Pennsylvania Central should be forthcoming, and he
came, and effectually aided General Butler, then at Annapolis
with his Massachusetts men, to build the road which opened
the way and restored the line of communication, and so saved
Washington from capture. He remained at his desk in the
War Department, unless when called off to superintend the vast
military transportation of the army at other points, until the
crisis was over, and then returned to his post at Philadelphia,
surrounded with the confidence and gratitude of every branch
of the government, executive and legislative. His cheerful and
buoyant temper, his bright face, genial, gentle manners, and,
above all, the readiness with which he answered every request,

and the grace with which he would say No, as he had frequently to do, proved that official labors came easy and natural to
him, and that the cares so sure to break down an ordinary man
bore lightly upon him.   It was pleasant to note how quietly he
met the leaders of armies and the leaders of the Senate, and
how in every circle, no matter what the theme, he was unconstrained and self-poised.   Perhaps one of the secrets of his
popularity was his avoidance of all political discussions.   Intensely attached to his country, Colonel Scott is claimed by no
party, and has as many friends in one as in the other.   His
early training was among Democrats, though many of his nearest connections were Old-line Whigs, and are Republicans.
As the real head of an enterprise which is gradually assuming
more than international proportions, and must depend for its
success upon the support of the whole people, he has little time
to play at the petty party politics of the hour.   He possesses
two inborn gifts, uncommon to one who has not seen the inside
of a school-house since his eleventh year—intuitive mathemat-
ical perception and singular ability in preparing legislation.
He dispatches business with electric facility.   He dictates to
his short-hand reporter as rapidly as an expert, and when he
rises to speak in any of the business conventions, his suggestions are so many flashes of intellect, and his sentences short,
terse, and clear.   He is happy in the capacity of getting rid of
difficult questions in a moment.   One subject dropped he seizes
the other at the proper time, and is as punctual to a promise,
an engagement, or a contract, as he is faithful to a friend.

Some time ago, in one of the managers' cars of the Pennsylvania Central, I sat by, a surprised and amused observer.   At
every station dispatches would be brought to him, which he
tore open and promptly answered, and then resumed the thread
of the conversation.   Sometimes a railroad president or official,
belonging to another State, would come in at the door while
the train waited, state his case, and receive his reply.   Some-

times a negotiation would be conducted between the stations, and yet, at the end of every such passage, he would move over to me, where I sat, and renew his pleasant and instructive talk.

Such are some of the leading traits of Thomas Alexander Scott, or "Aleck," as he used to be called while transacting business for his friend, Metcalf, in Franklin County. It is proper to add that no man has ever been more endeared to his associates in business. I wish I could refer to instances of his generosity to his family and to his friends, but this is a subject upon which he is a little sensitive, and yet he never seems to tire in doing good—never forgets the intimates of his early career, the men who served with him when he was a clerk, agent, or superintendent. Although overwhelmed with engagements, he never allows a case of suffering or misfortune to pass him unheeded. It deserves to be said that in his capacity as the active head of a gigantic corporation, he has never gambled with its great interests at the stock exchange, never corrupted judges or juries, never turned what belonged to others to selfish or mercenary ends; and it is undoubtedly to his exact, accurate, and inflexible business principles that the sound and permanent prosperity of the Pennsylvania Central is chiefly indebted.

I conclude this hasty sketch of my old friend by relating an incident of his promptitude. Some years ago, when his presence was necessary at an extraordinary crisis in the affairs of the company, he started from Pittsburgh on an express train, and found himself, after some hours' travel, obstructed by another train, which had run off the track. The *débris*, the fragments, and confusion produced by the accident would have required at least a day for their removal. The engineers were in despair. After a moment's reflection the Colonel directed that the whole of the wreck *should be burned*, and the torch was applied to the valuable machinery, cars, and goods that lay scattered around. Of course he made his destination; but when he

reached the company and told his story, there was some indig
nation at what they regarded a waste of property. Colonel
Scott sat down and soon convinced them, by a calculation estimating the loss that would accrue by the delay of trains, etc.,
that he had really saved a considerable sum by the transaction.

The brain-work of a man like Colonel Scott is immense, but
he enjoys the rare facility of dismissing troublesome questions
from his mind. He never takes his sorrows with him to bed.
When his day's work is done he retires with a sunny face to his
home, enjoys the society of his family, plays croquet or whist,
rides around the park, looks in at the opera, and now and then
mingles with a company of his friends. Of simple habits and
refined tastes, he ought to live a long life. That he may so live
is my sincere and earnest prayer.

[June 18, 1871.]

XXIV.

A FASCINATING volume might be written of the men who were
identified with Government newspapers in Washington under
the old *régime*, beginning with Joseph Gales and William Winston Seaton, and running on to Duff Green, Amos Kendall, Francis P. Blair, John C. Rives, Thomas Ritchie, Robert Armstrong,
A. O. P. Nicholson, Roger A. Pryor, Charles Eames, Wm. M.
Overton, George S. Gideon, Simeon M. Johnson, William M.
Browne, George W. Bowman, Alexander C. Bullet, and others.
Of this long list those who survive. are Duff Green, now at a
very advanced age ; Francis P. Blair, the generous host at Silver Spring, Maryland, near Washington ; A. O. P. Nicholson,
residing at Columbia, Tennessee ; George S. Gideon and Simeon M. Johnson, of Washington ; Roger A. Pryor, practicing
law in New York ; George W. Bowman, Pennsylvania, and Will-

iam M. Browne, who was in the South when last heard from. All the papers with which they were connected have passed out of existence excepting *The Globe*, now the almost exclusive record of Congressional debates, published by F. & J. Rives and George A. Bailey, to whom it is a source of enormous revenue.

In former times what was called the national organ was liberally sustained by the advertising and the printing of the Government, and the proprietors, who ought to have grown rich, were most generous in the treatment of their editors. It is a grave question whether there has been any actual saving by divorcing the public printing from the press. Certain it is that ever since newspapers at Washington have had to depend upon their own energies they have had a hard struggle. Several attempts have been made to build upon the great profits of *The Congressional Globe* a permanent organ, representing the political party in the possession of the Government for the time being, but they have failed in succession; yet I do not doubt that if ever the Democracy get control of the Government they will accomplish precisely what the Republicans have not had the courage or strength to carry through. No class of men do harder work for less pay than the political writers at Washington, and none, if properly sustained, can exert a wider or better influence. Proprietors of newspapers at the national capital must now spend vast sums of money for editorial assistance, news, correspondence, etc., yet their incomes are comparatively small. They have no large population around them, and as yet no active, progressive States south of them. If the old system were resumed, or another adopted by which, under proper regulations, the profits of the public printing could be secured to the organ of the party in the majority, I have not the slightest doubt the treasury would be the gainer in the end. Abundant experience has shown, at least in this country, that whenever Government undertakes to carry on business which belongs to individuals, it does so at a dead loss.

When James K. Polk was elected President, in 1844, he resolved, under the advice of the Southern politicians, to supersede the old Jackson and Van Buren firm of Blair & Rives, and to invite the veteran Thomas Ritchie, for many years the editor of the ancient Virginia organ, the *Richmond Enquirer*, to assume the responsibility of defending the measures of his Administration. There can be no doubt that the anti-slavery inclining of Mr. Blair was the motive for this change. Martin Van Buren had twice offended the Southern Democracy—once when in his inaugural, in 1837, he declared in favor of the constitutionality of the abolition of slavery in the District of Columbia, and again when he pronounced against the annexation of Texas in 1843. Renominated in 1840, and defeated by General Harrison, his name was again presented as a candidate in 1844; but his Texas letter raised a host of enemies against him in the National Convention of that year, who, after a long and harassing contest, united upon James K. Polk—the Blairs, the Riveses, the Bentons, the Tappans, the Allens, the Hoffmans, and the Silas Wrights all ranged on the side of the New York statesman. The new Tennessee President felt that his Administration would not be heartily supported by men who had sympathized with Van Buren in regard to the abolition of slavery in the District of Columbia and in opposition to the annexation of Texas, and hence he called for the services of Father Ritchie. The wound inflicted by this change of national editors was deep and rankled long. It undoubtedly created the Free-Soil party; it soured Thomas H. Benton; it organized a fierce internal opposition to General Cass when he was the Democratic candidate against General Taylor in 1848; it vitalized the able and vindictive pens of Mr. Blair and his associates; it put Prince John Van Buren on the stump as the advocate of his own father, who ran as the third candidate on the Buffalo platform. It did much to inspire David Wilmot to offer the Wilmot Proviso in 1846. It was one of the early elements which gradually and surely prepared the way for the political uprising of 1854, on the repeal of the Missouri Compromise—a convulsion which would have become universal had not James Buchanan in 1856 promised that the people of Kansas should be permitted to vote on the subject of slavery without interruption or violence—a promise which, broken in his term, was avenged by the political revolution of 1858, which destroyed the Democratic party effectually, gave victory to the Republicans, carried Lincoln into the Presidential chair, and so maddened the South as to drive it into that rebellion, the defeat of which ended in the complete and eternal abolition of human slavery. So it will be seen that so trifling a thing as a change in the editor of a political organ originated a movement that culminated in the most remarkable event of the century.

Thomas Ritchie, the successor of the Blairs, though he changed the name of the national Democratic organ from *The Globe* to *The Union*, was, nevertheless, the unconscious harbinger of disunion. A more amiable, simple-minded, honorable gentleman, never existed ; but he had lived too long in a narrow sphere to figure on the national stage. He was a conscientious believer in the extreme doctrine of State rights—the kindest and most genteel old fogy who ever wore nankeen pantaloons, high shirt-collars, and broad-brimmed straw hats. He was the delight of every social circle, not for his wit, which was dull, but for his chronic Virginia peculiarities. He was the Grandfather Whitehead of the politicians ; the Jesse Rural of the diplomats—his efforts at making peace between contending rivals generally ending in the renewal of strife, and his paragraphs in defense of the Administration awakening new storms of ridicule. He was a firm believer in the now happily exploded habit that nothing better became an editor than to be at war with his contemporary; and thus it was that *The Union* was filled with contradictions of accusations against the Administration, many of which had been invented by the practical jokers on the other side. Among these practical jokers, none was more busy than the German Austrian, Francis J. Grund, for a long time the "Observer" of the *Philadelphia Ledger*, and the "X" of the *Baltimore Sun*. A versatile genius, of enormous energy and inexhaustible resources—a linguist, an orator, a conversationalist, a writer with few rivals in his day and time—he was a knight of the Free Lance, mingling with all parties (to nearly all of which he had belonged and abandoned in turn), he was the terror of public men. Welcomed in every circle, especially among the diplomatists, where his large fund of information in regard to foreign politics gave him the *entrée*, and where he gathered stores of intelligence for the newspapers whose correspondent he was, he seemed to sport with questions that troubled others. Nothing gave him so much delight as to worry Father Ritchie, and nothing worried Father Ritchie more than Mr. Grund; and I am sure it can be no irreverence to the memory of the excellent old man to add that nothing excited more merriment in official coteries than the skill with which the accomplished German tantalized and taunted the high-strung Virginian. For Mr. Ritchie, like many other men, could not realize such a thing as a practical joke. Every thing was serious to him; and it was amusing to note how the most trifling allusion to the President and his Cabinet would quicken his facile pen, and how he would pour his almost unintelligible manuscript into the hands of the printer. He wrote much—not always clearly, but always honestly; and when he left the tripod to which he had been tempted by large promises, he was neither as comfortable nor as rich a man as when he broke up his household at Richmond to share the gay society and the heavy burdens of Washington journalism. He was too old when he exchanged places. He was never, though often called, the flatterer of power. His instincts were so pure, his relations to men so honest, that he could not discriminate in the support he gave to the Administration. He believed so utterly in the unselfishness of others that he could not understand that his support of them might be characterized as sycophancy. He reached Washington when Gales & Seaton, of the *National Intelligencer*, began their decline, and, if I understand aright, he sustained the kindliest relations to them. In more than one respect he has not been so fortunate as the illustrious twain, who, like himself, have now gone forth to learn the great secret. He had not a gentle and graceful annalist like William Winston Seaton, whose lately printed biography, from the genial pen of one of his own household, may happily be classed, not simply among the best productions of modern literature, but among the most precious tributes with which gratitude has crowned the well-earned fame of one who was alike father, counselor, and friend.

[June 25, 1871.]

XXV.

IT was fifteen years last December since the meeting of the first session of the Thirty-fourth Congress. Its business was delayed from the 2d of December, 1855, to the 3d of February, 1856, by the failure of the House to elect a Speaker. The revulsion produced by the repeal of the Missouri Compromise in the previous year, increased by the Know-Nothing frenzy, gave the opposition large accessions, and made it exceedingly doubtful who would control the House. The Democrats had enjoyed a long and almost unbroken reign, and this uprising was the first signal of its close. As Clerk of the popular branch of the previous Congress, it was my lot to act as presiding officer during the protracted contest. My position was most peculiar. I had had no experience in Parliamentary tactics—indeed, there were no rules for the discipline of that tumultuous body—and I could only rely on common-sense as my guide. I was one

of the editors of the *Washington Union*, the organ of President
Pierce, and the active advocate of James Buchanan, then American Minister at the British court, for the Presidential succession, and I was the personal friend of Andrew H. Reeder, who
had just been removed from the governorship of Kansas for
refusing to join the conspiracy to force slavery into that Territory.   Our relations had not changed, and I had earnestly, but
vainly, protested against his sacrifice.   He was on the floor
contesting the seat of J. W. Whitfield, who had secured the certificate of delegate from Kansas.   The struggle for the Presidency was at fever heat.   All the candidates had friends among
the members, and the canvassing between them was incessant.
The South was wrought to the highest pitch of excitement.
The bold attitude of the Free-State men in Congress and the
country, the extraordinary proceedings in Kansas, the close-
ness of parties in the House, added to the other perplexities of
my position.   The opposition looked upon me at first with a
very natural distrust, and the Democrats relied upon me to
exert every influence to forward their designs.   Nor was this
perplexity lessened by the fact that my political associates were
generally in the wrong.   Their hatred of my friend Reeder was
terrible.   He was charged with every possible corruption, and
I soon found that my unconcealed confidence in him made me
an object of general distrust among the Southern leaders.
Cobb and Stephens, of Georgia ; Garnett and Edmundson, of
Virginia ; Rust, of Arkansas ; Alexander K. Marshall and Burnett, of Kentucky ; Barksdale, of Mississippi ; Keitt and Brooks,
of South Carolina, backed by Slidell, Toombs, Iverson, J. M.
Mason, Hammond, Butler, Wigfall, Benjamin, Yulee, and C. C.
Clay, in the Senate, with Jefferson Davis in the Cabinet, all felt
that if the House was lost all was imperiled.   Every day the
same scene was enacted.   Interminable ballotings, points of
order, debates, threats of violence upon the Northern members,
consumed two months of the public time, and at last resulted

in the election of Nathaniel P. Banks, Speaker, by a vote of one hundred and three to one hundred for Aiken, of South Carolina.   The opposition soon saw that I was resolved to act honestly at every hazard, and at this distance from that embittered session I can recall no one decision that I would not repeat under similar circumstances.   Never shall I forget the last act of the drama—the fierce assaults of the fire-eaters upon my rulings, nor yet the ample and unanimous vindication of my course as I retired from a trying and thankless position.   These revengeful men recollected all these things when Buchanan was nominated, and demanded and secured from him a secret pledge, before his election, that, in the event of his being chosen President, I should never be called to Washington in any capacity.   They declared I was unsound on "the peculiar institution," and could not be trusted even in the only post to which I ever aspired, that of editor of the national organ, authorized to enforce Buchanan's solemn covenant of justice to the people of Kansas.   He gave this secret assurance reluctantly, and of course without my knowledge; and he kept it faithfully.   "There is a destiny that shapes our ends," and that which I believed at the time an act of unspeakable perfidy, proved to be a blessing to me and mine.   It threw me upon my own resources, made me an independent journalist, and enabled me to convince my fellow-citizens that I could live without party patronage.

Of the extreme men in that stormy interval, Cobb, Keitt, Brooks, Barksdale, Garnett, Soulé, Burnett, Butler, James M. Mason, have gone to their long account.   Slidell, Benjamin, and Wigfall are still, I believe, in foreign lands.   Toombs, Davis, and Stephens, having failed in one great act of treason, are busily engaged in the work of destroying the Democratic party, an enterprise in which they promise to be more successful.

[July 2, 1871.]

XXVI.

The short career of Felix Grundy McConnell, of Alabama, who died by his own hand in Washington, D.C., in September, 1846, in his thirty-seventh year, was in some respects a memorable one.   He was a singularly handsome man, and possessed abundant animal spirits and a native wit that made him popular with all parties.   His speeches were not numerous, but were original and forcible.   He was elected to two Congresses, but had not served out his full term when he died.   When James K. Polk was inaugurated President, on the 4th of March, 1845, one of his first visitors was McConnell, and I shall never forget the way he introduced himself: "I have called to pay you my respects, Mr. President, and to say that if you believe in the Virginia and Kentucky Resolutions, love the Union, and follow in the footsteps of Captain Andrew Jackson, of Tennessee, now at the Hermitage preparing to go to Heaven, then, sir, I hang my hammer on your anvil."   Though too careless of himself, he had many sterling traits.   Once, in a bar-room of the National Hotel, he heard an infidel blaspheming the Bible.   "Stop, sir," said the angry Felix—"stop! I am not a good man, but my mother used to read the Bible to me, and prayed that I might always believe in it; and d—n me if I will ever allow any body to attack it in my presence!   It must be all right, for it was her guide and comfort."

Of another type was Dixon H. Lewis, Representative in Congress from the same State from 1829 to 1843, and United States Senator from 1844 to October of 1848, when he died in New York.   He was the largest man I ever saw.   A chair for his especial use had to be made, and few public conveyances could accommodate him.   He was a man of first-rate talents, a forcible speaker, a sound lawyer, and a close reasoner.   Mr. Calhoun had no more devoted follower or friend.   He was a sincere believer in the whole theory of State rights and secession. Amiable, and generous to a fault, he was sensitive in regard to his enormous size, which undoubtedly shortened his life. He died aged forty-six, having been in Congress a continuous term of nineteen years. Once, on his return from Washington, the steamer in which he was a passenger was wrecked. The small boat was ordered out, but he refused to enter it, fearing that his huge weight would jeopard the safety of others. After they were saved he was rescued, but for a time he was in great danger.

Not unlike McConnell was Mike Walsh, of New York. Born in Youghall, Ireland, and brought to this country when a child, he spent his boyhood as a wanderer. His newspaper, *The Subterranean*, printed in New York, was the terror of the politicians, and finally cost him an imprisonment of two years for libel, but this punishment increased his popularity, and he was sent to the Legislature, and for two years to Congress. I was Clerk while he was a member, and found him full of good impulses. He was a satirist by nature. Nothing provoked him so much as a snob. He spared no pretender. He was especially severe upon the airs of the chivalry of the South, and, Democrat as he was, he had no patience with them. He never rose to speak without saying something new or odd. He read much and wrote strongly. He disliked Buchanan and loved Douglas. A sad man at times, nothing could exceed his bright humor on occasion. Had he lived, I believe he would have been, like Broderick, James T. Brady, and Sickles, in hearty hostility to the rebellion. After he left Congress he made a tour of Europe, visited the camps of the great contending powers in the Crimea, and was for a time the guest of the Hon. Carroll Spence, American Minister at Constantinople. He reached there from Sebastopol penniless, and without suitable clothing. I have heard Mr. Spence describe his bearing among the polished people of the diplomatic circles. His anecdotes of men and women, his tenacious memory, his genial nature, and, above all, his dry and irresistible humor, captivated them. Some of his letters, written while he was abroad, were unrivaled in their way. For many years he bore uncontested sway in the politics of New York, especially in the famous Empire Club. He was a proud and honest man, and had he shaped his course by a more moderate standard, he would, I believe, be still living. He was found dead on the 17th of March, 1859. Peace to the ashes of Mike Walsh!

[July 9, 1871.]

XXVII.

WRITING about "public men," I am not willing to exclude myself from the opportunity of saying something about the celebrated women who have figured in American history. First among these, among my own recollections, was the versatile and original Frances Wright, or Madame Frances d'Arusmont, still better known as "Fanny Wright," a Scotchwoman, who visited this country in 1818, 1820, and 1825, and died in Cincinnati on the 13th of January, 1853, aged fifty-seven. She excited much comment by her leveling doctrines and her extravagant language. But she had many followers and courtiers, among them the still living Robert Dale Owen. The well-known Amos Gilbert wrote a memoir of her in 1855, two years after her death, entitled, "The Pioneer Woman, or the Cause of Woman's Rights." She was a person of immense energy and uncommon versatility. The list of her works is something unusual. She wrote a tragedy called "Altorf," in 1819; "Views of Society and Manners in America," which ran through four editions, and was translated into French, published in 1820, and republished, with alterations and additions, in 1821 and 1822; "A Few Days in

Athens," being a translation of a Greek manuscript found in Herculaneum, and a defense of the Epicurean Philosophy, published in London in 1822, and republished in Boston in 1822. These were followed by a course of popular lectures, spoken in all the leading cities North, West, and South, and printed for circulation, and running through six editions. She was also the author, in company with Robert Dale Owen, of certain popular tracts, and in 1844 her biography was published in England, including her notes and political letters. I shall always remember the effect produced by the lectures of this indefatigable and really gifted woman, as she traveled through Pennsylvania many years ago. Controverted and attacked by the clergy and the press, she maintained an undaunted front, and persevered to the last. That she was a woman of great mind is established by the number of her followers, including some of the best intellects of the country, and by the repeated publication and very general reading of her tracts and essays. It is related that when she came to her death-bed she recanted the most of her free-love and socialistic theories.

Very different from Fanny Wright was the notorious Annie Royall, who died on the 1st of September, 1854, on Capitol Hill, in the city of Washington. She was the terror of politicians, and especially of Congressmen. I can see her now tramping through the halls of the old Capitol, umbrella in hand, seizing upon every passer-by, and offering her book for sale. Any public man who refused to buy was certain of a severe philippic in her newspaper, *The Washington Paul Pry*, or in that which succeeded it, *The Huntress*. "We have the famous Mrs. Royall here," writes Justice Story to Mrs. Story, on the 8th of March, 1827, "with her new novel, 'The Tennesseans,' which she has compelled the Chief Justice and myself to buy to avoid a castigation. I shall bring it home for your edification." She wrote and printed a great deal, but seemed to rely almost entirely upon her ability to blacken private character. Among her productions were "Sketches of History, Life, and Manners in the United States," published in 1826 ; the "Black Book," published in 1828, and continued in 1829 ; and her "Southern Tour," the second series of the "Black Book," which appeared in 1830–31; "The Tennesseans," a novel, and "Letters from Alabama" on various subjects, in 1830.

Mrs. Royall's career was a rough one, and she seemed to live for the purpose of revenging her misfortunes upon others. She was a native of Virginia, and at an early age was stolen by the Indians, with whom she remained about fifteen years. Shortly after her release she married a Captain Royall, and removed to Alabama, where she learned to read and write, subsequently taking up her residence in Washington. Dying at an advanced age in 1854, she was present during the administrations of John Quincy Adams, General Jackson, Martin Van Buren, Harrison and Tyler, James K. Polk, Taylor and Fillmore. Her newspapers were badly printed and badly written, and her squibs and stories more remarkable for bitterness than for wit. She was a woman of great industry and astonishing memory; but at last she seemed to tire of a vocation which grew more and more unprofitable with better times and milder manners.

There is no better evidence of the sure and permanent improvement of the public press than the difference between the lady writers of the present day and these two memorable examples. Correspondence, and even editorship, has risen to a profession among educated women in the United States ; and with the exception of a few, who do not find the circulation of scandal or of socialistic doctrines in any sense a profitable pastime, most of them are generously and substantially rewarded. No Fanny Wright frightens the proprieties in the States ; no Annie Royall terrifies the statesmen in the Capitol.

The female correspondents of to-day are welcomed and honored in every circle. They write generally from a conscientious love of their vocation, and they are popular because their style is more *spirituelle* than the rough rhetoric of the trained Bohemians. Avoiding all scandal and preserving the delicacy of the sex, they present a contrast to the startling theories of Fanny Wright and the rude vituperation of Annie Royall. Their energy and perseverance are making journalism and correspondence a permanent vocation for their sisters; and as the press grows in influence it will need all sorts of auxiliaries, and none will give it more of the variety, which is the spice of life, than the sparkle, the wit, the grace, and the impulse of intellectual womanhood.

[July 16, 1871.]

XXVIII.

THE Democratic National Convention which met at Baltimore on the 27th of May, 1844, was one of the most exciting political conventions I ever attended. I was there as a reporter of my newspaper, the *Lancaster Intelligencer and Journal*, and had a seat near the president, Andrew Stevenson, of Virginia, father of the present Senator in Congress from Kentucky, and witnessed the struggle of the two-thirds rule introduced into the convention by Hon. Robert J. Walker for the purpose of defeating Martin Van Buren, who was a candidate for the Presidential nomination of his party. The Hon. Benjamin F. Butler—not the present intellectual giant of that name, Representative from the Fifth Massachusetts district, but General Jackson's Attorney-General from December 27, 1831, to June 24, 1834, after the retirement of Roger B. Taney, who was appointed Chief Justice of the Supreme Court of the United States —was Van Buren's champion. Butler was at that time a man of about fifty years of age, with a handsome, intellectual face, of large reputation as orator and jurist ; but he was no match for the little Mississippian. That was the first time I had ever seen Robert J. Walker. I had read his speeches while he was a Senator in Congress, and knew a good deal of his history ; but I was not prepared to see so small and insignificant-looking a person, nor yet for the marvelous power which he exercised in the convention, and the effect produced by his speech in reply to the Van Buren leader. He had not spoken twenty minutes before it was evident, from the cheers of the convention, that the doom of the Kinderhook statesman was sealed. James K. Polk received the nomination, which would have been conferred upon Pennsylvania, in the person of James Buchanan, if the latter had not timidly withdrawn his name from the list of candidates, in the belief that the party was united upon Van Buren. It is true there were many elements in Pennsylvania opposed to Buchanan ; but he had strength enough to unite the South, and as no man could then be made President without the consolidated vote of that section, all domestic opposition would have been baffled.

The wound inflicted on the Van Buren faction rankled until it came to a head, in 1848, in the organization which made him a third candidate and defeated Lewis Cass. Polk was elected, chiefly through the influence of Silas Wright, who consented to resign his place as a Senator in Congress, and to run for Governor of New York—a concession and a sacrifice which satisfied the Van Burenites, and postponed their outbreak upon the Southern Democracy for four years.

No personage in politics ever led a more active life than Robert J. Walker. Born at Northumberland, in the State of Pennsylvania, in 1801, he entered the University in Philadelphia, and graduated in 1819 ; studied law, was admitted to practice in 1821, and became chairman of the Democratic committee when only twenty-two years of age. He was one of the earliest supporters of General Jackson for the Presidency, and effectually aided to bring about the action of the Harrisburg Convention, which nominated the hero of New Orleans for that office in 1824.   In the spring of 1826 he removed to Mississippi, and practiced his profession without taking any political office until ten years later, when he was chosen a Senator in Congress, and served until 1845, when he was called to the Treasury Department by President Polk.   He excelled as a writer for the newspapers, and as a popular orator ; was capable of prodigious mental toil ; had unequaled memory, rare enthusiasm, and intense convictions.   Large reading, polished manners, singular generosity, and simplicity of character completed the qualities of a successful leader.   His arguments in the Senate were masterpieces.   He there brought to the discussion of every question all his peculiar powers.   Without considering his free-trade ideas, which are still the subject of animated controversy, it is simple justice to state that he contributed immensely to many important reforms in the public service.   He was the advocate of a liberal land policy, the champion of public improvements, the antagonist of religious intolerance, the fearless enemy of nullification, and he will perhaps be better remembered for the part he acted when he reluctantly accepted the position of Governor of Kansas in 1857.   Sent there by an Administration which betrayed the solemn pledge upon which alone it was elected, he was believed by the pro-slavery men to be in hearty sympathy with their plans ; but sustained by his independent secretary, Hon. Frederick P. Stanton (still living in Washington, where he was born, and deservedly prospering in the practice of his profession of the law), he soon discovered that he could not second that betrayal without the loss of his own honor.   He revolted from the unblushing frauds sought to be perpetrated in the endeavor to force slavery into Kansas.   But what Reeder and Geary had done under Pierce in the same position, he did under Buchanan, with even more courage and effect.   At that time my paper, *The Press*, was in the throes

of its first great conflict with the pro-slavery Democracy. Holding Buchanan steadily to the pledge of justice to Kansas, day
after day I waited for the report of Robert J. Walker with inexpressible solicitude, and when finally it came in a telegraphic
dispatch, which he sent me from the town of York, Pennsylvania, while on his way to Washington to protest against the conspiracy to which Mr. Buchanan had surrendered, I felt that our
battle was won.   Walker's repudiation of the frauds in Kansas,
which he was solemnly enjoined to assist, in a private letter
written to him by President Buchanan, followed by his manly
resignation of an office which he could no longer hold, thrilled
the people of the whole country, and, in the election which ensued, aided to demolish the Democracy in nearly all the free
States.   It revolutionized Berks County by electing the venerable John Schwartz, in 1858, by nineteen votes, notwithstanding
the Democratic majority of 6004 two years before, defeating
Buchanan's favorite, J. Glancy Jones, now a citizen of the
State of Delaware, patiently preparing to step into the Senate
whenever the people of that little Commonwealth are ready to
employ him.   It gave us a Republican Representative in William E. Lehman, in the first Pennsylvania district.   It gave us
a Republican in the Montgomery district, and it left but four
Administration Congressmen from Pennsylvania.   It swept
New Jersey.   It destroyed the Democratic prestige in New
York, and almost changed the aspect of the National House of
Representatives.   It confessedly paved the way to the freedom
of Kansas and to the complete annihilation of the whole pro-
slavery plot.

Of course, a statesman bold and brave enough to take issue
with an Administration determined upon such a wrong could
not expect to escape the persecutions of the South, and so, after
Abraham Lincoln was elected, Robert J. Walker was found
among the firmest supporters of the policy of his Administration.   The same Jefferson Davis who had apologized for the

repudiation of the debt of Mississippi, was the leader of a rebellion founded upon the nullification doctrines which Walker
had always opposed.   Walker's labors through the press, on
the hustings, and in personal appeals against the rebellion, were
wonderful.

The sagacious Lincoln, fully convinced that the war for the
Union could not be carried to success without the aid of the
Douglas Democracy—and who would have conferred upon Stephen A. Douglas, if he had lived, one of the most important
commands in the army—called Robert J. Walker to his aid,
and sent him forth to Europe, in 1863, for the purpose of presenting our country's cause to the people of the Old World, and
especially for the purpose of spreading before them incontesti-
ble proofs of our ability to maintain ourselves, and of our inexhaustible financial resources.   One of his first acts was to print
in the *London Times* a caustic reply to John Slidell, then Jefferson Davis's Minister at Paris, who attempted to vindicate his
master against the charge of having assisted in the repudiation
of the State bonds of Mississippi.   As I write I have before
me this magnificent paper ; and now that the great brain that
conceived and the ready hand that penned it are silent in the
grave, it deserves to be laid as an enduring wreath upon his
tomb :

"Here, then, are eight judges, all chosen by the people of
Mississippi, concurring in 1842, as well as in 1853, as to
the validity of these bonds, and yet Jefferson Davis justifies
their repudiation.   The judges of Mississippi all take an oath
to support the Constitution, and it is made their duty to interpret it.

"The Legislature is confined to law-making, and forbidden
to exercise any judicial power ; the expounding this supple-
mental law, and the provisions under which it was enacted, is
exclusively a judicial power, and yet the Legislature *usurps* this
power, repudiates the bonds of the State, and the acts of the

three preceding Legislatures, and the decision of the highest tribunals of the State.   Jefferson Davis sustains this repudiation, and the British public are asked to take new Confederate bonds, issued by the same Jefferson Davis, and thus to sanction and encourage and offer a premium for repudiation.   These so-called Confederate bonds are issued in open violation of the Constitution of the United States ; they are absolute nullities, they are tainted with treason, they never can or will be paid, and yet they are thrust on the British public under the sanction of the same great repudiator, Jefferson Davis, who applauds the non-payment of the Mississippi bonds, and thus condemns hundreds of innocent holders, including widows and orphans, to want and misery.   Talk about *faith*, about *honor*, about *justice*, and the *sanctity of contracts;* why, if such flagrant outrages, such atrocious crimes can be sustained by the great public of any nation, small indeed must be the value of their bonds, which rests exclusively on good faith."

Now read the following appeal to the English government and people, and remember that the very men here denounced are once more engaged in an attempt to seize the government of the Union :

"The blasphemous doctrine of the divine right of kings was discarded by England in the Revolution of 1688.   The British throne reposes now on the alleged basis of the welfare and happiness of the people.   What form of government will best promote that end?   This is the only question.   I believe it is ours —but only with slavery extinguished, and universal education —schools—schools—schools—common schools—high schools for all.   Education the criterion of the right of suffrage, not property.   I do not believe in a government of ignorance, whether by the rich or poor, the many or the few.   With the constant and terrible opposing element of slavery, we have certainly achieved stupendous results in three fourths of a century; and to say that our system has failed, because slavery now

makes war upon it, is amazing folly.   Why predict that, when
reunited and with slavery extinguished, we would bully the
world?   Who were our bullies?   Who struck down Charles
Sumner, the Senator from Massachusetts, the eminent scholar
and orator, on the floor of the Senate, for denouncing the
horrors of slavery?   A South Carolina member of Congress,
while all slavedom approved the deed.   Who endeavored to
force slavery on Kansas by murder and rapine, and the forgery
of a constitution?   Who repealed the Missouri Compromise, in
order to force slavery upon all the Territories of the United
States?   Who are endeavoring now to dissolve the Union, and
spread slavery over all this wide domain?   Who conspired to
assassinate the American President on his way to Washington?
Who murdered, in Baltimore, the men of Massachusetts, on
their way to the defense of the Capital of the Union?   Who
commenced the conflict by firing upon the starving garrison of
Sumter, and striking down the banner of the Union which
floated over its walls?   Who, immediately thereafter, announced
their resolution to capture Washington, seized the national
arms and forts and dock-yards and vessels and arsenals and
mints and treasure, and opened the war upon the Federal Government?   There is a plain answer to all these questions.   It
is the lords of the whip and the chain and the branding-iron
who are our bullies; who insist upon forced labor, and repudiate all compensation to the toiling millions of slaves—who repudiate among slaves the marital and parental relation, and
class them by law as chattels—who forbid emancipation—who
make it a crime to teach slaves to write or read, aye, even the
Bible—who keep open the inter-State slave-trade (more horrible than the African, making Virginia a human stock-farm),
tearing husband from wife, and parents from children—found-
ing a Government boldly announcing the property in man based
avowedly on the divinity, extension, and perpetuity of slavery—
these are our bullies, and when they are overthrown we shall

commence a new career of peaceful progress and advanced civilization.   And why sow the seeds of international hatred between England and America?   Is war really desired between
the two countries, or is it supposed that we will yield to foreign
intervention without a struggle?   No; the North will rise as
one man, and thousands even from the South will join them.
The country will become a camp, and the ocean will swarm
with our privateers.   Rather than submit to dismemberment or
secession, which is anarchy and ruin, we will, we must fight until
the last man has fallen.   If the views of a foreign power have
been truly represented in Parliament, and such an aggression
upon us is contemplated, let him beware, for in such a contest
the political pyramid resting upon its apex, the power of one
man, is much more likely to fall than that which reposes on
the broad basis of the will of the people."

This first article was a bombshell in the ranks of the conspirators sent to Europe to poison our credit and blast our
fame, and it was followed by a number of even greater force
and ability, in one of which he said :

"Why, the legal-tender notes of the so-called Confederate
government, fundable in a stock bearing eight per cent. interest, are now worth in gold, at their own capital of Richmond,
less than ten cents on the dollar (two shillings on the pound),
while in two thirds of their territory such notes are utterly worthless ; and it is treason for any citizen of the United States,
North or South, or any alien resident there, to deal in them or
in Confederate bonds, or in the cotton pledged for their pay-
ment.   No form of Confederate bonds or notes or stock will
ever be recognized by the Government of the United States,
and the cotton pledged by slaveholding traitors for the pay-
ment of the Confederate bonds is all forfeited for treason, and
confiscated to the Federal Government by act of Congress."

On the 26th of November, 1863, at a great Thanksgiving
dinner of the loyal Americans in London, in accordance with

the proclamation of Abraham Lincoln, of which Robert J. Walker was president, he used the following inspiring language, which I quote, not only to revive the recollection of his great services, but as most pertinent at the present hour:

" This day has been set apart by the President of the United States for thanksgiving to Almighty God for all the blessings which he has vouchsafed to us as a people. Among these are abundant crops, great prosperity in all our industrial pursuits, a vast addition, even during the war, to our material wealth, and augmented immigration to our shores from Europe. Our finances have been conducted with great ability and success by the Secretary of the Treasury, Mr. Chase, who has also succeeded in giving us, for the first time in our history, a uniform national currency, which, as a bond of union and as an addition to our wealth and resources, is nearly equal to all the expenses of the great contest. [Loud cheers for Mr. Chase.] During the present year nearly four hundred million dollars of the six per cent. stock of the United States has been taken at home, at or above par, while within the last few months European capitalists, unsolicited by us, are making large investments in the securities of the Union. But, above all, we have to thank God for those victories in the field which are bringing this great contest to a successful conclusion. This rebellion is, indeed, the most stupendous in history. It absorbs the attention and affects the political institutions and material interests of the world. The armies engaged exceed those of Napoleon. Death never had such a carnival, and each week consumes millions of treasure. Great is the sacrifice, but the cause is peerless and sublime. [Cheers.] If God has placed us in the van of the great contest for the rights and liberties of man ; if he has assigned us the post of danger and of suffering, it is that of unfading glory and imperishable renown. [Loud cheers.] The question with us, which is so misunderstood here, is that of national unity [Hear, hear], which is the vital element of our existence; and any settlement which does not secure this, with the entire integrity of the Union and freedom throughout all its borders, will be treason to our country and to mankind. [Loud cheers.] To acknowledge the absurd and anarchical doctrine of secession, as is demanded of us here ; to abdicate the power of self-preservation, and permit the Union to be dissolved, is ruin, disgrace, and suicide. There is but one alternative—we must and will fight it out to the last. [Loud and prolonged applause.] If need be, all who can bear arms must take to the field, and leave to those who can not the pursuits of industry. [Hear, hear.] If we count not the cost of this contest in men or money, it is because all loyal Americans believe that the value of our Union can not be estimated. [Hear, hear.] If martyrs from every State, from England, and from nearly every nation of Christendom, have fallen in our defense, never, in humble faith we trust, has any blood since that of Calvary been shed in a cause so holy. [Cheers.]

*   *   *   *   *   *   *

" The Union will still live. It is written by the finger of God, on the scroll of destiny, that neither principalities nor powers shall affect its overthrow, nor shall 'the gates of hell prevail against it.' But what as to the results? It is said we have accomplished nothing ; and this is re-echoed every morning by the pro-slavery press of England. We have done nothing! Why we have conquered, and now occupy, two thirds of the entire territory of the South, an area far larger (while overcoming a greater resisting force) than that traversed by the armies of Cæsar or Alexander. The whole of the Mississippi River, from its source to its mouth, with all its thirty thousand miles of tributaries, is exclusively ours. [Cheers.] So is the great Chesapeake Bay. Slavery is not only abolished in the Federal district, containing the Capital of the Union, but in all our vast territorial domain, comprising more than eight hundred million acres, and nearly half the size of all Europe. The four slave-

holding States of Delaware, Maryland, Kentucky, and Missouri
are devotedly loyal, and thoroughly sustaining the Union. And
how as to Virginia? Why all the counties of Virginia east of
the Chesapeake are ours; all that vast portion of Eastern Virginia north of the Rappahannock is ours also. But still more,
all that great territory of Virginia, from the mountains to the
Ohio, is ours also; and not only ours, but, by the overwhelming
voice of her people, has formed a State government. By their
own votes they have abolished slavery, and have been admitted
as one of the free States of the American Union. [Loud
cheers.] And where is the great giant State of the West—
Missouri? She is not only ours, but, by an overwhelming majority of the popular vote, carried into effect by her constitutional convention, has provided for the abolition of slavery, and
enrolls herself soon as one of the free States of the American
Union. [Cheers.] And now, as to Maryland. The last steamer brings us the news of the recent elections in Maryland, which
have not only sustained the Union, but have sent an overwhelming majority to Congress and to the State Legislature in favor
of immediate emancipation; and Delaware adopts the same
policy. [Loud applause.] Tennessee is also ours. From the
Mississippi to the Cumberland and Tennessee rivers; from
Knoxville, in the mountains of the east, to Nashville, the capital, in the centre, and Memphis, the commercial metropolis, in
the west, Tennessee is wholly ours. So is Arkansas. So is
Louisiana, including the great city of New Orleans. So is
North Alabama. So is Western Texas. So is two thirds of
the State of Mississippi; and now the Union troops hold Chattanooga, the great impregnable fortress of Northwestern Georgia. From Chattanooga, which may be regarded as the great
geographical central point of the rebellion, the armies of the
Republic will march down through the heart of Georgia, and
join our troops upon the sea-board of that State, and thus terminate the rebellion. [Loud cheers.] Into Georgia and the

Carolinas nearly half a million slaves have been driven by their masters in advance of the Union army. From Virginia, from Kentucky, Missouri, Arkansas, Louisiana, Mississippi, Tennessee, and North Alabama, thousands of their slaves have been driven and huddled together in the two Carolinas and Georgia; because, if they had been left where they were, they would have joined the Northern armies. They preferred to be free men rather than slaves; they preferred to be men and women rather than chattels; they preferred freedom to chains and bondage; and just so soon as that Union army advances into the Carolinas and Georgia will the slaves rush to the standard of freedom, and fight, as they have fought, with undaunted courage for liberty and the Union. [Loud applause.]

"But how is it with the South? Why, months ago they had called out, *en masse*, all who were capable of bearing arms. They have raised their last army. And how as to money? Why they are in a state of absolute bankruptcy. Their money, all they have, that which they call money, according to their own estimation, as fixed and taken by themselves, one dollar of gold purchases sixteen dollars of Confederate paper, which must soon cease to circulate at any rate. The price of flour is now one hundred dollars a barrel, and other articles in like proportion. No revenue is collected, or can be. The army and the government are supported exclusively by force, by seizing the crops of farmers and planters and using them for the benefit of the so-called Confederate government. Starvation is staring them in the face. The collapse is imminent, and, so far as we may venture to predict any future event, nothing can be more certain than that before the closing of the ensuing year the rebellion will be brought entirely to a close. [Hear, hear.] We must recollect, also, that there is not a single State of the South in which a large majority of the population (including the blacks) is not now, and always has been, devoted to the Union. Why, in the State of South Carolina

alone the blacks who are devoted to the Union exceed the whites
more than one hundred thousand in number. The recent elections have all gone for the Union by overwhelming majorities,
and volunteering for the army progresses with renewed vigor.
For all these blessings the President of the United States in-
vites us to render thanks to Almighty God. Our cause is that
of humanity, of civilization, of Christianity. We write upon our
banners, from the inspired words of Holy Writ, 'God has made
of one blood all the nations of the earth.' We acknowledge all
as brothers; we invite them to partake with us alike in the grand
inheritance of freedom, and we repeat the divine sentiment
from the Sermon on the Mount, 'Do unto others as you would
have them do unto you.' [Loud cheers.] Nor let it be supposed that we, as Americans, are entirely selfish in this matter.
We believe that this Union is the most sacred trust ever confided by Almighty God to man. We believe that this American
Union is the best, the brightest, the last experiment of self-
government, and as it shall be sustained and perpetuated, or
broken and dissolved, the light of liberty shall beam upon the
hopes of mankind, or be forever extinguished, amid the scoffs
of exulting tyrants and the groans of a world in bondage.
[Loud applause.] All nations and ages will soon acknowledge
that, in this contest, we have made greater sacrifices of blood
and treasure in the cause of human freedom than was ever before recorded in history. We will have suppressed the most
gigantic and the most wicked rebellion, a task that could have
been accomplished by no other government. We have succeeded, because our institutions rest on the broad basis of the
affections, the interests, and the power of the people. No other
nation could bring a million of volunteers to the field—[loud
cheers]—and millions more would come if necessary. As a
result of this war we will extinguish slavery, we will perpetuate
and consolidate the Union, we will prove that man is capable
of self-government, and secure the ultimate ascendency of free

institutions throughout the world.   This, therefore, is a day in which all humanity may unite with us in the hymn of praise, and the toiling millions of the earth join with us in fervent thanksgiving to Almighty God for the approaching redemption of our race from slavery and oppression.   [Loud and long-continued cheering and applause.]"

Mr. Walker was not a member of the Republican party, although he supported Mr. Lincoln in 1864, but he was a patriot in the largest sense, and, like many of his school, after giving half a century of his time to his country, he died poor.   A generous government ought to seize an early occasion to prove, at least in this case, that "Republics are *not* ungrateful."

[July 23, 1871.]

XXIX.

WE are all the unconscious actors and spectators in the world's theatre.   The parts we play, and the scenes we applaud, are the double substance of the current attraction.   In 1844 we had the drama of the Native American riots in Philadelphia; in 1854 the sensation of Know-Nothingism; and seven years later the tragedy of the rebellion.   And now, at the end of another decade, the curtain rises before the New York outbreak of the 12th of July, 1871.   This last is too fresh for the historian, and so we refer it to the tribunal of time, content to let its seeds work their way among the minds of men, and sure of the harvest for the right.   For as the riots of 1844, and the frenzy of 1854, and the tragedy of 1861 – 65 were each followed by good results, so will the last sad evidence of bad passions attain its ultimate compensation.   In our happy country our better nature secures the final mastery.   Evil men and evil measures dominate for a while, but they are finally crushed, inevitably, and without exception.

Leaving the authors of the rebellion to the fate they deserve, it seems to me a not inopportune task to recall some of the leaders of the excitements of 1844 and 1854. They are nearly all in their graves; but they are keenly remembered in the light of recent events. The face and form of Lewis C. Levin rise before me as I write. In this section, at least, for six years the uncontested Native American chief, he is conceded to have been the founder of his party. Born in South Carolina, on the 10th day of November, 1808, and dying in Philadelphia on the 14th of March, 1860, he was qualified for a longer career, though it may be claimed that in his day he filled a large space in the public eye. He had an immense following. Blending religious with political passions, he dominated in our conventions, electing himself and others to Congress, carrying most of the local officers in Philadelphia, and erecting in the First Pennsylvania district, now the stronghold of the very Catholics he opposed, a power that was, while it endured, really invincible. Perhaps the very ferocity of the onset of Mr. Levin and his cohorts gave the sympathy of others to the Catholics. A fervid speaker and nervous writer, he was conspicuous on the open platform, the Congressional forum, and in the public press. Some of his speeches in the House were models of popular oratory. One of his finest was that of the 2d of March, 1848, from which I take these passages :

"If Rome will not come to America, America must go to Rome! This is the new doctrine of an age of retrogressive progress. If the Pope will not establish a republic for his Italian subjects, we, the American people, must renounce all the ties of our glorious freedom, and indorse the Papal system as the perfection of human wisdom, by sending an embassador to Rome to congratulate 'His Holiness' on having made—what? The Roman people free? Oh, no! but on having made tyranny amiable ; on having sugared the poisoned cake. And for this, the highest crime against freedom, we are to commission an embassador to Rome! Is there an American heart that does not recoil from the utter degradation of the scheme?

"The flood of immigration is sweeping its millions of foreign Roman Catholic voters over the land. The past is gloomy enough, the present awfully portentous—but the future is black 'with shadows, clouds, and darkness.' This country seems destined to be the grand theatre of Roman Catholic power—not American Papistry, but the Papistry of Rome, of the Old World, of Austria, and of the Pope. Shall we grow wise in time, or shall we surrender our rights without resistance? Shall we make a stand now, or a Government proposition to unite this free Republic with absolute Rome? or shall we surrender in anticipation of the day of trial, and ask the Pope, in despair, to fetter our hands before we strike a blow?

"Sir, if it be written in the black book of fate that this great Republic is yet to become a dependency of the Court of Rome, let us not hasten our infamy by any premature weakness, by any act that shall expedite our downfall or accelerate our bondage. We are now asked to become voluntary agents in enthralling ourselves; we are implored to send an embassador to Rome, to have our manacles forged in the furnaces of the imperial city, under the special care of the Holy Father, who acknowledges no human authority in matters of government, but who pleads a divine right to bow down the neck of a man in the dust and yoke him to the iron car of absolute power.

"Will gentlemen who propose to rivet this religious chain think of the future? for it is to the future that we are to look for bonds, fetters, and disfranchisement — that future which in a few years will expand our population to a hundred millions; when our wild Indian lands, embracing Oregon and the far West, shall have been settled by foreign Roman Catholics and their children, all under the guidance and control of Jesuit leaders, bound to obey their general, the Pope's nuncio, whose headquarters are to be the seat of government, and that seat of government the city of Washington! Let us imagine for a moment all this expanse of empire, embracing some fifty or sixty States, to be settled by its proportion of the foreign slaves of foreign Jesuits; and, inferring the future from the past, that they have been successful in extending their invasions upon the spiritual and political rights of the American people, what would be the direful consequences of this dreadful overshadowing of the moral and intellectual world?

"Are the religious wars and relentless persecutions of fire, rack, and other bloody demonstrations of bigotry, with which Popery has deluged Europe for ages, again to be acted over here, on the fair and unstained bosom of our vast and free Republic? Heaven forbid this foul desecration of our equal rights! And yet what hope of exemption gleams in the future, unless the friends of civil and religious liberty, animated by a sublime devotion to the welfare of their children and the freedom of prosperity, now combine to arrest the march of Papal usurpation before it overspreads the land, and plants its 'garrisons' of power deep into the bosom of our valleys, irresistible and unresisted?

"And here, sir, I may be permitted to ask, Why is it that the Jesuits have made such strenuous efforts to drive that Bible from our public schools? Why those dark insinuations of the unfitness of Bible truths for the daily duties of life? We claim for the American-born child of the foreign Roman Catholic the same glorious privileges our own children enjoy—to read, examine, investigate for themselves; to reject or adopt it as they see fit, unawed by any human power. Shall there be one code of morals for one class, and another for a higher or a lower one? Shall the Jesuit clergy coin a construction of the Bible for the people which the people have no right to test by their own understandings, and thus establish a human tariff for crime, adjusted by mere human authority, in opposition to the commandments of God, and meet with no resistance? Or rather, so far from resistance, the approving smiles and generous encouragement of the representatives of the American people?

" Sir, we have lived to see the Bible driven from our public schools and burned in the public streets—that Bible, so inseparably interwoven with the genius and spirit of American institutions. The Congress of 1777 distributed thirty thousand copies of that Bible among the American people—that same Bible that Mary gave to her little George, whose precepts and whose principles led him, at the head of the American troops, to achieve that freedom which we now enjoy. Do what you may, I tell you that the American-born citizens of this country, at least the native-born Americans, will, at all hazards, keep that Bible in the hands of their little Georges too.

" Sir, we do not protest against this religious link between our free Republic and the Papal throne ; a throne, unlike all others, built upon power, spiritual and temporal, political and religious ; a throne which makes man a slave, and transforms kings into fiends, priests into tormentors, a people into drones, a country into a desert ; a throne which extinguishes the fire on the altar of domestic love in a form peculiar, fatal, revolting ; snatching its votaries away from the homage of nature to the cold convent, the repulsive abbey, the gloomy cell of the anchorite, the horrid dungeon of the Inquisition, and the demoralizing edict of celibacy ; stirring up sedition, rebellion, and civil war, as the only means of extending a power which reason revolts from, and persuasion fails to diffuse ; which mankind have resisted in every age, at the peril and under the penalty of the cannon's mouth, the edge of the sword, the fire of the fagot, the torments of the stake, and the tortures of the rack !

" Sir, in the name of the American people, I protest against this innovation, which would make us a by-word among the nations. It is almost an obsolete but still a venerated and solemn custom, appropriate to all great and imminent conjunctures of public import, to invoke the special protection of a Superior

Being, and, in the same spirit that animated our sires of 1776, I exclaim, God save the Republic !''

Parties reeled, politicians changed and cowered before the fiery eloquence of this daring reformer, whose words, repeated to-day, have a strange and almost prophetic significance. I am proud to claim that I was not one of those who feared to take issue with his doctrines, and this the more because now I find myself arrayed against the dangerous dogmas enunciated by certain grave potentates, and too sadly illustrated by their ignorant and misguided followers.

The fires lighted by Mr. Levin were subdued before other questions, but they were not extinguished. When he had almost passed from the stage of politics, and the Democrats regained their lost power, they broke out again in 1854, extending over a wider field, and for a time threatening a more permanent demolition of parties; but, like its progenitor, Know-Nothingism was too fierce and illogical to last. It died of its secrecy, and when this was dissolved the whole organization passed away like an exhalation. The Aaron's rod of anti-slavery swallowed up all other issues, and Know-Nothingism was lost in Secession, which even in 1854 began to project its black shadow, like a monstrous demon, upon the scene.

If Levin was the master-spirit who organized Native-Americanism in 1844, Henry A. Wise, of Virginia, was the fearless knight who did most to put down Know-Nothingism ten years later. The two men were marked antipodes—contrasts in demeanor as in doctrine. Levin was a stout and well-built man, with a sonorous voice and a commanding and flowing diction. Wise was lean, tall, and cadaverous, with vehemence and tones not unlike John Randolph's, and a steel-spring energy that, despite feeble health, never bent or broke. His campaign for Governor in 1855 was one of the most successful in politics. The new party was carrying every thing before it. It had enlisted some of the first intellects of the time—men like Henry

Winter Davis, Henry W. Hoffman, and J. Morrison Harris, of
Maryland ; Henry M. Fuller, of Pennsylvania ; John S. Carlile,
of Virginia ; Zollicoffer and Etheridge, of Tennessee ; George
Eustis, of Louisiana ; Humphrey Marshall, A. K. Marshall, and
W. L. Underwood, of Kentucky. Maryland, Delaware, Ken-
tucky, Alabama, Georgia, Tennessee, had in whole or in part
bowed to the torrent, when Wise came forth and breasted and
broke it. His speeches were unique, original, and resistless.
He traversed his State from the Alleghanies to the sea. He
was ubiquitous. He became more than ever a national figure.
Thousands of dollars were lost and won on the issue. The only
money I ever wagered on an election was five hundred dollars
I ventured on Wise. The following extract from a speech of
Governor Wise, delivered at Liberty Hall, Alexandria, on Saturday, February 3, 1856, may not be out of place, if only as a
counterpart to Levin's :

"I was saying when interrupted that the State of Virginia
has every element of commerce, of agriculture, of mining, and
of manufacturing. On Chesapeake Bay, from the mouth of the
Rappahannock to the capes of the Chesapeake, you have road-
steads and harbors sufficient to float the navies of the world.
From the River of Swans, on whose margin we are, down to the
line of North Carolina, you have the Potomac, the Rappahannock, the Piankatank, from Mobjack Bay to James River, and
the Elizabeth River—all meeting in the most beautiful sheet
of water of all the seas of the earth. You have the bowels of
your western mountains—rich in iron, in copper, in coal, in salt,
in gypsum ; and the very earth is rich in oil, which makes the
very rivers inflame. You have the line of the Alleghany—
that beautiful Blue Ridge which stands there, placed by the
Almighty, not to obstruct the way of the people to market, but
placed there in the very bounty of Providence to milk the
clouds, to make the sweet springs which are the source of your
rivers—[great applause]—and at the head of every stream is

the waterfall murmuring the very music of your power. [Applause.] And yet Commerce has long ago spread her sails and sailed away from you. You have not as yet dug more than coal enough to warm yourselves at your own hearths. You have set no tilt-hammer of Vulcan to strike blows worthy of gods in the iron founderies. You have not yet spun more than coarse cotton enough, in the way of manufacture, to clothe your own slaves. You have had no commerce, no mining, no manufactures. You have relied alone on the single power of agriculture—and such agriculture ! [Great laughter.] Your ledge-patches outshine the sun. Your inattention to your only source of wealth has seared the very bosom of Mother Earth. [Laughter.] Instead of having to feed cattle on a thousand hills, you have had to chase the stump-tailed steer through the ledge-patches to procure a tough beefsteak. [Laughter.]

"With all this plenitude of power she has been dwarfed in the Union; but, by the gods ! I say that she has power now, the energy, the resources—may I say the men?—to be put upon the line of progress to eminence of prosperity, to pass New York yet faster in the Union than ever New York has passed her. [Cheers.] You have been called the 'Old Dominion.' Let us, as Virginians, I implore you, this night resolve that a new era dawn, and that henceforth she shall be called the New Dominion. [Cheering.]

"The present condition of things has existed too long in Virginia. The landlord has skinned the tenant, and the tenant has skinned the land, until all have grown poor together. [Laughter.] I have heard a story—I will not locate it here or there—about the condition of our agriculture. I was told by a gentleman in Washington, not long ago, that he was traveling in a county not a hundred miles from this place, and overtook one of our citizens on horseback, with perhaps a bag of hay for a saddle, without stirrups, and the leading-line for a bridle, and he said: 'Stranger, whose house is that?' 'It is mine,' was

the reply.   They came to another, 'Whose house is that?'
' Mine, too, stranger.'   To a third, ' And whose house is that?'
'That's mine, too, stranger ; but don't suppose that I am so
darned poor as to own all the land about here.'

"What more do you want?   Why, you are in the habit of
discussing Federal politics ; and permit me to say to you, very
honestly and very openly, that, next to brandy, next to card-
playing, next to horse-racing, the thing that has done Virginia
more harm than any other in the course of her past history has
been her insatiable appetite for Federal politics.   [Cheers and
laughter.]   She has given all her great men to the Union.   Her
Washington, her Jefferson, her Madison, her Marshall, her gal-
axy of great men, she has given to the Union.   When and where
have her best sons been at work, devoting their best energies
to her service at home?   Richmond, instead of attending to
Richmond's business, has been too much in the habit of attending to the affairs of Washington City, when there are plenty
there, God knows, to attend to them themselves.   [Laughter.]
If you want my opinions upon Federal politics, though, I shall
not skulk them.

"The most prominent subject is that of the foreign war.   It
is said that this Administration is a 'do-nothing Administration.'   To its honor I can claim of every fair-minded man of
you—to its honor I can claim that it is at least preserving our
neutrality in the foreign war.   [Loud and prolonged cheers.]   I
concur with them in that policy ; and here let me say that, so
far as I am concerned, my sentiments are utterly opposed to
any filibustering in any part of the world.   [Cheers.]

"There is a Know-Nothing member elect from Massachusetts to the Congress of the United States.   There is a United
States Senator elect of the Know-Nothings who confesses the
accusation which I make, that the new party of Know-Nothings
was formed especially for the sake of abolitionism.   [Cheers
and hisses.]   And there is a Know-Nothing governor, one of

the nine, who are all ready to take the same ground. [Stamping of feet and some hissing.] Then, gentlemen, I have here an act of the Know-Nothing Legislature of Pennsylvania, which proposes to give citizenship to the fugitive slaves of the South. I have here, also, an article, which is too long for me to read, exhausted as I am, from the *Worcester Evening Journal*, an organ of Governor Gardner and Senator Wilson, which says to you boldly that the American organ at Washington is a pro-slavery organ, that it is not a true Know-Nothing organ, and that they speak for the North when they claim that they have already one hundred and sixty votes of the non-slaveholding States organized, eleven more than sufficient to elect a President of the United States without a single electoral vote from the slaveholding States.

"Now, gentlemen, having swept the Northern and the Northwestern non-slaveholding States of the Union, the next onset is on the soil of Virginia. This *Worcester Journal* boasts that Maryland and Virginia are already almost Northern States; and pray, how do they propose to operate on the South? Having swept the North—Massachusetts, New York, Pennsylvania, and all those other States—the question was: How can this ism be wedged in the South? And the devil was at the elbow of these preachers of 'Christian politics,' to tell them precisely how. [Cat-calls, derisive cheers, and other manifestations of the Know-Nothing element of the meeting.] There were three elements in the South, and in Virginia particularly, to which they might apply themselves. There is the religious element —the Protestant bigotry and fanaticism (for Protestants, gentlemen, have their religious zeal without knowledge as well as the Catholics). [A voice, 'True enough, sir.'] It is an appeal to the 103,000 Presbyterians, to the 30,000 Baptists, to the 300,000 Methodists of Virginia. Well, how were they to reach them? Why, just by raising a hell of a fuss about the Pope. [Laughter.] The Pope! The Pope, 'now so poor that none

can do him reverence,' so poor that Louis Napoleon, who requires every soldier in his kingdom to be at Sebastopol, has to
leave a guard of muskets at Rome!   Once on a time crowned
heads could bow down and kiss his big toe, but now who cares
for a Pope in Italy? Gentlemen, the Pope is here. Priestcraft
at home is what you have to dread more than all the Popes in
the world. I believe, intellectually, and in my heart as well as
my head, in evangelical Christianity. I believe that there is no
other certain foundation for this Republic but the pure and un-
defiled religion of Jesus Christ of Nazareth; and the man of
God who believes in the Father, in the divinity of the Son and
the Holy Ghost; the preacher in the pulpit, at the baptismal
font, by the sick-bed, at the grave, pointing

> 'The way to heaven and leading there,'

I honor; no man honors him more than I do.   But the priest
who deserts the spiritual kingdom for the carnal kingdom, he is
'of the earth, earthy.'   Whoever he be—Episcopalian, Baptist,
or Methodist—who leaves the pulpit to join a dark-lantern, secret political society, in order that he may become a Protestant
Pope by seizing on political power, he is a hypocrite, whoever
he be. [Some applause, and cries of 'Good.'] Jesus Christ of
Nazareth settled the question himself. I have his authority
on this question. When the Jews expected him to put on a
prince's crown and seat himself on the actual throne of David,
he asked for a penny to be shown him.   A penny was brought
to him, a metal coin, assayed, clipped, stamped with the image
of the State's representative of the civil power, stamped with
Cæsar's image. 'Whose is this image and superscription?' 'It
is Cæsar's.' 'Then render unto Cæsar the things which are
Cæsar's, and unto God the things that are God's.' [Applause.]
'My kingdom is not of this world. My kingdom is a spiritual
kingdom.' Cæsar's kingdom is political—is a carnal kingdom.
And I tell you that if I stood alone in the State of Virginia, and
if priestcraft—if the priests of my own mother-Church—dared

to lay their hands on the political power of our people, or to use their churches to wield political influence, I would stand, in feeble imitation of, it may be, but I would stand, even if I stood alone, as Patrick Henry stood in the Revolution, between the parsons and the people. [Applause, and a cry, 'I'm with you.'] I want no Pope, either Catholic or Protestant. I will pay Peter's pence to no Pontiff, Episcopalian, Presbyterian, Baptist, Methodist, or any other. [Applause, and cries of 'Good.'] They not only appeal to the religious element, but they raise a cry about the Pope. These men—many of them are neither Episcopalians, Presbyterians, Baptists, Methodists, Congregationalists, Lutherans, or what not—who are men of no religion, who have no Church, who do not say their prayers, who do not read their Bible, who live God-defying lives every day of their existence—are now seen with faces as long as their dark-lanterns, with the whites of their eyes turned up in holy fear lest the Bible should be shut up by the Pope! [Laughter, applause, and derisive cheers.] Men who were never known before, on the face of God's earth, to show any interest in religion, to take any part with Christ or his kingdom, who were the devil's own, belonging to the devil's church, are all of a sudden very deeply interested for the Word of God and against the Pope! It would be well for them that they joined a Church which does believe in the Father, and in the Son, and in the Holy Ghost. ['Good.'] Let us see, my friends, what Know-Nothingism believes in. Do you know that, gentlemen?

"But, gentlemen, these Know-Nothings appeal not only to the religious element, but to the political element; not only to the political element, but to the agrarian element. Not only do they appeal to Protestant bigotry; not only do they ask Protestants to out-Herod Herod, to out-Catholic the Catholics, to out-Jesuit the Jesuits by adopting their Machiavelian creed, but they appeal to a forlorn party in the State of Virginia—a minority party—broken down at home and disorganized, be-

cause their associates have become abolitionized at the North
—they appeal to them as affording them a house of refuge.
[Cheers and laughter.] There is a paper published in this
town by one of the most respectable gentlemen of the State,
who some time ago published an article which I must confess I
did not expect to see in print from his pen. The *Alexandria
Gazette*, one of the most respectable of the Whig papers of the
United States, edited by one of the most conservative and respectable gentlemen that I know of among my acquaintances,
one who has been advocating the doctrines and practice of conservatism ever since I knew him, is now proposing a fusion between the Know-Nothing and the Whig parties, simply for the
reason that 'the Whigs are tired of standing at the rack without fodder.' [A voice in the crowd, 'Oh, go along,' and laughter.] One who used (as I well remember) to denounce corruption and the spoils very sweepingly, is now actually maintaining
that the Whigs will not and can not go upon principle any
longer and adhere to conservatism, because they are tired of
waiting for office.

"And, sir, before George Washington was born, before Lafayette wielded the sword, or Charles Carroll the pen of his
country, six hundred and forty years ago, on the 16th of June,
1214, there was another scene enacted on the face of the globe,
when the general charter of all charters of freedom was gained,
when one man—a man called Stephen Langton—swore the
barons of England, for the people, against the orders of the
Pope and against the powers of the King—swore the barons on
the high altar of the Catholic church at St. Edmundsbury, that
they would have Magna Charta or die for it—the charter which
secures to every one of you to-day the trial by jury, freedom of
press, freedom of pen, the confronting of witnesses with the accused, and the opening of secret dungeons. That charter was
obtained by Stephen Langton against the Pope and against the
King of England, and if you Know-Nothings do not know who

Stephen Langton was, you know nothing, sure enough. [Laughter and cheers.] He was a Catholic Archbishop of Canterbury. [Renewed cheers.] I come here not to praise the Catholics, but I come here to acknowledge historical truths, and to ask of Protestants, What has heretofore been the pride and boast of Protestants? Tolerance of opinions in religious faith. [Applause.] All we ask is tolerance. All we ask is that, if you hate the Catholics because they have proscribed heretics, you won't out-proscribe proscription. If you hate the Catholics because they have nunneries and monasteries, and Jesuitical secret orders, don't out-Jesuit the Jesuits by going into dark-lantern secret chambers to apply test oaths. If you hate the Catholics because you say they encourage the Machiavelian expediency of telling lies sometimes, don't swear yourselves not to tell the truth.

"If you place me with your sword in hand by that great pillar of Virginia sovereignty, I promise you to bear and forbear to the last extremity. I will suffer much, suffer long, suffer almost any thing but dishonor. But it is, in my estimation, with the union of the States as it is with the union of matrimony—you may suffer almost any thing except dishonor; but when honor is touched the union must be dissolved. [Loud and prolonged cheers.] I will not say that; I take back the words. I will not allow myself to contemplate a dissolution of the Union. [Renewed cheering.] No; we will still try to save it. But when the worst comes to worst, if compelled to draw the sword of Virginia, I will draw it; and, by the gods of the State and her holy altars, if I am compelled to draw it, I will flesh it or it shall pierce my body. [Enthusiastic cheering.] And I tell you more, we have got Abolitionists in this State. [Voice in the crowd, 'D—n the Know-Nothings,' and great laughter.] If I should have to move, some of the first, I fear, against whom I should have to act would be some within our own limits. But if forced to fight, I will not confine myself to the State of Virginia. My motto will be:

> " ' Woe to the coward that ever he was born,
> That did not draw the sword before he blew the horn.'

[Loud cheers.]"

Mr. Levin died, as I have stated, in March of 1860, in his fifty-second year, but Henry A. Wise is still living in his sixty-fifth. His has been a stormy experience. He graduated at Washington College, Pennsylvania, at the age of nineteen, was admitted to the bar at Winchester, Virginia, in 1828, and removed the same year to Nashville, Tennessee, where he practiced his profession for a short time. Returning to his native county of Accomac, Virginia, he was elected a Representative in Congress in 1833, and served until 1844. He was an extreme Whig up to the time John Tyler quarreled with that party, after which he gradually united with the Democrats, and in 1855 became their candidate for Governor of Virginia and was elected. He held that position until 1860. He was a Confederate brigadier-general, and did his utmost to excite the people of the South against the Government. The extract I take from his speech is a fair specimen of his oratory. Intense, impetuous, and rapid, he is a very formidable adversary on the hustings and at the bar. His opposition to General Jackson was exceedingly virulent and able. He figured prominently in the lamentable duel at Bladensburg, Maryland, on the 24th of February, 1838, between Jonathan Cilley, of Maine, a Democrat, and William J. Graves, of Kentucky, a Whig. Few events ever excited greater horror. It was the first of many tragedies growing out of the arrogant insolence of the slaveholders. They fought with rifles, at eighty yards, and when Cilley fell, in the thirty-sixth year of his age, a bright light was extinguished and a noble heart stilled. Wise was the undoubted dictator of the Tyler Administration. Standing between the two great parties in the House, he delighted in his isolation and rioted in the eccentricities of his genius. Sent as Minister to Brazil in 1844, and remaining there until 1847, he made himself notorious by some of the maddest diplomatic explosions. He had been appointed Minister to France in 1843, and resigned his place to accept the post, but the Senate would not confirm him, and his constituency immediately returned him to Congress. He was Governor of Virginia when John Brown was executed, and made the worst use of that event in preparing the people for the coming rebellion. He lost one or two sons in that struggle, and is now, I believe, in the active practice of his profession.

The fatal error in the Native American and Know-Nothing excitements was that the first warred against all Catholics, and the second against all foreigners. We must wait to see how the present assault by Irish Catholics upon Irish Protestants will end. It is a new phase, and must work out new results, especially in view of late developments in Italy, France, Germany, and Spain, in all of which Republican members of the Church of Rome, like Hyacinthe in France, Garibaldi in Italy, Döllinger in Germany, and Castelar in Spain, have taken arms boldly against the extraordinary assumptions of the Pope and his College of Cardinals. Döllinger is already being called the Luther of his time, and Garibaldi is the soldier who fights for liberty in the name of the crucified Saviour.

Should this movement crystallize, it may revolutionize by liberalizing the Catholic Church. Let us not despise these signs of the times. They are numerous. The past history of the American sentiment is a profound philosophy—worthy of the statesman's careful study. The appointment of so many foreigners in New York by the Democratic party in the spring of 1844 was so odious that the Native Americans carried that great city in all its departments, electing James Harper (the venerable head of the publishing house of that name, now deceased) Mayor, and carrying the Board of Aldermen. The contagion then spread to Philadelphia, when Levin took up the cause, and, as I have shown, carried it to a great success. Defeated for a season, it is again revived by causes that have a deeper root and extend over the whole area of civilization. How these will germinate and grow, whether into a creed or a faction, into a great mission or a new mischief, is one of the mysteries of the age.

[July 30, 1871.]

XXX.

How to win friends and keep them is the secret of a success-ful public man. Andrew Jackson possessed it, without abso-lutely courting the people. His strict integrity, generous nat-ure, high honor, military character and history, were the chief elements of his prestige. Henry Clay possessed and knew how to use it. His charms were unrivaled eloquence, supreme am-bition, innate patriotism, commanding presence, and magnet-ism of men and women. John Quincy Adams, Martin Van Buren, and James Buchanan were cold and formal men, who inspired admiration by their talents, but never awakened real affection. Abraham Lincoln captured every body by seeming to be indifferent to the very qualities in which he was eminent. His simplicity and naturalness, so to speak, were resistless. But no character, certainly no candidate for our highest office, was a completer master of the gift of securing tenacious friends than Stephen A. Douglas. He had scarcely touched the floor of Congress before he became an object of interest. His ex-treme youth, his boyish appearance, his ready wit, his fine memory, his native rhetoric, above all, his suavity and heart-iness, made him a favorite long before he was named for Pres-ident. He delighted in pleasant company. Unused to what is called "etiquette," he soon adapted himself to its rules, and took rank in the dazzling society of the capital. Many a time have I watched him leading in the keen encounters of the

bright intellects around the festive board. To see him thread-
ing the glittering crowd with a pleasant smile or a kind word
for every body, one would have taken him for a trained courtier. But he was more at home in the close and exciting thicket
of men. That was his element. To call each one by name,
sometimes by his Christian name; to stand in the centre of a
listening throng, while he told some Western story or defended
some public measure; to exchange jokes with a political adversary; or, ascending the rostrum, to hold thousands spell-bound
for hours, as he poured forth torrents of characteristic eloquence—these were traits that raised up for him hosts who
were ready to fight for him. Eminent men did not hesitate to
take their stand under the Douglas flag. Riper scholars than
himself, older if not better statesmen, frankly acknowledged
his leadership and faithfully followed his fortunes.

But among them all none came into Congress more devotedly attached to Douglas than James A. McDougall, who died
shortly after the close of his term as a Senator in Congress
from California. Born at Bethlehem, New York, on the 19th
of November, 1817, he removed to Pike County, Illinois, when
he was just twenty years of age, and when Stephen A. Douglas
was registrar of the Land Office in that State. There was four
years' difference between the men, and they loved each other
like brothers. McDougall was chosen Attorney-General of
the State in 1842, and re-elected in 1844. In 1849 he origi-·
nated and accompanied an exploring expedition to Rio del
Norte, Gila, and Colorado; afterward emigrated to California,
where he followed his profession until he was chosen Attorney-
General of that State in 1850. He was sent to Congress for
one term, from 1853 to 1855, but declined a re-election, and remained out of public life until he was made a Senator in Congress in 1861, the term of which he served out. He entered
the Senate as a War Democrat of the advanced school, and
was for a while the representative of the ideas for which Brod-

erick fell at the hands of Terry in 1859. He advocated the
extremest measures against the rebellion, and sustained the
Lincoln Administration. But as the excitement grew, and
sterner measures were demanded, he gradually fell back into
the ranks of the old Democracy, and died in that faith. It can
be no irreverence to his memory to say that James A. McDougall would have been living now if he had not yielded to the
destroyer. When I first saw him in 1853, as a Representative
from California, he was the picture of health and strength.
Public life, with all its fascinations, was too much for him.
Generous to a fault, unusually disinterested, the enemy of all
corruption, he had the material for a long and useful life. Had
he not discarded the opportunities in his path, and surrendered
to the allurements around him, he might have been still among
us. Unlike some in the same body, McDougall rarely forgot
his place. If he committed excesses, it was outside the Senate
chamber. Every body loved him. I think he had not a personal enemy, and those who opposed him politically admired
his genius and deplored his weakness. Some of his arguments
were specimens of complete logic. He was an adept in the
law. He seldom forgot an authority, and his opinion on the
gravest questions was frequently sought and followed. Well
versed in the classics, familiar with ancient and modern poetry, his tastes, whether of books or men, were always refined.
One of his last speeches is that which follows, pronounced from
his seat in the Senate on the 11th of April, 1866, on the proposition of Senator Wilson, of Massachusetts, to prohibit the
sale of liquor in the Capitol building. It is given exactly as
it fell from his lips, and is a sad explanation of the cause which
called him too early from life to death, and of his peculiar habits of thought at a period when he seemed to have entirely
abandoned all hope of self-redemption :

"MR. PRESIDENT: It was once said that there are as many
minds as men, and there is no end to wrangling. I had oc-

casion some years since to discourse with a reverend doctor of
divinity from the State which has the honor to be the birth-
place, I think, of the president of this body. While I was dis-
coursing with him a lot of vile rapscallions invited me to join
them at the bar. I declined, out of respect to the reverend
gentleman in whose presence I then was. As soon as the occasion had passed, I remarked to the reverend doctor: 'Do
not understand that I decline to go and join those young men
at the bar because I have any objections to that thing, for it is
my habit to drink always in the front and not behind the door.'
He looked at me with a certain degree of interrogation. I
then asked him, 'Doctor, what was the first miracle worked by
our great Master?' He hesitated, and I said to him, 'Was it
not at Cana, in Galilee, where he converted the water into wine
at a marriage feast?' He assented. I asked him then, 'After
the ark had floated on the tempestuous seas for forty days and
nights, and as it descended upon the dry land, what was the
first thing done by Father Noah?' He said he did not know
that exactly. 'Well,' said I, 'did he not plant a vine?' Yes,
he remembered it then.

"I asked him, 'Do you remember any great poet that ever
illustrated the higher fields of humanity that did not dignify
the use of wine, from old Homer down?' He did not. I
asked, 'Do you know any great philosopher that did not use it
for the exaltation of his intelligence? Do you think, Doctor,
that a man who lived upon pork and beef and corn-bread could
get up into the superior regions—into the ethereal?' No, he
must

    " 'Take nectar on high Olympus,
     And mighty mead in Valhalla.'

"I said to him again: 'Doctor, you are a scholarly man, of
course — a doctor of divinity, a graduate of Yale ; do you remember Plato's Symposium?' Yes, he remembered that. I
referred him to the occasion when Agatho, having won the

prize of Tragedy at the Olympic games at Corinth, on coming
back to Athens was fêted by the nobility and aristocracy of
that city, for it was a proud triumph to Athens to win the prize
of Tragedy. They got together at the house of Phædrus, and
they said, 'Now, we have been every night for these last six
nights drunk; let us be sober to-night, and we will start a
theme,' which they passed around the table as the sun goes
round, or as they drank their wine, or as men tell a story. They
started a theme, and the theme was love—not love in the vulgar sense, but love in the high sense—love of all that is beautiful. After they had gone through, and after Socrates had pronounced his judgment about the true and beautiful, in came
Alcibiades with a drunken body of Athenian boys, with gar-
lands around their heads to crown Agatho and crown old Socrates, and they said to those assembled : 'This will not do; we
have been drinking, and you have not;' and after Alcibiades
had made his talk in pursuance of the argument, in which he
undertook to dignify Socrates, as I remember it, they required
(after the party had agreed to drink, it being quite late in the
evening, and they had finished their business in the way of discussion) that Socrates should drink two measures for every
other man's one, because he was better able to stand it. And
so, one after another, they were laid down on the lounges in
the Athenian style, all except an old physician named Aristo-
demus, and Plato makes him the hardest-headed fellow except
Socrates. He and Socrates stuck at it until the gray of the
morning, and then Socrates took his bath and went down to
the groves and talked academic knowledge.

"After citing this incident, I said to this divine : 'Do you remember that Lord Bacon said that a man should get drunk at
least once a month, and that Montaigne, the French philosopher, indorsed the proposition ?'

"These exaltants that bring us up above the common measure of the brute—wine and oil—elevate us, enable us to seize

great facts, inspirations which, once possessed, are ours forever;
and those who never go beyond the mere beastly means of animal support never live in the high planes of life, and can not
achieve them.

"I believe in women, wine, whisky, and war."

Let us not, with this curious specimen of his last ideas, judge
harshly of James A. McDougall; let us rather sympathize with
his weakness, and remember him for those qualities of heart
and head which, with a little self-restraint, would have made
him a shining light in the councils of the nation.

As showing how tranquillity and good temper promote happiness and long life, turn to the contrasting character of Gerritt
Smith, of New York, who came into Congress with McDougall
in 1853, and went out with him in 1855. Gerritt Smith was
born in Utica, New York, March 6, 1797, and is therefore in
his seventy-fifth year. He is living at Peterboro, New York, in
fine health. I saw him several months ago in Washington, the
picture of ripe, vigorous, well-preserved old age. The possessor
of immense wealth, which he distributes with princely generosity, he delighted in gathering men of opposite opinions, and
especially the Southern leaders, to his dinner parties. His
handsome face and elegant manners, his kind heart, native wit,
and graceful hospitality were made strangely attractive by the
fact that he never allowed a drop of wine or liquor at his entertainments. Every thing else was in profusion, and it was amusing to hear the comments of those who never knew what it was
to accept an invitation without anticipating copious draughts
of champagne, sherry, or madeira. Bold and manly in his opposition to slavery in all its forms, a powerful speaker, a conscientious legislator, he mingled with the extreme men of the South
like a friend. Combating what he believed to be their heresies,
he extended as free a toleration to them as he demanded for
himself. When he met McDougall first, the latter was one of
the promising men in the nation; and I doubt not, when his

career was prematurely closed, no one mourned him more or made a more generous allowance for his frailties than Gerritt Smith, of New York.

[August 6, 1871.]

XXXI.

JOHN SLIDELL'S death freshens a memory that ought to live forever—the memory of the short and last session of the Thirty-sixth Congress—when the work of secession preceded the work of rebellion. What was said in those short three months would fill many volumes ; what was done after them filled hundreds of thousands of graves. The defiance of Wigfall, now in a foreign land ; the threats of Jefferson Davis, now utterly despised by his former followers ; the prolonged plea for treason of Clingman, of North Carolina, now in safe obscurity ; the vulgar abuse of Jim Lane, of Oregon, now utterly out of sight —were nothing to the speech of Senator Slidell, of Louisiana, on the 4th of February, 1861, after he presented the ordinance of secession adopted by the Legislature of that State. I allude to it, not by way of reproach, but to point the solemn moral of a tragedy which began with so many loud prophecies of success from the wrong-doers, and ended in such a complete catastrophe of their hopes and plans. A few passages will therefore be useful :

"We have no idea that you will ever attempt to invade our soil with your armies ; but we acknowledge your superiority on the sea, at present, in some degree, accidental, but in the main natural and permanent, until we shall have acquired better ports for our marine. You may, if you will it, persist in considering us bound to you during your good pleasure ; you may deny the sacred and indefeasible right, we will not say of secession, but of revolution—aye, of rebellion, if you choose so to call our action—the right of every people to establish for itself that form of government which it may, even in its folly, if such you deem it, consider best calculated to secure its safety and promote its welfare. You may ignore the principles of our immortal Declaration of Independence; you may attempt to reduce us to subjection, or you may, under color of enforcing your laws or collecting your revenue, blockade our ports. This will be war, and we shall meet it, with different but equally efficient weapons. We will not permit the consumption or introduction of any of your manufactures; every sea will swarm with our volunteer militia of the ocean, with the striped bunting floating over their heads, *for we do not mean to give up that flag without a bloody struggle—it is ours as much as yours;* and although for a time more stars may shine on your banner, our children, if not we, will rally under a constellation more numerous and more resplendent than yours. You may smile at this as an impotent boast, at least for the present, if not for the future; but if we need ships and men for privateering, we shall be amply supplied from the same sources as now almost exclusively furnish the means for carrying on with such unexampled vigor the African slave-trade—New York and New England. Your mercantile marine must either sail under foreign flags or rot at your wharves.

"But enough, perhaps somewhat too much, of this. We desire not to speak to you in terms of bravado or menace. Let us treat each other as men, who, determined to break off unpleasant, incompatible, and unprofitable relations, cease to bandy words, and mutually leave each other to determine whether their differences shall be decided by blows or by the code, which some of us still recognize as that of honor. We shall do with you as the French Guards did with the English at the battle of Fontenoy. In a preliminary skirmish, the French and English Guards met face to face; the English Guards courteously saluted their adver-

saries by taking off their hats ; the French Guards returned the
salute with equal courtesy.   Lord Hay, of the English Guards,
cried out, in a loud voice, 'Gentlemen of the French Guards,
fire !'   Count d'Auteroche replied in the same tone, 'Gentlemen, we never fire first!'   The English took them at their
word, and did fire first.   Being at close quarters, the effect was
very destructive, and the French were for a time thrown into
disorder; but the fortunes of the day were soon restored by the
skill and courage of Marshal Saxe, and the English, under the
Duke of Cumberland, suffered one of the most disastrous de-
feats which their military annals record.   *Gentlemen, we will not
fire first.*

   " Senators, six States have now severed the links that bound
them to a Union to which we were all attached, as well by many
ties of material well-being as by the inheritance of common
glories in the past, and the well-founded hopes of still more
brilliant destinies in the future.   Twelve seats are now vacant
on this floor.   The work is only yet begun.   It requires no
spirit of prophecy to point to many, many chairs around us that
will soon, like ours, be unfilled ; and if the weird sisters of the
great dramatic poet could here be conjured up, they would present to the affrighted vision of those on the other side of the
chamber, who have so largely contributed to 'the deep dam-
nation of this taking off,' a 'glass to show them many more.'
They who have so foully murdered the Constitution and the
Union will find, when too late, like the Scottish Thane, that
'for Banquo's issue they have filed their minds ;' 'they have
but placed upon their heads a fruitless crown, and put a barren
sceptre in their gripe, no son of theirs succeeding.'

   " In taking leave of the Senate, while we shall carry with us
many agreeable recollections of intercourse, social and official,
with gentlemen who have differed with us on this, the great
question of the age, we would that we could, in fitting language,
express the mingled feelings of admiration and regret with which

we look back to our associations on this floor with many of our Northern colleagues. They have, one after the other, fallen in their heroic struggle against a blind fanaticism, until now but few—alas! how few—remain to fight the battle of the Constitution. Several even of these will terminate their official career in one short month, and will give place to men holding opinions diametrically opposite, which have recommended them to the suffrages of their States. Had we remained here, the same fate would have awaited, at the next election, the four or five last survivors of that gallant band ; but now we shall carry with us at least this one consoling reflection—our departure, realizing all their predictions of ill to the Republic, opens a new era of triumph for the Democratic party of the North, and will, we firmly believe, re-establish its lost ascendency in most of the non-slaveholding States."

It is hard to believe that the author of these sentiments was born and lived to manhood in the North, and that all this hate and scorn should have been cherished by one who ought to have been filled with gratitude to a government that had so long protected and so frequently honored him. Yet these are very characteristic words. They describe the man like a photograph. He had really come to despise his native section, and the feeling finally so absorbed him that he would consort with none who did not agree with him about slavery. He made his own ideas the test in all cases, grading his likes and dislikes by the favor or disfavor with which these ideas were received. His animosity to Douglas, Broderick, and—while he was on the right side—to Andrew Johnson, was intense and unnatural ; while to those who opposed Buchanan and his Lecompton treachery in 1858, he showed no mercy.

The curious part of the above extract is the unconscious tribute to the old flag and the promise "not to fire first ;" and yet in a little more than two months the rebellion had not only adopted a new flag, but authoritatively began the war by firing upon ours! Not less mistaken was his idea that the withdrawal of the main body of the Democratic party from Congress would be the very best plan to give to that which was left the control of the North.

Mr. Slidell was a man of the world and a scheming politician, yet never a statesman. He had some reputation as a lawyer, but not as an advocate or pleader. Few men had more influence over James Buchanan, and none did so much to mislead that ill-starred President. His rule was implacable hostility to all who did not agree with him. He was faithful to those who followed him, but his prejudices always dominated his friendships. He had undoubted courage, but his mistake was a belief that the best way to adjust a dispute was by an appeal to the "code of honor." Born in New York in 1793, he did not adopt Louisiana as his home till he had passed his majority; but he soon rose to leadership in the Democratic party. He was successively United States District Attorney, member of the State Legislature, Representative in Congress, Minister to Mexico, and United States Senator. It is easy to understand, upon reading his speech, how well qualified he was for the Confederate service. He had some diplomatic experience, spoke French fluently, had been much in foreign countries, and was perhaps the very man to make Louis Napoleon the ally of Jefferson Davis. But he made slow progress on his mission. He was constantly baffled—the prey of false promises and undying remorse. His capture by Captain Wilkes of the *San Jacinto* and his imprisonment in Fort Warren were not auguries of a fortunate career; and, doubtless, when he saw his proud predictions disappointed, his State captured by the despised Yankees, his associates beaten on land and sea, and the Democratic party every where utterly broken, he was not sorry to hear the last call. His associate commissioner, James M. Mason, of Virginia, preceded him to the final rest by a very few months. His colleague, J. P. Benjamin, who with him left the

Senate on the same 4th of February, 1861, is a barrister before the London courts, and is now a foreigner, as he was before he became naturalized under the laws of a country he sought to destroy. The man he most disliked in Louisiana, poor Pierre Soulé, the brilliant and superficial Frenchman, passed away after the saddest closing years. His friend Howell Cobb has gone. His *confrère*, Jesse D. Bright, has left Indiana to become a member of the Kentucky Legislature. And James Buchanan sleeps his last sleep in the Lancaster cemetery. It is certain that Mr. Slidell desired to lay his bones among his kindred in America. He tired of life in Paris, wealthy as he was in his own right and in the success of his connections; but for some reason the efforts of his friends to make his return easy were not persisted in, and in his seventy-eighth year he died in a strange land.

[August 13, 1871.]

XXXII.

BETWEEN December, 1860, and the 19th of April, 1861, was crowded a series of events which, carefully preserved, would have constituted many chapters of absorbing interest. But neither side believed entirely in the absolute certainty of hostilities; few were sufficiently composed to keep a regular diary outside the daily printed reports, and these, at least at the immediate theatre of operations, the nation's capital, were relatively inferior to the full and exact reflections of the doings of the world in the newspapers of these times. Some persons did, perhaps, journalize their experience, but much that entered into the real history of the period can only be rescued from oblivion by utilizing unrecorded memories. I recollect that as early as December, 1860, I called upon the people of Pennsylvania to put themselves in the condition of armed assistance to the Government.   For this letter I was severely censured as an alarmist.   The most sagacious men did not give up the hope of reconciliation.   Mr. Lincoln's inaugural, conceived in the best Christian spirit, was easily construed into a prayer for compromise; and one of the most thoughtful speeches of Judge Douglas, in which he contended that the difficulties could be amicably arranged, was inspired by that inaugural.   In recurring to my letters of March, 1861, I find myself busily seconding these efforts.   The firing upon Sumter, on the 14th of April, however, dissipated all these expectations, and men began to look for the worst.   From that day Baltimore city became an obedient echo of the agitation throughout the South.   Lying directly across the great highway leading to Washington, it was soon evident that no troops could be sent to the defense of the latter without danger.   But even then few persons were willing to admit that the pro-slavery mob of the city would dare to attack the soldiers on their way to the immediate scene of peril.   Among these was Charles Sumner, Senator in Congress from Massachusetts, who relates an incident that typifies the prevailing sentiment in Baltimore, and his own characteristic firmness and self-reliance.   At noon on the 18th of April, 1861, he bought a ticket at Washington for Baltimore, and arriving there, entered his full name on the books of Barnum's Hotel.   Preferring a quiet hour, he crossed the street and ordered an early dinner at Guy's Monument House, always famous for its good fare, and a favorite resort of the celebrities when they visited the Monumental City.   Dinner over, he called on a New England friend and resident, remained to tea, and then returned through a by-street to Barnum's, entering at the side door.   In the hall he met a gentleman who seemed much excited by his presence, and anxious for his safety.   Conscious of his own rectitude, he walked up to the office and demanded the key of his room, to which he was soon followed by the proprietor of the hotel, the late lamented Zenos Barnum, and another gentleman. There he was informed that the fact of his being in the house had obtained publicity, and that a large and angry crowd was outside threatening violence and demanding his life. His answer was that he felt perfectly secure as long as he was under that roof, and that he would hold the proprietors responsible for any outrage that might be attempted upon him. Mr. Barnum did not conceal his apprehensions alike for his great establishment and for the safety of his guest. Under his advice Mr. Sumner consented to remove to a more inaccessible room, where he remained for some time, discussing the situation of the country with his kind-hearted and generous host. He could distinctly hear the threatenings of the surging mob outside, and he felt that there was little doubt that nothing was needed but the opportunity to stimulate them to the wildest violence. Baltimore was completely in the hands of reckless and blood-thirsty men. They thought the Government powerless. Freedom of opinion was only tolerated on one side. The newspapers, with the exception of the *Baltimore American*, added fuel to the fire, and Union men were constrained to silence to save person and property. The nation's capital was almost entirely unprotected, and, although the North was at last rousing to a full sense of the public peril, as yet no troops had gone forward in response to the call of the Executive. Acting under the advice and the exhortations of Mr. Barnum, Mr. Sumner rose early on the morning of the 19th, and in a private carriage crossed the then quiet streets of the city to the Philadelphia station, where he entered the first train eastward, reaching Philadelphia in a few hours. On the way, and I think at Havre-de-Grace, he met the men of the 6th Massachusetts going South, and saw their happy faces and heard their joyous shouts. When he got to Philadelphia he found the streets crowded with people discussing the crisis. To get exact information, he called at the office of *The Press*, 413 Chestnut Street,

near Fourth, where he met Mr. J. G. L. Brown, then as now my
business manager, and learned for the first time the particulars of the attack upon the 6th Massachusetts on their way
through Baltimore.   Had he taken the train of the 19th instead of the 18th, he would undoubtedly have been among the
first victims of the rebellion, and possibly Barnum's Hotel
would have fallen before the infuriated fiends who were seeking
for objects upon which to wreak their vengeance and their ingratitude.

Zenos Barnum is dead, but I can not withhold a tribute to his
memory, nor refuse to recall the many happy hours I spent in
his society, when he, McLaughlin, and Dorsey had charge of
the old hotel, still one of the best in the South.   In the days before the war, when politics were not divided or disturbed by
slavery, it was very agreeable to Northern men to stop over and
enjoy its superior comforts, spacious rooms, unrivaled table, and
really refined society.   Every such visit was followed by an entertainment at Guy's Monumental House, where the men of
both parties met in friendly consultation, and where Whigs and
Democrats canvassed candidates, prepared platforms, and laid
plans for future campaigns.

Baltimore was for many years the chosen spot for political
national conventions, and Barnum's and Guy's the head-quarters
of the respective factions.   It was in Baltimore that Martin Van
Buren was nominated and renominated.   It was in Baltimore
where Joseph Holt, of Kentucky, thrilled the nation by an electric speech in vindication of Richard M. Johnson, in 1840.   It
was in Baltimore that James K. Polk was nominated, in 1844.
It was in Baltimore, in 1848, that Lewis Cass was nominated.
It was in Baltimore that Franklin Pierce was nominated by the
Democrats, and Winfield Scott by the Whigs, in 1852.   It was
in Baltimore that John C. Breckinridge was presented as the
candidate of the slaveholders, and Stephen A. Douglas ratified
as the candidate of the Independent Democracy, in 1860.   It

was in Baltimore that Abraham Lincoln was renominated for President in 1864, with Andrew Johnson as Vice-President.

Perhaps it was the meeting of these quadrennial assemblages, their exciting debates, and the extreme personal animosities to which they gave rise, which made Baltimore the seat and centre of such persistent opposition to the Government when the war finally took place. In all these conflicts Zenos Barnum was never a partisan. He was the prince of good fellows, warmly welcoming his friends and making no enemies. I suspect he was an Old-line Whig in the days of Webster and Clay, but when the South resolved to take issue with the North, in 1861, it was natural that he should sympathize with his own people; yet, if he did, it was always with due regard to the feelings of others. As the war progressed, Baltimore became more than ever an important point to the Government, and the responsibilities of a hotel-keeper like Barnum, in the midst of an inflammable community, were painfully increased. On one occasion the general in command of the Department closed the hotel, and Mr. Barnum came to Washington to ask me to intercede for him, which I did promptly and effectively, by appealing to President Lincoln and Secretary Stanton. After the doors of the old hotel were reopened, I received from my good friend a letter abounding in grateful expressions. He regarded it as an unusual obligation, and I revive the circumstance now, not because I had a hand in relieving an innocent man from the follies of one or two of his youthful employés, but to show that the humane and gentle spirit which induced him to interfere to protect Charles Sumner from the cruelty of the pro-slavery mob was not forgotten in darker or more exciting times, either by himself or by the men in command of the Government at Washington.

[August 21, 1871.]

XXXIII.

STEAM is your real revolutionist.   It has altered the physical geography of the civilized world.   It has bridged the seas, partially annihilated space and time, opened new highways into and redeemed the wilderness, neighbored far-distant States, converted old cities into new ones, changed deserted villages into thriving towns, leveled the forest, crossed chasms and connected mountains, and elevated skilled labor into a science. Imagination is baffled by its present, and vainly attempts to anticipate its future triumphs.   But in nothing has steam so transformed the face of the country and the habits of the people as in the substitution of railroads for turnpikes.   While I was preparing my last sketch, in which I recalled the genial Zenos Barnum, of Baltimore, to the thousands who knew him in bygone days, the famous hotel and inn keepers of the past rose before me, with the stage-coach, the Conestoga wagon, and the ancient system of land transportation.   Where are they now? Who that has passed his half-century does not remember them with pleasure?   In my young manhood their decay had begun, but it requires no strong effort to revive the long train of canvas-covered wagons passing through my native town on their way to and from Pittsburgh and Philadelphia, carrying the produce of the West in exchange for the merchandise of the East, with their hale, rough drivers, and their long leather whips, the coronal of bells on their horses, and their stoppage at the old taverns for food and water.   They were to the more ostentatious stage-coach what the baggage train is to the lightning express of the present day.

And when these coaches dashed into Lancaster, and rushed down the streets, the driver winding a merry air on his horn, accompanied by the crack of his long whip, women, children, and dogs rushed out to greet the meteoric chariot as it drew up with its foaming steeds at Slaymaker's old hotel, on East King Street, and began to throw off the mails, while the passengers alighted, thirsty, hungry, and covered with dust. It was the event of the day. Repeated at every other station and in every other town, it was one of a thousand similar pictures in other States and countries. Old England's great highways were made jocund with post-chaises, fast horses, daring drivers, uniformed guards, and jolly passengers. It was a favorite amusement for the nobility to mount the box and hold the reins with four in hand, and to course along the level roads, excelling in feats of daring drivership. They were as ambitious to lead in this sort of exercise as their descendants are in boat and foot races, in pugilistic encounters, and general gymnastics. Of these scenes the central figure was always the inn-keeper, who did not hold it beneath his dignity to stand in his doorway, en-girthed in his white apron, to "welcome the coming and speed the parting guest." That class is nearly extinct, though happily not forgotten. The old-fashioned publican aspired to be a gentleman, and was generally the associate of gentlemen, a connoisseur of wines, a judge of horse-flesh, a critical caterer, and in politics so unexceptionally neutral that, when the probable votes of a town were estimated, it was generally "so many Whigs, so many Democrats, and so many tavern-keepers." These Sir Roger De Coverleys—for they were men of substance and hospitable to the extreme—have given way to a generation as different as the Conestoga wagon differs from the locomotive, the old stage-driver from the car-conductor, the railroad director from the stockholder of the turnpike company. They are the *dilettanti* of the hotels, and, like the Pontiff's robe, rarely seen and much wondered at. Living in gorgeous private residences, away from the splendid palaces which bear their names, they in fact vicariously feed, room, and care for more human beings in one day than the men of the past did in six months. One of these men was John Guy, who may be called

the hero of three cities—known alike in Philadelphia, Baltimore, and Washington, though better appreciated in Baltimore.
Born in Lancaster County, Pennsylvania, I believe, he was the
founder of a family of unrivaled hotel-keepers. He still lives in
Guy's, on Seventh Street, Philadelphia, now in course of reha-
bilitation, and soon to expand into an ostentatious establish-
ment on the European plan, and in the unequaled Monument
House, nearly opposite Barnum's, in Baltimore. When I think
of him I think also of Dorrance and Pope Mitchell of the
United States Hotel, of Joseph Head of the Mansion House on
Third Street, of Dunlap of the City Hotel, of Hartwell of the
Washington House, and Jones of the old Jones Hotel, in
Philadelphia; of Gadsby in Washington, Stetson of the Astor
House, in New York, and many, many more. There is not a
State in the Union, north or south, which could not furnish
anecdotes of its representative inn-keepers, of their relations to
public men—to Calhoun in South Corolina, to Webster in Massachusetts, to Clay in Kentucky, to Sergeant S. Prentiss in Mississippi, to George D. Prentice in Louisville, and to the lawyers,
divines, and orators who for half a century dominated in those
sections. If these Bonifaces could have kept records of their
experience, what anecdotes they could relate of the giants of
the past, of their private troubles, their public ambitions, their
contrivances and their caucuses, their friends and their foes!
I knew many of them, and could relate many interesting incidents if I had space and time.

Let me recall one in regard to this same John Guy, sometimes told by my friend Dougherty, when we can win him to
social familiarity and make him forget professional responsibilities. Guy bore a striking resemblance to General Lewis Cass,
and while he was proprietor of the National Hotel, in Washington, the Michigan Senator was among his favored guests. Guy
dressed like Cass, and although not as portly, his face, including the wart, was strangely similar. One day a Western friend

of the house came in after a long ride, dusty and tired, and, walking up to the office, encountered General Cass, who was quietly standing there. Mistaking him for Guy, he slapped him on the shoulder, and exclaimed, "Well, old fellow, here I am; the last time I hung my hat up in your shanty, one of your clerks sent me to the fourth story; but now that I have got hold of you, I insist upon a lower room."

The General, a most dignified personage, taken aback by this startling salute, coldly replied: "You have committed a mistake, sir. I am not Mr. Guy; I am General Cass, of Michigan," and angrily turned away. The Western man was shocked at the unconscious outrage he had committed; but before he had recovered from his mortification, General Cass, who had passed around the office, confronted him again, when, a second time mistaking him for Guy, he faced him and said, "Here you are at last. I have just made a devil of a mistake; I met old Cass and took him for you, and I am afraid the Michigander has gone off mad." What General Cass would have said may well be imagined, if the real Guy had not approached and rescued the innocent offender from the twice-assailed and twice-angered statesman.

[August 27, 1871.]

XXXIV.

PARALLELS or contrasts of character are the most useful of biographies. They are like studies of different pictures placed side by side. Take Abraham Lincoln and Andrew Johnson. Lincoln was almost untrained in statecraft. He had been postmaster of a little town, had served four successive terms in the Legislature of Illinois, and one in Congress; was the only Whig from Illinois from 1847 to 1849, taking his seat just as Douglas took his in the Senate. Looking through the debates, we find Lincoln among the most modest of members. His utterances were forcible and few. It is easy to detect the quaint humor that figured so prominently in his after actions, but there was no frequency or ostentation of speech. In the same body sat Andrew Johnson, the Democratic head of the delegation from Tennessee. Less than two years older than Lincoln, his motions, measures, and spoken opinions would cover a hundred times the space allotted to his Illinois contemporary. Six years in the State Legislature, ten years in Congress, four years Governor, five years United States Senator, with several intermediate positions, he was constantly aspiring to a higher station. How significantly the huge library of Andrew Johnson's talk compares with the little casket of Lincoln's ideas! The loudness and length of the one, the brevity and silence of the other. These two men were alike in one thing only: in the obscurity of their origin and in the hard toil of their early lives. In every other respect they were opposites. I will not imitate the sad business of impugning or doubting motives. Let us hope that both were honest, as indeed the just judgment of all classes and writers now concedes Abraham Lincoln to have been. But how differently they used their weapons! Lincoln, without seeming to aspire, reached the highest station in the world; while Johnson, always reaching forth for the golden fruit, got it, and lost it in a fit of inconceivable madness. Abraham Lincoln died at the best moment for himself; Andrew Johnson lives to prove how great opportunities may be wasted.

In many respects Abraham Lincoln had few parallels. He was most considerate of the feelings and deservings of others. I have related how, before I ever saw or knew him, he wrote me a letter, directly after his election in 1860, thanking me for what he was pleased to call my services in resisting the proscriptions of the Buchanan Administration, and proffering a friendship which never abated. When the Baltimore Convention, which renominated him for President, was about to meet, and Mr. Hamlin declined being a candidate for Vice-President in order that the Democratic element might be represented, Mr. Lincoln personally advocated Andrew Johnson, and was backed by Mr. Seward, who was, however, interested in the defeat of Daniel S. Dickinson, pressed for the same post by his opponents in New York. Although Douglas defeated Lincoln for Senator in 1858, he gave him his confidence immediately after his inauguration, and never failed in generosity to his widow and children. When I was defeated for Clerk of the House in March, 1861, he called in person upon a number of Senators and asked them to vote for me for Secretary of that body. When Stonewall Jackson was killed, and one of my assistant editors spoke kindly of the better part of his character, Abraham Lincoln wrote me commending the tribute to a brave adversary. If you visited Lincoln he never wearied you with dreary politics or heavy theories, or glorified himself or his doings. In every crisis he sought the advice, not of his enemies, but of his friends. To his convictions he was ever true, but his opinions were always subject to revision. He delighted in parables, and especially in the rude jokes of the South and the West. He hailed Artemus Ward and Petroleum Nasby as benefactors of the human race, and no witticism, whether delicate or broad, escaped his keen appreciation. He was, withal, a man of sentiment, reading Shakespeare like a philosopher, and remembering the best passages. A little poem written by Francis De Haes Janvier, of Philadelphia, called "The Sleeping Sentinel," was an especial favorite ; and "The Patriot's Oath" and "Sheridan's Ride," by Thomas Buchanan Read, were always recited at his request by Mr. Murdoch, whenever that loyal actor visited the metropolis. He was neither boisterous nor profane. He cared little for the pleasures of the table ; and, although reared among a frontier people largely addicted to intoxicating drinks, he preferred water as a beverage. He liked the theatre, especially when Edwin Forrest, Joseph Jefferson, John Brougham, or John S. Clarke was the star. Though he frequently accompanied Mrs. Lincoln to the opera, it was rather in obedience to a social demand or an eagerness for rest in the corner of his box than a taste for scientific music. He was a capital peacemaker, and was especially resolute in refusing to adopt the enemies of his friends. He had a horror of making speeches, although a fine colloquial orator, and when he did address the people it was in short sentences, and only for a few moments at a time. In these addresses, as well as in his messages and letters, he said things that will survive for many generations. I give a few at random:

From his first annual message, March 9, 1861:

" There are already among us those who, if the Union be preserved, will live to see it contain two hundred and fifty millions. The struggle *of* to-day is not altogether *for* to-day—it is for a vast future also. With a reliance on Providence, all the more firm and earnest, let us proceed in the great task which events have devolved upon us."

From his remarks at a Union meeting in Washington, D. C., August 6, 1863:

" There has been a very widespread attempt to have a quarrel between General McClellan and the Secretary of War. Now I occupy a position that enables me to observe that these two gentlemen are not nearly so deep in the quarrel as some pretending to be their friends. General McClellan's attitude is such that, in the very selfishness of his nature, he can not but wish to be successful, and I hope he will ; and the Secretary of War is in precisely the same situation. If the military commanders in the field can not be successful, not only the Secretary of War, but myself, for the time being the master of them both, can not but be failures."

From his letter to Horace Greeley, August 22, 1862:

" The sooner the national authority can be restored, the near-er the Union will be — the Union as it was.

"If there be those who would not save the Union unless they could at the same time save slavery, I do not agree with them.

"If there be those who would not save the Union unless they could at the same time destroy slavery, I do not agree with them.

"*My paramount object is to save the Union, and not either to save or destroy slavery.*

"If I could save the Union without freeing any slave, I would do it; and if I could save it by freeing all the slaves, I would do it; and if I could save it by freeing some and leaving others alone, I would also do that.

"What I do about slavery and the colored race, I do because I believe it helps to save the Union; and what I forbear, I forbear because I do not believe it would help to save the Union.

"I shall do less whenever I shall believe what I am doing hurts the cause, and shall do more whenever I believe doing more will help the cause.

"I shall try to correct errors when shown to be errors, and I shall adopt new views so fast as they shall appear to be true views."

From his letter to the Illinois Convention, August 26, 1863:

"Peace does not appear so distant as it did. I hope it will come soon, and come to stay; and so come as to be worth the keeping in all future time. It will then have been proved that among freemen there can be no successful appeal from the ballot to the bullet, and that they who take such appeal are sure to lose their case and pay the cost. And there will be some black men who can remember that, with silent tongue and clenched teeth and steady eye and well-poised bayonet, they have helped mankind on to this great consummation, while I fear there will be some white ones unable to forget that, with malignant heart and deceitful speech, they have striven to hinder it."

From his letter to Colonel Hodges, of Kentucky, April 4, 1864:

"I claim not to have controlled events, but confess that

events have controlled me. Now, at the end of three years' struggle, the nation's condition is not what either party, or any man, devised or expected. God alone can claim it. Whither it is tending seems plain. If God now wills the removal of a great wrong, and wills also that we of the North, as well as you of the South, shall pay fairly for our complicity in that wrong, impartial history will find therein new causes to attest and re- vere the justice and goodness of God."

From his speech at the Philadelphia Fair, June 16, 1864 :

" It is a pertinent question, often asked in the mind privately, and from one to the other, When is the war to end?   Surely, I feel as deep an interest in this question as any other can, but I do not wish to name a day, a month, or a year when it is to end.   I do not wish to run any risk of seeing the time come without our being ready for the end, for fear of disappointment because the time had come and not the end.   We accepted this war for an object, a worthy object, and the war will end when that object is attained.   Under God, I hope it never will end until that time.   Speaking of the present campaign, Gen- eral Grant is reported to have said, ' I am going through on this line if it takes all summer.'   This war has taken three years ; it was begun or accepted upon the line of restoring the national authority over the whole national domain ; and for the Ameri- can people, so far as my knowledge enables me to speak, I say we are going through on this line if it takes three years more."

From his second annual message :

" The dogmas of the quiet past are inadequate to the stormy present.   The occasion is piled high with difficulty, and we must rise with the occasion.   As our case is new, so we must think anew and act anew.   We must disenthral ourselves, and then we shall save our country.

" Fellow-citizens, *we* can not escape history. We, of this Con- gress and this Administration, will be remembered in spite of ourselves.   No personal significance, or insignificance, can spare one or another of us. The fiery trial through which we pass will light us down, in honor or dishonor, to the latest generation. We *say* we are for the Union. The world will not forget that we say this. We know how to save the Union. The world knows we do know how to save it. We—even *we here*—hold the power and bear the responsibility. In *giving* freedom to the *slave* we *assure* freedom to the *free*—honorable alike in what we give and what we preserve. We shall nobly save, or meanly lose, the last, best hope of earth. Other means may succeed ; this could not fail. The way is plain, peaceful, generous, just—a way which, if followed, the world will forever applaud, and God must forever bless."

From his address at the consecration of the National Cemetery at Gettysburg, November 19, 1864 :

" But in a larger sense we can not dedicate, we can not consecrate, we can not hallow this ground. The brave men, living and dead, who struggled here, have consecrated it far above our power to add or detract. The world will little note nor long remember what we say here, but it can never forget what they did here. It is for us, the living, rather to be dedicated here to the unfinished work that they have thus far so nobly carried on. It is rather for us to be here dedicated to the great task remaining before us, that from these honored dead we take increased devotion to the cause for which they here gave the last full measure of devotion ; that we here highly resolve that the dead shall not have died in vain ; that the nation shall, under God, have a new birth of freedom, and that the government of the people, by the people, and for the people, shall not perish from the earth."

From his letter to a committee of New York workingmen, March 21, 1864 :

" None are so deeply interested to resist the present rebellion as the working people. Let them beware of prejudices working disunion and hostility among themselves. The most notable feature of a disturbance in your city last summer was the hanging of some working people by other working people. It should never be so. The strongest bond of human sympathy, outside of the family relation, should be one uniting all working people, of all nations, tongues, and kindreds. Nor should this lead to a war upon property or the owners of property. Property is the fruit of labor; property is desirable; is a positive good in the world. That some should be rich shows that others may become rich, and hence is just encouragement to industry and enterprise. Let not him who is houseless pull down the house of another, but let him labor diligently and build one for himself; thus by example assuring that his own shall be safe from violence when built."

To a club of Pennsylvanians, November 8, 1864:

"I am thankful to God for this approval of the people; but, while deeply gratified for this mark of their confidence in me, if I know my heart, my gratitude is free from any taint of personal triumph. I do not impugn the motives of any one opposed to me. It is not pleasure to me to triumph over any one; but I give thanks to the Almighty for this evidence of the people's resolution to stand by free government and the rights of humanity."

To political clubs of Washington, D. C., December 10, 1864:

"But the election, along with its incidental and undesired strife, has done good too. It has demonstrated that a people's government can sustain a national election in the midst of a great civil war. [Renewed cheers.] Until now it has not been known to the world that this was a possibility. It shows, also, how sound and how strong we still are. It shows that, even among candidates of the same party, he who is most devoted to the Union and most opposed to treason can receive most of the people's vote. [Applause.]

"It shows, also, to the extent yet unknown, that we have more men now than we had when the war began. Gold is good in its place, but living, brave, patriotic men are better than gold. [Cheers and other demonstrations of applause.]"

On the adoption of the anti-slavery amendment this speech from the Presidential Mansion, February 1, 1865 :

" A question might be raised whether the proclamation was legally valid. It might be urged that it only aided those who came into our lines, and that it was inoperative as to those who did not give themselves up ; or that it would have no effect upon the children of slaves born hereafter ; in fact, it would be urged that it did not meet the evil. But the amendment is a king's cure-all for all the evils. [Applause.] It winds the whole thing up."

On being officially notified of his re-election :

" Having served four years in the depths of a great and yet unended national peril, I can view this call to a second term in nowise more flattering to myself than as an expression of the public judgment that I may better finish a difficult work, in which I have labored from the first, than could any one less severely schooled to the task. In this view, and with assured reliance on that Almighty Ruler who has so graciously sustained us thus far, and with increased gratitude to the generous people for their continued confidence, I accept the renewed trust with its yet onerous and perplexing duties and responsibilities."

From his second inaugural address :

" If we shall suppose that American slavery is one of those offenses which, in the providence of God, must needs come, but which, having continued through his appointed time, he now wills to remove, and that he gives to both North and South this terrible war, as the woe due to those by whom the offense came, shall we discern therein any departure from those divine attri- butes which the believers in a God always ascribe to him? Fondly do we hope, fervently do we pray, that this mighty scourge of war may speedily pass away. Yet, if God wills that it continues until all the wealth piled by the bondsmen's two hundred and fifty years of unrequited toil shall be sunk, and until every drop of blood drawn with the lash shall be paid by another drawn with the sword, as was said three thousand years ago, so still it must be said, 'The judgments of the Lord are true and righteous altogether.'

"With malice toward none, with charity for all, with firmness in the right, as God gives us to see the right, let us strive on to finish the work we are in; to bind up the nation's wounds, to care for him who shall have borne the battle, and for his widow and his orphan—to do all which may achieve and cherish a just and lasting peace among ourselves and with all nations."

On the slaves fighting for the rebels, March 11, 1865:

"There are but few aspects of this great war on which I have not already expressed my views by speaking or writing. *There is one*—the recent effort of 'our erring brethren,' sometimes so called, to employ the slaves in their armies. The great question with them has been, 'Will the negro fight for them?' They ought to know better than we, and doubtless do know better than we. I may incidentally remark, however, that having in my life heard many arguments—or strings of words meant to pass for arguments—intended to show that the negro ought to be a slave, that if he shall now really fight to keep himself a slave, it will be a far better argument why he should remain a slave than I have ever before heard. He, perhaps, ought to be a slave, if he desires it ardently enough to fight for it. Or if one out of four will, for his own freedom, fight to keep the other three in slavery, he ought to be a slave for his selfish meanness. I have always thought that all men should be free; but if any should be slaves, it should be first those who desire it for *themselves*, and secondly those who desire it for *others*. Whenever I hear any one arguing for slavery, I feel a strong impulse to see it tried on him personally."

On Victory and Reconstruction, the last speech of his life, April 11, 1865:

" Some twelve thousand voters in the heretofore slave State of Louisiana have sworn allegiance to the Union, assumed to be the rightful political power of the State, held elections, organized a State government, adopted a free State constitution, giving the benefit of public schools equally to black and white, and empowering the Legislature to ĉonfer the elective franchise upon the colored man. Their Legislature has already voted to ratify the constitutional amendment recently passed by Congress abolishing slavery throughout the nation. These twelve thousand persons are thus fully committed to the Union and to perpetual freedom in the State ; committed to the very things and nearly all the things the nation wants, and they ask the nation's recognition and its assistance to make good that committal. Now, if we reject and spurn them, we do our utmost to disorganize and disperse them. We, in effect, say to the white men, 'You are worthless, or worse ; we will neither help you nor be helped by you.' To the blacks we say, 'This cup of Liberty which these, your old masters, hold to your lips, we will dash from you, and leave you to the chances of gathering the spilled and scattered contents in some vague and undefined when, where, and how.' If this course, discouraging and paralyzing both white and black, has any tendency to bring Louisiana into proper practical relations with the Union, I have, so far, been unable to perceive it. If, on the contrary, we recognize and sustain the new government of Louisiana, the converse of all this is made true.

" We encourage the hearts and nerve the arms of the twelve thousand to adhere to their work, and argue for it and proselyte for it and fight for it, and feed it and grow it and ripen it to a complete success. The colored man, too, seeing all united for him, is inspired with vigilance and energy and daring to the same end. Grant that he desires the elective franchise, will he not attain it sooner by saving the already advanced steps toward it than by running backward over them? Concede that the new government of Louisiana is only to what it should be as the egg is to the fowl; we shall sooner have the fowl by hatching the egg than by smashing it.

"Again, if we reject Louisiana, we also reject one vote in favor of the proposed amendment to the National Constitution. To meet this proposition it has been argued that no more than three fourths of those States which have not attempted secession are necessary to validly ratify the amendment. I do not commit myself against this further than to say that such a ratification would be questionable, and sure to be persistently questioned; whilst a ratification by three fourths of all the States would be unquestioned and unquestionable."

I think I never saw him out of temper but once, and that was when I presented him the unanimous confirmation of a certain personage for a high office. "Why did the Senate not confirm Mr. —— and Mr. ——? My friends knew I wanted this done, and I wanted it done to-day;" and then he used certain strong expressions against the successful person. I looked at him with some surprise, never having seen him in such a mood, and said, "Why, Mr. Lincoln, you seem to hold me responsible for the act of the Senate, when you must be aware of the custom under which that body acted." "Oh, no," was his reply; "I was not scolding you, my friend, but I fear I have been caught in a trap."

Many a fierce conflict took place in his presence between angry politicians, but it required a very strong provocation to overbalance his judgment or his equanimity. Not so, however, with an appeal for mercy; not so with a petition from the poor. Here he was as weak as woman, and more than once mingled his tears with the gentler sex.

There are few parallels to such a character, but many contrasts.

The contrast between Lincoln and Johnson may be illustrated by an incident connected with the unhappy fourth of March, 1865, when Andrew Johnson was inaugurated Vice-President in the Senate chamber. I do not desire to see the curtain rise before a scene that both parties seem willing to expunge—the Republicans, who apologized for it when it occurred, and the Democrats, who regretted it after Johnson joined their despairing columns. But I can never forget President Lincoln's face as he came into the Senate Chamber while Johnson was delivering his incoherent harangue. Lincoln had been detained signing the bills that had just passed the old Congress, and could not witness the regular opening of the new Senate till the ceremonies had fairly commenced. He took his seat facing the brilliant and surprised audience, and heard all that took place with unutterable sorrow. He then spoke his short inaugural from the middle portico of the Capitol, and rode quickly home. Bitter maledictions were immediately hurled against the new Vice-President. I hastened to his defense to the best of my abilities, believing the affair to have been an accident. Threats of impeachment were common in both parties, especially among the Democrats; and the crusade got so fierce at last that I found myself included among those who had helped Mr. Johnson to his exposure. But no voice of anger was heard from Abraham Lincoln. While nearly all censured and many threatened, Mr. Lincoln simply said, "It has been a severe lesson for Andy, but I do not think he will do it again."

In a little more than a month, Lincoln was in his grave and Johnson his successor. Both have had their trial before the same people. The verdict on each is irreversible. What was at first a parallel has become a contrast. And this contrast grows stronger with every hour, and will stand through all time as a warning to the nations.

[September 3, 1871.]

XXXV.

VERY many people are exercised about the growth of monopolies. Do they ever think of the monopoly of government and legislation by the lawyers? I do not repeat a prejudice, but a fact. Take a seat in the gallery of the Senate or the House in Washington, or in any of the State Legislatures, and you will note that the controlling minds, with very few exceptions, are lawyers. All our Presidents were educated at the bar except Washington, Harrison, Taylor, and Grant. Most persons forget that Andrew Jackson's early life, even beyond his thirtieth year, was given to the law, as United States District Attorney for the Territory of Western North Carolina, and as Judge of the Supreme Court of the new State of Tennessee ; that James K. Polk was one of the busiest men on his circuit; that Millard Fillmore (at first a tailor's apprentice), Franklin Pierce, James Buchanan, and Abraham Lincoln were distinguished lawyers. It is true that Andrew Johnson was in no sense a lawyer, but he had been long in politics and knew how to avail himself of lawyers. The Southern politicians of the generation after Washington, Jefferson, and Monroe, such as Clay, Calhoun, Crittenden, Thomas H. Benton, George Poindexter, Bailie Peyton, Henry A. Wise, Jefferson Davis, Robert Toombs, and W. H. Roane, were famous at the bar before entering public life. Sam Houston, of Texas, was not a lawyer, nor Lewis F. Linn, Colonel Benton's handsome colleague from Missouri, nor William M. Gwin, Senator from California, nor his martyr-colleague, David C. Broderick; but such exceptions only strengthen the rule that the legal profession is, after all, the sure secret of successful leadership. I have often been struck with the dogmatism of the attorneys who came into Congress after a prosperous career, and the deference paid to them by those of stronger minds and larger experience. They assert their old habits while they were advocates or judges. W. Pitt Fessenden, of Maine, Jacob Collamer, of Vermont, Reverdy Johnson, of Maryland, Thaddeus Stevens and John Hickman, of Pennsylvania, were signal illustrations. Their opinions were given with an *ex cathedrâ* air, and generally submitted to. The privileges of lawyers in Congress have often excited complaint. They can practice in the courts, even in cases upon which they may have voted in Congress. Many do not scruple to attend to business in the Departments and take fees for their services, but the laymen—the merchants, the physicians, and the manufacturers—can not, uncensured, follow their example, while holding a place in the national councils. What was true in this respect in the past is more true at the present, and will be truer of the future. The law is the royal road to eminence in this country, whatever men may say to the contrary ; and it is natural that it should be so, as government, property, and personal rights are vitally dependent upon law : thus all Americans ought to include something of legal knowledge in their early education. In England every statesman is reared, if not to the bar, at least to a knowledge of jurisprudence. First take a thorough classical education as a foundation, and build on it a complete insight into the common law and of the laws of nations. Such is the British ideal. Ordinary minds, thoroughly conversant with legal precedents and authorities, wield a large influence in public bodies. Every man of business consults his lawyer more frequently than his physician. The youth who varies his collegiate course by lessons in the law academy, emigrates to the West with rare advantages over those who are not so equipped. Our Delegates, Senators, and Representatives from the new States and Territories are lawyers almost without exception. A profession which clothes its disciples with so many facilities deserves more attention than it has received from scholastic institutions. I do not insist that all our young men should study the law, but where the acquisition of it is so easy and the possession of it so useful, it certainly deserves consideration at the hands of those who direct the instruction of the people.   No citizen is any the worse for such an acquisition.

More than a year ago I sat among the spectators at the commencement of the Howard University in the city of Washington, while Professor John M. Langston presided over the exercises of a class of colored young men, just completing their legal studies.   Some of them had only a year before been unable to read and write, and one bright, black fellow was especially patronized by the Professor, because six months before he did not know his alphabet.   Nearly all had been slaves.   There were oral and written arguments.   The manner in which they spoke or read their productions displayed extraordinary talent. I thought I could detect in their flowing cadences and graceful gestures close copies of the old Southern statesmen, who in past years lorded it over both parties.   There was scarcely an error of grammar or pronunciation.   The logic and the appreciation of the subjects treated, which included landlord and tenant, titles to real estate, divorce, borrowing and lending, promissory notes, etc., proved not only careful study, but intense determination to succeed.   Among the candidates was a woman who read a clear and compact treatise on a difficult legal problem, in the enunciation and preparation of which she exhibited the precision of an expert and the condensation of a thinker. I doubt whether the older and more extensive Law School connected with Columbia College, where the offspring of the other, and what is called the superior race, are educated, could show, all things considered, an equal number of graduates as well grounded and as completely armed for the battle of the future. There are colored lawyers in most of our courts, even in the highest judiciary.   They are the pioneers of an interesting and exciting destiny.   With them, unlike their more fortunate white brethren, the bitterest struggle begins when they receive their sheepskins.   They go forth to war against a tempest of bigotry and prejudice.   They will have to fight their way into society, and to contend with jealousy and hate in the jury-box and in the court-room, but they will win, as surely as ambition, genius, and courage are gifts, not of race or condition, but of God alone.

[September 10, 1871.]

XXXVI.

HENRY CLAY never fully forgave James Buchanan for the part he played in 1824–25 in the celebrated bargain and sale by which it was charged that Clay gave the vote of Kentucky to John Quincy Adams for President instead of General Jackson, in consideration of his subsequent appointment by Adams to the Department of State.   Buchanan was then a Representative in Congress from the old Lancaster, Chester, and Delaware district in Pennsylvania.   Chosen originally as a Federalist, he became a Democrat under the influence of Jackson's popularity, while Clay, originally a Democrat, became a violent Whig antagonist of Jackson and his party.   In 1824–25 Buchanan was in his thirty-fifth year, and Clay in his forty-eighth. The accusation that Clay had supported Adams for a place in his Cabinet, long insisted upon by his adversaries, aroused the bitterest passions, and was haughtily and indignantly repelled by himself.   He was made to believe that the story was started by the young member from Lancaster, but this was always denied by the latter, and he wrote several letters effectually disproving it, but they were not satisfactory to the imperious Kentuckian.   It will be remembered that John Randolph, of Virginia, was one of Clay's fiercest assailants, and he carried his enmity so far that it led to a duel between them, which terminated without bloodshed.

Some ten years later Clay and Buchanan were both in the United States Senate together, and the latter was one of the leaders of the Democracy.   Clay did not conceal his dislike of the Pennsylvanian, and sought every occasion to show it.   One memorable day he rose and made a studied attack upon the Democrats, and especially upon General Jackson.   Mr. Buchanan was put forward to answer him, which he did with his best ability.   When he took his seat Mr. Clay rose with well-feigned surprise, and sarcastically remarked that "he had made no allusion to the Senator from Pennsylvania.   He was referring to the *leaders*, not to the subordinates of the Democracy." Upon which Buchanan took the floor and said that the Senator from Kentucky was certainly in error, because he had pointedly and repeatedly looked at him while he was speaking.   Clay quickly and sneeringly retorted by alluding to Buchanan's slight obliquity of vision.   "I beg to say, Mr. President," he remarked, "that the mistake was the Senator's, not mine.   Unlike him, sir, I do not look one way and row another."   It was a cruel thrust; and when a gentleman reproached Clay for his harshness, he shrugged his shoulders and said, "Oh, d—n him! he deserved it.   *He writes letters!*"   On another occasion Buchanan defended himself against the charge of hostility to the second war with England by showing that he had formed a troop of Lancaster horse, and rode to Baltimore to resist the invader.   "Yes, Mr. President," was Clay's prompt rejoinder, "I remember that event, and I remember also that by the time the Senator got into Maryland the enemy had fled.   Doubtless they heard of the approach of the distinguished gentleman, and retired before the prestige of his courage."

But time, if it does not make all things even, mollifies the passions of men.   Mr. Buchanan was too much a man of the world—too accomplished a courtier—not to soften the asperity of as proud a spirit as Clay.   They frequently met in society in after years, especially at the dinner-table.   If they did not become friends, they at least ceased to be enemies. And in 1856, when Buchanan became the Democratic candidate for President, he had no more hearty supporter than the son of the Great Kentuckian, James B. Clay, who, after having served in the Confederate army, died at Montreal on the 26th of January, 1864.

Benton, who had always opposed Buchanan's aspirations, because he regarded him as weak and timid, powerfully championed him in that year even against his own son-in-law, Fremont. Rufus Choate, Webster's nearest friend, was on the same side; so were John Van Buren and his father, notwithstanding both held Buchanan's friends accountable for the nomination of Polk in 1844. Webster himself, had he lived, would, I think, have voted the same way; and perhaps Henry Clay would have preferred the man who so solemnly pledged himself to put an end to the slavery agitation. They both died, Clay in September and Webster in October of 1852, and so were spared the mortification of Choate, Benton, and the Van Burens, when James Buchanan yielded to the fire-eaters, and tried to force slavery into Kansas.

[September 17, 1871.]

XXXVII.

CEMETERIES are of modern origin. One of the oldest is *Père la Chaise*, near Paris, the arrangements of which have been generally followed in English and American cities. The dead of the ancients became so numerous at last that the bodies were burned, and the ashes preserved in urns, which it appears from recent excavations had accumulated in incalculable numbers. It is believed that the fine burial grounds of the Turks, extending over large tracts, adorned by cedars and other trees, suggested the prevailing plans of the Europeans. Our places

of interment are surrounded by beautiful and elevating influences, decorated by foliage and flowers, monuments and statuary, and always located in the midst of exquisite natural scenery. Greenwood, near New York; Mount Auburn, Boston;
Laurel Hill, Philadelphia; Buenaventura, Savannah, may be
called the patterns from which many have been copied, so that
there is not a considerable town, North or South, that does not
boast of one of these cities of the dead. Among the most picturesque is undoubtedly that founded by W. W. Corcoran —
"Oak Hill Cemetery," at Georgetown, D. C. The marble pile
awaiting his own remains is a work of consummate majesty
and symmetry. The plan is entirely different from that adopted in other cemeteries. A series of natural ravines have been
handsomely terraced and planted with shrubbery. No railings
are allowed around the different lots, so that the whole presents the appearance of a handsome private park. Many of
the monuments are noted specimens. Prominent among the
latest is that erected by the family of Edwin M. Stanton. It is
of silver-tinged granite from the quarries near Concord, New
Hampshire. The inscription reads: " Edwin M. Stanton, born
December 19, 1814; died December 4, 1869."

No modern character possesses more interest than Stanton.
The time has not come when his biography may be faithfully
and dispassionately written. Up to the rebellion he lived a
life of singular tranquillity. Discarding office and avoiding
politics, his ambition was in the line of the law, in which he
soon became a giant. A close student, a clear, compact logician, a bold and impetuous advocate, his best powers were given
to his profession. Sought after far and near, and employed in
most of the great cases, his reputation and large influence, in
his native State of Ohio and in his adopted State of Pennsylvania, assumed national proportions when he removed to the
city of Washington. He towered in the Supreme Court a
leader of leaders. An authority of wide acceptation, he was a

genius of his school. Forced finally into public position at the close of Buchanan's Administration, his bearing as Attorney-General was so fearless and conscientious that when General Cameron retired from the War Department, popular opinion pointed him out as the fittest man for that responsible post, and when President Lincoln selected him, the whole country cried Amen.

I knew him well. Long before his name was cited in the catalogue of great lawyers, I met and learned to love him, wondered at his mind, and gathered instruction from his counsels. He had strong convictions. He hated slavery from the start, although co-operating with the Democratic party. Once he was sent to Columbus as a delegate to a Young Men's State Convention, and when the chairman endeavored to disregard the sentiment to which the majority were pledged, Stanton, who was in the second or third tier, made several efforts to obtain a hearing. At last he caught the chairman's eye, and commanded his attention by beginning his speech as follows : "I address you to-day as the meanest man among the thousands of young men of Ohio whom you have attempted to betray." When he accepted the portfolio of War Minister it was in the spirit of the generals of Cromwell's Puritan army. The first thing he did was to put himself out of sight. In the long catalogue of calumnies heaped by bad men upon his honored name, not even a suspicion of personal ambition is found. They hated him because he loved his country—because that love was sincere, vigilant, exacting. He was rough in his manners to those he had reason to believe corrupt, but he was sweet as summer to the poor, the humble, and the brave. By his own example he conquered. Asking nothing for himself, he refused every thing to others that was not just. After several generals had failed, I heard him say, more than once, " I will find a leader for these armies, if he must be taken from the ranks." The intensity with which he was identified with his client's cause was in accordance with his intense devotion to the Republic. I have seen him more than once order back the laggard to camp in tones of stern rebuke, and immediately afterward take the mother of a private soldier by the hand and cheer her for the loss of her son. Utterly regardless of social pleasure, he had no hope, no object, no time but for the cause. He worked harder than any of his subordinates, and stayed longer in his Department. It was astonishing how this man, who had never participated in party warfare, comprehended the political situation. Fertile of suggestion, he was a mine of information to an editor. He thought quickly and wrote strongly. He would give a key-note for a campaign, which, sounded in the columns of a newspaper, would thrill a continent. He was no respecter of persons. Frequently, to prove his iron impartiality, he reproached his nearest friends when he feared they were faltering. He studiously abstained from public speaking. His reports were brief, but clear and cogent; his letters few and simple; his gazettes announcing a victory were marked by all the Covenanter's fire. I reproduce that in which he promulgated the decisive victories of Grant before Richmond :

"WAR DEPARTMENT, WASHINGTON, D.C., }
"*Lieutenant-General Grant:*   "April 9, 1865—9:30 P.M. }

"Thanks be to Almighty God for the great victory with which he has this day crowned you and the gallant army under your command! The thanks of this Department, and of the Government, and of the people of the United States, their reverence and honor, have been deserved, and will be rendered to you and the brave and gallant officers and soldiers of your army for all time.   EDWARD M. STANTON, Secretary of War."

In these two sentences you have an insight into the character of Edwin M. Stanton. Every word seems to have been coined out of the pure gold and weighed in the nicest scales of gratitude. They are short, but how ponderous! Written for the living millions, they will be read by the coming millions. As we ponder them, and recollect that in five little days Abraham Lin-

coln slept in death, and that a little more than five years later—
after that terrible struggle with Andrew Johnson, which may be
said to have literally crushed the heart of the great statesman—
Stanton himself was summoned to his last account, let us never
cease to cherish and follow his matchless example.   Had he
lived to take his seat upon the bench of the Supreme Court of
the United States, the words of Daniel Webster, applied to the
illustrious John Jay, would have been equally true of Edwin M.
Stanton : " When the spotless ermine of the judicial robe fell
upon him it touched nothing less spotless than itself."

[September 24, 1871.]

XXXVIII.

GENERAL McCLELLAN'S father, the famous Philadelphia surgeon, Dr. George McClellan, was one of the most devoted of
Whigs, and one of Henry Clay's sincerest friends.   His lectures
at our great Philadelphia Medical College, in which he was an
eminent professor, were models of terse statement and lucid
analysis.   His influence in society was large and commanding.
Shortly after the defeat of Mr. Clay, in 1844, I was the guest of
my friend, Hon. Morton McMichael, the present editor of the
Philadelphia North American, who then resided in Filbert Street,
near Broad, in that city.   Like Dr. McClellan, he had fervently
supported the Kentucky statesman.   At that time I was the
editor of the Democratic organ at Lancaster, Pennsylvania, and
bore a very near relation to James Buchanan.   Politics had
never interfered with my intimacy with Mr. McMichael, which,
beginning when we were both very young, has continued without pause to this hour.   One day after dinner there was a
quick, sharp ring at the door-bell, when my host said with a
laugh, " Look out! there is Dr. McClellan ;" and with that the

distinguished surgeon came bustling in. The defeat of Mr. Clay was still keenly felt by the Whigs, though my generous and genial friend, McMichael, did not allow his hospitality to be less because I had opposed him. But Dr. McClellan could not restrain his feelings. He held Buchanan responsible for the vote of Pennsylvania, and, though most courteous to me, did not spare the Wheatland leader. We soon got over our little difference, however, and closed the controversy in a glass of wine. The Doctor possessed rare traits. Abounding in anecdote and information, he was an unrivaled wit and conversationalist. His son, Dr. J. H. B. McClellan, and his grandson, young Dr. George, both in fine practice in Philadelphia, have inherited his high professional skill and in a considerable degree his lively and vivacious nature.

There is a well-known physician in Washington, Dr. J. C. Hall, who relates many incidents of the public men he has attended in his long and brilliant experience. At the head of his profession, he has attained old age almost without an enemy. I know no man more universally beloved. A happy temperament, fine manners, and a thorough scholar, his sketches of the leading characters of other days would make a charming volume if he would write them out. Fond of polite literature and of cultivated people, he is almost out of practice, and may be said to live among his friends and his books. He, too, was an "Old-line Whig," and shared the feelings, if not the prejudices, of Dr. McClellan, whom he knew and admired, especially as he was a graduate of Jefferson College, Philadelphia. Dr. Hall has known the leaders of both, in fact, of all the great parties, and was frequently consulted by them. He attended General Jackson on several occasions, though not his family physician. It is one of the Doctor's peculiarities that he does not trouble himself with money matters, and is careless about collecting his fees. Once, however, during a temporary absence, his clerk made out some bills, and among others sent one to the President. On his return the Doctor found a note from General Jackson inclosing a check for the amount, deducting an old charge which had been called for and settled, and for which he held a receipt. The fact that the bill had been sent was not less a mortification to Dr. Hall than the error in the account itself. But on looking at the President's check he found that the General had forgotten to sign it! He therefore returned it, with the expression of his regret that the bill had been sent, and pointed out the General's omission. The check was duly signed and sent back inclosed in a note with this remark:

"DEAR DOCTOR,—The best of men is liable to mistakes.

"ANDREW JACKSON."

Dr. Hall testifies to the old hero's kindness to all his people, especially to his servants. Once when the small-pox broke out among them, and nearly every body else fled, the President remained in the White House, and waited on black and white with unremitting attention.

Few physicians enter public life, though many of them are active politicians. They seem to prefer the field of science to the field of party. Yet there is no class capable of exercising more power. They are the depositories of many a sacred trust; and if they dared to relate what they know of the great ones they have attended in sickness and in their last hours, they would shed a wonderful light upon the characters of men and the mysteries of governments.

[October 1, 1871.]

XXXIX.

I WAS introduced to Charles Carroll, of Carrollton, grandson of the illustrious patriot of that name, at Barnum's Hotel, Baltimore, in the spring of 1855, and after a friendly conversation

upon public affairs he cordially invited me to visit his estate at
Doughoregan Manor, in Carroll County, Maryland. There was
something so sincere in his manner that I yielded to his wish,
and one afternoon in July of the same year I took the cars for
Ellicott's Station, in company with a young friend. When we
reached it, on a bright moonlight night, we found a carriage
waiting to convey us to the farm of the Hon. Edward Hammond, then a Representative in Congress, and the neighbor
and confidential friend of Mr. Carroll. Mr. Hammond had
been an invalid, and was confined to his room, but came forth
and greeted us with an old-fashioned Southern welcome. A
number of the young men of the vicinity came in on horseback
to join our merry party, and it was very late when we retired.
The next morning we passed over to see our host at Doughoregan Manor. He received us like a knight of the olden time.
We found ourselves in the midst of a vast estate, into which all
the modern improvements in agriculture had been introduced.
He showed me a thousand acres devoted to the cultivation of
corn, then in full leaf and tassel, promising a bounteous crop;
he carried us through his slave-quarters, and when I remarked
that this system could not last, he turned to me with an expression I shall ever remember, and said, "So far as I can help it,
it shall not." He was a Catholic, like his great ancestor, Charles
Carroll of Carrollton, who was born at Annapolis, September
20, 1737, and who died November 14, 1832, in his ninety-sixth
year. He pointed out the exquisite marble effigies of his deceased relatives in the beautiful chapel, without seeming to
think that he would soon be one of the occupants of that beautiful chamber of the dead. Of gentle, polished manners, handsome presence, large acquirements, and generous, even profuse
hospitality, he was a type of the patriotic school of which his
grandfather was one of the finest ideals. As a citizen of intrin-
sic and historic merit, an authentic sketch of his career may not
be out of place:

Charles Carroll, grandson of Charles Carroll of Carrollton, and son of Charles Carroll, of Homewood, and Harriet Chew, a daughter of the late Chief Justice Chew, of Pennsylvania, was born in Baltimore on July 25, 1801. He had one brother older than himself, who died in his infancy, and he remained an only son with four sisters.

The preparatory studies of Mr. Carroll were made at home under a tutor, from which he was sent to St. Mary's College, Baltimore, and afterward to Mount St. Mary's, Emmettsburg, in Maryland. In 1818, in company with his cousin, Charles Harper, a son of the late General Harper, he went to Europe under the charge of a tutor, and was placed at the College of St. Stanislaus, in Paris. He remained there until 1821, when he returned and entered Harvard University, Cambridge, Mass. A few months before the graduation of his class, in 1823, owing to some difficulty with the professors, a large portion of that class was dismissed, and their degrees were not given to them for many years afterward.

Mr. Carroll, returning home, entered the law-office of the late General Harper, and in 1825 he married Mary Diggs Lee, granddaughter of the late Thomas Simon Lee, Governor of Maryland. At the death of Charles Carroll of Carrollton, Mr. Carroll came into possession of the estate called Doughoregan Manor, which he held undivided until his death. A large number of slaves were bequeathed to him by his grandfather's will, and he set himself to work to renovate and improve the lands, which were considerably run down by being leased for long terms of years.

He greatly improved the mansion-house and grounds, and succeeded in a very short time in bringing nearly the whole estate, consisting of two thousand acres, under prosperous cultivation.

For many years he was a Whig in political sentiment, and although always posted and taking a great interest in public matters, he never held any position of political preferment, but devoted his life to the development of his property for the benefit of his family. His slaves were always treated with that kindness and consideration which he felt was their due, and, having always professed the Catholic faith, their religious education was guarded with the same care as was that of his own family.

In 1860 an affection of the heart, from which he had long been disturbed, developed more fully, and in December, 1862, he died, devising his estate of Doughoregan Manor, and all the rest of his property, equally among his seven representatives. He left as heirs three sons and three daughters, and the infant children of a son who died a few months previous to himself. His views upon the subject of slavery are perhaps best set forth in his will, which is thus transcribed:

" I have always regarded slavery as a great evil, producing injury and loss in grain-growing States, but an evil for which we are not responsible who now hold slaves, considering that God in his wisdom placed them here and permitted them to be introduced. My experience and full convictions are that as long as we have that class of labor among us, they are as a mass better cared for and happier than if they were free and providing for themselves. I therefore give all my slaves to all my children, with these positive injunctions, that none of them shall ever be sold except among themselves, and except for those crimes for which they would be punishable by the laws of the State, or for gross insubordination. I also direct that they shall continue to have the advantages of the religious education they now receive, and that their morals and habits be watched over like those of children. It may hereafter be found advisable to remove them to the South to cultivate cotton, where the climate is more congenial to their health, while it removes them from the pernicious influence of the low whites, who now corrupt them. In this way they can be made profitable, and eventually

a fund provided to establish them at some future day in Africa
or in the West Indies. It is my wish that my children shall not
transmit them to any of my grandchildren."

It was a sad yet happy day and a half I spent among these
interesting men. Amid their abounding hospitality there was
still a presentiment upon me, and so when I returned to Washington, and found Sydney Webster, private secretary of President Pierce, waiting for me at the station, I knew something
had happened. He had come to announce that Andrew H.
Reeder had been that day removed as Governor of Kansas. It
was the beginning of the end. Jefferson Davis, of Mississippi,
was too powerful for either Hon. Asa Packer or myself, and our
gallant friend was ejected from his place only because he had refused to consent to the conspiracy to make Kansas a slave State.

We had jointly recommended the appointment of Andrew H.
Reeder to this post, really in response to President Pierce's
suggestion, who was anxious to give it to a Pennsylvanian.
When Reeder accepted he was in high favor with the Democracy of the old Tenth Legion of Pennsylvania. An extreme
sympathizer with the South at all times, his experience in Kansas completely converted him. Honest, independent in his
circumstances, a very able lawyer, and an entrancing speaker,
he was just the character for a new country, just the man to
save the Administration from fatal complications. When the
President nominated him, Hon. Richard Brodhead, then one of
the Pennsylvania Senators, and always the rival of Reeder, or
Reeder of him, did not conceal his disappointment, but Judge
Packer, who lived in the same Congressional district, was too
strong for Brodhead to fight, and Reeder was confirmed. Then
our friend went forth to Kansas, free, fair, and unprejudiced.
He had not been there long before he wrote back to us, denouncing the open frauds of the slaveholders. I well remember
the effect produced upon our minds. But Jefferson Davis's
friends were potent with the Executive ; their falsehoods were

credited ; Reeder's statements discredited, and a brave, honest
man sacrificed. The news of his dismissal, after my agreeable
visit to Charles Carroll of Carrollton, was the gloomy sequel
of a happy day. What rendered it more unpleasant was the
fact that I was at that time one of the editors of the *Washington
Union,* the Democratic Administration organ. Many will blame
President Pierce for consenting to the proscription of Governor
Reeder ; but I can never forget that when I told him I could
not remain in the *Union,* and write in support of the policy
which had displaced Governor Reeder, or even consent to let
others do so, he refused to accept my resignation, and I continued under the proffered generous condition that the paper
should remain silent on the subject. And so it did, until I formally retired, and returned to Pennsylvania to make James
Buchanan President.

Of the parties to this event I have named, incidentally and
otherwise, three only survive ; Charles Carroll of Carrollton,
Andrew H. Reeder, Richard Brodhead, and Franklin Pierce
have been gathered to their fathers.

[October 8, 1871.]

XL.

THERE is always something grotesque in the manners and
habits of the old Southern slaveholders. Every body has noticed
how the negro dialect pervades the conversation of the so-called
superior race. A beautiful Georgia, South Carolina, Virginia,
or Louisiana woman is made more interesting by the infusion
of the plantation *patois* into her liquid language. Long and
constant communication between the master and the slave created and crystallized affinities and eccentricities that will require generations to modify. As some friends and myself were

passing through one of the Southern States, a little more than two years ago, an odd incident illustrative of the characteristics of the old-time school took place in one of the smoking-cars. A venerable gentleman, with white hair and gold-headed cane, got in at one of the stations, took his seat, and drew from his large coat-pocket a long pipe, which he proceeded to fill and light. He was soon followed by another of the same school, a little older, who took his seat next to him and lit a cigar. They were evidently near neighbors, and the dialogue ran about as follows : " How are you all at home, sah?" "Well, sah !" "Is Miz Smith well ?" "Very well, sah !" " Is Miz Jones well ?" " Yes, sah," question and answer being rapidly punctuated with alternate puffs. Then came the more serious topic. " Mr. Smith," said the one to the other, " I notice that Tom has gone back on you, sah. I never had any opinion of Tom, and I am not surprised that he did go back on you, sah !" " Yes, sah," was the reply, " he has gone back on me. Is it not an astonishing thing, sah, that this boy of mine should now be representing me in the Legislature, sah, when I am prevented from voting by this d—d Radical Congress and Government, sah? ˙He was a first-rate servant ; wrote a good hand, sah ; frequently kept my books, sah, and yet he sits in the Legislature, sah, and I can not even vote, sah." On inquiry I learned that Tom was a former slave of our worthy Polonius, but, after emancipation and reconstruction, was elected a member of the Legislature, and was then at Raleigh doing the work that the masters had done for a century. The simple-hearted old man did not seem to know that in every complaint against Tom he was paying the highest tribute to his qualifications.

During the same trip one of the same class came into our special car and regaled us with a long catalogue of his sufferings and losses. Like most Southern men and women, he was full of talk and full of politics. It is the characteristic of these people that they hardly ever hold a conversation which is not

interlarded with their own affairs.   Addicted to it before the
war, they enlarge upon it now.   I had barely been presented to
my new friend before he opened his budget.   We were passing
over some of the historic fields of the rebellion, and it was
amusing to note, in the midst of his lamentations, how he
stopped to say, "Well, sah, here's the spot whar we gave the
Yankees h—, sah."   "Now we are coming to the place where
you uns rather got the advantage of us, sah, and here is whar
we had to fly to when Wilmington fell;" and then he would
resume his wail.   I listened a good hour without interruption.
The oblivious simplicity of the man rather pleased me, and
when there was a pause in the torrent, I said, "Pray, Mr. ——, in
all your accusations of the National Government, have you ever
once reflected upon the part you played against it?   Do you
ever think that all these sufferings have been brought upon you
by yourselves?"   I think if I had struck him in the face he
would not have been more surprised.   This honest, kind-hearted
man was so completely absorbed in his grievances that he had
never taken account of his own offenses.   And so it is with
the entire class.   Naturally generous, confiding, and brave, they
are so much absorbed in themselves, and have lived so long in
their exclusive world, that they have finally come to believe in
nothing but their own wrongs, and never indulge the habit of
self-examination.   Herein we have the source of their steady
resistance to mental and material progress.   They do not feel
the world move.   They do not see the vast improvements all
around them.   They will retain thousands of acres without going out of their way for purchasers, and even when they find
them, they are very apt to forfeit a bargain on account of politics.   To them every advance in science and in government is
a Radical innovation.   They can't be called malignant, although
their exclusiveness operates precisely as if they were.   They are
generous as long as their vanity is flattered.   Very brave in
personal combat, they fought gallantly on the rebel side, but,

lacking true courage and self-respect, they do not admit that they committed the slightest wrong against their Government, even while they expect that Government to extend its blessings over them. It remains to be seen whether the children of these men and women will follow their example. Happily for themselves, and happily for the country, the Government of the United States and the welfare of all its citizens do not depend upon the fiat of the old slaveholders.

But I was talking of the peculiar dialect of these people rather than their opinions. Henry Clay's speaking was strongly marked by it. James M. Mason, of Virginia, seemed to delight in the African accent. But there was no better specimen than the late Thomas H. Bayley, for many years the Representative in Congress of the Accomac district. He was a man of considerable force and education, and I can easily recall his tall form, his expressive face and ringing voice, as, spectacles on nose, he would address "Mr. Speakah," and refer to the honorable member who had just had the "flo'." Keitt, of South Carolina, had the same accent and pronunciation. So, too, Linn Boyd, of Kentucky, and Howell Cobb, of Georgia. All these men, and most of the former leaders of opinion in the South, are in their graves, but Toombs, Stephens, Henry A. Wise, Bocock, John Forsyth, and Jeff Davis, still live, as warnings, if not as examples.

[October 15, 1871.]

XLI.

JOHN SERGEANT is one of the many Philadelphians whose memory will always be honored. His reputation, ripened by culture, integrity, and winning manners, became national before he was forty, and when he died, in his seventy-third year, he had filled out a life of rare usefulness and success. He was born in 1779, less than a year before Horace Binney, who is still living, and who was his contemporary for fifty years at the bar and in public life. The tribute of the latter, a few days after the death of his friend, at a meeting of the members of the legal profession of Philadelphia, in November, 1852, is a classic of obituaries. At a period when so many are rushing into the law as a profession, Horace Binney on John Sergeant may not be unprofitably read. I quote:

"Mr. Sergeant was born in Philadelphia, and lived there for seventy-three years, during fifty-three years of which he was an advocate and counselor—one of the ministers of justice. He has been known and honored for half a century. In learning, integrity, and in liberal fairness, in habitual courtesy, he has maintained the reputation of the bar of Philadelphia and supported the inherent dignity of the profession. He continued every year during his whole life increasing his titles to respect and honor every day, until he achieved the highest degrees of both—as wise men estimate degrees of honor and respect—by merit, not by accident or fortune, or the breath of popular applause. He has rounded the whole circle of his life fully, completely, perfectly."

As marking the difference between the lawyers of the past and the present, I heard an anecdote of Mr. Sergeant the other day, which shows how the giants estimated their professional services and by what sensitive and scrupulous rules they squared their actions. A distinguished merchant, still living, called upon Mr. Sergeant for his opinion in an important case, which was duly prepared and sent by one of the students of the great lawyer. The merchant opened the letter, and after glancing over it asked the student for the charge. He said he did not know the contents of the paper and could not answer. The merchant then signed a blank check, and sent it back to Mr. Sergeant by the same hand, with a message that he should

fill it up with the amount of his fee. This very student, now
one of the leading members of the Philadelphia bar, graphically
describes the effect of the communication. He says he never
saw a little man (Mr. Sergeant was of slight stature) so suddenly tower into a giant. "Mr. —— entirely misunderstands me,
sir! Go back to him, sir, and say for me that I am the last
person living to fill up another man's check. If he will carefully examine the paper I sent, he will find my fee written in
one of the corners." With this somewhat considerable flea
in his ear the young man retraced his steps to the merchant,
when the opinion was carefully inspected, and written in very
small letters, in the angle of one of the pages, were the figures
"$30."

I fear the fee of our reigning legal magnates for similar services would be at least ten times thirty dollars.

In illustration of Sergeant's mode of life, I quote again from
the venerable Binney's eulogy : " His honor and integrity in all
that regarded his profession or management of his cause were
not only above impeachment or imputation, but beyond the
thought of it. So distinct and universal was this impression,
that if any man had directed a battery of that sort against him,
the recoil would have prostrated him to the earth. His heart,
his mind, his principles, his conscience, his bond to man, his
bond to Heaven, which he had given early, and which to the
last he never intentionally violated, would have made it, hu-
manly speaking, impossible for him to swerve from his integrity.
It is the best example for the rising generations to have before
them. He was perfectly fair. There was no evasion, no strat-
agem, no surprising, no invocation of prejudice, no appeal to unworthy passions—he was far above all these. Mr. Sergeant
had too much strength indeed to make use of such arts, to say
nothing of his virtue. He was charitable in doing work at the
bar without pecuniary compensation—though not without reward. He did that which, in his judgment, was best, but he

did not do it ostentatiously. He did not do it by proclamation, informing the court in the presence of the bystanders that he did not receive a fee, but that it would make no difference to him. He never let his left hand know what his right hand did —still less did he ever impose upon the left hand of others by informing it of what his right hand had *not* done."

We must not forget, in perusing such a character in the light of such an eulogy, that Horace Binney was himself, during his active career, a fair illustration of his own sentiments. Mr. Binney sat in Congress while Andrew Jackson was President, and was, perhaps, the ablest advocate of the Bank of the United States, and therefore one of the stanchest opponents of General Jackson's Administration ; but he understood how to antagonize measures without assailing men—how to arraign a public policy without traducing private character—a rare quality, which might be profitably copied by our modern teachers. One day he was surprised by a note from the President soliciting an interview, and the more so because he had just finished an exhaustive protest against the President's course in regard to the United States Bank.   General Jackson met him with all his grace, dignity, and cordiality, and said : "I have taken the liberty of sending for you, Mr. Binney, to say that I have read your speech, which is the most powerful yet made on your side of the House.   I can not, of course, thank you for the strength of your argument, but I am happy to know you as an adversary who does not conceive it necessary to employ invective against a public officer who believes he has discharged his duty faithfully."   I have this interesting fact from good authority.

John Sergeant and Horace Binney moved together in politics and in their profession.   Let me employ Mr. Binney's language in 1852 once more : "I honored and respected him to the end of his life.   I shall honor and respect his memory to the end of my own.   No trivial incongruities of feeling or opinion, no misrepresentations, however arisen ; no petty gust ; no cloud of a hand's breadth, which may and will chill or overcast the summer sky of the truest friends; in a life of fifty-five years not a single accident disturbed the foundations of my regard for him, or even reached the depths in which they were laid. These foundations were laid upon his principles as I well knew them fifty years ago. They were laid deep upon that sure basis, and they were beyond the reach of change or chance, as his principles were."

Binney was a member of the State Legislature sixty-one years ago, in 1806–7 [do not forget he is still living at his old home in the city of Philadelphia], and declined a re-election. He was a Representative in Congress from Philadelphia from 1833 to 1835, served as a member of the Committee of Ways and Means, and again declined a re-election. Sergeant was in Congress from 1815 to 1823, from 1827 to 1829, and from 1837 to 1842. He was especially famous for his part in the great Missouri Compromise of 1820. He was selected by President John Quincy Adams to represent the United States on the Panama Commission. He was the Whig candidate for Vice-President in 1832, on the same ticket with Henry Clay. He was tendered the mission to England by General Harrison, which he declined.

For half a century these two interesting men were associates at the bar, harmonizing in politics, and generally supporting the same measures and the same candidates. Their joint experience, their blended patriotism, their high sense of honor, their fidelity to convictions and to the interests of their city, state, and country, can not be too frequently reproduced. We tread the path of duty more bravely in the lustre shed from examples so unselfish and pure.

[October 22, 1871.]

XLII.

A GOOD story is told of the celebrated George Kremer, who figured conspicuously during the "bargain and sale" excitement forty-five years ago, about the time Henry Clay was appointed Secretary of State by President John Quincy Adams. Mr. Kremer represented the old Union and Northumberland Congressional district in Pennsylvania, and was a fine type of the primitive manners and rugged Democracy of that period. He was firmly convinced that Mr. Clay threw his influence against General Jackson, by which the electoral vote of Kentucky was given to Mr. Adams, for a consideration; and when the first place in the Cabinet was tendered to and accepted by the Kentucky statesman, honest George "cried aloud and spared not." The sensation he created disturbed the politics of the whole country, and led to many differences between public men. John Randolph of Roanoke dilated upon the accusation against Clay to such an extent that the new Secretary of State was compelled to challenge him to mortal combat. But I do not propose a chapter on the "bargain and sale." That episode is happily ignored by the retiring generation, and is no longer recalled as a reproach on the memory of Henry Clay. I write simply to revive an incident between Randolph and Kremer characteristic of both. After one of the peculiar speeches of the eccentric Virginian, which he interlarded with copious quotations in Latin and Greek, Kremer rose, and, in a strain of well-acted indignation, poured forth a torrent of Pennsylvania German upon the head of the amazed and startled Randolph. His violent gesticulations, his loud and boisterous tones, his defiant manner, were not more annoying to the imperious Southerner than the fact that he could not understand a word that was spoken. And when honest George took his seat, covered with perspiration, Randolph rose and begged the honorable gentleman from Pennsylvania to enlighten the House and the country by translating what he had just uttered. Kremer retorted as follows: "I have only to say in reply to my friend from Virginia that when he translates the dead languages, which he is constantly using for the benefit of us country members, into something like English, I will be equally liberal in translating my living Pennsylvania Dutch into something that the House can understand." The laugh was completely against Randolph.

Apart from the beauty of well-written and well-spoken German, and the benefits conferred upon the human race by German philosophers and scholars, there is something irrepressibly odd in the *patois* of Pennsylvania Dutch, so called. Under the influence of my learned friend, Charles Godfrey Leland, this mingled dialect has recently acquired a world-wide celebrity. His "Hans Breitmann," even including the "dog Latin" he weaves into it, is becoming one of the comic classics of English-speaking nations. Whether read at the fireside or acted in the theatres, it excites irrepressible mirth. Jefferson's *Rip Van Winkle* is a signal illustration of this remark. His inimitable acting, although the story itself amounts to nothing, reaches all hearts, inspiring alternate tears and smiles. Clinton Lloyd, Esq., the accomplished chief clerk of the National House of Representatives, has memorized "Hans Breitmann" entire. He is a native Pennsylvanian, reared in a community where this curious admixture of English and German was once largely spoken. He is, besides, a cultivated gentleman, and perhaps the best-known interpreter of Leland's famous creation. I know of few things more pleasant than to sit by and hear Lloyd going through the experiences of *Hans*, the soldier and the traveler. I have seen him entertain hundreds of persons of all nationalities at one time with this grotesque production. Sympathizing fully with the poet, he gives additional flavor to his peculiar wit, because he knows the character he describes, whom you almost see passing before you in his diversified guises. Mr. Leland is now a resident of London, the friend and associate of most of the literary leaders. It must be extremely gratifying to him that the amusing poems which he threw off in his leisure moments should be read and admired in all intellectual circles, and that every stanza he adds increases their deserved popularity. I can only hope that he is fortunate in something more than mere fame, and that his writings are contributing to his substantial comfort in the Old World.

Almost as interesting is it to hear Mr. Lloyd reciting James Russell Lowell's "Hosea Biglow;" but the Yankee idiom is not so cosmopolitan as the *patois* of English and German. The same remark applies to negro melodies and plays. The New-Englander and the black man are Americans, while Hans Breitmann is the citizen of the world; his poetry is a medley of the tongues of the oldest and most civilized nations, and, as he plays many parts and borrows a little from each, he will be remembered when the accent of Brother Jonathan and Uncle Tom is lost in the universality of the language that must ultimately control the whole American continent.

[October 29, 1871.]

XLIII.

SLAVERY and its mysterious inner life has never yet been described. When it is, Reality will surpass Fiction. Uncle Tom's Cabin will be rebuilt and newly garnitured. A book detailing the operations of the Under-ground Railroad is soon to be published in Philadelphia by William Still, Esq., an intelligent colored gentleman, which, composed entirely of facts, will supply material for indefinite dramas and romances. It will disclose a

record of unparalleled courage and suffering for the right. The
narrative of Professor John M. Langston, of Howard University, at Washington, famous as orator and scholar; his birth as
a slave, the education of himself and brother by his white father; his return, after many years, to his native town in Virginia,
as the champion of his race and of their newly acquired freedom; the thrilling story of Frederick Douglass, told by himself;
the eventful career of Stephen Smith, the rich colored man of
Philadelphia, who voted for Jackson in 1832, was afterward dis-
franchised by the insertion of the word "white" in the constitution of Pennsylvania in 1838, and again voted under the immortal act of emancipation; the experience of Ebenezer D. Bas-
sett, our resident Minister at Hayti; the struggle for self-im-
provement of Octavius V. Catto, and the tragedy of his assassination; the early efforts of John Brown, long before he was
known to the world as the willing martyr of his ideas; the
sketch of the inner life of William J. Wilson, vice-president of
the Freedmen's Savings Institution at Washington, including
his story of the industry, patience, and economy of his race;
the long conflict with slavery of Senator Revels, of Mississippi;
the stormy life of Lieutenant-Governor Dunn, of Louisiana; and
last, not least, the memoir of Robert Purvis, the accomplished
gentleman and scholar, residing at Byberry, in Philadelphia—
a memoir which, written by himself, would surpass in the intensity of its interest many of the famous autobiographies of the
day—these and their companion pictures might be called the
genuine "Romance of Reality." The time is coming when
they can be published without fear and read without prejudice.
In the light of a civilization which liberated millions, as well
the slaves of others as the slaves of mere bigotry, men will ponder these volumes with an indignation and surprise not less sincere because felt for the first time. In the sanctity which surrounded the institution of slavery—a sanctity resulting from the
arguments of the clergy, the politicians, and the capitalists, the

habits and luxuries of the society created by the submission of its fettered millions, and its influence upon commerce in Europe and America—the still small voice of conscience was hushed. And if the men who had grown rich and great had not finally been maddened by the idea that they were irresistible and inviolable, slavery would have finally accomplished the overthrow of the Government. That idea carried into war saved the nation and destroyed its enemies.

Among the thousand novel incidents of emancipation, one of curious interest, familiar to myself and many others, may be related:

John Queen was a light mulatto, five feet ten inches high, about thirty-five years of age. He had lived a slave in Anne Arundel County, in the State of Maryland, and several years before emancipation obtained his free papers. He was harmless, quiet, and inoffensive; but when he was jokingly told that the traders were coming to take him back to slavery his eyes would flash, and his whole demeanor would change. He would exclaim, "Dey neber take me back to slabery. I die in de blood first—I die in de blood! *cut out dere heart, eat der liber.* Is'e free-born, I tell you, Is'e free-born;" and when asked to show his papers, he would repeat something like these words: "Do you know de H——d's?" "Yes, I know them." "Do you know Squire C——?" referring to certain old Maryland families. "Do you mind de mornin' old Squire H—— said, 'Go, John, go down to de stable, hitch up old Baldy and de silber gray, put em in de coach, go to 'Napolis to make out de free papers?' Den old Squire H—— came down, all dressed up, dressed in black silk breeches, silber buckle on de knee, silber buckle in de shoes, hair powdered, hanging down de back; John Queen jump on de step behind de coach, and den we all go to 'Napolis. When we got dere we all go to de *court,* and dere, in de face of de whole court, Squire H—— he kiss de Book and do declare dat John Queen is a free-born." Upon being asked to show his papers, which he never would consent to do, the poor half-witted fellow, who had long years before committed them and locked them in his memory, while he himself did keep the key, in a monotonous recitative repeated something like the following, never varying in the slightest degree, and always reiterating "dat I'se free-born:" "In de State of Maryland, de Ann Arundel County, and de Anno Domini, in de year of our Lord, de one tousand and de eight hundred and de forty-seven. In de face of de whole court, I do now declare dat John Queen, who is five feet ten inches in de height, wid de long, straight, black hair, yaller in complexion, wid a mole on de right upper lip, which is de free-born, in de testimony whereof I do hereby, in de State of Maryland, in de County of Ann Arundel, in de year of our Lord, de Anno Domini one tousand eight hundred and forty-seven, set my hand and de great seal of de court, and do hereby now declare dat de aforesaid John Queen is free-born."

John never paused until he finished this indubitable proof of his freedom, and always seemed to glean satisfaction from having the original in his possession, which he said he never would part from save with his heart's blood. Only a few evenings ago I heard this incident described in the presence of some of the connections of the Maryland families referred to, and they instantly recognized the picture and the persons preserved in the memory of this simple freedman. If I suppress the names, it is only because it is unnecessary to revive individual relations to a system which does no credit to those who subsisted upon it, however unconsciously or innocently.

[November 5, 1871.]

XLIV.

SHORTLY after I took possession of the *Lancaster Intelligencer*, more than thirty-four years ago—before I had reached manhood—Mrs. Dickson, the amiable and gentle postmistress of that place, handed me a soiled letter directed to "the editor of a newspaper," which she said had been in her possession for more than a year, and had not been delivered because it had no definite address. Upon opening it I found it dated Logansport, Indiana, and signed by George W. Ewing, United States Indian Agent. He stated that he had only recently stopped at an Indian wigwam for the night on the banks of the Mississinewa, about fifty miles south of Fort Wayne, and found it occupied by a family who were rich for Indians, and boasted of considerable property in houses and lands. He went on to say that in the course of the evening he noticed that the hair of one of the women was light, and her skin under her dress white, and so he entered into conversation with her, which was not difficult, as he spoke the language of the tribe. She told him she was white, but had been carried away when a very small girl. She could only remember that her name was Slocum ; that she had lived in a little house on the banks of the Susquehanna ; also the number of her father's family, and the order of their ages ; but she could not recall the name of the town from which she was taken. Fascinated by this romantic story, yet undecided how to let the facts be known, he wrote a letter and sent it to my native town of Lancaster, as the place nearest the Susquehanna that he could remember of any importance. After, as I have said, sleeping in the post-office for many months, it came out through the columns of my little journal, and in that way got to the Slocums of Wilkesbarre, being the first intelligence of the child which had been stolen from them sixty years before. The brother of Frances, who was only two years and

a half old when his sister was carried off by the Indians, started
for the Indian country in company with his eldest sister, who
had aided him to escape, and another brother, then living in
Ohio, born after the captivity of Frances. After a long journey
they found a little wigwam among the Miami Indians. "We
shall know Frances," said the sister, "because she lost the nail
of her first finger. You, brother, hammered it off in the blacksmith shop when she was four years old." They entered and
found a swarthy woman who looked to be seventy-five. She was
painted, jeweled, and dressed like an Indian in all respects.
Nothing but her hair and her covered skin indicated her origin.
They got an interpreter, asked her name and where she was
born. "How came that nail gone?" said the eldest sister. She
answered, "My elder brother pounded it off when I was a little
child in the shop." They had discovered the long-lost sister.
They asked her Christian name. She had forgotten it. "Was
it Frances?" As if smitten by a revelation, she answered
"Yes." It was the first time she had heard it pronounced in
sixty years. Here they were met, two brothers and two sisters,
after having been separated for more than half a century. The
brothers were walking the cabin, unable to speak, the sister was
drowned in tears, but the poor Indian sat motionless and pas-
sionless. She could not speak a word of English. She did not
know when Sunday came. Was not this the consummation of
ignorance in a descendant of the Puritans? She was carried
off by the Indians, and when she grew up she married one of
their number. He either died or ran away, and then she married a Miami chief, since dead. She had two daughters, both
married, who, thirty-four years ago, lived in all the glory of
Indian cabins, deer-skin clothes, and cow-skin head-dresses.
They had horses in abundance, and when the Indian sister accompanied her new relatives, she bridled her horse and mounted it astride. At night she slept on the floor, with her blanket
around her. They could not persuade her to return to Wilkes-

barre, even when the invitation was extended to her children. She had always lived with the Indians, they had been kind to her, and she promised her last husband on his death-bed she would never leave them. It is now nearly ninety-five years since this white child was torn from her parents' home in Wyoming Valley. She herself has been gathered to her fathers, and most of her double family who were living in 1838, with the exception, I believe, of Mr. Joseph Slocum, now one of the most influential and respectable citizens of Scranton. Among all the changes that have taken place in this long interval, few are more interesting than this transformation from civilization to barbarism.

A coincidence even more romantic is soon to be revealed in the pages of the remarkable book of William Still, of Philadelphia, entitled the "Under-ground Railroad," referred to in my last number. Mr. Still kept a careful memorandum of the sufferings and trials of his race during the existence of the fugitive-slave law, in the belief that they would be instructive to his posterity rather than from any hope of the overthrow of the revolting system of human servitude. But when that passed away, and speech became as free as thought, and the printing-press, the school-house, the ballot, and every civil right, were secured to the colored race, he resolved to spread before the world this unprecedented experience. When his book appears it will accomplish more than one object. Interesting to the literary world, it will undoubtedly facilitate the reunion of other colored families, long divided, long sought for, and perhaps to this day strangers to each other. The curious similarity between the case of the wealthy Slocums in Wyoming Valley and the experience of Mr. Still will be intensified when this book is published. Here we find the story of Peter Still, torn from his mother when a little boy of six, and for more than forty years a slave in Alabama, totally destitute of all knowledge of his parents. We are told how by extreme economy and overwork he saved about five hundred dollars with which to buy his ransom —how he started in search of his mother and kindred—how he reached Philadelphia, where, by having notices read in the colored churches that more than forty years before "two little boys were kidnapped and carried South," he obtained information in regard to them—how, after traveling sixteen hundred miles, the first man Peter Still sought advice from was his brother, the author of this very book on the Under-ground Railroad, whom he had never seen or heard of—how, after this mutual recognition, the self-ransomed captive was destined again to suffer the keenest pangs of sorrow for his own wife and children, whom he had left in Alabama in bondage—how, finally, a brave white man, Seth Conklin, proceeded to Alabama, carried off this wife and children, and was retaken with them, in Indiana, and perished while he was being carried in irons back to the South, by leaping from the boat in which they were confined. The volume, containing this and other equally romantic yet truthful stories, will soon be out, and, my word for it, no book of the times will be more eagerly read or more profitably remembered.

[November 12, 1871.]

XLV.

David Paul Brown, of Philadelphia, has been for half a century the favorite orator of the American bar. His renown was national before he was thirty; and as he not only never sought but resolutely declined office, and rarely practiced in the courts of other States, his fame is mainly the outgrowth of professional efforts in his native city. He is still living in Philadelphia, in his seventy-seventh year, the most active veteran of his time. Who can not recall him in the flush of his manhood?

Of middle height, compactly made, with a full, round chest; his forehead high and broad, eyes black, mouth large, and filled with the finest teeth, he is frequently seen on the streets, almost as erect and graceful as when he thrilled our court-rooms and was followed by crowds of admirers. Mr. Brown was always rather an exquisite in his dress, and to this day his blue coat and brass buttons, buff vest and light pantaloons, gloved hands, neat boots, and rather rakish hat, prove the youthfulness of his tastes and the gayety of his disposition. He is, perhaps, too fond of dress; but he defends his peculiarity by saying "that he had never known a man to speak well in clumsy boots, nor to have a clear mind with dirty hands and face; that he had known many a fop that was not a fool, and many a sloven that was not a Solomon." "A becoming decency of exterior," he says, "may not be necessary for ourselves, but is agreeable to others; and while it may render a fool more contemptible, it serves to embellish inherent worth. It is like the polish of the diamond, taking something, perhaps, from its weight, but adding much to its brilliancy and attraction."

Another peculiarity of David Paul Brown is his disregard of money. He has often been heard to say that he never was so rich and happy as in his early youth; for then, in the language of Socrates, he wanted least, and therefore approached nearer to the gods, who wanted nothing. He is not extravagant in the mere pleasures of the world. His attire is rich, but his habits simple and abstemious. To these he attributes his entire freedom from pain and diseases of every sort. Money has no value in his eyes. Its receipt gives him no pleasure—its expenditure no annoyance. From his early manhood to the present, though his professional income has exceeded a quarter of a million, the same indifference, the same recklessness, in regard to wealth, has marked his career. A characteristic anecdote is told in this connection. He studied law with the late William Rawle, a lawyer of universal celebrity, whose writings and example are fondly treasured by the profession. The preceptor and student met one day, after the latter had attained a high position at the bar. "My dear Mr. Rawle," said Mr. Brown, "fifteen years ago I gave you my check for $400, in return for your valuable legal instruction; since that time I find I have received for professional services upward of $100,000." "I know," replied the preceptor (himself a most liberal-minded man), "you have been very busy, and it is necessary to be very busy for a young man to make such a sum in so short a time." "Oh! but," rejoined Mr. Brown, "you don't know how busy I have been. I have spent all; there is not a dollar left. Yes, I have spent it on *principle*. There are two kinds of extravagance: that which arises from a love of display, and that which springs from contempt of wealth. *Mine* is the last. If I could become rich, I should become indolent, and lose in fame what I gained in money. This is not the case, perhaps, with all, but it is with me." The old gentleman laughed heartily at the amusing candor of his former *élève*. To show the high estimation in which the pupil was held by his revered preceptor, I transcribe the following letter, written by him to Mr. Brown some ten years after his admission. The applause of such a man is worth more than that of a whole theatre of critics :

"MY DEAR SIR,—You borrowed of me some time ago the first volume of Guthrie's Quintilian. Will you allow me to send you the second, with the request that you will receive them both into your library?

"The plain binding will not affect the internal merit of an author who, the first that is known to us, systematically and fully laid down the precepts not only of forensic but of general oratory, and who, were he now living, would be delighted to perceive a full illustration of what he requires to form an accomplished orator in yourself.

"With unfeigned respect and esteem, I am, dear sir,
"Your affectionate friend,   W. RAWLE.

"March 31, 1828.
"To DAVID PAUL BROWN, Esq."

And it is as an orator that he deserves to be remembered.

As a criminal lawyer he has few equals. His examination of witnesses and his appeals to the jury illustrate his peculiar talents. A voice of rare compass and sweetness; a command of the best phrases; a master of action, his pathos melts and subdues, his invective startles and dismays. Once, on a celebrated trial, he objected to a certain witness being heard because the witness was a convict. Great consternation ensued. The witness was indignant, spoke of his good character, and defied his accuser. But he had met his master. Mr. Brown fixed his searching eye upon him, and then spoke : "I have objected to your evidence, sir. This objection is founded upon a knowledge of your character. Answer me, sir. Were you not convicted and punished in the State of Delaware for a heinous crime?" "No, sir !" This was uttered with an evidently assumed boldness. "Now," said the lawyer, "if I were to strip up the sleeves of your coat, and point to the letter *R* branded on your right arm, near the shoulder, and say this was done at New Castle, Delaware, what answer would you make?" The poor wretch was crushed; his artificial courage melted away before the fire of an intellectual eye. It is scarcely necessary to add that Mr. Brown won his cause. Industrious and persevering, he never was the slave of the black-letter. He always delighted in literature, and was a consummate Shakespearian interpreter. Chief Justice Gibson, of Pennsylvania, a very eminent authority, said, "He does not quote Shakespeare—he speaks Shakespeare." It was natural that he should affect the drama. His rhetoric, his manner, his voice, were modeled after the best standards, and he firmly believed that the very best case was improved by being set forth gracefully and eloquently. Hence he alternated, or rather relieved the heavy toil of his profession by reading and writing poetry, by lectures on "Hamlet," by orations on patriotic subjects, and by a mass of miscellaneous composition. "How is it possible you can do so much business?" was the question of a friend. "Because," was the practical reply, "I have got so much to do." "But," was the rejoinder, "how can you indulge in poetry and general literature?" "Because," he replied—"because it enables me to return to my more rugged pursuits with greater alacrity and renewed strength. The mind takes its direction from habit; if you wish to strengthen it you must direct it for a time into other channels, and thereby refresh and improve it. A mere lawyer is a mere jackass, and has never the power to unload himself; whereas I consider the advocate—the thoroughly accomplished advocate—the highest style of a man. He is always ready to learn, and always ready to teach. Hortensius was a lawyer, Cicero an orator. The one is forgotten, the other is immortal." He wrote "Sertorius, or the Roman Patriot," a tragedy, in 1830; "The Prophet of St. Paul," a melodrama; and a farce called "Love and Honor, or the Generous Soldier." The elder Booth took the leading character in the first, which was represented nine times. Mr. Brown was not vain of these productions. He said, quaintly enough, "I must say they derived greater celebrity from their author than their author will derive from them."

He has written much on other subjects. "The Forum, or Forty Years' full Practice at the Philadelphia Bar," a work published by subscription, in 1856, in two large volumes, is a mine of learning to student and statesman. After a review of the practice of the law before the Revolution, and its history from the Declaration of Independence to the year 1856, we have a series of biographical sketches of distinguished American lawyers, with an entertaining description of their personal appearance, manners, dress, etc. Justices Washington, Tilghman, Breckinridge, and others, now deceased, are passed in review, and then he takes up the living. The celebrated trials which have occurred in our civil and criminal courts (in many of which he took part) are described, with anecdotes of the giants of the bench and bar, and a chapter on legal wit. "The Golden

Rules for the Examination of Witnesses," "Capital Hints in Capital Cases," and "Instructions from a Father to his Son," are still in demand, and have passed through several editions.

He can not yet be said to have left the arena in which, for fifty-six years, he has been so conspicuous an actor. He lives in honored and vigorous old age, keenly alive to all the great events of an eventful era. Even as I write I have some of his MSS. before me. His thoughts are clearly stated, and his contributions practical and pleasing. He is still averse to party politics, though, as ever, an ardent Republican patriot. His passion for literature is unabated, and if he touches public questions, it is only in a tolerant and judicial spirit. Few men have enjoyed life more thoroughly; few have seen more of our mighty minds; and none survive with a warmer love of country or a larger share of the love of their countrymen. He has passed the Psalmist's age, and bids fair to live to see the hundredth anniversary of that Declaration of Independence of which he has been one of the most gifted of interpreters and champions.

[November 19, 1871.]

XLVI.

JULY 4, 1876, will be a proud and happy day to those who shall live to see it, especially in Philadelphia, where it is to be celebrated under peculiar historical and national auspices, as the hundredth anniversary of our independence. A little more than four years and a half remain to digest plans and to execute them. These will be various and numerous, and many will be visionary and impracticable. The primal conditions to success should be discrimination against pretenders—a cultivated knowledge of and taste for art, and a resolute resistance to every thing selfish or corrupt. Happily the men at the head of Fairmount Park, which, with its twenty-eight hundred acres, is to-day the largest of its kind in the world, and in a few years will be the completest and loveliest, are generally citizens of national and local reputation. As they will have much to do with the preliminaries and control of the Centenary, I give their names for the benefit of those who may want some assurance that their efforts and interest in this important movement shall not be wasted: Morton McMichael (president), journalist; General George G. Meade (vice-president), topographical engineer; Samuel W. Cattell, manufacturer; Theodore Cuyler, attorney-at-law; Daniel M. Fox, real-estate agent; Frederick Graeff, civil engineer; Joseph Harrison, Jr., manufacturer; Henry Huhn, coal shipper; Strickland Kneass, surveyor; Henry M. Phillips, attorney-at-law; Eli K. Price, attorney-at-law; Jonathan H. Pugh, locksmith; Gustavus Remak, attorney-at-law; William Sellers, machinist; John Welsh, merchant; James McManes, gentleman. There is hardly one name in this list that is not a guarantee of integrity and responsibility. Several are connoisseurs of art, the owners of fine pictures and statuary, and nearly all men of wealth. They represent different vocations and both parties. Having no other motive but that which concerns the public, and no temptation but to honor themselves and the country, they will be to Philadelphia what the New York Central Park Commission was before Sweeny and Tweed polluted it with their creatures, and removed Colonel Stebbins, its president, and Mr. Green, its incorruptible treasurer. The confidence crystallized around the New York Park Commission, under the administration of these excellent men, was such that at one time it was proposed to place the best portion of the city government in their hands. Two short years avenged the wrong inflicted in their rude removal. The people rose against Tammany, and the historical Committee of Seventy, their agent in the rescue and redemption of their great State and city, had Colonel H.

G. Stebbins for its president, and Mr. Green as his most efficient auxiliary; and now both are to go back to the Central Park Commission, as if to complete their own vindication and the retribution of the spoilers. Let us take care to maintain the Philadelphia Park Commission, soon to enter upon a wider field of action, and to act in conjunction with the preparations for the grandest national event of the country, so that, with commensurate dignity and energy, it may fulfill the mission assigned to it.

One suggestion is made in connection with the Centenary of Independence which deserves the consideration of the Fairmount Park Commission. There is not a county in Pennsylvania that can not point to names of national and even worldwide renown. I need not recount a catalogue brilliant with the services of Benjamin Franklin, Robert Morris, Anthony Wayne, Robert Fulton, Lindley Murray, David Rittenhouse, Peter Muhlenberg, and their contemporaries and successors in war and peace, in science and in statesmanship, in art, in law, in medicine, in religion, in manufactures, and in skilled labor. The suggestion is that every county should select one of these departed worthies, and have a colossal statue to represent him, in bronze, marble, or iron, ready for Fairmount Park in season for the Centenary, there to remain during all time. The tribute would be graceful, and the cost comparatively small. There is not a county in Pennsylvania that could not easily afford to perpetuate the features of one of its illustrious sons. The condition precedent, however, should be that the work itself should be done by an accomplished artist. Save us, O Park Commission! from the effigies and caricatures that have so often disfigured and disgraced our lovely cities, and that still dishonor our nation's capital. "Art is long," says the poet. Art is not the growth of the hour, but of the ages. As it is created to endure, it can not graduate at once. If years of toil, study, and patience are essential to ripen a statesman, a scholar, a philosopher, a poet, or a complete mechanic, so are they essential to the creation of an artist, who should be a combination of varied learning. We have some fine specimens of American genius. Our Powers, Story, Rogers, Rothermel, Miss Hosmer, Reade, Ball, Baillie, Miss Stebbins, Church, Bierstadt, etc., are acknowledged leaders. But we should not be ashamed to lay under contribution the best minds of Europe when we come to the preservation of the memorials of those who have done so much for the liberty and the elevation of the whole human race. No crude brain or 'prentice hand should be employed, simply because it is of domestic growth, and no acknowledged master should be excluded because he was born under French, Italian, German, or English skies. As we shall invite the liberal thinkers of all nations to join us on the Fourth of July, 1876—as we shall look for John Bright, Louis Kossuth, Edouard Laboulaye, Guiseppe Garibaldi, Victor Hugo, Emilio Castelar, Guiseppe Mazzini, Alfred Tennyson, Charles Reade, and the republican teachers of Germany, we must extend a welcome, at least as warm, to the ripe and aspiring minds who are beautifying the galleries, churches, and streets of Paris, London, Berlin, Dresden, Munich, Brussels, Cologne, Frankfort, Dusseldorf, Florence, Naples, Venice, Turin, and Imperial Rome. Art knows no party and no country. America is eventually and inexorably the chief of civilization. Opening her arms to all the children of men, she will gather to her side with a precious love those fortunate ones whom God has most generously crowned with his richest gifts. An able writer, in a late number of a London magazine, *Temple Bar*, thus sets forth the verdict of enlightened Europe, in a contrast between this country and France. We can not be unmindful of the duty here taught us in our relations to the rest of mankind:

" America, not France, has been the propagandist of democracy, and has instituted the only successful republic of ancient or modern times—a republic of which the foundations have

been cemented by no unrighteously spilled blood, nor under-
mined by fantastic social theories ; a republic founded on reason, on the unalterable principles of humanity, neither twisted
nor forced from their natural channels to harmonize with individual ideas ; on the purely normal development of certain
conditions of society and their only practical solution.   American republicanism means the advancement of the human race ;
French republicanism its destruction.   Commerce and the arts
of peace are the weapons of the one ; fire and sword are the
weapons of the other."

[November 26, 1871.]

XLVII.

MORE than twenty years ago I made the acquaintance of
David Hoffman, of Baltimore, the eminent lawyer and legal
writer, who died of apoplexy shortly after in the city of New
York, seventy years old.   I was introduced to him at the dinner-table of Charles Jared Ingersoll, then living in Walnut
Street, near Fifth, in the city of Philadelphia, an equally interesting character, of more experience, if not profounder learning,
who was born in 1782, and died on the 14th of May, 1862, at
the great age of eighty.   Marked deeply in my memory of that
afternoon were two anecdotes of General Washington, whom
these interesting veterans had known in their youth.   Mr. Hoffman, while playfully reminding his contemporary and friend of
his ancient Federalism [Mr. Ingersoll was one of the ablest of
the Democratic leaders at the time], took special pains to illustrate his own consistent attachment to what he was pleased to
call the doctrines and teachings of Washington, by relating how,
as a lad of twelve, he had met the Father of his Country at
Beltzhoover's Hotel, in Light Street, Baltimore.   An immense

crowd had assembled to greet the patriot. Hoffman, with two other boys, lingered after the concourse had dispersed, for an opportunity to see and converse with the honored guest. Washington had retired to his chamber, but answered the knock of the boys by opening his door and inviting them in. In those days the French republicans had a large class of imitators and followers in the United States, and Hoffman's two companions wore what was known as the Jefferson or French cockade in their caps. After Washington had asked their names, he turned to Hoffman and said, "I see that you have no cockade; will you allow me to make one for you?" And calling a servant, he directed him to purchase a piece of *black* ribbon, and "with this," said Mr. Hoffman, "he cut out for me a black cockade, which he pinned to my cap with his own hands; and that is why I have remained a Washington Federalist to this day, and why I shall die one." Mr. Ingersoll followed with an incident not less interesting. In his thirteenth year he had seen General Washington in Philadelphia. Playing around his residence in Market Street, near Fifth, with some of the children connected with the Washington family, he was persuaded into the house, and dined at the table with the great man, his wife, Mrs. Martha Washington, and his military aids or secretaries. Mr. Ingersoll described Washington as stately and austere. No conversation took place during the meal. He filled his own glass of madeira silently, passed the decanter to his lady, and then took wine with the guests, the boys inclusive. It was a long and quiet repast, and the boys were glad when it was over. Washington rose first, and passed to his front door, where three horses were in waiting in the hands of the grooms; the General mounted one, the aids the others, and all three rode rapidly out of Fifth Street.

There are not many living who could relate similar experiences. Mrs. Mary Ellet, whose memoir I had the honor of writing, and who lived to be nearly ninety, dying in the city of

Philadelphia about two years ago, was full of these reminiscences.   There are doubtless old families whose records and recollections abound in stories of the Revolutionary and ante-Revolutionary heroes and statesmen.   As we approach the Centennial Anniversary of American Independence these materials ought to be collected and edited.   Our Historical Societies could in no better way honor the day and increase their usefulness than by publishing every thing pertaining to the immortal characters who deliberated at Philadelphia during the early stages of the Revolution, and down to the period when the seat of the National Government was finally removed to the city of Washington, at the beginning of the century.   There is hardly an old State, from Maine to South Carolina, that is not instinct with private and personal recollections of these men and their works.   In the five years between now and the 4th of July, 1876, much could be gathered from these sources to add to the interest of that auspicious anniversary, and to perpetuate our gratitude for those who first destroyed the British power, and then laid the foundations of American liberty on this continent.

[December 3, 1871.]

XLVIII.

FROM the month of December, 1860, to the 19th of April, 1861, we made history like magic.   Parties dissolved and sections consolidated.   Professed politicians became practical patriots; professed patriots became practical traitors.   Andrew Johnson struck the first blow on the 19th of December, 1860, in the Senate, and continued pounding against the Secessionists all through the war, insanely changing his course only when assassination and accident made him President—throwing away the ripest fruits of what seemed to be honest endeavors, and that golden opportunity which rarely comes more than once in a lifetime. Of Buchanan's Cabinet, General Cass, Howell Cobb, and John B. Floyd all resigned at an early day, and Jacob Thompson later—Cass in the spirit of profound attachment to the Constitution ; the others with defiance and threats. The two Houses of Congress were two theatres. The galleries were filled with excited spectators. Few speeches were made by the Union men, and almost none by the Republicans, until honest Ben Wade, of Ohio, broke silence and gave tongue to the feelings of an outraged people. Especially was Philadelphia an interesting scene during these initial months. The meeting at the Board of Trade Rooms on Thursday, the 3d of January, 1861, called to decide "What measures should be adopted in the present condition of our national affairs," was an extraordinary event. The veteran Colonel Cephas G. Childs presided. There were some differences between those who participated, but the sentiment of devotion to the Union was almost unanimous. That meeting resulted in a committee to make preparations for a larger demonstration at National Hall, on the evening of the Saturday succeeding, January 5, 1861. In looking over the names of those who took part in that monster and electric popular upheaval I find representatives of all parties. Many have passed away. We no longer see the familiar forms of Commodore Charles Stewart, Evans Rogers, J. Murray Rush, Joseph R. Ingersoll, Edward Coles, George W. Nebinger, John B. Myers, John Grigg, Oswald Thompson, Henry Horn, Cephas G. Childs, Edward Gratz, George A. Coffey, John M. Butler, James Landy, Edward G. Webb, Robert T. Carter, and George W. Thorn. All these have gone. Among the resolutions adopted and indorsed by the Republicans and many of the Democratic leaders of Philadelphia, was the following axiomatic and fundamental declaration :

"That all persons who wage war against the United States for the purpose of destroying the Government established by our fathers, and for any other purpose whatever, or who aid, sanction, counsel, or encourage them, can not be regarded in any other light than as public enemies."

The gentleman who introduced the resolutions was J. Murray Rush, since deceased, son of the late venerable Richard Rush, widely known as a consummate statesman. Co-operating with him were such Philadelphia Democrats as General Robert Patterson, Lewis C. Cassidy, William A. Porter, George Northrop, Benjamin Rush, and George W. Nebinger. The veteran William D. Lewis, who presided, and whose speech was as full of fire as any of the younger orators, and Horace Binney, who wrote a glowing appeal, now almost a centenarian, are yet among us.

Other cities and towns were equally prompt and outspoken, but Philadelphia, with Boston, took the start and maintained it. When war was inevitable, Philadelphia, like Boston, became a rendezvous of loyal spirits. She symbolized her purpose by her memorable reception of Mr. Lincoln at Independence Hall, on the 22d of February, 1861; by her first welcome to the Union troops as they passed along Washington Avenue to the national capital; by the impromptu organization of the Cooper-Shop Refreshment Saloon, which soon became a national Mecca; by her magnificent Sanitary Fair; and her great Union League, beginning with a few gentlemen at a social meeting, and increasing into a brotherhood of seventeen hundred, wielding a potential influence in local, State, and general politics—a society not less distinguished for the culture of its members than for the gracious hospitalities extended to liberal strangers of every sect and clime.

On the day after the firing upon Fort Sumter I met Stephen A. Douglas upon Pennsylvania Avenue, in the city of Washington. Naturally anxious to ascertain what part he would take in coming events, I put the question to him, "What is now to be done? My dear friend, what are we to do?"

I shall never forget his answer : "We must fight for our country and forget all differences.   There can be but two parties— the party of patriots and the party of traitors.   We belong to the first."   Abraham Lincoln was President.   His old adversary, who had defeated him for Senator in 1858, and whom he (Lincoln) had defeated for President in 1860, called that very day at the White House and proffered his counsel and his services.   The firing upon Sumter on the 14th of April, followed by the attack upon the Massachusetts troops on the 19th of the same month, raised the question how the soldiers of the North were to reach the capital, already beleaguered by the prepared hosts of the South.   It was in the discussion of this question that Mr. Lincoln made the memorable remark, "If we can not pass over Baltimore, or under Baltimore, we must necessarily pass *through* Baltimore;" and it was in one of his interviews that Judge Douglas pressed the suggestion which originated in Massachusetts that we might go *round Baltimore*, and reach Washington *viâ* Annapolis by water—a suggestion subsequently successfully carried out.   During this cordial intercourse Mr. Lincoln solicited Judge Douglas to go to the West and raise his voice in favor of the Government; and it was in response to this request that the great Senator turned his face homeward, and made the magnetic speech which aroused his followers, and gave to the Administration that timely support which helped to fill our armies, to increase the Republican column, and to add to Republican counsels the culture and courage of the flower of the Democratic party.   Let me quote this his farewell speech at Chicago on the first of May, 1861— the faithful echo to Mr. Lincoln's affectionate appeal in the preceding April.   These golden words should never be forgotten:

" The election of Mr. Lincoln is a mere pretext.   The present secession movement is the result of an enormous conspiracy formed more than a year since—formed by leaders in the Southern Confederacy more than twelve months ago.   They use the slavery question as a means to aid the accomplishment of their ends. They desired the election of a Northern candidate by a sectional vote, in order to show that the two sections can not live together. When the history of the two years from the Lecompton question down to the Presidential election shall be written it will be shown that the scheme was deliberately made to break up this Union.

"They desired a Northern Republican to be elected by a purely Northern vote, and then assign this fact as a reason why the sections can not live together. If the Disunion candidate in the late Presidential contest had carried the united South, their scheme was, the Northern candidate successful, to seize the capital last spring, and, by a united South and a divided North, hold it. Their scheme was defeated in the defeat of the Disunion candidate in several of the Southern States.

" But this is no time for a detail of causes. The conspiracy is now known; armies have been raised; war is levied to accomplish it. There are only two sides to the question. Every man must be for the United States or against it. There can be no neutrals in this war—only patriots or traitors."

A little more than a month after (June 3, 1861), Stephen A. Douglas died at Chicago, aged forty-eight years and two months. But Abraham Lincoln did not forget him. He directed the Departments to be clothed in mourning and the colors of the different Union regiments to be craped. Nor did his sympathy end in words. He seized the first occasion to honor the sons of Douglas—an example fitly followed by General Grant. Robert Martin Douglas is one of the President's private secretaries, and his brother, Stephen A. Douglas, Jr., a leading Republican in North Carolina, in full accord with the Administration. It is gratifying to add, as I feel I may now do by authority, that had Judge Douglas lived he would have been called into the Administration of Abraham Lincoln, or placed in one of the highest military commands. The relations of the present Chief

Magistrate to the friends of Douglas were closer and more intimate than those of Mr. Lincoln, and it is more than probable that had Douglas survived he would to-day be one of the counselors of President Grant, who himself was a citizen of Illinois at the time Judge Douglas was sweeping the Buchanan hosts out of the field. John A. Rawlins, the nearest friend and Secretary of War of Grant, was also the nearest friend of Douglas. What a power Douglas would have been, enlisted on the right side, with all his prophecies proved, all his Southern enemies crushed, with his plan of transcontinental railroads vindicated and increased, with our new Territories controlled and freed by the voice of the people, with the Mormon problem he so boldly attacked on the eve of solution, and the great West realizing every day his hopes of supreme empire!

[December 10, 1871.]

XLIX.

No member of the Geneva Conference raised under the Treaty of Washington to adjust questions arising out of that convention will attract more notice than the senior counsel of the American members, Caleb Cushing, of Massachusetts. Born on the 17th of January, 1800, and therefore on the verge of seventy-two, he is, for his years, one of the most vigorous intellects in the world. His long career of more than half a century has been singularly varied. A graduate of Harvard College in 1817, subsequently a tutor of mathematics and natural philosophy, he studied law at Cambridge, and settled at Newburyport, still his Massachusetts residence, to practice the profession which he formally entered in 1822. In 1825–26 he served in the Legislature of the State, in 1829 visited Europe and published on his return "Reminiscences of Spain," a delightful book, and a profound review of the Revolution in France. He was also one of the favorite writers of the old *North American Review.* In 1833–34 he was again elected to the Legislature, and was a Representative in Congress from 1835 to 1843. Appointed by President Tyler commissioner to China, he negotiated an important treaty. On his return, in 1846, he was again elected to the State Legislature. In 1847 he was chosen colonel of volunteers in the Mexican war, and was afterward made brigadier-general by President Polk. In 1850 he was elected for the fifth time to the State Legislature, and in 1851 made a Justice of the Supreme Court of Massachusetts. When President Pierce was elected, Caleb Cushing was made his Attorney-General, and at the end of his term he returned to Massachusetts, and was again elected to the Legislature. He was president of the Democratic Charleston Convention in 1860 to nominate a President, and in July, 1866, was appointed by Andrew Johnson one of the three commissioners to codify and revise the laws of the United States. When he accepted the post of American counselor to the commissioners under the English treaty he was the advocate of the Mexican Government before the United States and Mexican Claims Commission. Few men living can point to such an experience —few are better qualified by varied acquirements and personal address to cope with the ripe and thorough statesmen sent by Great Britain to Geneva.

General Cushing was for a long time one of the ablest of the Whig leaders; and when John Tyler severed his connection with that party, he and Henry A. Wise, and one or two more, constituted what was called the Tyler Guard in the House. After that he gradually changed his course, and became as prominent a leader of the Democrats. At present, without any special party proclivities — having reached what Mr. Sumner calls "the philosophic age" — he devotes himself to law and literature. It is not denied that he is frequently employed at the Department of State, and no doubt by other Departments, in the preparation of important papers. I have heard him at a dinner-table conversing in French, Spanish, English, and German. His style of speaking is exceedingly fascinating. Some eighteen years ago I was present at an oratorical combat between him and Jefferson Davis at Newark, N. J., where President Pierce halted on his way to the opening of the Crystal Palace at New York. They were well matched. Davis had the reputation of being one of the most graceful of the Southern debaters, but he found more than an equal in the Massachusetts dialectician. As a newspaper writer he is unsurpassed. While I was one of the editors of the National Democratic organ during Pierce's Administration, Attorney-General Cushing, although deeply immersed in the business of his Department, hardly let a day pass without sending me an editorial on some subject, and he frequently aided me on the *Washington Chronicle*. He was at home on finance, on law, and especially on foreign questions. In society he is delightful. Excelling in conversation, his reminiscences are original and graphic. It is very interesting to sit by and hear him talk of the characters of the past without hatred or prejudice. A man of large wealth, inherited and self-earned, a widower without children, fond of labor, of matchless excellence as a practitioner in the Supreme Court of the United States, he is also a great student—devouring every new book as it comes out, novels inclusive, and remembering every thing he reads. His health is good, his activity remarkable, his habits temperate. Invited every where in Washington, he is the ornament of every circle, and it is not going too far to say that, gracious, polite, and agreeable as all educated Englishmen are—especially those reared in high life—among his associates in the Geneva mission he will be one of the most popular. I could run this notice of Caleb Cushing into several columns, but I will close my hasty tribute to a remarkable man with an extract from one of his speeches in 1836, while he was a Whig member of the House of Representatives, as a specimen of his style. In all that has been written against the enemies of the Union, nothing finer can be found. I commend it to the special consideration of his old friend, Mr. Jefferson Davis :

"I pray to God, if in the decree of his Providence he have any mercy in store for me, not to suffer me to behold the hour of its dissolution; its glory extinct; the banner of its pride rent and trampled in the dust; its nationality a moral of history; its grandeur a lustrous vision of the morning slumber vanished; its liberty a disembodied spirit, brooding like the genius of the Past amid the prostrate monuments of its old magnificence. To him that shall compass or plot the dissolution of this Union, I would apply language resembling what I remember to have seen of an old anathema : Wherever fire burns or water runs; wherever ship floats or land is tilled; wherever the skies vault themselves or the lark carols to the dawn, or sun shines or earth greens in his ray; wherever God is worshiped in temples or heard in thunder; wherever man is honored or woman loved— there, from thenceforth and forever, shall there be to him no part or lot in the honor of man or the love of woman. Ixion's revolving wheel, the overmantling cup at which Tantalus may not slake his unquenchable thirst; the insatiate vulture gnawing at the immortal heart of Prometheus; the rebel giants writhing in the volcanic fires of Ætna—are but faint types of his doom."

[December 17, 1871.]

L.

CHRISTMAS is one of the holidays when childhood joyously looks forward, and manhood solemnly looks back. The one lives in anticipation of happy years to come—the other lives

over the years that have gone.   In this, the fiftieth number of
these anecdotes, which, when commenced, I did not suppose
would extend to twenty, I am reminded of a season every where
celebrated by the Christian world, and I quietly turn over the
leaves of memory to see if I can not restore a few of the events
that mark this time in former years.   My first visit to Washington was in the holidays of 1839, thirty-two years ago, when
Martin Van Buren was President, Richard M. Johnson Vice-
President, John Forsyth Secretary of State, Levi Woodbury
Secretary of the Treasury, Joel R. Poinset Secretary of War,
James K. Paulding Secretary of the Navy, John M. Niles Postmaster-General, Felix Grundy Attorney-General; when Henry
Clay, Daniel Webster, James Buchanan, Silas Wright, John C.
Calhoun, Robert J. Walker, Samuel L. Southard, and William
C. Preston were Senators in Congress; when James K. Polk
was Speaker of the House, William R. King President *pro tem-
pore* of the Senate, and Roger B. Taney Chief Justice of the
Supreme Court.   Not one of these names now figures on the
roll of living men.   Washington was then little more than a
straggling village, fulfilling painfully the idea of a city of dreary
distances.   The avenues were poorly paved, and the streets almost impassible and miserably lighted at night.   The leading
hotel was Gadsby's—a vast barn or caravanserai; the chief
amusements gambling-houses and a poor theatre; and no public halls with the exception of Carusi's.   The only creditable
buildings were the Capitol, the President's House, and the Departments.   When I was here first the snow lay deep upon the
ground, the cold was intense; sleighs were the ordinary conveyances, and Senators and members were generally huddled
into ordinary boarding-houses, in which a sort of gipsy life was
led, only tolerable to those who had fortunes of their own.   It
was a cheerless city, simply endurable by political and public
receptions.   Society was pleasant enough for those who had
time to stay, but a casual visitor like myself had to be content

with a seat in the gallery of Congress, a presentation to the President among a mob, or a loiter in the East Room. Twenty years made comparatively little change in the character of the city. Old men died and new men rose. One set of giants was succeeded by another. Modern improvements came in slowly, for slavery was spread like a shroud over the whole district. Population grew apace, but enterprise was stagnant. The newspapers were didactic and dull. Gales & Seaton still quietly vegetated in their genteel *Intelligencer*, its prestige gone, and they struggled vainly against the huge and ponderous issues then projecting their dark proportions upon the scene. James Buchanan was President, trying with feeble force to quell the storm he aided to raise, while Stephen A. Douglas, Charles Sumner, John J. Crittenden, Benjamin F. Wade, Salmon P. Chase, Wm. H. Seward, John C. Breckinridge, Robert Toombs, John Slidell, and Andrew Johnson were leading different divisions of men—each contending for his own theories, and all irresistibly floating into that great conflict which abolished slavery, purified the Constitution, redeemed the whole government, and, for the first time since the Declaration of Independence, established and fortified a consolidated nation. Then the strong, warm blood began to circulate in the District of Columbia. Still the progress was slow. The *débris* of the battle had to be removed. The local municipality had to be changed. Free labor had to be organized and rewarded. The experiment of the ballot had to be tried. New men, when they came in to push old incapables from their stools, had to be accustomed to the demands and the progress of the times. Summoned to the helm of a Washington Republican daily in 1862, I gladly echoed the popular cry for improvement. Still years passed before there was any substantial response. It was only when General Grant succeeded Andrew Johnson that men were found to undertake responsibilities and bear misrepresentations, and place Washington City on the high plane of vigorous competition

with its sisters.   A few days since, after an absence of several
months, I returned, to realize the vast difference between the
Washington of 1839 and the Washington of 1871.   During these
few months a magical transformation has been wrought.   The
desolation, decay, and retrogression of thirty-two years have
been succeeded by a diversified and miraculous development.
The inertness of the past is put to shame by the activity of the
present.   Youth has superseded age, enterprise enervation.
Ten years ago its churches were hospitals, its parks camping-
grounds, many of its public places barracks or prisons.   Its
avenues and streets trembled under the march of embattled
thousands, and were torn and lacerated by long trains of artil-
lery and huge processions of army wagons.   Nothing maintained its character but the marble Capitol, and that, as if to
prefigure the new era, extended its wings in all the wonders of
its classic beauty amid the shock of conflict and of death.   And
now, on the eve of that anniversary of the birth of Him whose

> " Blessed feet
> Which nineteen hundred years ago
> Were nailed for our advantage on the bitter cross,"

the visitor, whether American or foreigner, stands in the midst
of something more than a material metamorphosis.   It was said
of one of the Roman emperors that he found Rome brick and
left it marble.   Not less true is the eulogy that the Republicans
found Washington in chains and made it free.   They found it
a miserable mockery and converted it into a magnificent metropolis.   My companions, most of whom had not seen Washington for years, and easily recalled its former wretchedness,
stood in amazement in the midst of the trophies of its present
splendor.   After riding along Pennsylvania Avenue and observ-
ing the new residences going up in every quarter, and the broad
streets laid with enduring composite, we stopped on the noble
walk before the north front of the Treasury Department and
stood opposite the Freedmen's Savings Bank.   Its history will

form a striking chapter in the annals of these times.   On the east corner of the same block I pointed out the famous banking-house of Corcoran & Riggs—now managed, I believe, by Mr. George W. Riggs.   The contrast between these two edifices is a contrast between two ideas, and suggests a moral better than an argument.   Let us take two living men—men whose names are immediately associated with these institutions—W. W. Corcoran, the former head of the little old banking-house at the corner, and William J. Wilson, cashier of the new savings bank—the one white and the other colored, both natives of the United States, and both sympathizers with the South in the rebellion—Corcoran with the Confederates and Wilson with the slaves.   It can be no offense to the white man to say that, like his colored brother, he was of humble origin, and it is equally true that while he flourished under our institutions, William J. Wilson was oppressed and degraded.   The white man grew in riches and in graces with his years.   Under former Administrations, before the Sub-Treasury, he was the principal depositary of the national funds, and to this day his name is a letter of credit in all financial circles.   Belonging to the age that is fast passing away, he does not forget that most of his wealth is the result of the confidence of his Government; and in the rapid growth of Washington, although he himself has resisted many of the recent efforts in that direction, there are no more beautiful objects than his noble Art Gallery and the Louisa Home for Indigent Ladies.   The black man had none of these chances.   When Congress, early in 1865, passed a charter of incorporation for the Freedmen's Savings Bank, William J. Wilson, the present indomitable cashier, was teaching school on Twelfth Street, near R, in Washington City, without remuneration.   The trustees called upon him to make the bank known to the colored people of America, and he undertook the work. His first office was a rented room in a small brick house in G Street, where he remained for a few months stemming the tide of bigotry against his race, and untiring in teaching them the necessity of hoarding their surplus wages in some institution that would keep them safely and profitably. A freedman, in 1866, told Wilson that his father's box had been broken into and two hundred dollars stolen, but that the old man had still twenty-four dollars left, and this was the first investment, under Wilson's advice, in the Freedmen's Savings Bank. It was the seed from which has grown what is already a gigantic and must become an overwhelming corporation. Other deposits followed in rapid succession, and real estate was purchased at the corner of Nineteenth and I Streets in Washington. The operations of the concern became too large in a short time, and it was finally moved to the northwest corner of Pennsylvania Avenue and Nineteenth Street. During this period colored soldiers began to deposit something of their pay, and those who were wise enough to do so now reap the benefit of their wisdom. In the winter of 1867 the bank was moved to Seventh Street, between E and F, where it remained for fourteen months, until finally it was located in the new building opposite the Treasury Department, to which I have referred. There are few banking-houses in America equal to it, and yet, large, commodious, and beautiful as it is, it is to be still further extended, inasmuch as the company has purchased the whole of the western portion of the lot, and are even now ambitious to buy out Corcoran & Riggs, so that the entire square may be given up to them. It may be called a tree of many branches, extending through the South and the Southwest. They have fine buildings, with capable officers engaged in the good work of collecting the savings of the freedmen, and so hoarding and investing them as that in the course of time the institution will be second to none on the continent. The Washington depositors are from one hundred and fifty to two hundred a day, and the daily amount of business varies from six to twenty thousand dollars. In four weeks these deposits have exceeded the drafts by sixty thousand

dollars.   No discounts are made for the public or for any of
the officers of the bank, and advances are made only on security of real estate.   It is unnecessary to give further details.
The concern itself stands first among financial institutions.   Its
future may be judged from its present.   With ordinary care
and integrity it must distance all competitors, inasmuch as it
has secured the confidence of the great race which, united for
one object, can accomplish almost any thing.   Imagine these
millions of colored men, women, and children, all resolved upon
hoarding their earnings in one banking institution, and then
contrast this unity of action with the savings banks in other
cities and States which have grown rich because they have been
preferred by only a portion of the whites, and you have the story in a nutshell.   The architect of all this prosperity is William
J. Wilson, the cashier, an earnest, hard-headed, true-hearted
man, with the intelligence, vigor, and the directness of a John
W. Garrett or a George Law, and the conviction of an Oliver
Cromwell.   As a Pennsylvanian I am proud to record the fact
that perhaps the most efficient and persevering of the coadju-
tors of Mr. Wilson in the administration of the affairs of this
magnificent institution is Colonel D. L. Eaton, of Pittsburgh.
But Wilson is the W. W. Corcoran of the colored men of the
South, successfully emerging from a deadlier struggle, fighting
against sterner obstacles, and perhaps surer of a grander future.
Who knows but that in the years that lie beyond, a reputation
as pure, a credit as high, may await the posterity of the colored
banker as that which has a thousand times rewarded the white
capitalist?   I said at the beginning that Christmas is that holiday on which childhood looks joyously forward, and when manhood solemnly looks backward ; and, as I conclude this striking contrast, may not both child and man be instructed by its
lessons, and alike anticipate the glorious destiny of our country?

[December 24, 1871.]

LI.

NEW-YEAR'S calls had their origin in Continental Europe. The custom was brought to New York by the Dutch and Huguenots as one of their peculiar institutions. It has never been naturalized, until recently, in towns of a more purely English origin or population. Christmas is the favorite holiday all through the Middle States, especially in districts originally settled by the English and the Germans. New-year's receptions have latterly become universally fashionable, but the cities of New York and Washington are more particularly abandoned to this growing and pleasant custom. On Friday, the first of January, 1790, the Government of the young United States, then located in the city of New York, the first President, George Washington, was waited upon by the principal gentlemen of the metropolis. Mrs. Washington held her levee as on other Friday evenings, but this special reception was one of unusual elegance. The weather was almost as gentle as May, and the full moon shone brightly into the chambers of the President's stately mansion. It was not the general custom for visitors to the President to sit, but on this particular evening, as I learn from a diary of the period, there were chairs in the rooms where Mrs. Washington met her friends, and, after they were seated, tea and coffee and plum and plain cake were served. Mrs. Washington afterward remarked that none of the proceedings of the day so pleased " the General " (by which title she always designated her husband, differing in that respect from Mrs. Grant, who nearly always speaks of our present President as "Mr. Grant ") as the friendly greeting of the gentlemen who had called upon him. Washington asked if New-year's visiting had always been kept up in New York, and when he was answered in the affirmative, he paused a moment and said, " The highly favored situation of New York will in the progress of years at-

tract numerous emigrants, who will gradually change its customs and manners; but, whatever changes take place, never
forget the cordial and cheerful observance of New-year's-day."
Mrs. Washington stood by his side as the visitors arrived and
were presented, and when the clock in the hall struck *nine* she
advanced and said, with a pleasant smile, "The General always
retires at nine, and I usually precede him," upon which the
company made their parting salutations, and said good-night.
This was the second session of the First American Congress,
and the last ever held in New York. It was closed on the 12th
of August, 1790, and on the 30th the President set out for Virginia.

The population of Boston at this time was about eighteen
thousand, that of New York thirty-three thousand, of whom
twenty-three hundred were slaves, and that of Philadelphia forty-
two thousand, of whom less than three hundred were slaves.
One of the great questions of the day was in which of the cities
or sections the capital of the nation should be fixed. It is
amusing to note the efforts made to retain it in New York
and to prevent its transfer to Philadelphia, and to compare
them with the late endeavor of the gentle Mr. Reavis, of St.
Louis, and his very few associates, against keeping the seat of
the National Government where it is to-day. The first Congress had just closed at New York, and Washington prepared,
in accordance with the decision of that body, to fix his new residence at Philadelphia, where the Executive, Legislative, and
Judicial Departments were to be retained until the close of the
century. It was known that Washington and the Southern
men generally were anxious that the political centre of the Republic should be on the River Potomac, while Pennsylvania
wished it on the banks of the Delaware, and New York vainly
tried to keep it on the Hudson. Dr. Rush, in a letter to General Muhlenberg, said, "I rejoice in the prospect of Congress
leaving New York. It is a sink of political vice. Do as you

please, but tear Congress away from New York in any way. Do not rise without effecting this business." But the New-Yorkers did not hesitate to retort upon Philadelphia. Captain Freneau, afterward Mr. Jefferson's great editorial advocate, and the assailant of General Washington in the *Philadelphia National Gazette*, wrote some verses, in which he made a Philadelphia house-maid, in a letter to her friend in New York, speak of Philadelphia as follows:

> " Six weeks my dear mistress has been in a fret,
> And nothing but Congress will do for her yet.
> She says they must come, or her senses she'll lose ;
> From morning to night she is reading the news,
> And loves the dear fellows that vote for our town,
> Since no one can relish New York but a clown.
>
> " She tells us as how she has read in her books
> That God gives the meat but the devil the cooks ;
> And Grumbleton told us, who often shoots flying,
> That fish you have plenty, but spoil them in frying ;
> That your streets are as crooked as crooked can be,
> Right forward three perches he never could see ;
> That his view was cut short with a house or a shop
> That stood in his way and obliged him to stop."

To which the New York maid responds to her friend :

> " Well, Nannie, I'm sorry to find, since you writ us,
> That Congress at last has determined to quit us ;
> You now may begin with your dish-cloths and brooms,
> To be scouring your knockers and scrubbing your rooms.
>
> " As for us, my dear Nannie, we're much in a pet,
> And hundreds of houses will be " To be Let ;"
> Our streets, that were just in a way to look clever,
> Will now be neglected and nasty as ever.
> This Congress unsettled's a very sad thing,
> Seven years, my dear Nannie, they've been on the wing.
> My master would rather saw timber or dig,
> Than to have it removed to Conogocheague,
> Where the houses and kitchens are yet to framed,
> The trees to be felled, and the streets to be named."

Then came the hurry and excitement of moving the different Departments of the Government, complaints on the part of members of Congress of high prices of rents and provisions, and all the numerous intrigues incidental to such a transition. The appearance of Philadelphia was monotonous enough, though Christ Church had quite a cathedral air, and the Dutch church was magnificent. But the city, plain and unpretending, was chiefly attractive to visitors by its markets, which were declared to be the best in the world. The Pennsylvania politicians, including such men as Robert Morris, felt that if they could make Congress, the President, and the Departments comfortable in Philadelphia, the project of removing to the South would be abandoned, and therefore some amusing expedients were resorted to, especially to propitiate the President, but without effect. He was exceedingly careful about committing himself, would receive no favors of any kind, and scrupulously paid for every thing. The house of Mr. Robert Morris had been taken by the corporation for his residence. " It is," said Washington to his private secretary, Mr. Lear, " the best they could get, and is, I believe, the best single house in the city." A larger house was set apart for him on Ninth Street, on the grounds now covered by the Pennsylvania University, which he refused to accept.

The house he occupied while he was President was a large double house, on the south side of High Street, near Fifth, was three stories, thirty-two feet wide, four windows in the second as well as in the third story, and three in the first, approached by three heavy steps of gray stone to a single door. It was situated in a vacant lot, used as a garden, and surrounded with trees and shrubbery.

On Saturday, the 28th of November, 1790, the President and Mrs. Washington arrived from Mount Vernon, and took possession of this their new mansion, and on Christmas-day, the 25th of December, they gave their first formal levee. The President was surrounded by members of his Cabinet or other distinguished

men, his hair powdered and gathered behind in a silk bag, coat
and breeches of plain black silk velvet, white or pearl-colored
vest, yellow gloves, a cocked hat in his hand, silver knee and
shoe buckles, and a long sword, with a finely wrought and glittering steel hilt, the coat worn over it and its scabbard of polished white leather.   On these occasions he never shook hands
even with his most intimate friends.   Every name was distinctly
announced, and he rarely forgot it after the owner had been
introduced.   At Mrs. Washington's receptions the President
appeared as a private gentleman, without hat or sword, conversing without restraint, generally with the ladies, who had few
other opportunities of meeting him.

The winter of 1790–91, including the New-year's receptions
and levees, was unusually brilliant in Philadelphia.   "I should
spend a very dissipated winter," writes Mrs. John Adams, "if
I were to accept one half the invitations I receive."   Another
correspondent wrote as follows: "I never saw any thing like the
frenzy which has seized upon the inhabitants here.   They have
been half mad ever since this city became the seat of Government, and there is no limit to their prodigality, and, Ellsworth
might say, profligacy.   The probability is that some families
will find they can not support their dinners, suppers, and losses
at loo a great while ; but generally, I believe, the sharp citizens manage to make the temporary residents pay the bills,
one way or another.   They have given a good many delightful
parties, and I have been at Chew's, McKean's, Clymer's, Dallas's, Bingham's, and a dozen other houses lately.   Among your
more particular friends there is more quiet and comfort, and it
is not impossible that the most truly respectable people are
least heard of."

Few will think of the New-year of 1790–91 as they greet
to-morrow ; and yet, though eighty years have gone, it is not
difficult, after a little reading and reflection, to recall it.   "The
belle of the period" was Anne Willing, afterward Mrs. William

Bingham.   She was the princess of society before whom Jefferson, Hamilton, Jay, and John Adams gladly bowed.   Of rare personal attractions, fine intelligence, and unlimited resources, supplied by husband and father, she dazzled society in both continents.   Dying at thirty-seven, she has left a deathless reputation for loveliness of person and of mind.   A chief favorite of Washington, who saw her alike at her town and country home —the latter the famous Lansdowne on the Schuylkill, the glory of the great Fairmount Park—she was the star of Mrs. Washington's levees.   It is not difficult to picture her now, the queen of the ladies of her own age and sphere, and the admired of the great leaders of the time.   There will be lovely women and eminent men to-morrow at the White House in Washington, and in the many great houses of New York, Philadelphia, Boston, Cincinnati, New Orleans, Charleston, Baltimore, and Richmond ; but will the women be more attractive than those who attended the first levee of President Washington in Philadelphia in 1790–91?   There were Mrs. Vice-President John Adams, the dazzling Mrs. Bingham and her beautiful sisters, the Misses Allen, the Misses Chew, and a constellation of others. The eldest of the Allens became the lovely Mrs. Greenleaf. Mrs. Theodore Sedgwick, and Miss Wolcott, of New England, added singular grace to the scene.   Miss Sally McKean, afterward the Marchioness d'Yrujo (wife of the Spanish Minister), whose portrait, by Gilbert Stuart, is still in possession of Pratt McKean, in Philadelphia, wrote to a friend in New York : "You never could have had such a drawing-room ; it was brilliant beyond any thing you can imagine, and though there was a great deal of extravagance, there was so much of Philadelphia taste in every thing that it must be confessed the most delightful occasion ever known in this country."   In fact, all the great women of this country, North and South, and of the foreign legations, figured in the decade between 1790 and 1800 in these historical assemblies.

At these Washington receptions and levees also might be found the public men of the Revolutionary era—the leaders in the Senate and in society, beginning with Washington's Cabinet, which included Jefferson, Hamilton, Knox, Timothy Pickering, John Marshall, Oliver Wolcott, and Edmund Randolph; and his immediate personal friends, at the head of whom stood John Jay, Governor Clinton, and Robert Morris. There, too, might have been seen Colonel Trumbull, the eminent historical painter. The Philadelphia celebrities living at that time were Dominie Proud, the historian of Pennsylvania, tall, thin, with a nose like a hook, and overhanging brows, a striking figure, with his ivory-headed cane, as he walked about among the new generation; Benjamin Chew, at seventy years preserving the distinguished air and high-bred courtesy which forty years before had arrested the admiration of Washington; Edward Shippen, in his sixty-second year—just called to a position on the bench —the ancestor of his esteemed and universally beloved namesake now living in Philadelphia, and exercising a salutary and generous influence; Dr. Rush, though not in the Washington circle, still a great favorite with the people; the facetious Judge Peters, in his fiftieth year, with his good nature and unfailing wit; the genial and humorous Francis Hopkinson, author of "The Battle of the Kegs;" the sage Rittenhouse, in his sixtieth year; William Bartram, at his famous botanic garden; John Fitch, the inventor of the steam-boat; the eminent Bishop White; Charles Brockden Brown, not yet twenty-one years old, with Hugh H. Breckinridge, Peter S. Duponceau, Dr. Caspar Wistar, and many more unforgotten in our annals, though long since gathered to their fathers.

[December 31, 1871.]

LII.

Who will ever forget Friday, the 22d of February, 1861, when Abraham Lincoln rode down Chestnut Street, Philadelphia, from the Continental Hotel, for the purpose of raising the American flag in front of Independence Hall? The spot, newly sanctified by that patriotic deed, has recently been additionally hallowed by an exquisite marble life-size statue of Washington, executed by that fine artist, Bailly, and paid for by the contributions of the public-school children of the First School District of Pennsylvania.

All his speeches on his way to Washington seemed to be pervaded by consciousness of his danger and determination to do his duty. He was greeted by affectionate crowds at every station, but as he approached Philadelphia he became more serious and resolved. In his reply to Mayor Henry, of that city, on the 21st of February, he said : "You have expressed the wish, in which I join, that it were convenient for me to remain long enough to consult, or rather to listen to, those breathings arising within the consecrated walls in which the Constitution of the United States, and, I will add, the Declaration of Independence, were originally framed and adopted. All my political warfare has been in favor of those teachings. *May my right hand forget its cunning and my tongue cleave to the roof of my mouth if ever I prove false to those teachings.*"

The next day he was escorted to Independence Hall. It was an early winter morning, and as the President had to visit the Legislature at Harrisburg in the afternoon, in a special train that was to leave at 8:30, what was to be done had to be done quickly. In front of the ancient Temple of Liberty a platform was erected, from which Mr. Lincoln was to raise the national flag with its thirty-four stars. As he approached the sacred spot, in a carriage drawn by four white horses, escorted by the Scott Legion, with the flag they had carried to victory in Mexico twelve years before, the whole scene was highly dramatic. The whole population was in the streets, and their excitement and enthusiasm baffled description. It recalled Shakespeare's picture of Bolingbroke's entrance into London :

> "You would have thought the very windows spake,
> So many greedy looks of young and old
> Through casements darted their desiring eyes
> Upon his visage; and that all the walls,
> With painted imagery, had said at once :
> 'Jesu preserve thee !   Welcome, Bolingbroke !'
> Whilst he, from one side to the other turning,
> Bareheaded, lower than his proud steed's neck,
> Bespake them thus : 'I thank you, countrymen;'
> And this still doing, thus he passed along."

Leaving the carriage at the door, he entered, uncovered, the sacred Hall of Independence.   And there it was that he used the language that now sounds like a solemn prophecy :

"That Declaration of Independence gave liberty, not alone to the people of this country, but hope for the world for all future time.   It was that which gave promise that in our time the weights should be lifted from the shoulders of all men, and that *all should have an equal chance.*   This is the sentiment embodied in the Declaration of Independence.   Now, my friends, can this country be saved upon that basis?   If it can, I will consider myself one of the happiest men in the world if I can save it. If it can not be saved upon that principle, it will be truly awful. *But if this country can not be saved without giving up that principle—I was about to say I would rather be assassinated on this spot than surrender it."*   And then, after a few more words, he added solemnly, as he drew his tall form to its fullest height, *"I have said nothing but what I am willing to live by, and, in the pleasure of Almighty God,* TO DIE BY."

He had just been freshly warned of his peril, and when he walked forth to face the mighty concourse outside, and mounted

the platform, "his tall form rose Saul-like above the mass."
He stood elevated and alone before the people, and, with his
overcoat off, grasped the halyards to draw up the flag. Then
arose a shout like the roar of many waters. Mr. Lincoln's expression was serene and confident. Extending his long arms,
he slowly drew up the standard, which had never before kissed
the light of heaven till it floated over the Hall of Independence.
Tears, prayers, shouts, music, and cannon followed, and sealed
an act which few knew was only the beginning of unspeakable
sufferings and sacrifices, ending in his own martyrdom. That
same afternoon, at Harrisburg, he spoke of his part in the morning's drama as follows :

"This morning I was for the first time allowed the privilege
of standing in Old Independence Hall. Our friends had provided a magnificent flag of our country, and they had arranged
it so that I was given the honor of raising it to the head of its
staff, and when it went up I was pleased that it went to its place
by the strength of my own feeble arm. When, according to the
arrangement, the cord was pulled, and it flaunted gloriously to
the wind, without an accident, in the bright glowing sunshine
of the morning, I could not help hoping that there was, in the
entire success of that beautiful ceremony, at least something of
an omen of what is to come. Nor could I help feeling then, as
I have often felt, that in the whole of that proceeding I was a
very humble instrument. I had not provided the flag. I had
not made the arrangement for elevating it to its place. I had
applied a very small portion even of my feeble strength in raising it. In the whole transaction I was in the hands of the people who had arranged it. And if I can have the same generous co-operation of the people of this nation, I think the flag of
our country may yet be kept flaunting gloriously."

After the reception of Mr. Lincoln by the State authorities at
Harrisburg, Pennsylvania, preparations were immediately made
for his return to Philadelphia. It was impossible to conceal

the events of his journey to the capital. Fully advised of these events, the rebels prepared to take his life in Baltimore. Accurate information of their intentions had been received and conveyed to him. Supposing that he would proceed by the Northern Central road, they lay in wait for him at the Calvert Street dépôt of that road in Baltimore. To baffle them he took the Pennsylvania Central from Harrisburg, and reached Philadelphia just in time to enter the sleeping-car of the 11:30 train, at the Broad and Prime dépôt, in that city, by which means he was conveyed through Baltimore at night, and safely landed in Washington on the morning of the 23d of February, 1861. To prevent the knowledge of this change of programme from being telegraphed to Baltimore, Henry Sanford, Esq., one of the officers of Adams's Express, suggested that the wires should be cut some distance from Harrisburg, which was accordingly done. And now for a statement not generally known, and for the first time published in the very interesting book entitled "Massachusetts during the War," prepared by General William Schouler, adjutant-general under Governors Banks and Andrew (a monument of industry and patriotism), which, notwithstanding its length, will be read with deep interest. This true history of Mr. Lincoln's perilous journey to Washington, in 1861, and the way he escaped death, have never been printed before. The narrative was written by Samuel M. Felton, late president of the Philadelphia and Baltimore Railroad Company, in 1862, at the request of Mr. Sibley, librarian of Harvard University, but it was not completed until lately, when it was sent to General Schouler, with other valuable material, by Mr. Felton. Mr. Felton is a native of Massachusetts, and a brother of the late president of Harvard University. He was born in West Newbury, Essex County, Massachusetts, July 17, 1809, and graduated at Harvard in the class of 1834. His services in the cause of the Union and good government are therefore a part of the renown of that Commonwealth. His narrative is as follows:

"It came to my knowledge in the early part of 1861, first by rumors and then by evidence which I could not doubt, that there was a deep-laid conspiracy to capture Washington, destroy all the avenues leading to it from the North, East, and West, and thus prevent the inauguration of Mr. Lincoln in the Capitol of the country; and if this plot did not succeed, then to murder him while on his way to the capital, and thus inaugurate a revolution which should end in establishing a Southern Confederacy, uniting all the slave States, while it was imagined that the North would be divided into separate cliques, each striving for the destruction of the other. Early in the year 1861, Miss Dix, the philanthropist, came into my office on a Saturday afternoon. I had known her for some years as one engaged in alleviating the sufferings of the afflicted. Her occupation had brought her in contact with the prominent men South. In visiting hospitals she had become familiar with the structure of Southern society, and also with the working of its political machinery. She stated that she had an important communication to make to me personally; and, after closing my door, I listened attentively to what she had to say for more than an hour. She put in a tangible and reliable shape, by the facts she related, what before I had heard in numerous and detached parcels. The sum of it all was that there was then an extensive and organized conspiracy throughout the South to seize upon Washington, with its archives and records, and then declare the Southern conspirators *de facto* the Government of the United States. The whole was to be a *coup d'état*. At the same time they were to cut off all modes of communication between Washington and the North, East, or West, and thus prevent the transportation of troops to wrest the capital from the hands of the insurgents. Mr. Lincoln's inauguration was thus to be prevented, or his life was to fall a sacrifice to the attempt at inauguration. In fact, troops were then drilling on the line of our road, and the Washington and Annapolis line, and other lines; and they were

sworn to obey the command of their leaders, and the leaders
were banded together to capture Washington. As soon as the
interview was ended, I called Mr. N. P. Trist into my office, and
told him I wanted him to go to Washington that night and communicate these facts to General Scott. I also furnished him
with some data as to the other routes to Washington that might
be adopted in case the direct route was cut off. One was the
Delaware Railroad to Seaford, and thence up the Chesapeake
and Potomac to Washington, or to Annapolis, and thence to
Washington; another to Perryville, and thence to Annapolis
and Washington. Mr. Trist left that night, and arrived in Washington at six the next morning, which was on Sunday. He immediately had an interview with General Scott, who told him he
had foreseen the trouble that was coming, and in October previous had made a communication to the President, predicting
trouble at the South, and urging strongly the garrisoning of all
the Southern forts and arsenals with forces sufficient to hold
them, but that his advice had been unheeded; nothing had been
done, and he feared nothing would be done; that he was powerless, and that he feared Mr. Lincoln would be obliged to be
inaugurated into office at Philadelphia. He should, however,
do all he could to bring troops to Washington sufficient to make
it secure; but he had no influence with the Administration, and
feared the worst consequences. Thus matters stood on Mr.
Trist's visit to Washington, and thus they stood for some time
afterward. About this time—a few days subsequent, however
—a gentleman from Baltimore came out to Back River bridge,
about five miles this side of the city, and told the bridge-keeper
that he had come to give information which had come to his
knowledge of vital importance to the road, which he wished
communicated to me. The nature of this communication was
that a party was then organized in Baltimore to burn our bridges
in case Mr. Lincoln came over the road, or in case we attempted to carry troops for the defense of Washington. The party

at that time had combustible materials prepared to pour over the bridges, and were to disguise themselves as negroes, and be at the bridge just before the train in which Mr. Lincoln traveled had arrived. The bridge was then to be burned, the train attacked, and Mr. Lincoln to be put out of the way. This man appeared to be a gentleman, and in earnest, and honest in what he said; but he would not give his name, nor allow any inquiries to be made as to his name or exact abode, as he said his life would be in peril were it known that he had given this information; but, if we would not attempt to find him out, he would continue to come and give information. He came subsequently several times, and gave items of information as to the movements of the conspirators; but I have never been able to ascertain who he was. Immediately after the development of these facts I went to Washington, and there met a prominent and reliable gentleman from Baltimore, who was well acquainted with Marshal Kane, then the Chief of Police. I was then anxious to ascertain whether he was loyal and reliable, and made particular inquiries upon both these points. I was assured that Kane was perfectly reliable; whereupon I made known some of the facts that had come to my knowledge in reference to the designs for the burning of the bridges, and requested that they should be laid before Marshal Kane, with a request that he should detail a police force to make the necessary investigation. Marshal Kane was seen, and it was suggested to him that there were reports of a conspiracy to burn the bridges and cut off Washington, and his advice was asked as to the best way of ferreting out the conspirators. He scouted the idea that there was any such thing on foot; said he had thoroughly investigated the whole matter, and there was not the slightest foundation for such rumors. I then determined to have nothing more to do with Marshal Kane, but to investigate the matter in my own way, and at once sent for a celebrated detective, who resided in the West, and whom I had before employed on an important matter. He was a man of great skill and resources. I furnished him with a few hints, and at once set him on the track with eight assistants. There were then drilling upon the line of the railroad some three military organizations, professedly for home defense, pretending to be Union men, and, in one or two instances, tendering their services to the railroad in case of trouble. Their propositions were duly considered; but the defense of the road was never intrusted to their tender mercies. The first thing done was to enlist a volunteer in each of these military companies. They pretended to come from New Orleans and Mobile, and did not appear to be wanting in sympathy for the South. They were furnished with uniforms at the expense of the road, and drilled as often as their associates in arms; became initiated into all the secrets of the organization, and reported every day or two to their chief, who immediately reported to me the designs and plans of these military companies. One of these organizations was loyal, but the other two were disloyal, and fully in the plot to destroy the bridges and march to Washington to wrest it from the hands of the legally constituted authorities. Every nook and corner of the road and its vicinity was explored by the chief and his detectives, and the secret working of secession and treason laid bare and brought to light.

"Societies were joined in Baltimore, and various modes known to and practiced only by detectives were resorted to to win the confidence of the conspirators and get into their secrets. This plan worked well, and the midnight plottings and daily consultations of the conspirators were treasured up as a guide to our future plans for thwarting them. It turned out that all that had been communicated by Miss Dix and the gentleman from Baltimore rested upon a foundation of fact, and that the half had not been told. It was made as certain as strong circumstantial and positive evidence could make it, that there was a plot to burn the bridges and destroy the road, and

murder Mr. Lincoln on his way to Washington, if it turned out
that he went there before troops were called.   If troops were
first called, then the bridges were to be destroyed and Washington cut off and taken possession of by the South. · I at once
organized and armed a force of about two hundred men, whom
I distributed along the line between the Susquehanna and Baltimore, principally at the bridges.

"These men were drilled secretly and regularly by drill-mas-
ters, and were apparently employed in whitewashing the bridges,
putting on some six or seven coats of whitewash saturated
with salt and alum, to make the outside of the bridges as nearly
fire-proof as possible.   This whitewashing, so extensive in its
application, became the nine-days' wonder of the neighborhood.
Thus the bridges were strongly guarded, and a train was arranged so as to concentrate all the forces at one point in case
of trouble.   The programme of Mr. Lincoln was changed, and it
was decided by him that he would go to Harrisburg from Philadelphia, and thence over the Northern Central road by day to
Baltimore, and thence to Washington.   We were then informed
by our detective that the attention of the conspirators was turned from our road to the Northern Central, and that they would
there await the coming of Mr. Lincoln.   This statement was
confirmed by our Baltimore gentleman, who came out again and
said their designs upon our road were postponed for the present, and, unless we carried troops, would not be renewed again.
Mr. Lincoln was to be waylaid on the line of the Northern
Central road, and prevented from reaching Washington, and
his life was to fall a sacrifice to the attempt.   Thus matters
stood on his arrival in Philadelphia.   I felt it my duty to communicate to him the facts that had come to my knowledge, and
urge his going to Washington privately that night in our sleeping-car, instead of publicly two days after, as was proposed.   I
went to a hotel in Philadelphia, where I met the detective, who
was registered under an assumed name, and arranged with him

to bring Mr. Judd, Mr. Lincoln's intimate friend, to my room in season to arrange the journey to Washington that night.   One of our sub-detectives made three efforts to communicate with Mr. Judd·while passing through the streets in the procession, and was three times arrested and carried out of the crowd by the police.   The fourth time he succeeded, and brought Mr. Judd to my room, where he met the detective-in-chief and myself.

"We lost no time in making known to him all the facts which had come to our knowledge in reference to the conspiracy, and I most earnestly advised that Mr. Lincoln should go to Washington that night in the sleeping-car.   Mr. Judd fully entered into the plan, and said he would urge Mr. Lincoln to adopt it. On his communicating with Mr. Lincoln, after the services of the evening were over, he answered that he had engaged to go to Harrisburg and speak the next day, and he would not break his engagement even in the face of such peril, but that after he had fulfilled the engagement he would follow such advice as we might give him in reference to his journey to Washington.   It was then arranged that he would go to Harrisburg the next day and make his address, after which he was to apparently return to Governor Curtin's house for the night, but in reality to go to a point about two miles out of Harrisburg, where an extra car and engine awaited to take him to Philadelphia.   At the time of his returning, the telegraph lines, east, west, north, and south, were cut, so that no message as to his movements could be sent off in any direction.   Mr. Lincoln could not possibly arrive in season for our regular train that left at eleven P. M., and I did not dare to send him by an extra for fear of its being found out or suspected that he was on the road ; so it became necessary for me to devise some excuse for the detention of the train. But three or four on the road besides myself knew the plan. One of these I sent by an earlier train, to say to the people of the Washington branch road that I had an important package

I was getting ready for the eleven P.M. train; that it was necessary that I should have this package delivered in Washington early the next morning, without fail; that I was straining every nerve to get it ready by eleven o'clock, but, in case I did not succeed, I should delay the train until it was ready, probably not more than half an hour, and I wished as a personal favor that the Washington train should await the coming of ours from Philadelphia before leaving. This request was willingly complied with by the managers of the Washington branch, and the man whom I had sent to Baltimore so informed me by telegraph in cipher. The second person in the secret I sent to West Philadelphia with a carriage, to await the coming of Mr. Lincoln. I gave him a package of old railroad reports, done up with great care, with a great seal attached to it, and directed, in a fair, round hand, to a person at Willard's. I marked it 'Very important. To be delivered, without fail, by eleven o'clock train,' indorsing my own name upon the package. Mr. Lincoln arrived in West Philadelphia, and was immediately taken into the carriage and driven to within a square of our station, where my man with the package jumped off, and waited till he saw the carriage drive up to the door and Mr. Lincoln and the detective get out and go into the station. He then came up and gave the package to the conductor, who was waiting at the door to receive it, in company with a police officer. Tickets had been bought beforehand for Mr. Lincoln and party to Washington, including a tier of berths in the sleeping-car. He passed between the conductor and the police officer at the door, and neither suspected who he was. The conductor remarked as he passed, 'Well, old fellow, it was lucky for you that our president detained the train to send a package by it, or you would have been left.' Mr. Lincoln and the detective safely ensconced in the sleeping-car, and my package safe in the hands of the conductor, the train started for Baltimore nearly fifteen minutes behind time. Our man No. 3, George ——, started with the train to go to Baltimore, and hand it over with its contents to man No. 1, who awaited its arrival in Baltimore. Before the train reached Gray's Ferry bridge, and before Mr. Lincoln had resigned himself to slumber, the conductor came to our man George, and said, 'George, I thought you and I were old friends; and why did you not tell me we had Old Abe on board?' George, thinking the conductor had in some way become possessed of the secret, answered, 'John, we are friends; and, as you have found it out, Old Abe is on board; and we will still be friends, and see him safely through.' John answered, 'Yes, if it costs me my life he shall have a safe passage.' And so George stuck to one end of the car and the conductor to the other, every moment that his duties to the other passengers would admit of it. It turned out, however, that the conductor was mistaken in his man. A man strongly resembling Mr. Lincoln had come down to the train, about half an hour before it left, and bought a ticket to Washington for the sleeping-car. The conductor had seen him, and concluded it was the veritable Old Abe. George delivered the sleeping-car and train over to William in Baltimore, as had been previously arranged, who took his place at the brake, and rode to Washington, where he arrived at six A.M., on time, and saw Mr. Lincoln in the hands of a friend, safely delivered at Willard's, where he secretly ejaculated, 'God be praised!' He also saw the package of railroad reports, marked 'important,' safely delivered into the hands for which it was intended. This being done, he performed his morning ablutions in peace and quiet, and enjoyed with unusual zest his breakfast. At eight o'clock, the time agreed upon, the telegraph wires were joined; and the first message flashed across the line was, 'Your package has arrived safely, and has been delivered. Signed, William.' Then there went up from the writer of this a shout of joy and a devout thanksgiving to Him from whom all blessings flow; and the few who were in the secret joined in a heartfelt amen. Thus began and ended a chapter in the history of the rebellion that has never before been written, but about which there have been many hints, entitled ' A Scotch Cap and Rid-ing-cloak,' etc., neither of which had any foundation in truth, as Mr. Lincoln traveled in his ordinary dress. Mr. Lincoln was safely inaugurated, after which I discharged our detective force, and also the semi-military whitewashers, and all was quiet and serene again on our railroad. But the distant booming from Fort Sumter was soon heard, and aroused in earnest the whole population of the loyal States. The seventy-five thousand three-months' men were called out, and again the plans for burning bridges and destroying the railroad were revived in all their force and intensity. Again I sent Mr. Trist to Washington to see General Scott, to beg for troops to garrison the road, as our forces were then scattered and could not be then got at. Mr. Trist telegraphed me that the forces would be supplied, but the crisis came on immediately, and all, and more than all, were required at Washington. At the last moment I obtained and sent down the road about two hundred men, armed with shot-guns and revolvers—all the arms I could get hold of at that time. They were raw and undisciplined men, and not fit to cope with those brought against them—about one hundred and fifty men, fully armed, and commanded by the redoubtable reb-el, J. R. Trimble."

To confirm this careful statement of Mr. Felton, who is now living in honored retirement near Thurlow, Delaware County, Pennsylvania, I need only refer to subsequent events: To the attack upon the Massachusetts Sixth, to the after attempts of the rebels to burn the bridges across the Susquehanna, to the necessity of placing Baltimore under military rule, and to the authoritative admission of the *Baltimore Sun* of Monday, the 25th of February, 1861, proving that if President Lincoln had taken the Northern Central, and had reached Baltimore by the Calvert Street dépôt, he would undoubtedly have been murdered in cold blood, and the conspiracy foreshadowed and exposed by Mr. Felton carried out and consummated. I shall never forget the sensations of the Union men and the consternation of the rebels when Abraham Lincoln entered Washington on Saturday, the 23d of February. We all breathed freer and deeper. We felt that our leader had reached the citadel in safety. Few indeed anticipated what incredible effort and what incalculable loss of life would be necessary to maintain the capital, and none, perhaps, outside the few persons who had knowledge of the dark and dreadful plot herein revealed, believed that among these sacrifices would be our beloved President, Abraham Lincoln.

[January 7, 1872.]

LIII.

ON the 19th of March, 1791, President Washington wrote from Philadelphia to General Lafayette as follows : " My health is now quite restored, and I flatter myself with the hope of a long exemption from sickness. On Monday next I shall enter upon your friendly prescription of exercise, intending at that time to begin a long journey to the southward." He had been invited by many of the leading characters of the Southern States, who promised him every where the cordial and enthusiastic greeting which two years before marked his triumphal progress through New England. The carriage in which he traveled was that in which he usually appeared on public occasions in Philadelphia. This carriage was built by Mr. Clarke, of that city, and was carefully preserved in a house built especially for its reception, where it remained for half a century. It is described as "a most satisfactory exhibition of the progress of American manufactures." It was drawn by six horses, carefully selected for

their handsome appearance and endurance. Washington started
from his residence, in Market Street, at twelve o'clock, on Monday, the 21st of March, 1791. Mr. Jefferson and General Knox
escorted him into the State of Delaware, and there left him.
Major Jackson, one of his private secretaries, accompanied him
until he returned to Philadelphia, the capital of the nation. He
arrived at Annapolis, Maryland, on the 25th of March, and remained two days. He stopped at Georgetown, thence proceeded to Mount Vernon, where he remained a week, thence to
Fredericksburg, Virginia, where he dined with his old friends
and neighbors, recalling, with Chancellor Wythe, the scenes of
his youth and early manhood. The party arrived at Richmond
at eleven o'clock on Monday, the 11th of April, where, as at Annapolis, Washington was greeted with acclamations and public
illuminations. They visited Halifax, Newbern, Wilmington,
and other places in North Carolina. Leaving Wilmington,
Washington was rowed across Cape Fear River in an elegantly
decorated barge. He arrived at Charleston, South Carolina,
on Monday, the 2d of May. Charleston was then the gayest of
cities. Milliners and tailors corresponded directly with inventors of dresses in London and Paris. Women preferred French
fashions, and often improved upon them. Gentlemen were partial to blue, the product of their staple, indigo. Pantaloons had
been introduced, and were worn by some of the younger men,
but in a few years were entirely laid aside, and breeches resumed. Duels were frequent. " Drunkenness," says Dr. Ram-
sey, " was the endemic vice." There were periodical races, hunting and fishing, and luxurious dinners, followed by dancing and
music. The Duc de Rochefoucauld Liancourt observed that
" from the hour of four in the afternoon the people of Charleston
rarely thought of any thing but pleasure. They had two gaming-
houses, both constantly full. The inhabitants had acquired
great knowledge of European manners, and a stronger partiality
for them than was found in New York. A foreign style of life

prevailed." This view of the inner society of Charleston is interesting as the key to a future largely controlled by the political opinions there nurtured and disseminated. Here the President had a royal greeting. A twelve-oared barge, commanded by thirteen captains of American ships, conveyed him, with several distinguished gentlemen, from Hadrill's Point, surrounded by a fleet containing an instrumental band and a choir of singers, which greeted him with triumphant airs and songs on his way to the city, where he was received by the Governor, the Society of the Cincinnati, and the military, amid ringing of bells, firing of cannon, and public acclamations. He remained a week the centre of affection and admiration. At the corporation ball two hundred and fifty ladies wore sashes decorated with his likeness. A part of their head-dress was a fillet or bandeau, with the inscription "Long live the President," in gilt letters. He sat for his portrait to Colonel Trumbull, the same that now adorns the City Hall in Philadelphia. On Monday, the 9th of May, he left Charleston, accompanied by a committee from Savannah, and was escorted on board a richly decorated boat, rowed down the river by nine sea captains, dressed in light-blue silk jackets, black satin breeches, white silk stockings, and round hats with black ribbons, inscribed "Long live the President," in gold letters. Ten miles from Savannah they were met by other barges, in one of which the gentlemen sung the popular air, "He comes, the Hero comes!" Here new honors and festivities awaited him. He passed on to Augusta, where the populace rapturously received him; returned into South Carolina, visited Columbia, dined at Camden, passed through Charlotte, Salisbury, Salem, Guilford, and other towns in North Carolina, and arrived at Mount Vernon on the 12th of June. On the last day of that month he started for Philadelphia by way of Frederick, York, and Lancaster, and arrived at the Presidential residence about noon on the 6th of July, having been absent nearly three months, during that period performing a journey of one thousand eight hundred and eighty-seven miles. It was said of Washington that "no man in the army had a better eye for horses." This long tour was a severe test of the capacity of his steeds, and before reaching Charleston he wrote to Mr. Lear, his secretary, "that, though all things considered, they had got on very well, yet if brought back they would not cut capers as they did on setting out. My horses, especially the two I bought just before I left Philadelphia, and my old white one, are much worn down, and yet I have one hundred and fifty or two hundred miles of heavy sand before I get into the upper roads."

While the President was in the South, Thomas Jefferson and James Madison were making a tour in the North. They proceeded to New York, sailed up the Hudson to Albany, visited the principal scenes of the British General Burgoyne's misfortunes, at Stillwater, Saratoga, and Bennington, Fort William Henry, Fort Ticonderoga, Crown Point, and other memorable Revolutionary places. Jefferson amused himself with his gun and hook and line, and indulged his strong taste for natural history.

I recall these facts to show that the custom of Presidential journeys did not originate with President Grant. The example of Washington was followed without censure or exception by all his successors, save Mr. Lincoln, who was constantly at work in the midst of a great war. Eighteen hundred and eighty-seven miles in three months was regarded as an extraordinary feat in 1791 ; and if the most hopeful of our statesmen had then predicted that the day would come when a successor of Washington would preside over thirty-seven States, with a population of nearly forty millions of people, and travel from Washington City to the Pacific and back, by way of New York and Philadelphia —a double distance of over seven thousand miles, with plenty of time to see and converse with the masses, all in one month —he would have been denounced as a lunatic.

Washington was pleased with his Southern tour. In one of his letters he said : "It was accomplished without any interruption by sickness, bad weather, or any untoward accident. Indeed, so highly favored were we that we arrived at each place where I proposed to halt on the very day I fixed before we set out. I am very much pleased that I undertook this excursion, as it has enabled me to see with my own eyes the situation of the country through which we traveled, and to learn more accurately the disposition of the people than I could through any information."

But these contrasts and comparisons do not end here. Official manners, customs, and costumes were different things when Washington lived in Philadelphia from what they are to-day. His habit, when the day was fine, was to take a walk, attended by his two secretaries, Mr. Lear and Major William Jackson, one on each side. He always crossed directly from his own door, on Market Street, near Fifth, to the sunny side, and walked down toward the river. He was dressed in black, and all three wore cocked hats. They were silent men, and seemed to converse very little. Washington had a large family coach, a light carriage, and a chariot, all light cream-colored, painted with three enameled figures on each panel, and very handsome. He went in the coach to Christ Church every Sunday morning, with two horses; used the carriage and four for his rides into the country, and the Lansdowne, the Hills, and other places. When he visited the Senate he had the chariot, with six horses. All his servants were white, and wore liveries of white cloth, trimmed with scarlet or orange. It was Mrs. Washington's custom to return calls on the third day. The footman would knock loudly and announce Mrs. Washington, who would then pay the visit in company with Mr. Secretary Lear. Her manners were easy, pleasant, and unceremonious. The late lamented Richard Rush, whom I knew well, and who occupied very many distinguished positions, local, State, national, and diplomatic, and who died July 30, 1859, aged seventy-nine, recalls a scene in Philadelphia in 1794–95, when Washington opened Congress in person, and which Mr. Rush saw as a boy. His words are almost mine. "The carriage of the President was drawn by four beautiful bay horses. It was white, with medallion ornaments on the panels, the liveries of the servants white turned up with red. Washington got out of the carriage, slowly crossed the pavement, ascended the steps of the edifice, corner of Sixth and Chestnut, upon the upper platform of which he paused, and, turning half around, looked in the direction of a carriage which had followed the lead of his own. Thus he stood for a minute, distinctly seen by every body in the vast concourse. His costume was a full suit of black velvet ; his hair, blanched by time, powdered to snowy whiteness, a dress sword hanging by his side, his hat in his hand. Profound stillness reigned throughout the dense crowd ; not a word was heard ; every heart was full. It seemed as if he stood in that position to gratify the assembled thousands with a full view of the Father of his Country. Not so; he paused for his secretary, who had got out of the other carriage, decorated like his own. The secretary ascended the steps, handed him a paper, probably a copy of the speech he was to deliver, when both entered the building. An English gentleman, a manufacturer, Mr. Henry Wansey, breakfasted with Washington and his family on the 8th of June, 1794. He was greatly impressed. The first President was then in his sixty-third year, but had little appearance of age, having been in his life exceedingly temperate. Mrs. Washington herself made tea and coffee for them ; on the table were two small plates of sliced tongue and dry toast, bread and butter, but no broiled fish, as is generally the custom. Miss Eleanor Custis, her granddaughter, a very pleasant young lady, in her sixteenth year, sat next to her, and next, her grandson, George Washington Parke Custis, about two years older. There were but few slight indications of form ; one servant only attended, who wore no livery. Mrs. Washington struck him as something older than the President, although he understood they were both born the same year. She was short in stature, rather robust, extremely simple in her dress, and wore a very plain cap, with her hair turned under it." This description of Mrs. Washington corresponds exactly with the portrait painted by Trumbull, now in the Trumbull gallery, at New Haven, Connecticut. In 1793 Washington left Philadelphia for nearly three months during the prevalence of yellow-fever, and stayed at Mount Vernon. The disease broke out in August, but he continued at his post until the 10th of September. He wished to stay longer, but Mrs. Washington was unwilling to leave him exposed, and he could not, without hazarding her life and the lives of the children, remain. Freneau, the editor who was charged with having written the bitterest things against Washington, complained in the following stanza that the physicians fled from Philadelphia to escape the plague :

> " On prancing steed, with sponge at nose,
>   From town behold Sangrado fly;
> Camphor and tar, where'er he goes,
>   The infected shafts of death defy–
> Safe in an atmosphere of scents,
> He leaves us to our own defense."

Among the public characters attacked by the yellow-fever were Mr. Willing and Colonel Hamilton, but they recovered. The officers of the government were dispersed, and the President even deliberated on the propriety of convening Congress elsewhere ; but the abatement of the disease rendered this unnecessary, and in November the inhabitants returned to their homes, and Congress reassembled on the 2d of December.

[January 14, 1872.]

LIV.

ONE Saturday afternoon in July, 1861, George H. Boker, now
on his way as American Minister to Constantinople, visited
Washington City and called with me upon President Lincoln.
It was a most interesting period of the war, just previous to the
battle of Bull Run. When I presented Boker to the President,
in his reception-room, up stairs, he asked, " Are you the son
of Charles S. Boker, of Philadelphia?" My friend answered,
" That is what I am believed to be." " Well," said the President, "I was your father's lawyer in Springfield, and I only wish
I had all the money I collected and paid to him, for I would
have a very handsome fortune." The Marine Band was playing on the green, south of the Presidential mansion, surrounded
by a gay and glittering crowd. Mr. Lincoln said, " The Kentucky commissioners are waiting for me on the balcony below.
They are here to protest against my sending troops through
their State to the relief of the Unionists of Tennessee, and I
would like you and Forney to come down and see them. They
say they want Kentucky to decide her relations to the General
Government for herself, and that any forces sent through their
State to the Unionists of Tennessee would certainly arouse the
elements of revolt." Then Boker told the President an anecdote of the British Minister at the Court of Frederick the Great,
who was anxious to persuade the King to take part in the
British conflicts with other European powers. Old Fritz steadily refused to be involved. His policy was against all part in
the quarrel. At a formal state dinner, when the British Minister was present, Frederick said, " Will my Lord Bristol "—the
name of the British plenipotentiary—" allow me to send him a
piece of capon?" to which the latter indignantly replied, " No,
sir; I decline having any thing to do with *neutral* animals."
The President enjoyed the joke hugely, and we walked down

stairs, where, on the balcony overlooking the joyous throng, stood the two Kentucky commissioners, one of them the eminent Judge Robertson, lately deceased. They renewed their appeals against sending troops across their State with much earnestness and ability. Mr. Lincoln quietly but resolutely combated their views, assuring them that neutrality did not become any of the friends of the Government—that while the citizen enjoyed his rights and the protection of the laws, he must also recognize his obligations and'his duties. Then turning to Boker, he asked him to repeat the incident between Frederick the Great and the British Minister, which, though it made the Kentuckians laugh, was evidently not agreeable to them. Mr. Lincoln added, " Gentlemen, my position in regard to your State is like that of the woodman, who, returning to his home one night, found coiled around his beautiful children, who were quietly sleeping in their bed, several poisonous snakes. His first impulse was to save his little ones, but he feared that if he struck at the snakes he might strike the children, and yet he dared not let them die without an effort. So it is with me. I know Kentucky and Tennessee are infested with the enemies of the Union ; but I know also that there are thousands of patriots in both who will be persecuted even unto death unless the strong hand of the Government is interposed for their protection and rescue. We must go in. The old flag must be carried into Tennessee at whatever hazard." Upon which the commissioners retired with unconcealed dissatisfaction. Unhappily for the good cause, it was many months before relief could be extended to the clamorous people of Tennessee. Kentucky lay athwart the road to their rescue, a dark and stubborn obstacle ; and now, six years after the overthrow of the rebellion—thanks to the dangerous doctrine of neutrality—the State most obdurate and obstinate in its opposition to all progress, most ready to resort to violence against the law, most eager in its opposition to the Union people, most intolerant to free opinion, most qualified to throw the largest vote against the Republican party—is this very State of Kentucky. So much for neutrality in politics and in war. In a few days came the first battle of Bull Run with all its attendant horrors, teaching to us the severest lesson of the great conflict—the lesson that a great people, armed for their own defense and for their own liberties, *must be prepared at all points.* Just at that period the genius of Boker broke out in a great poem, entitled "Upon the Hill before Centreville, July 21, 1861," from which I extract the following:

> "Awake, my countrymen! with me
> Redeem the honor which you lost,
> With any blood, at any cost!
> I ask not how the war began,
> Nor how the quarrel branched and ran
> To this dread height. The wrong or right
> Stands clear before God's faultless sight.
> I only feel the shameful blow,
> I only see the scornful foe,
> And vengeance burns in every vein
> To die, or wipe away the stain.
> The war-wise hero of the West,
> Wearing his glories as a crest
> Of trophies gathered in your sight,
> Is arming for the coming fight.
> Full well his wisdom apprehends
> The duty and its mighty ends;
> The great occasion of the hour,
> That never lay in human power
> Since over Yorktown's tented plain
> The red cross fell, nor rose again.
> My humble pledge of faith I lay,
> Dear comrade of my school-boy day,
> Before thee, in the nation's view;
> And if thy prophet prove untrue,
> And from thy country's grasp be thrown
> The sceptre and the starry crown,
> And thou and all thy marshaled host
> Be baffled, and in ruin lost—

O ! let me not outlive the blow
That seals my country's overthrow !
And, lest this woeful end come true,
Men of the North, I turn to you.
Display your vaunted flag once more,
Southward your eager columns pour !
Sound trump and fife and rallying drum ;
From every hill and valley come !
Old men, yield up your treasured gold ;
Can liberty be priced and sold ?
Fair matrons, maids, and tender brides,
Gird weapons to your lovers' sides ;
And, though your hearts break at the deed,
Give them your blessing and God-speed ;
Then point them to the field of fame,
With words like those of Sparta's dame !
And when the ranks are full and strong,
And the whole army moves along,
A vast result of care and skill,
Obedient to the master will ;
And your young hero draws the sword,
And gives the last commanding word
That hurls your strength upon the foe—
O, let them need no second blow !
Strike, as your fathers struck of old,
Through summer's heat and winter's cold ;
Through pain, disaster, and defeat ;
Through marches tracked with bloody feet ;
Through every ill that could befall
The holy cause that bound them all !
Strike as they struck for liberty !
Strike as they struck to make you free !
Strike for the crown of victory !"

"The war-wise hero of the West" was George B. McClellan,
son of the great surgeon, George McClellan, of Philadelphia.
He had been Boker's "dear comrade of the school-boy days,"
and after the first Bull Run was the nation's hope. His victories in West Virginia gave him the opportunity which others
had lost, to be lost by him in his own turn. Boker wrote sev-

eral great lyrics afterward, but whatever he may have said of other soldiers, the tribute he paid to McClellan in 1861 was the outpouring of a sincere and hopeful heart.

[January 21, 1872.]

LV.

THE first theatrical performance in Philadelphia of which there is any mention was in January of 1749, evidently conducted by home-made Thespians. In 1754 some genuine artists arrived, called "Hallam's Company," and got a license to open their "New Theatre in Water Street," in William Plumstead's store, corner of the first alley above Pine Street. Here they acted "The Fair Penitent" and "Miss in her Teens" as their first effort. Boxes, 6s.; pit, 4s.; gallery, 2s. 6d. In 1759 they opened at the corner of Vernon Street, then beyond the city bounds, so as to be out of the reach of the city authorities. They were violently assailed by the Friends, and they made every effort to evade this hostility by calling their entertainment a "Concert of Music," and by playing "George Barnwell" "for the benefit of the College of Philadelphia," and "to improve youth in the divine art of psalm and church music." The British occupation of Philadelphia revived the drama. They used the Southwark Theatre, the performers being officers of Howe's army, the proceeds going to the widows and orphans of the soldiers. Major André and Captain Delancy were the scene-painters. In 1793 the Chestnut Street Theatre, northwest corner of Sixth and Chestnut, was erected, under the name of the "New Theatre," in opposition to the Southwark Theatre, known afterward as the Old Theatre. This is the house patronized by Washington, the statesmen in Congress, and the Cabinet and their families.

The New Theatre was not opened, in consequence of the
yellow-fever, until the 17th of February, 1794. The manager
was Wigfall or Wignell, famous in the annals of the American
stage, and "the house was fitted up with a luxurious elegance
hitherto unknown in this country." The principal actors were
Whitlock, Harwood, Morton, Darley, Mrs. Oldmixon, Mrs.
Morris, and Mrs. Marshall. Harwood married Miss Bache,
granddaughter of Dr. Franklin. Mrs. Whitlock was a sister of
Mrs. Siddons. The illustrious John Jay writes from Philadelphia to his wife on the 13th of April, 1794, just previous to his
appointment as envoy extraordinary to the Court of London, as
follows: "Two evenings ago I went to the theatre with Mrs.
Robert Morris and her family. 'The Gamester,' a deep tragedy, succeeded by a piece called 'The Guardian,' were played."
An English traveler describes the theatre "as elegant, convenient, and large as that of Covent Garden. I should have thought
myself still in England. The ladies wore small bonnets of the
same fashion as those I saw in London, some of checkered
straw; many had their hair full dress, without caps, as with us,
and very few had it in the French style. Gentlemen had round
hats, coats with high collars, cut quite in the English fashion,
and many coats of striped silk." The motto over the stage,
"The eagle suffers little birds to sing," is explained by the fact
that when it was in contemplation to build the theatre, the
Quakers used all their influence with Congress to prevent it;
but Robert Morris and General Anthony Wayne successfully
advocated the establishment of theatres for the public amusement. Wigfall, the manager, fell under the displeasure of the
beautiful Mrs. Bingham. The cause of the quarrel seems to
have been because she desired to furnish and decorate her box
at her own expense, with the absolute condition that the key
should be kept by herself and no admission allowed to any
one, except on her assent. Wigfall refused the exclusive request, and in consequence Mrs. Bingham and her set rarely

attended the theatre. The great rival of the new Chestnut
Street Theatre was "the Grand Circus," controlled and owned
by the celebrated Ricketts. Washington and his family went
frequently to both their performances.

On Monday, the 27th of February, 1797, Benjamin Franklin
Bache's *Philadelphia Aurora and Advertiser* contained the following paragraph : "The President of the United States, we
understand, intends to visit the theatre THIS EVENING, *for
the last time.*" The performance was the celebrated new comedy, for the fourth time, called "The Way to Get Married," "as
performed at Covent Garden (I copy from the advertisement)
thirty-nine nights without intermission, the first season, and
since upward of one hundred and fifty nights, with unbounded
applause. At the end of the comedy the pantomime ballet,
composed by Mr. Byrne, called 'Dermit Kathleen,' to which
will be added a farce called 'Animal Magnetism.' Boxes,
$1 25 ; pit, seven eighths of a dollar ; gallery, half a dollar.
The doors of the theatre will open at five o'clock, and the curtain will rise precisely at six o'clock. Ladies and gentlemen
are requested to send their servants to keep places a quarter
before five o'clock, and to order them, as soon as the company
are seated, to withdraw, as they can on no account be permitted
to remain."

The first President and all his successors were constant attendants at the theatres, although it was some years before such
an institution was built in Washington City after it became the
national capital.

The habit of attending places of public amusement had no
exception in our Presidents. It was a good way to see and to
be seen by the people. Mrs. John Adams wrote in eulogy of
the New Chestnut, in Philadelphia, and her husband, the second President, attended of course. Jefferson's residence in
France, his musical tastes, his fondness for polite literature, all
made him like the stage. Madison, Monroe, and John Quincy

Adams were all men of letters, and the latter as late as 1845 had quite a discussion with James H. Hackett on the character of *Hamlet*. Jackson went frequently to the play, and Van Buren followed his example. So of John Tyler, Polk, Taylor, Fillmore, Pierce, and Buchanan. Lincoln was killed in the theatre. Andrew Johnson liked the drama when he was in Congress, and did not give it up when he was Chief Magistrate. General Grant conforms to the custom of his predecessors.

Actors have always wielded a large influence, though few have been politicians. It was Talma, I believe, who boasted that he had played to " a whole pit full of kings." Jefferson, the grandfather of Joseph, who, by acting a single character, has made himself rich in fortune and fame, was a rare favorite with the leading men of Pennsylvania, especially with Chief Justice John Bannister Gibson, who wrote the impressive words upon his tombstone at Harrisburg, Pennsylvania. Forrest has been welcome in every social circle, where, by his humor and genius, he has surpassed all rivals. John Brougham is perhaps the finest of dinner-table companions, only excelled by the late John Van Buren and John T. Sullivan. There is no more genial gentleman than Davenport, whom you meet at most of the great parties in Philadelphia. Edwin Booth is exceedingly popular in New York society. Nobody, during his lifetime, was so much sought after as Power, the incomparable Irish comedian. The late William B. Wood was even more interesting off than on the stage. William E. Burton, in his time, distinguished himself by uncommon versatility as a writer and a comedian. The Wallacks have made fame for themselves by scholarship and success as managers and actors. Fanny Kemble, the last of a long list of great artists, shone with equal brilliancy in private and public life. It is natural that such people should be attractive to statesmen. Students of the manners and habits of other countries, and mimics of the manners and habits of our own, where can the wearied public servant find a

surer and a better rest than in listening to the words of the great
men of the past as these are echoed from the stage by cultivated
students? The President, who visits the theatre, not only sees
the people and is seen by them, but reposes, so to speak, without interruption, upon the delightful utterances of deathless
minds. Mr. Lincoln liked the theatre not so much for itself
as because of the rest it afforded him. I have seen him more
than once looking at a play without seeming to know what was
going on before him. Abstracted and silent, scene after scene
would pass, and nothing roused him until some broad joke or
curious antic disturbed his equanimity. We are in the habit of
saying that the drama of the present is not equal to the drama
of the past—a truism, like many others, easily contradicted.
Turn to New York, Philadelphia, or any of the great cities,
and compare the number of amusements offered every night
with the scarcity of the same attractions fifty years ago; the
delightful repetition of the works of the great masters; the
endless inventions of modern playwrights; the infinite variety
of opera, comedy, tragedy, and spectacular pantomime; and no
other fact is needed to enforce the argument that if we are not
wiser than our ancestors, we certainly ought to be.

[January 28, 1872.]

LVI.

MUCH of the recreation of the public men at the capital of
the nation in former times was entertaining and instructive.
The era of lectures seems to have superseded these symposia—
perhaps for the better; but I always recur to them as the unforgotten and unsurpassed pleasures of my life. There were
cards and wine, of course; but the real attractions were impromptu wit and humor, recitations, magnetic speeches, music,

and songs; and as the participants were generally cultivated and representative men, it needed no formal rule to exclude vulgarity. Every one had a constituency of some sort to respect and fear, even if he did not respect himself; and, as they were of all sides in politics, many meeting for the first time, and never to meet again, they did their best to leave the best impressions. Ah, could those "Noctes Ambrosianæ" have been taken down in short-hand, or recorded by a faithful scribe like Pepys, Boswell, or Crabbe Robinson, what a delicious repast would have been left to posterity! When William E. Burton came to Washington to play, and after the curtain fell would join one of these assemblies, and give us his raciest things spontaneously; when Charlie Oakford, of Philadelphia—clever, genial, and ever-ready Oakford—rolled out Drake's "Ode to the American Flag," with a voice so rich and mellow; when Murdoch moved us to tears with Janvier's "Sleeping Sentinel," or stilled us with the sweet drowsiness of Buchanan Read's "Drifting;" when John Hay recited one of his fine creations, or Fitz-James O'Brien or Charles G. Halpine thrilled us with a song of war or of love; when Jack Savage sung us "The Temptation of St. Anthony," or rare Forrest dropped the tragedian, and played for us the mimic and the comedian; or Jefferson sung his "Cuckoo Song;" or Nesmith of Oregon left the Senate to set our table in a roar; we had no thought of phonography, and no time that was not crowded with ecstacy. Some of these are dead, and all are absent from the scenes of these happy evenings. Other forms crowd the saloons; other voices wake the echoes of other hearts; other eyes glisten with responsive smiles and tears. Every night we had something new, for the inventors of our amusements were artists, who worked for the best of all rewards—the happiness of their fellows.

At one time it was an opera sung by a corps of amateurs, with a houseful of Congressmen in the choruses. Then we "Buried Joe Sanders," to illustrate the sin of idleness. This was the late John L. Dawson's great story. Joe was a village nuisance, who would not work, and lived upon what he could borrow or beg. At last it was resolved to bury him alive, and so relieve the village. A coffin was duly prepared, with a place for him to see and breathe, and the procession started, Joe inside, resigned to his fate. Passing by the blacksmith, who stood at his shop-door, Vulcan asked who was to be buried. The chief mourner answered, "Joe Sanders." "What! is poor Joe dead?" "Oh no! but he is so great a nuisance that, rather than support him any longer, we have resolved to put him in the grave alive." "Oh, that won't do," says the smith; "I have enough corn to keep him going for some time, and he shall have it." Joe overhears the dialogue, lifts the coffin lid, and quietly asks, "Is the corn shelled?" "No," is the indignant reply. "Well, then," says the disgusted Joe, "*go on with the funeral.*" Dawson used to tell this as a joke upon the Southerners, to prove that they lived without labor. To play this piece was quite an event, and required a first-rate Joe and a very considerable procession, with a good feast after the dead man was in his grave—generally the back parlor.

One memorable night in January of 1859 deserves to be specially embalmed. It has been recorded in a volume for private circulation, but has never had any public place. Albert Pike, a name well known in poetry and journalism, though not so well remembered in the North for his part in the rebellion, yet withal one of the most genial of men, was reported killed by an accident, to the great grief of his very many friends in Washington. The report was proved to be false by the sudden appearance of Pike himself, whereupon John F. Coyle, of the *National Intelligencer*, determined to honor him by an Irish "wake" at his residence. More than a hundred people participated. It was called "The Life Wake of the fine Arkansas Gentleman who died before his time." The "obituary" was read by Alexander Dimitry, of New Orleans, after which Coyle sang a capital parody on Pike's own rare parody of the "Fine Old English Gentleman," a few verses of which will show its quality. Pike had lived a varied life, especially among the Indians of Arkansas, which will account for the allusions to the red men :

" The fine Arkansas gentleman restored to life once more,
 Continued to enjoy himself as he had done before ;
 And, tired of civilized pursuits, concluded he would go
 To see some Indian friends he had, and chase the buffalo.
   This fine Arkansas gentleman,
   Who died before his time.

" The rumor of his visit had extended far and near,
 And distant chiefs and warriors came with bow and gun and spear ;
 So when he reached the council-grounds, with much delight he sees
 Delegations from the Foxes, Sioux, Quapaws, Blackfeet, Pottawatomies,
  Gros Ventres, Arrapahoes, Comanches, Creeks, Navajoes, Choctaws,
  and Cherokees.
   This fine Arkansas gentleman, etc.

" They welcomed him with all the sports well known on the frontier,
 He hunted buffalo and elk, and lived on grouse and deer ;
 And having brought his stores along, he entertained each chief
 With best Otard and whisky, smoking and chewing tobacco, not forgetting
  cards, with instructions in seven-up, brag, bluff, and was whooped
  whoo-oo-ooo-oooped till he was deaf.
   This fine Arkansas gentleman, etc.

" He went to sleep among these friends, in huts or tents of skin,
 And if it rained or hailed or snowed, he didn't care a pin,
 For he'd lined his hide with whisky and a brace of roasted grouse,
 And he didn't mind the weather any more than if he slept in a four-story
  brown-stone front, tip roof, fire-proof Fifth Avenue house.
   This fine Arkansas gentleman, etc.

" Now while he was enjoying all that such adventure brings,
 The chase and pipe and bottle, and such like forbidden things,
 Some spalpeen of an editor, the Lord had made in vain,
 Inserted in his horrible accident column, among murders, robberies, thefts,
  camphene accidents, collisions, explosions, defalcations, seductions,
  abductions, and destructions, under a splendid black-bordered notice,
  the lamentable news that—he was dead again.
   This fine Arkansas gentleman, etc.

" But far above the common grief—though he was good as gold—
  His creditors, like Jacob's wife, refused to be consoled ;
  They granted him a poet, and a warrior, if you will,
  But said they had extensive experience in generals, commodores, orators,
      statesmen, congressmen, actors, editors, letter-writers, route agents,
      conductors, and other public characters who—rarely paid a bill.
        This fine Arkansas gentleman, etc.

" Behold, in this excitement our distinguished friend arrived,
  We 'knew from a remark he made' that he was still alive ;
  Then every journal joyously the contradiction quotes,
  The tailors take his measure, and the banks renew his notes.
        This fine Arkansas gentleman, etc."

A racy song in such a voice electrified the dead man, who
woke and spoke at length, and in part as follows :

" If any of us have unfortunately, and even by their fault, become estranged from old friends, and if in this circle we miss
any of the old familiar faces that were once welcomed among
us with delight, surely I shall not be deemed to tread upon forbidden ground if, thinking aloud, I murmur that at some time
hereafter, when perhaps it is too late, perhaps not until the por-
tals of another life open to us, but surely then, at the furthest,
all the old kindly feelings will revive, and the misunderstanding
of the past will seem to have been only unreal shadows.

" Let us remember that ' we love but to lose those we love,
and to see the grave-yards become populous with the bodies of
the dead, where in our childhood were open woods or cultivated
fields ;' and that we can not afford to lose any of our friends
while yet they live. ' Every where around us, as we look out
into the night, we can see the faces of those we have loved, and
who have gone away before us, shining upon us like stars.'
Alas ! for us, if, besides these that we have lost, there are other
faces of the living looking sadly upon us out of the darkness,
regretting that they too could not, even if it be their own fault,
have been with us here to-night, beaming with pleasure and
sympathy as of yore. Must not I, at least, always feel how true

it is that if men were perfect they might respect each other more, but would love each other less? and that we love our friend more for his weaknesses and failings, which we must overlook and forgive, than for his rigid virtues, which demand our admiration more than our affection? Let the memories of the dead soften our feelings toward the living, and while by experience we grow in knowledge, let us also, knowing that we all fall short of perfect excellence, grow in love—from within, like the large oaks, as well as from without, like the hard, cold crystals.

"I submit it to your indulgence to decide whether, desiring to be at peace with all the world and to serve my fellows, I may not be forgiven for wishing to live a little longer. If I desired to live for myself alone, the judgment rendered against me ought to be affirmed. In that case I would already have lived too long. I wish, and I am sure we all wish, to work for the men of the future, as the men of the past have lived for us, and to plant the acorns from which shall spring the oaks that shall shelter those who will live after we are dead. It is as natural as to enjoy the shade of those our fathers planted.

"I detain you too long. May the memory of each of you, when it comes to you to die, be as kindly cherished and as gently dealt with as mine has been ; and if you, like me, should have the good fortune to read your own obituaries, may you have as good cause to be grateful for the consequences of the mistake as I have ! You deserve no less fortune, and I could wish you none better."

Afterward John Savage sung Pike's own song on his own demise, in a noble tenor, a strain of which I quote :

" A gentleman from Arkansas, not long ago, 'tis said,
    Waked up one pleasant morning and discovered he was dead;
    He was on his way to Washington, not seeking for the spoils,
    But rejoicing in the promise of a night at Johnny Coyle's.

" He waked and found himself aboard a rickety old boat;
    Says the ferryman, when questioned, 'On the Styx you are afloat.'

'What! dead?' said he.   'Indeed you are,' the grim old churl replied.
'Why, then, I'll miss the night at Coyle's,' the gentleman replied.

" Old Charon ferried him across the dirty, sluggish tide,
  But he swore he would not tarry long upon the farther side;
  The ancient ghosts came flocking round upon the Stygian shore;
  'But,' said he, 'excuse me; I must have at Coyle's one frolic more.'

" He crossed the adamantine halls and reached the ebon throne,
  Where gloomy Pluto frowned, and where his queen's soft beauty shone.
  'What want you here?' the monarch said.   'Your Majesty,' said he,
  'Permission at one frolic more at Johnny Coyle's to be.

" "'Tis not for power or wealth or fame I hanker to return,
  Nor that love's kisses once again upon my lips may burn;
  Let me but once more meet the friends that long have been so dear,
  And who, if I'm not there, will say, " Would God that he were here !" '

" ' If it's good company you want,' the King said, 'we've the best—
  Philosophers, poets, orators, wits, statesmen, and the rest,
  The courtiers of the good old times, the gentlemen most rare.'
  Says he, 'With those I'll meet at Coyle's *your* folks will not compare.'

" Says the King: 'There's Homer here, and all the bards of ancient Greece,
  And the chaps that sailed away so far to fetch the Golden Fleece;
  We've Tully, Horace, and Montaigne.'   Says he, 'I'll match the lot,
  If you'll let me go to Johnny Coyle's and fetch them on the spot.'

" ' Enough !' old Pluto cried; 'the law must be enforced. 'Tis plain,
  If with those fellows once you get, you'll ne'er return again;
  One night would not content you, and your face would ne'er be seen,
  After that night at Johnny Coyle's, by me or by my queen.

" ' And if all these fellows came at once, what would become of us ?
  They'd drown old Charon in the Styx, and murder Cerebus;
  Make love to all the women here, and even to my wife;
  Drink all my liquor up, and be the torment of my life.' "

The portraits in the private volume before me of the chief
actors in this humorous drama are preceded by that of Pike
himself, who is described by one of them, Dr. Shelton Mackenzie, as " a stalwart figure, large and lofty, with keen eyes, a nose
reminding one of an eagle's beak, a noble head firmly placed
between a pair of massive shoulders, and flowing locks nearly

half way down his back." He may be seen in Washington City any day, where he now practices his profession, in company with ex-Senator R. W. Johnson, of Arkansas, whose fine face smiles upon me from the same pages. Here we have Elias Rector, the famous Indian agent of the same State, whose life has been almost as romantic as that of Pike, and whose conversation was as unique as his anecdotes were fresh; then kind-hearted Arnold Harris, of Tennessee, whose well-remembered song, "Miss Patsey," accompanied by his odd negro dance, recalls his features, even better than his photograph, from beyond the grave; then "Father" Kingman, the rich and retired "Ion" of the *Baltimore Sun;* then Alexander Dimitry, "that peripatetic encyclopedia," says Dr. Mackenzie, "who is popularly believed to have intimate acquaintance with all the dead languages, and also with the tongues of nearly every undiscovered country in the world. He translates their books, he speaks their tongues, he knows the variety of their dialects, he remembers their ballads, and sings them splendidly, occasionally translating them into good Anglo-Saxon verse for the benefit of the unlearned. I shall not soon forget the *ore rotundo* swell of his organ-like tones, deep and resonant as those which Lablache used to pour out from his capacious chest." There are many more of these portraits, but these will suffice to give some idea of the pleasant and profitable pastimes of the men of thought and action at the nation's capital ten, fifteen, twenty years ago.

[February 4, 1872.]

LVII.

Is it not true that the public men best abused are the best remembered? Certainly Andrew Jackson looms up through all the mists and misrepresentations of the past like a great

statue founded as if to last forever. Witness the tribute paid
to his memory by Henry A. Wise in his just-published book—
a book bitter enough as regards Benton and others, but abounding in compliments to the hero President, of whom Wise, during
his early career in Congress, was perhaps the most violent
assailant. Witness, also, the extraordinary memoir of James
Parton, the most caustic and remorseless of critics. Never
shall I forget the eulogy of George Bancroft, pronounced twenty-six years ago, while he was Secretary of the Navy under
President Polk, after the intelligence of the death of Jackson had
been received in Washington. The affluence of genius never
produced a more exquisite offspring. The rapidity with which it
was prepared, the fervor with which it was pronounced, and its
effect upon the public mind, excited the wonder and delight of
the followers of Old Hickory ; and if you turn to it now you
will find it surpassed by nothing in the interesting volume which
preserves the " Jackson Obsequies."   At the end of nearly a
generation, we find the ardent expressions of a partisan Cabinet
Minister equaled by the more deliberate praise of former political adversaries.   Why is this ?   Simply because Andrew Jackson's inspiration through his whole life was a passionate love
of the Union—a fixed and even ferocious determination to put
down its enemies at whatever hazard or cost.   Henry Clay and
Daniel Webster live in the affections of posterity more because
they were animated by the same principle, than because of the
fame of the one as an orator and the other as a statesman and
jurist.   They forgot party when their country was in peril, bury-
ing or postponing animosities as against even their severest foe,
Andrew Jackson, when he struck the key-note and declared
that " the Union must and shall be preserved."   Something
like this was the scene between George Wolf and Thaddeus
Stevens, some thirty-six years ago, when in the midst of the
anti-Masonic excitement which Stevens headed against Wolf,
Dallas, Rev. Mr. Sprole, and other Masonic dignitaries—even

to the extent of threatening them with imprisonment—Wolf and Stevens forgot their envenomed quarrel in the ardor with which they together pressed forward the great cause of popular education. No name can perish from memory or history that is truly identified with civilization and liberty. I was talking of these things the other day with an old Ohio Whig, at present a Republican, when he related an anecdote of Old Hickory which I had never heard before, and which I think worth preserving. After Jackson's first election in 1828, a strong effort was made to remove General ——, an old Revolutionary soldier, at that time postmaster in one of the principal New York towns. He had been so fierce an Adams man that the Jackson men determined to displace him. He was no stranger to Jackson, who knew him well, and was conscious of his private worth and public services ; but as the effort to get his place was a determined one, General —— resolved to undertake a journey to Washington for the purpose of looking after his case. Silas Wright had just left his seat as a Representative in Congress from New York. Never was the Empire State more ably represented. Cool, honest, profound, and subtle, Mr. Wright was precisely the man to head a movement against the old postmaster. His influence with Jackson was boundless. His force in debate made him a match for the giants themselves ; and as Mr. Van Buren was then Jackson's Secretary of State, the combination was powerful. The old postmaster, knowing that these two political masters were against him, called upon the President immediately upon his arrival, and was most courteously received and requested to call again, which he did several times, but nothing was said about the post-office. Finally the politicians finished their protest, and sent it forward to Mr. Wright, with the request that it should be delivered at the first opportunity. The old postmaster heard from his friends at home that the important document was on its way, so he resolved on a *coup de main.* The next day there was a Presidential reception, and among the early visitors was General ——. After a cordial greeting by Jackson, he quietly took his seat, and waited until the long train of visitors had duly saluted the nation's Chief and passed through the grand East Room on their way home. The President turned to his venerable guest with some surprise as he noticed him still seated on one of the sofas, and entered into familiar conversation with him, when, to his amazement, the old soldier said, " General Jackson, I have come here to talk to you about my office. The politicians want to take it from me, and they know I have nothing else to live upon." The President made no reply, till the aged postmaster began to take off his coat in the most excited manner, when Old Hickory broke out with the inquiry : " What in Heaven's name are you going to do? Why do you take off your coat in this public place ?" " Well, sir, I am going to show you my wounds, which I received in fighting for my country against the English !" " Put it on at once, sir !" was the reply ; " I am surprised that a man of your age should make such an exhibition of himself," and the eyes of the iron President were suffused with tears, as without another word he bade his ancient foe good-evening. The very next night the crafty and able New York politician called at the White House and sent in his card. He was immediately ushered into the presence, and found Jackson, in loose gown and slippers, seated before a blazing wood fire, quietly smoking his long pipe. After the ordinary courtesies had been exchanged, the politician opened his budget. He represented the district from which the venerable postmaster hailed ; said the latter had been known as a very active advocate of John Quincy Adams ; that he had literally forfeited his place by his earnest opposition to the Jackson men, and that if he were not removed, the new Administration would be seriously injured. He had hardly finished the last sentence, when Jackson sprung to his feet, flung his pipe into the fire, and exclaimed, with great vehemence, " I take the consequences, sir ; I take

the consequences.   By the Eternal! I will not remove the old
man—I can not remove him.   Why, Mr. Wright, do you not
know that he carries more than a pound of British lead in his
body?"   That was the last of it.   He who was stronger than
courts, courtiers, or cabinets, pronounced his fiat, and the
happy old postmaster next day took the stage and returned
home rejoicing.

[February 11, 1872.]

<hr/>

LVIII.

WHILE I was editor of the *Washington Union,* under the administration of President Pierce, a very interesting incident
took place at a dinner at my former residence, now the Census
Bureau, on Eighth Street, near F.   It was attended by a number of the Democratic leaders, including John C. Breckinridge,
of Kentucky, Lawrence M. Keitt, of South Carolina, Jesse D.
Bright, of Indiana, John Slidell, of Louisiana, and several whose
names I can not remember.   Hon. Samuel S. Cox, then a very
young man, just known for his book, "The Buckeye Abroad,"
and for his talents as an occasional lecturer, was among the
guests, and did me the honor to write an editorial against the
Know-Nothings—the proof of which was sent to us while we
were at the table, and read aloud for the general delectation.
Mr. Keitt was full of humor, and took special delight in teasing
Mr. Breckinridge by his raillery of the Kentuckians—their peculiar habits and ideas.   The retort of Breckinridge was recalled to me the other evening at the reporters' banquet in
Washington by Mr. Cox, who, after having been appointed Secretary of Legation to Peru, in 1855, was chosen a Representative in Congress from Ohio for three successive terms, and then,
on his removal to the city of New York, chosen several terms

to the same body, in which he now figures as one of the ablest
advocates of the Democratic party. Breckinridge wittily described a recent trip to South Carolina, and his meeting with
several of the original Secessionists—one of them a militia officer in Keitt's district, who had just returned from a training,
clothed in faded regimentals, with a huge trooper's sword at his
side, and a chapeau surmounted with a very long plume. He
was full of enthusiasm for " the cause," and descanted with particular eloquence upon what he called the wrongs of the South.
" I tell you, sah, we can not stand it any longer; we intend to
fight; we are preparing to fight; it is impossible, sah, that we
should submit, sah, even for an additional hour, sah." " And
from what are you suffering?" quietly asked Breckinridge.
"Why, sah, we are suffering under the oppressions of the Federal Government. We have been suffering under it for thirty
years, and will stand it no more." " Now," said Breckinridge,
turning to Keitt, " I would advise my young friend here to invite some of his constituents, before undertaking the war, upon
a tour through the North, if only for the purpose of teaching
them what an almighty big country they will have to whip before they get through!" The effect was irresistible, and the
impulsive but really kind-hearted South Carolina Hotspur
joined in the loud laughter excited by Breckinridge's retort.
Somehow the name of Baker is always associated in my mind
with that of Breckinridge. You have not forgotten my description of the thrilling scene between these two men, after the
battle of Bull Run, in the Senate of the United States—the
eloquent attack of Breckinridge upon the administration of
Mr. Lincoln, and the magnetic reply of Baker, who had just
come in from his camp in time to hear the outburst of the Kentuckian, and to answer it on the spot with such overwhelming
force. He was killed in one of the Virginia battles, October
21, 1861, and on the 28th of that month I reproduced in an
" Occasional" letter one of his fugitive poems, which is so beau-

tiful, and the last verse of which applies so strikingly to his untimely death, that I copy it here :

"TO A WAVE.

"Dost thou seek a star with thy swelling crest,
    O wave, that leavest thy mother's breast?
    Dost thou leap from the prisoned depths below
    In scorn of their calm and constant flow?
    Or art thou seeking some distant land,
    To die in murmurs upon the strand?

"Hast thou tales to tell of the pearl-lit deep,
    Where the wave-whelmed mariner rocks in sleep?
    Canst thou speak of navies that sunk in pride
    Ere the roll of their thunder in echo died?
    What trophies, what banners, are floating free
    In the shadowy depths of that silent sea?

"It were vain to ask, as thou rollest afar,
    Of banner or mariner, ship or star :
    It were vain to seek in thy stormy face
    Some tale of the sorrowful past to trace ;
    Thou art swelling high, thou art flashing free,
    How vain are the questions we ask of thee.

"I too am a wave on the stormy sea ;
    I too am a wanderer, driven like thee ;
    I too am seeking a distant land,
    To be lost and gone ere I reach the strand—
    For the land I seek is a waveless shore,
    And those who once reach it shall wander no more."

[February 18, 1872.]

LIX.

SHORTLY after my return from Europe, in 1867, I met the present Chief Justice Cartter of the Supreme Court of the District of Columbia, and Hon. John M. Thayer, then Senator in

Congress from Nebraska, corner of Tenth and Pennsylvania Avenue. Andrew Johnson was doing his level best to destroy the Republican party, and the chief hope of patriots and politicians was a Republican candidate for President who could secure a majority of electoral votes. Johnson had so utterly demoralized politics as to make it an even chance whether the Republicans could elect anybody. He had consolidated the South against us, and had corrupted enough of the North to render it exceedingly doubtful whether a Republican successor could be elected with the power of the National Government against him. He came into the Presidency under tragic circumstances, and his plans were so well laid that if our institutions had not been singularly elastic, and our people intensely patriotic, he would have undoubtedly transferred the Government to the hands of those who rushed to arms to destroy it. I saw enough after he had rejoined the Democrats—after he had yielded to the rebel element—to convince me that unless we could secure some good strong name the Republican party was bankrupt. And there was a vast deal in Johnson's theory to captivate Republicans as strong as Doolittle, of Wisconsin, Cowan, of Pennsylvania, and Foster, of Connecticut. Aided by that extraordinary intellect, William H. Seward, Johnson made the most decided onset against the Republican party that has ever been or ever can be made. Full of these apprehensions, there was something of a coincidence when I met Justice Cartter and Senator Thayer, and was not much surprised when they said, "Why can we not make General Grant the Republican candidate for the Presidency?—every body is for him ; his star is the star of victory. There are two things necessary—his own consent and an approved Republican record. Now, will you not apply yourself to a thorough examination into the political declarations of Grant since he left Galena as a volunteer against the rebellion?" I answered with perfect frankness, "that I had had quite enough to do with making Presidents. I had assisted somewhat in the election of James Buchanan in 1856, and had contributed to the nomination of Andrew Johnson as the Republican candidate for Vice-President in 1864 ; and that, with my experience of public men generally, I did not feel warranted to undertake such a task ;" but the earnest appeals of my good friends prevailed, and I retired to my rooms on Capitol Hill, and prepared the five-column article which appeared in the *Washington Chronicle* and the *Philadelphia Press* of November 7, 1867. After it was in type, Senator Thayer and myself called upon John A. Rawlins, Chief of General Grant's staff, and read it to him. He instantly advised that it should appear the very next day ; but I answered that "General Grant was not a candidate for President, and did not desire to be, and if I printed it without authority, there was little doubt that some superserviceable politician would call upon him and ask him if he had been made a candidate with his sanction. He will, of course, reply that he never saw the article till it was in print, and so all your schemes to make him President will *gang a gley*." Then Rawlins took it in to General Grant, and stayed a long time. When he returned he said, "General Grant is quite pleased with your statement of his political record, and surprised that he proves to be so good a Republican." Upon this hint I printed. But this is not the real point. My misgivings were correct ; for on that very day an elaborate dispatch was sent from Washington to the *Boston Post*, stating that "a distinguished friend of General Grant had called upon him with the article, and inquired if it met his approval or was published with his sanction. He promptly denied all knowledge of the publication, and expressed his indignation at the liberty taken by his self-styled friend who had concocted the article in question. In speaking of the Hon. E. B. Washburne, who would like to be considered the conscience-keeper and guardian of General Grant, the latter expressed his detestation of Mr. Washburne's patronizing airs, and said he could not understand why he was so constantly annoyed by his presence, as he had never known Mr. Washburne before the war, and that Mr. Washburne knew quite as little of him." The dispatch concluded as follows :

"The report of the conversation I obtained directly from General Grant's friend, with full permission to publish the same, that the country may know how far the Radicals are authorized to shelter themselves from the storm under General Grant's wing."

I immediately telegraphed to Washington, and got the following authorized contradiction of the dispatch in the *Boston Post:*

" General Grant expressed neither indignation nor annoyance at the appearance of the article in *The Chronicle* and *The Press*, nor did he intimate to any one that it misrepresented his political position. As to the remarks attributed to him relative to Mr. Washburne, they are so palpably untrue as to stamp the character of the entire dispatch. General Grant has never uttered a word against Mr. Washburne which could have afforded the slightest foundation for these atrocious statements. General Rawlins says that the sentiments attributed to General Grant in *The Chronicle* are undoubtedly those he has held, and holds still, and he asserts unequivocally that the italicized words, introducing his own words, are true."

When Rawlins came back from General Grant with the editorial, he told us with great emphasis, " General Grant does not want to be President. He thinks the Republican party may need him, and he believes, as their candidate, he can be elected and re-elected ; but," said Rawlins, " what is to become of him after his second Presidential term—what, indeed, during his administration ? He is receiving from seventeen to twenty thousand dollars a year as General of the armies of the Republic—a life salary. To go into the Presidency at twenty-five thousand dollars a year for eight years is, perhaps, to gain more fame ; but what is to become of him at the end of his Presidency ? He is not a politician. He does not aspire to the place. Eight years from the 4th of March, 1869, he will

be about fifty-six years old. Of course he must spend his salary as President. England, with her Wellington, her Nelson,
and her other heroes on land and sea, has never hesitated to
enrich and ennoble them through all their posterity. Such a
policy is in accordance with the character of the English government, but in our country the man who fights for and saves
the Republic would be a beggar if he depended upon political
office; and mark it, if Grant takes any thing from the rich,
whose vast fortunes he has saved, after he is President, he will
be accused as the willing recipient of gifts." Just now, when
General Grant is struggling out of his first term of the Presidency and struggling into his second, I thought it might not be
out of place to revive this incident. Is it not true that when
we elect a man to office we at the same time unconsciously encourage others to tear him to pieces? What public character
can escape investigation? What public character can escape
calumny? Our best candidates for office are not saints—our
best Representatives and Senators in Congress are not divini-
ties. I have shown that even President Washington when he
closed his second term was regarded as an usurper, and the end
of his administration declared a great national relief. Please
understand that in selecting this incident I am simply trying to
show my countrymen that if we establish an angelic standard
for our public men, we are not only sure to fail, but perhaps to
end in making an hereditary monarchy necessary to govern and
subdue a dissatisfied people.

Poor Rawlins did not live long after his friend was made
President. I was one of the last he recognized. No knight
of the days of chivalry surpassed him in integrity of soul and
nobility of nature. He was an original Douglas Democrat, but
no man was more truly influenced by the conscience of the
fight, and none was ever called before his Creator with a more
spotless character—public and private.

[February 25, 1872.]

LX.

Is there such a thing as unconscious courage? Of bravery against volition? A coward will fight for his life; but I know a case where a single man routed a large armed force while he was in a tremor of fear. The death of General Andrew Porter, U. S. A., at Paris, France, a few weeks ago, recalled the story, and I tell it as it fell from the lips of one of my old transcribing clerks in Washington eighteen years ago—the popular and witty Dr. W. P. Reyburn, of New Orleans. He was a surgeon in a Louisiana regiment during the Mexican war, and a close friend of Andrew Porter, one of the captains in the Mounted Rifles, and, if I mistake not, attached to that celebrated corps. He was hand-in-glove with all the Southern notables, a welcome visitor at every social circle—a fellow of quick wit, with a contagious laugh, fond of pleasure of every kind, and, to complete the picture, a very fat man, who loved his leisure and his friends, and hated work consumedly. He is dead, too; but I often think of him rolling into my room on his short legs, with his broad face aglow, his large mouth streaming with tobacco, full of some quaint story, which he would relate, till every body roared with the merriment he always started in his explosive way—fairly screaming over his own fun. One of these incidents, and one of the best, was the way he charged and dispersed a squadron of Mexican rancheros. I have seen a roomful of celebrities enjoying this really original story, as thus told by my departed friend: "You will all recollect that Andy Porter's company of mounted rifles was detailed as the escort of the American commissioners, who were to carry the treaty of Guadaloupe-Hidalgo from the city of Mexico, then occupied by the victorious American forces, under General Winfield Scott, to the city of Queretaro, for ratification by the Mexican government, which, driven out of their capital, had taken up its quar-

ʲers in that city.   Among these commissioners were Ambrose
H. Sevier, of Arkansas, and Nathan Clifford, of Maine [at present a Justice of the Supreme Court of the United States].   We
had whipped the Mexicans, taken their fortresses, subdued their
country.   That magnificent empire lay at our feet.   We ought
to have gobbled it then, as we shall have to absorb it hereafter.
The war was over, but the entire country was swept by preda-
tory parties, and no American was safe within a few miles of the
city of Mexico.   The route from the capital to Queretaro, distant some sixty or eighty miles, was beset by guerrillas, and the
commissioners, with their attendants, occupying several handsome coaches, drawn by fine horses, could not proceed on their
errand without due military escort.   Captain Andy Porter was,
as I have said, in command, and I was selected as surgeon, no
doubt because I liked him and he liked me.   Before starting,
a very fine-looking filly was set apart for me; for you must recollect, gentlemen, that we laid under contribution the best animals the vicinage could afford.   I am fond of a good horse, and
you can imagine my displeasure when I saw the animal that
had been assigned me was considered too light by the owner,
who came to me, saying: 'Dr. Reyburn, you have a long journey before you, and would not like to find your horse lame.   I
have, therefore, brought with me a handsome roadster, capable
of carrying you comfortably.   As I am the owner of both, and
as you would be certain to destroy the filly by your heavy
weight, without helping yourself, why not take the easy and safe
roadster, and therefore subserve your own comfort and my interests?'   Captivated by the candor of my friend, and not knowing that his only object was selfish, and, above all, not knowing
that the roadster, as he called it, had been an old campaigner,
I gladly mounted him, and the *cortége* proceeded on its way,
headed by Captain Porter.   It was a beautiful day, and our
course ran through a picturesque country.   The commissioners
were happy, the command in good order, the surgeon (that is

myself) in the rear—none happier than our gallant leader, and
none more perfectly at ease than myself. But you must recollect, gentlemen, that I make no professions to intrepidity;
the fact is, I suspect I am a coward; at any rate, I always kept
myself in the rear of my valor.   In the midst of our pleasant-
ries we heard the ring of the bugle in the front, then the quiet
roll of drums, and now and then a dropping shot.   I, of course,
regarded this as among the pyrotechnics of the journey; but as
the noise proceeded I felt a quick tremor of my horse, and noticed a strange movement of his ears, till at last the firing became more brisk, and the roll of the drums and the blasts of
the bugle more frequent, when he became ungovernable, until I
lost all control, and he burst ahead with me, past the commissioners, past the escort, past the gallant Captain Andrew Porter—when, to my horror, I found stretched across the road a
large body of Mexicans, arms in hand, resolved to dispute our
passage.   You may well imagine my consternation,

> " 'Never having set a squadron in the field,
> Nor the division of a battle knew,
> More than a spinster !'

Conceive my feelings when I saw myself, single-handed and
alone, without an effort of my own, and certainly without my
consent, facing the enemies of my country ; yet judge of my relief when, supposing me to be the advanced guard of a charging
column, they divided on both sides of the road and fled up the
hills, leaving our way unobstructed.   I never was in the same
danger before, and yet I can not express to you my relief at the
escape when, drawing in my veteran charger, he having accomplished his work, I quietly turned back to the escort, feeling
somewhat like an unconscious conqueror, yet unprepared for
the salute I received from my good Captain Andrew Porter,
who was scarcely able to articulate between his amusement at
my unexpected courage and his rage at the loss of a chance to
distinguish himself. 'What, in God's name, did you mean?

Why, sir, did you dare to leave your position in the rear and attack the enemy in the front? Who gave you orders to charge? Are you aware that you spoiled a fine chance for my men to unload their muskets, and to rid the road of a set of infernal scoundrels who are violating the truce between two nations?' 'Well, sir,' was my respectful reply to my good friend Andy, 'all I have to say in self-defense is, that you must not accuse me of courage; I make no pretensions to it; I am not a fighting man; I am simply Doctor Reyburn, of New Orleans; and if I have shown any thing like pluck on this occasion, you must attribute it to the infernal Mexican who was afraid to allow me the use of his good horse, and who put upon me an old cavalry charger, without giving me notice in advance that he would be sure to respond to the first bugle call or rouse at the first tap of a drum.'" You may imagine, for I can not describe, the effect of this story told by the genial, generous, frank-hearted Southerner, himself punctuating his points by his own laughter, and therefore awakening the merriment of all who heard him.

[March 3, 1872.]

LXI.

" Most history is false, save in name and dates, while a good novel is generally a truthful picture of real life, false only in names and dates." I often think of this sensible remark of a veteran statesman, now in Europe, as I glance into the pages of some of the numberless volumes born during and since the rebellion. Many of their writers seem to have no other object than to make gods of their favorites and devils of their adversaries. Perhaps there can be no true philosophy of that tragic interval. Passion and prejudice have given way before judicial impartiality and tranquil reflection. Carlyle's "French Revolution" of 1793, one of the most remarkable of that strange man's productions, as wonderful for its flashes of individual character as for its accuracy in describing events, was made up from personal investigation and from a careful review of the journals of the day. It inspired Dickens's "Tale of Two Cities," one of the most grotesque and thrilling of all his creations. Exactly such a mind is required to give us a faithful picture of the inner life of the rebellion. There are several collections of the newspapers of both sides, one that was preserved for some years in the National Library, and, I think, one or two in New York and Boston. Add to these the letters of private soldiers to their families at home, thousands of which are laid away for reference. But who will distill the essence from this mass of material? Who will digest the endless collection? It should be a patriotic and laborious man, a student like Carlyle, blessed with a pleasant style, large sympathies, and a strict and conscientious sense of justice. The incidents of the war, set forth in these private letters of the soldiers and narrated in the newspapers, would make up not only what would be the best of all histories, but reading as absorbing as any romance.

One of these incidents occurs to me as I write. While I was Secretary of the Senate there was hardly an hour during any day that I was not called upon to help somebody who had friends or kindred in the army, or had business in the Departments, or was anxious to get some poor fellow out of the Old Capitol Prison. These constant appeals were incessant demands upon the time of a very busy man, but the labor was a labor of love, and I am glad to remember that I never undertook it reluctantly. One day a very energetic lady called on me to take her to the President, and aid her to get a private soldier pardoned who had been sentenced to death for desertion, and was to be shot the very next morning. We were much pressed in the Senate, and she had to wait a long time before I could

accompany her to the White House. It was late in the afternoon when we got there, and yet the Cabinet was still in session. I sent my name in to Mr. Lincoln, and he came out evidently in profound thought, and full of some great subject. I
stated the object of our call, and, leaving the lady in one of the
ante-chambers, returned to the Senate, which had not yet adjourned. The case made a deep impression on me, but I
forgot it in the excitement of the debate and the work of my
office, until, perhaps, near ten o'clock that night, when my female friend came rushing into my room, radiant with delight,
the pardon in her hand. "I have been up there ever since,"
she said. "The Cabinet adjourned, and I sat waiting for the
President to come out and tell me the fate of my poor soldier,
whose case I placed in his hands after you left; but I waited in
vain—there was no Mr. Lincoln. So I thought I would go up
to the door of his Cabinet chamber and knock. I did so, and,
as there was no answer, I opened it and passed in, and there
was the worn President asleep, with his head on the table resting on his arms, and my boy's pardon signed by his side. I
quietly waked him, blessed him for his good deed, and came
here to tell you the glorious news. You have helped me to
save a human life."

This is the material, if not for solemn history, at least for
those better lessons which speak to us from the lives of the just
and the pure.

[March 10, 1872.]

LXII.

CONGRESSIONAL debates and Departmental reports, too often
dreary enough, are not without a large leaven of romance and
humor. Time and patience are required, however, to winnow

the wheat from these piles of dust. It is almost like digging
for gold or searching for jewels—you must endure much before
you reach the precious deposits. The records of our former
wars by land and sea, of the Treasury, State, Interior, Postal,
and Law Departments, conceal an infinite variety of material,
now utterly forgotten, and almost entirely unknown. As you
pass through the lofty spaces of the Capitol, or the dim clois-
ters of the executive buildings, you see aged men with busy
pens bending over and filling large folios of this increasing
history. If you could catch one of these veterans after hours,
he would spare you a world of pains by gossiping through the
avenues of his experience, not a few of which are full of the
flowers and fragrance of a cultivated life. William L. Marcy
used to be such a man, as, with snuff-box in hand, he sat cross-
legged in his place as War Minister under Polk, and Foreign
Secretary under Pierce. Robert J. Walker, vastly like that delicious literary canary, Dr. Oliver Wendell Holmes, of Boston,
would crowd his talk with the pictures of the people he had
known. James Buchanan was no mean delineator of the characters of the past. Mr. Seward loved to philosophize, or rather
dogmatize, by the hour. Doubtless General Spinner, the United States Treasurer, could tell you a thousand stories about the
romance of the Greenbacks. The beloved First Auditor, Thomas L. Smith, who died recently after half a century's honest
service, wrote and spoke of departed leaders with rare facility;
Admiral Joseph Smith is a treasure-house of sea-legends; Quar-
termaster-General Meigs will relate what would fill a volume
of his work on the extension of the Capitol, and his relations to
the rebellion; General David Hunter will take you back to the
primitive days of Washington City, and repeople many of the
old houses on Capitol Hill. The other day I called on Commodore Daniel Ammen, Chief of the Bureau of Navigation and
Detail, and asked him to tell me about the celebrated mutiny
on board the California steamer, the *Ocean Queen,* in May, of

1864. This event, though of a recent date, has been literally
sponged from the slate of the general memory, though still preserved among the records of the navy. A contingent of over
200 men, most of them " roughs " who had served in the army,
and had volunteered for naval service on the Pacific coast, were
shipped for their destination on board the *Ocean Queen*, in
charge of Commodore Ammen and a subordinate officer.
There were over a thousand other passengers, including many
women and children. Justice Field, of the United States Supreme Court, was among the cabin passengers. The vessel
itself was commanded by a fine old seaman, Captain Tinklepaugh. On the first day out the new recruits began to show
dissatisfaction with their accommodations and food, and it was
soon evident that, under the counsel of two or three desperate
leaders, they were preparing to seize and rifle the steamer and
the passengers. The Captain proposed to run into one of the
nearest ports and get rid of the dangerous conspirators, but this
was resisted by Commodore Ammen, who had the turbulent
men in charge. He quietly reasoned with them, and assured
them that, as he was responsible for their good conduct, he would
see to their proper comfort, but that if they resorted to violence
they would be severely punished. He was so cool and kind as
he made this statement, that they did not think him in earnest,
and proceeded with their plans. Their chief, Kelley, was a
young fellow of six feet four inches, very athletic and determined. When the first demonstration was made Commodore Ammen was in a distant part of the vessel, and on hearing the noise
proceeded to the scene of action. There he found Captain
Tinklepaugh in the hands of Kelley, who was surrounded by
the other mutineers, all evidently under his orders, and ready to
proceed to the worst extremities. The crisis had come, and
Ammen, seeing that prompt action was necessary to save the
steamer and perhaps the lives of the female passengers, drew
his revolver and shot Kelley dead on the spot. One of his im-

mediate followers was killed at the same time. The effect on the others was instantaneous. They saw that the quiet man who had them in charge was resolved to enforce his authority, and they quailed. He then briefly addressed them, telling them of his determination, exhorted them to remember their duty and their flag, and was greeted with three hearty cheers. After which, under his advice, they went to their dinner. There was, of course, great consternation among the cabin passengers, but they were soon reassured by the calm demeanor of Commodore Ammen. His next step was to go straight among the remainder of the mutineers, and to call out the leaders and put them in irons. One or two attempted to resist, but when they saw that they would soon be made to follow their dead companions, who had by this time been sewed in canvas and cast overboard, they submitted. The whole affair occupied very little time; and the commander, crew, and passengers were so impressed by the resolute courage of Commodore Ammen that they joined in a hearty commendation of his course. Justice Field himself addressed a strong letter to the Department in earnest vindication of the wisdom and energy of his action. I do not pretend to tell the story as it fell from Commodore Ammen—so modest and so clear. His printed defense before the court-martial, which he demanded, is a model of candor, and was followed by his unanimous acquittal. Had he been weak or impulsive, the scene would have ended in a grand tragedy, and perhaps hundreds of innocent persons would have perished. Men like Ammen, though beloved and honored in their own circle, and by the Government they bravely and unostentatiously serve, are rarely heard of in the great outside world; and it is simple justice that they should not be wholly lost sight of in the loud rush and conflict of these busy times.

[March 17, 1872.]

LXIII.

"WHAT constitutes a State?" is the title of one of the most familiar poems in the English language.   I could not help thinking of the constantly quoted answer during my visit to Boston last autumn in company with my friend Dougherty, who repeated his fine lecture on "Oratory," at Music Hall, in that city. The next day Senator Sumner invited us to dine with him at a place called Taft's, on the ocean beach, a few miles outside of the town, and when we got there I found among the company assembled Professor Agassiz, Henry W. Longfellow, Richard H. Dana, Dr. Oliver Wendell Holmes, ex-Governor Clifford, George S. Hilliard, Samuel Hooper, and one or two more.   The dinner itself was a rare curiosity—thirteen courses in all, consisting of seven varieties of fish, taken from the neighboring waters, each of which was familiarly and graphically described by Professor Agassiz in an exceedingly interesting manner, and six courses of game, gathered from far and near, all of different species, expressly stated on a written label, as they were sent in hot from the kitchen, and as exquisitely prepared as if they had been so many varieties of French cooking, and had been ushered in under French titles, so that it would have been difficult to tell whether the fish was not fowl, and whether the fowl was not something else than itself.   The wines were choice, old, and historical, and they were thoroughly enjoyed, although with that moderation which always marks the gentleman at a dinner-table who knows the wise stop, and never forgets himself.   But I do not desire to speak of what was to me, a plain Pennsylvanian, the mere novelty of the substantials of the feast, as of my patient study of the interesting men by whom I was surrounded. Here was Professor Agassiz at sixty-four, looking younger than most men at forty-four ; Longfellow, with his streaming locks. revealing in a snowy framework a face of enchanting and ven-

erable beauty; Sumner, who, to use the remark of another, always looks like the classic statue of some great Roman; Hooper,
the living type of the solid men of Boston; Richard H. Dana,
the author of "Two Years before the Mast," keen, congenial,
and receptive, and equally distinguished as the leader of the
bar; Dr. Holmes, with his charming sparkle, and his endless
and spontaneous humor.   Their conversation was the flavor of
the afternoon and evening.   Unconstrained, without coarseness;
animated, without intolerance; if it could have been reported
for future reading it would have furnished a precious page in
some new "Noctes Ambrosianæ."   Professor Agassiz was filled
with enthusiasm, and appeared to have realized the acme of his
ambition in the proposed scientific trip he was soon to make
under the auspices of our Government, and aided by the liberality of enterprising citizens of Boston.   He rejoiced in the fact
that America had taken the initiative in these important investigations, and explained in a clear and lucid manner, devoid of
technical phrases, the object of his mission.   England had for
many years considered the propriety of exploring the wonders
of the deep, but it was reserved for America to carry into practical effect a scheme that would not fail to be followed by good
results, and which would add materially to the development of
science.   He said he proposed to survey the geography of the
bed of the ocean.   The topography of the earth had long since
been discovered, but we were yet in darkness as to the foundation of the great waters, which is supposed to present the same
indentations, elevations, and irregularities.   All the requisite
appliances and every conceivable comfort had been furnished
Agassiz, a ship had been placed at his disposal, and he entered
upon his work with all the eagerness and fervor of a young man
just in the prime of life.   The affectionate and loving passage
between Longfellow and himself, when the former left his chair
to bid the Professor farewell and God-speed on his long voyage,
which commenced a few days afterward; the skill, the learning,

and the wit displayed in the discussion of the private character of Franklin, by Sumner and Dana; the frank and manly interchange of views on all questions affecting men and measures, answered the question so frequently asked in regard to Massachusetts. What is it that constitutes this great State? What is it that has made New England so powerful, with her barren soil and inhospitable clime? Her men. Here were the offspring of generations; the sons and grandsons of some of those who have laid deep the foundations of civil and religious liberty; who initiated the war of the Revolution, and fought it through to the end; who lighted the fires against slavery, and when slavery flew to arms were the first to rush to its overthrow; whose colleges, schools, charities, municipal management, internal finance, and the general order, propriety, and safety of whose government has no parallel in the world. It is very easy to sneer at the habit of laudation of New England and of Massachusetts, but facts are better than fables, plain experience better than theory; and as I sat in this goodly company I reverted to the condition of the South, that fought in the war against Great Britain a hundred years ago, under the leadership of men confessedly as great, and many of them greater than the great chiefs of cold New England. They were venerated every where; but what effect has their example had upon posterity? And why? Simply because, whereas the New England foundation of schools in peace and in war produced an increasing popular intelligence, there has never been in the South such a thing as popular intelligence until, perhaps, to-day, when the most benighted class, elevated to freedom, is outstripping the ignorant minority which held it so long in slavery. But the lesson is capable of a more elaborate and extended notice.

[March 24, 1872.]

LXIV.

PREMATURE death is always sad. The fall of a brave, bright spirit, as we perhaps profanely phrase it, "before his time," awakens a sharper pain than when the ripe fruit drops of itself, or is kindly gathered in. Douglas died when millions, who would once have been glad of his death, prayed that he might live ; died when his brain would have been a treasure to his country. Henry Winter Davis pássed away in the flush and prime of his usefulness. The Rupert of debate, the Rienzi of the people, the model of manly beauty—yet he faded out at the moment when he was filling the hearts and eyes of men. I have two or three such precious memories of my own—memories that can never die, memories that never waken but to stir every fibre and to start every throb. Oh! what a career was closed to them by the sudden shutting of the vital gates. How splendidly they were equipped for the race ! They were armed personally and mentally ; they loved life ; they inspired love in others ; they reveled in books and in society ; they were fired by ambition. And they are gone, as utterly forgotten by the mass who flattered and followed them as if they had never existed. But to me they are deathless :

> " The loveliest of their race,
> Whose grassy tombs my sorrows steep ;
> Whose worth my soul delights to trace ;
> Whose very loss 'tis sweet to weep."

It is only a few weeks since I sat with my old friend, Simeon M. Johnson, at Delmonico's, in New York. Johnson was a rare man. He read much and remembered what he read ; he had seen much, and knew how to describe what he had seen with eloquent tongue and ready pen. He was so kind and genial that you felt as if he must live to a great age. There are some men who so entirely absorb you that when they die you "can not make them dead." As with Johnson, when I saw that he was gone, so with our dear friend, James H. Orne, whom we carried into his vault one icy afternoon last December; and so, too, with William S. Huntington, whom you Washington people are just now mourning. I can see Orne now at the head of his dinner-table, or in his own parlors, or on Chestnut Street, or in his business—the air, the bearing, the tone of a gentleman; graceful, unselfish, polite, practical, and I "can not make him dead." I think it was two weeks ago this very Sunday that I was passing by the new club house, on New York Avenue, Washington City, with some friends, when Mr. Huntington saw us, came out on the steps, invited us in, showed us through the establishment, and asked us to enroll our names. He was most courteous, and, though not robust, seemed cheery and hopeful. He described to me his trip to St. Petersburg, Russia, and back; how many days it consumed; how much he had seen in his meteor flight. His face was always one of singular interest to me; its classic outlines indicated brain of the highest order; his whole bearing was *distingué*. And now *he* is gone, at thirty-one. Even on the threshold of an earthly future, crowded with hopes and honors, he is suddenly introduced into the mysteries of another world.

[March 31, 1872.]

LXV.

To preside over a large dinner-party is always a trying task to a woman. Those who recall the sparkling descriptions of the entertainments of Lady Blessington, by Nathaniel P. Willis, during his stay in London, many years ago, need not be told that the post is one which requires rare qualities. There is the necessity of knowing something of the guests, then the art of conversation, and, above all, easy address, refinement, and tact. When New York was the political capital of the United States, which embraced but one winter—that succeeding the formal ratification of the Constitution—President Washington's ill-health, the death of his mother, and other circumstances, prevented him from attending public balls, and Mrs. Washington had little inclination for such amusements, and was never present at grand entertainments. She was a plain, old-fashioned person, and rarely figured save in the subsequent Presidential receptions in Philadelphia, after the removal of the capital to that city.

Mrs. John Adams, wife of the second President, removed while her husband was Vice-President from Boston to Philadelphia to her new residence at Bush Hill, which she describes as a very beautiful place. She was fond of the theatre, having acquired the taste during her sojourn in Paris. "She was not without tenderness, and womanly, but her distinction was a masculine understanding, energy, and decision, fitting her for the bravest or most delicate periods of affairs, and in an eminent degree for that domestic relation which continued unbroken through so many changeful years, herself unchangeful—always making her own lot a portion of her husband's, in a manner that illustrates the noblest ideas that we have of marriage." She remained in Paris and London four years, and was forty-five when summoned to America by the election of her husband to the office of Vice-President. She was very intimate with Martha Jefferson, Thomas Jefferson's daughter, who had been intrusted to her care in Paris, and spoke of her as a young woman of uncommon delicacy and sensibility.

Mr. Jefferson kept a liberal table for his friends, but there is little note of the ladies who figured at his dinners. He was a widower when he entered the Presidency. He married Martha Skelton, the widow of Bathhurst Skelton, of Virginia, and daughter of John Wayles. The marriage took place at "The Forest," in Charles County. The bride was left a widow when very young, and was only twenty-three when she married Mr. Jefferson. She is described as having been very beautiful, a little above the middle height, with a lithe and exquisitely formed figure. She was well educated for her day, and a constant reader; inheriting from her father method and industry, as the accounts kept in her clear handwriting, still in the possession of her descendants, testify. Several other prominent men aspired to her hand, but Jefferson carried off the prize. She did not survive to enjoy the brilliant career of her husband, but died on the 6th of September, 1782, after the birth of her sixth child, leaving three female children. Jefferson wrote the following epitaph for his wife's tomb:

" To the memory of
Martha Jefferson,
Daughter of John Wayles;
Born October 19, 1748, O. S.;
Intermarried with Thomas Jefferson, January 1, 1772;
Torn from him by death, Septemper 6, 1782,
This monument of his love is inscribed.

———

" ' If in the melancholy shades below
The flames of friends and lovers cease to glow,
Yet mine shall sacred last; mine undecayed,
Burn on through death, and animate my shade.' "

These four lines Mr. Jefferson left in the Greek in the original epitaph. There is a photograph from a portrait by Sully in " The Domestic Life of Jefferson," compiled from family letters and reminiscences by his great-granddaughter, Sarah N. Randolph, of Virginia, which fully confirms the above description.

Mr. Jefferson thought it becoming a Republican that his inauguration should be as unostentatious and free from display as possible; and such it was. An English traveler, who was in Washington at the time, thus describes him : " His dress was of plain cloth, and he rode on horseback to the Capitol without a single guard, or even servant, in his train, dismounted without

assistance, and hitched the bridle of his horse to the palisades."
He was accompanied to the Senate Chamber by a number of
his friends, where, before taking the oath of office, he delivered
his inaugural address, whose chaste and simple beauty is so familiar to the student of American history.

Congress opened December 7, 1801. It had been the custom for the session to be opened pretty much as the English
Parliament is by the Queen's speech. The President, accompanied by a cavalcade, proceeded in state to the Capitol, took
his seat in the Senate Chamber, and, the House of Representatives being summoned, he read his address. Mr. Jefferson,
however, on the opening of this session of Congress (1801),
swept away all these inconvenient forms and ceremonies by introducing the custom of the President reading a written message to Congress. Soon after his inauguration he did away
with levees, and established only two public days for the reception of company, the first of January and the Fourth of July,
when his doors were thrown open to the public. He received
private calls, whether of courtesy or on business, at all other
times.

We have had preserved to us by his great-granddaughter an
amusing anecdote of the effect of abolishing levees. Many of
the ladies of Washington, indignant at being cut off from the
pleasure of attending them, and thinking that their discontinu-
ance was an innovation on former customs, determined to force
the President to hold them. Accordingly, on the usual levee
day, they resorted in full force to the White House. The President was out taking his habitual ride on horseback. On his
return, being told that the public rooms were filled with ladies,
he at once divined their true motives for coming on that day.
Without being at all disconcerted, all booted and spurred, and
still covered with the dust of his ride, he went in to receive his
fair guests. Never had his reception been more graceful or
courteous. The ladies, charmed with the ease and grace of his

manners and address, forgot their indignation with him, and went away, feeling that, of the two parties, they had shown most impoliteness in visiting his house when not expected. The result of their plot was for a long time a subject of mirth among them, and they never again attempted to infringe upon the rules of his household.

Madison succeeded Jefferson as President, and his wife, Dolly Payne, the Quakeress, is still remembered by surviving statesmen like Reverdy Johnson and Horace Binney. She was born in North Carolina, but had been educated under the strictest rules of the Friends of Philadelphia, where, at an early age, she married a young lawyer of this sect named Todd; but when she became a widow she threw off drab silks and plain laces, and was for several years one of the gayest and most attractive women in the city. She had many lovers, but she gave the preference to young Madison, whose wife she became in 1794. To this day there are anecdotes told of her peculiar fascinations in Washington City, and especially at dinner-parties and receptions. Mrs. Stephen A. Douglas (now Mrs. General Williams) is one of her descendants. She made a jolly and happy social administration. One of Mrs. Seaton's letters graphically describes a dinner at the President's, and a naval ball, under date of November 12, 1812:

"On Tuesday, William and I repaired to 'the place' between four and five o'clock, our carriage setting us down after the first comers and before the last. It is customary, on whatever occasion, to advance to the upper end of the room, pay your obeisance to Mrs. Madison, courtesy to his Highness, and take a seat; after this ceremony, being at liberty to speak to acquaintances, or amuse yourself as at another party. The party already assembled consisted of the Treasurer of the United States; Mr. Russell, the American Minister to England; Mr. Cutts, brother-in-law of Mrs. Madison; General Van Ness and family; General Smith and daughter, from New York; Pat-

rick Magruder's family; Colonel Goodwine and daughter; Mr.
Coles, the Private Secretary; Washington Irving, the author
of 'Knickerbocker' and 'Salmagundi;' Mr. Thomas, an European; Mr. Poindexter; William R. King, and two other gentlemen; and these, with Mr. and Mrs. Madison, and Payne
Todd, her son, completed the select company.

"Mrs. Madison very handsomely came to me and led me
nearest the fire, introduced Mrs. Magruder, and sat down between us, politely conversing on familiar subjects, and by her
own ease of manner making her guests feel at home. Mr. King
came to our side, *sans ceremonie*, and gayly chatted with us until
dinner was announced. Mrs. Magruder, by a priority of age,
was entitled to the right hand of her hostess, and I, in virtue of
being a stranger, to the next seat, Mr. Russell to her left, Mr.
Coles at the foot of the table, the President in the middle, which
relieves him from the trouble of receiving guests, drinking wine,
etc. The dinner was certainly very fine, but still I was rather
surprised, as it did not surpass some I have eaten in Carolina.
There were many French dishes, and exquisite wiñes, I presume, by the praises bestowed on them; but I have been so
little accustomed to drink that I could not discern the difference between sherry and rare old Burgundy madeira. Comment on the quality of the wine seems to form the chief topic
after the removal of the cloth and during the dessert, at which,
by-the-way, no pastry is countenanced. Ice-creams, macaroons, preserves, and various cakes are placed on the table,
which are removed for almonds, raisins, pecan-nuts, apples,
pears, etc. Candies were introduced before the ladies left the
table; and the gentlemen continued half an hour longer to
drink a social glass. Meantime Mrs. Madison insisted on my
playing on her elegant grand piano a waltz for Miss Smith and
Miss Magruder to dance, the figure of which she instructed
them in. By this time the gentlemen came in, and we adjourned to the tea-room; and here, in the most delightful man-

ner imaginable, I shared with Mrs. Smith, who is remarkably intelligent, the pleasure of Mrs. Madison's conversation on books,
men and manners, literature in general, and many special
branches of knowledge. I never spent a more rational or pleasing half-hour than that which preceded our return home. On
paying our compliments at parting we were politely invited to
attend the levee the next evening. I would describe the dignified appearance of Mrs. Madison, but I fear it is the woman
altogether whom I should wish you to see. She wears a crim-
son cap that almost hides her forehead, but which becomes her
extremely, and reminds one of a crown from its brilliant appearance, contrasted with the white satin folds and her jet-black
curls; but her demeanor is so far removed from the *hauteur*
generally attendant on royalty that your fancy can carry the resemblance no further than the head-dress. In a conspicuous
position every fault is rendered more discernible to common
eyes, and more liable to censure; and the same rule certainly
enables every virtue to shine with more brilliancy than when
confined to an inferior station in society. But I—and I am by
no means singular in the opinion—believe that Mrs. Madison's
conduct would be graced by propriety were she placed in the
most adverse circumstances in life.

" Mr. Madison has no leisure for the ladies, for every moment
of his time is engrossed by the crowd of male visitors who court
his notice; and, after passing the first complimentary salutations, his attention is unavoidably withdrawn to more important
objects. Some days ago invitations were issued to two or three
hundred ladies and gentlemen to dine and spend the day with
Colonel Wharton and Captain Stewart, on board the *Constellation*, an immense ship of war. This, of all the sights I have
ever witnessed, was the most interesting, grand, and novel.
William, Joseph R., and I went together, and as the vessel lay
in the stream off the point, there were several beautiful little
yachts to convey the guests to the scene of festivity. On reach-

ing the deck we were ushered immediately under the awning,
composed of many flags, and found ourselves in the presence
of hundreds of ladies and gentlemen. The effect was astonishing—every color of the rainbow, every form and fashion ; nature
and art ransacked to furnish gay and suitable habiliments for
the belles, who, with the beaux, in their court dresses, were
gayly dancing to the inspiring strains of a magnificent band.
The ladies had assured youth and beauty in their persons, taste
and splendor in their dress.   Thousands of dollars were ex-
pended by the dashing fair ones in preparation for this *fête*.

"At the upper end of the quarter-deck sat Mrs. Madison, to
whom we paid our respects, and then participated in the conversation and amusements with our friends, among whom were
Mrs. Monroe, Mrs. Gallatin, etc.

"It is customary to breakfast at nine o'clock, dine at four, and
drink tea at eight, which division of time I do not like, but am
compelled to submit. I am more surprised at the method of
taking tea here than any other meal. In private families, if
you step in of an evening, they give you tea and crackers or
cold bread, and if by invitation, unless the party is very splendid, you have a few sweet cakes and macaroons from the con-
fectioner's. Once I saw a ceremony of preserves at tea, but
the deficiency is made up by the style at dinner, with extravagant wines, etc. Pastry and puddings going out of date, and
wine and ice-cream coming in, does not suit my taste, and I
confess to preferring Raleigh hospitality. I have never even
heard of warm bread at breakfast.

"On Thursday last was the grand naval bill, given in honor
of Captains Hull, Morris, and Stewart, of which I must say a
few words. * * * The assembly was crowded with a more than
usual portion of the youth and beauty of the city, and was the
scene of an unprecedented event—two British flags unfurled
and hung as trophies in an American assembly by American
sailors. *Io triumphe!* Before we started, our house had been

illuminated in token of our cheerful accordance with the general joy which pervaded the city, manifested by nearly every window being more or less lighted. This was inspiring, and calculated to give every patriot and old officer in Washington an inclination to join in the festivities of an event devoted to the pleasing task of paying homage to the bravery and politeness of the naval heroes."

James Monroe, who succeeded with his "era of good feeling," did not follow the free-and-easy reunions, parties, balls, and dinners, under the auspices of Mrs. Madison, who saw everybody, visited everywhere, and allowed no distinction of sect or party. John Quincy Adams, Mr. Monroe's Secretary of State, drew up a severe series of rules of etiquette, which gave great offense. But when the President's daughter, Maria, was married to her cousin, Sam Gouverneur, of New York, she had quite a reception at the Presidential Mansion, Mrs. Monroe, her mother, yielding the post of honor to the bride, and mingling with the other guests. There was a grand birthnight ball at Washington on the 22d of February, 1821, at which the contrast between the plain attire of President Monroe and John Quincy Adams and the splendid costumes and decorations of the foreign legations was much remarked. They had a handsome foreigner present in the person of the new British Minister, Mr. Stratford Canning, cousin of George Canning, afterward the celebrated Viscount Stratford de Redcliffe.

Of course, the administration of John Quincy Adams was rather austere. His wife, Mrs. Louisa C. Adams, was a lady of high literary tastes and great precision ; and it is not going too far to say that their only son, the present Charles Francis Adams, owes almost as much to her care and attention to his manners and education as to his myriad-minded, indefatigable, and illustrious father. They succeeded Monroe, a man of peace with a peaceful administration, and they had a hot and violent time of it for four years. John Randolph openly charged Henry Clay with having traded off the vote of Kentucky for a place in the Adams Cabinet, and George Kremer cried aloud and spared not.   Andrew Jackson felt that he had lost the glittering prize, and took a lofty and imperious tone.   This was not a time for poor Mrs. Adams to show her social points, however graceful and numerous.

Mrs. Andrew Jackson seldom appeared at receptions and other public entertainments.   She was a plain, domestic woman, little accustomed to society and devoted to her husband, who, in turn, showed her the utmost affection.   The account of her burial, by Henry A. Wise, in his book lately published, is one of the most striking illustrations of Old Hickory's private character.   The first lady of the White House I ever saw was Mrs. James K. Polk, in 1846.   She presided at all the state dinners, and was the queen of her own social circle ; a woman of striking presence, stately and tall, perhaps a little too formal and cold, yet not the less an ornament and an example.   Mrs. President Pierce was in such ill-health as rarely to be seen save on her evenings with ladies.   Amiable, gentle, and long-suffering, she filled the picture of a good woman, and nothing in her husband's character stands more to his credit than his devotion to her during her painful invalid years.   Miss Harriet Lane was the most accomplished young mistress of the Presidential Mansion of modern times.   She was a valuable auxiliary to her uncle, the bachelor President, and did much to assuage the asperities of his unfortunate administration.   Mrs. Lincoln was always present with her husband at public dinners and receptions, conversed freely, and took pleasure in introducing the wives and daughters of members of Congress.   Mrs. A. Johnson was rarely seen on great occasions, but was beloved by all who knew her.   Of Mrs. Grant, the present lady of the White House, it only needs to be said that she sustains her delicate position with quiet dignity, and is never more interesting than when surrounded by her little family in the evening, with Mr.

Dent, her aged father, at her side. What are now known as great state dinners do not severely tax the hostess. The guests are so arranged that each lady is only called on to converse with her next neighbor, and thus an agreeable evening is passed and many pleasant acquaintances formed. The President is seated opposite Mrs. Grant, about the middle of the table, generally between two of the loveliest or most distinguished ladies, while Mrs. Grant is flanked by the two most eminent men, foreigners or natives, among the company. At the President's private dinners the same order is preserved, only that there is less restraint, and more of the freedom of the family.

In that delightful book, " Sir Henry Holland's Recollections," just published, there is a sketch of one of the famous leaders of British society, Lady Holland, which shows what peculiar qualities were required when the wife, so to speak, is empress of the household. Like Lady Blessington, Lady Holland is a historical character, and if there are any who resemble her in these days they have not perhaps the same opportunities for display and distinction.

[April 7, 1872.]

LXVI.

AN attack upon the policy of the Mexican war and the annexation of Texas always disposes me to direct attention to the results of the conquest or purchase of California and the opening of our way to the Pacific on the thirty-second parallel. When Robert J. Walker, who was perhaps the most active engineer of the annexation scheme, wrote his celebrated letter in its favor, he pleaded with prophetic ken for its effect on the whole country. The future vindicated his views, and gave him an opportunity to resist, on a broader field and with resplendent disinterestedness, the efforts of the Disunionists to use their new advantages for the overthrow of the Government. The slaveholders gave quick and earnest support to the Texas programme, and they sent their best material into the war against Mexico, but they soon realized that freedom could spread as well as slavery, and that the more it was distributed the stronger it was. They met a fearful fall when they tried to divide California in 1850, so as to reserve half of it for the peculiar institution; and they were still more disappointed when California refused to follow them in their spoliation of Kansas in 1855, '56, '57; and later still, in 1861,'62, when the Pacific State, set apart as an outlying fortress of slavery, became one of the chief bulwarks of the Union.

But I did not sit down to write politics, or to show how Providence overthrows the best-laid plans of ambitious men, but to restore to the memory of my readers some of those who figured in the early days of California. These were all in the prime of life, most of them young, and all of them seeking their fortunes. They came from various sections. Young Fremont, who in his twenty-seventh year explored the South Pass, and afterward penetrated to the Rocky Mountains and the Great Salt Lakes, and still later unfolded Alta California, the Sierra Nevada, the valleys of the San Joaquin and the Sacramento, was the first United States Senator after the war and the ratification of the treaty of Guadaloupe-Hidalgo. This was in 1850, when he was thirty-six years old. I remember him well, his quiet manners and his youthful figure. His colleague, Dr. William M. Gwin, of Mississippi, who had grown to be a veteran in the bitter conflicts of the South, where he had held any number of places, emigrated to California, like the rest, to better his condition, and was made a Senator in Congress in 1850 for six years. He was then just forty-five, full of vigor, resources, busy, continuous, and resolute, not over-scrupulous, and intensely ambitious. His wife was exactly the mate for such a man; fashionable, liberal, dashing, generous, and full of Southern partialities. Their house was as hospitable as plenty of money and pleasant people could make it. George H. Wright was then a Representative in the House in 1850–51. He is now a resident of Washington, and a sound Republican. In 1852 Milton S. Latham came to Washington as a Representative from California. He was just twenty-five when he took his seat—a handsome boy, who, after a short career in Alabama, had emigrated, in his twenty-third year, to the Golden State. He was modest and graceful, made a good sophomore speech, was never violent, and soon conciliated great favor. Few men have enjoyed more of the world's smiles and favors, and few deserved them more than this young man. He was clerk of the Recorder's Court of San Francisco in 1850, district attorney in 1851, Representative in Congress in 1852, and declined a re-election; was Collector of the Port of San Francisco in 1855, elected Governor of California in 1860, and three days after his inauguration chosen a Senator in Congress for six years. He was always moderate in his politics, though a Democrat; liked Douglas and Breckinridge; was a close friend of Andy Johnson, and never "fell out," I believe, with Hotspur Wigfall or dogmatic Toombs. He was even and genial to all; had no angular points, and made money with the ease of a fortune's favorite. He is now living at San Francisco, a millionaire at forty-five, having had an experience of a quarter of a century unusual in any man's history, with perhaps as many years before him in which to increase and enjoy his large possessions. Of a widely different type was E. C. Marshall, who went forth from Kentucky to California about the same time, and sat in the House with Latham as his colleague. He was a genius; impetuous, blind, reckless; a true scion of a gifted and eccentric race. Some of his speeches were gems; but he had no system, and wasted his gifts lavishly, while the more prudent Latham carefully garnered and added to his. Then came the big-brained James A. McDougall,

born in New York, thence removing to Illinois, and in 1850
settling down in California, where, after other service, he was
chosen to succeed Latham in the House.   What a handsome
fellow he was in 1853, in his thirty-seventh year, and how he
flamed in debate !   He ought to be living to-day, and would be
if he had been a little less selfish.   John B. Weller, of Ohio, trans-
planted himself to California in the exodus of 1846, succeeded
Fremont in the Senate in 1851, and was afterward Governor of
the State.   He is, I believe, still living in California.   Thomas
J. Henly, of Indiana, belonged to the same emigration.   He
made the longest and best stump speeches I ever heard, and
could hold a crowd together for four hours at a stretch.   Broderick, " the noblest Roman of them all," was, I think, in the
mines as early as 1845.   He fled from New York and its deg-
radations, and dug for a living in the gulches; but he was
soon called forth to lead in the formation of the constitution of
the new State, and to sit in and preside over the State Senate.
Chosen a Senator in Congress in 1856, and refusing to sanction
the treachery of Buchanan on the Kansas question, he was killed in a duel by a Southern Secessionist in September of 1859.
John Conness, one of the disciples of Broderick, was one of the
first emigrants to California, and served in various public positions till he was chosen a Senator in Congress in 1863.

The gold discovery, following directly after the conquest of
California, stimulated the rush from the old States, North and
South.   That revelation made the ancient Spanish settlement
the seat of a new American empire.   It seemed a providential
sequel to a great national event; and you will note how the
men I have named were moulded and mastered in the developments of the times.   Every one of them left home a pro-slavery
Democrat, with the exception of General Fremont; and they
were either forced into sympathy with the rebellion, and with
its collapse closed their political career, or took bold ground
against the rebellion, and so live in the gratitude of posterity.

California is no longer an outpost of slavery or Democracy. New men have succeeded the pioneers; men like Cole, Sargent, and Lowe. The bad influence that ruled the State has passed away. The old, slow ocean passage has yielded to the genius of the rail. Continents make treaties by telegraph and interchange commodities by steam. Distant nations are made neighbors, and thoughts that could only be spoken or written for a few, twenty years ago, fly in an instant into millions of minds in the remotest regions. The ideas of Broderick and Baker and Starr King survive the evil sophistries of Gwin and Weller, and leaven the whole mass of dogmas that came so near losing for us a country.

[April 14, 1872.]

LXVII.

IN 1853, when President Pierce nominated James Buchanan as Minister to England, the Senate was on the point of adjourning without confirming the Pennsylvania statesman, and he positively refused to accept unless he was confirmed. Hon. Richard Brodhead, a Senator in Congress from Pennsylvania, since deceased, was an opponent of Buchanan, and it was difficult to secure his vote for the new Minister; but Mr. Marcy, Secretary of State, and the President, finally succeeded in conciliating him, and J. B. was put through, and began to prepare for his mission. His first solicitude was to secure a competent Secretary of Legation, and he asked me if I had any such person in view. I said I had not; knowing that Mr. Buchanan was not easy to please in such matters, and believing that in the choice of his confidential assistant he ought to act for himself. Shortly after this conversation, however, I visited New York, and met a gentleman whose talents and address seemed

to fit him for the post. This was the present General Daniel
E. Sickles, then the prominent young leader of the Democracy
of the Empire State. He was in his thirty-fourth year, in the
flush of a full practice at the bar, and in the receipt of a large
income at the head of the law department of the city. I said
to him one day, "How would you like to be Secretary of Legation under Mr. Buchanan, the new Minister to London?"
"What's the pay?" "Twenty-five hundred dollars a year."
"Why, bless you, my dear fellow, that would hardly pay for my
wine and cigars. My annual income is fifteen times more than
that; I could not think of such a sacrifice." But the next day
he thought better of it. A year or two at the British Court,
with opportunities to see Paris and the Continent, began to be
attractive to him, and he said he would give up his splendid
business for the time and go. He had never seen Mr. Buchanan, and the latter only knew him as a brilliant lawyer, politician, and man of the world, who had a host of friends and not
a few enemies, like all men of force and originality. I wrote
to Wheatland, announcing that Mr. Sickles would accept the
post, and that he would call on him in a day or two. The veteran statesman was most favorably impressed, and nominated
Sickles as his Secretary of Legation. Sickles did not belong
to the Marcy wing of the party in New York, and the ancient
Secretary of State stoutly objected to his appointment; but General Pierce interposed, and the new Secretary of Legation got
his commission. I was, of course, anxious to know how the
bright and daring youngster got on with the staid old bachelor,
and at last I heard from the latter something like this: "*Your*
Secretary of Legation is a pleasant companion, but he writes a
very bad hand, and spends a great deal of money." And
again: "Sickles writes as bad a hand as you do, but I find him
a very able lawyer, and of great use to me." They got on very
well, though not without some amusing experiences. One is
worth referring to, and I wish my readers could hear General

Sickles tell it in his own inimitable way. The American legation, including the ladies, were invited to dine with a person of
high-rank, a duchess, residing near London, and they proceeded in their carriages to her residence. Their coachmen and
other attendants, under the direction of General Sickles, drove
back to the little inn hard by, to feed their horses and take care
of themselves till the hour for the return of the party; and the
young secretary told them to have "a good time." On the return of the legation Mr. Buchanan ordered the carriages to stop
at the English inn, that he might pay the bill of mine host, who
soon appeared with his "little claim." It was a startling array
of charges for all sorts of delicacies, including a full English
dinner, with "the materials," and amounted to five pounds, or
$25. " Five pounds!" exclaimed Old Buck in amazement; " I
never heard of such a thing in all my life." "Let me pay the
bill," said Sickles, in his cool way; "I told the boys to enjoy
themselves, and I am to blame." " No, sir," was the severe reply, " I will pay it myself, and will keep it as a *souvenir* of English extortion and of your economy. Why, my dear sir, do you
know I could have got just as good a dinner for twenty-five
cents apiece at John Michael's, sign of 'The Grapes,' in my own
town of Lancaster, as this man has charged a pound a head
for? No, sir; I will keep this bill as a curiosity of its kind, an
autograph worthy of historical mention." The incident marked
the difference between the men—the open-hearted generosity
of the Secretary and the exact business habits of the Minister.

Some men crowd a year into a month; others vegetate in
aimless and eventless routine. Some give a life to the collection of coins and insects; others are happy in the study of old
pictures, or busy themselves in figuring how to pay off the national debt, or lose themselves in vainly seeking for perpetual
motion; and one of the best I know spends most of his days in
collecting autographs, and especially in filling books with the
original letters and photographs of certain characters, so that

when he dies he may be remembered as the owner and com-
piler of volumes of which there can be no copies or duplicates.

But here is one still in his prime—he was fifty last October—
whose career has been as diversified and romantic as if he had
filled out a full century of endless action. He was a printer
before he read law; was a member of the New York Assembly
when he was twenty-six; a State Senator when he was thirty-five;
then Secretary of Legation at London, where he met and mingled with the best minds; afterward two terms in Congress; an
early volunteer against the rebellion, losing his leg at Gettysburg
in 1863; then one of the chief agents as Military Governor in the
reconstruction of North and South Carolina; and now American Minister to the Spanish Court. I do not refer to the saddest page of his experience save to prove that he has outlived
it, nor yet to his intermediate labors as orator, journalist, advocate, and counselor. He is what one might call a lawyer by
intuition; careful in reaching his conclusions, but quick and
bold in pushing them; as a speaker, incisive, clear, and logical;
as a controversialist, cool and wary. His recent *coup d'état*
against the Erie ring would alone make any man famous. Few
characters in our country, or in our history, have passed through
so many ordeals. Tried for his life, hunted by fierce and desperate foes, tabooed under a relentless though temporary ostracism, periling his life in battle, and saving it only at the cost
of a fearful mutilation, he survives to teach to his countrymen
the lesson beautifully set forth in his speech on the 2d of October, 1868, from the portico of the Union League of Philadelphia, and now most worthy of reproduction:

"I see thousands and thousands of men, formerly of the
Democratic party, who have determined no longer to be ruled
by it; and if the Democratic party determine not to see the future that shall lead them to a better course, the Union party of
this country will illumine the path that will lead them to a better conclusion. No disloyal party can ever gain control of this

country.   As well might George III. again stretch his long hand
to seize the starry coronet of the Colonies ; as well might the
Mohawks, the Cherokees, and the Mohicans claim again their
lost hunting-grounds, or attempt to drive back civilization to
the sea, as that old slave dynasty ever again attempt to resume
sway in this land of justice and loyalty."

[April 21, 1872.]

LXVIII.

CONGRESSIONAL habits and manners have changed with the
times, and the change is marvelous.   In fact, social life at the
nation's capital has itself been revolutionized.   If you look
down from the galleries of the two houses, or step into the old
Senate Chamber, now the Supreme Court-room, you will see
how thorough is the revolution.   Colored men in Congress,
colored men before the highest judicial tribunal, also colored
men in the local courts, deliberate and practice without insult
or interruption.   In 1857–58 a white man could not safely advocate ordinary justice to a black man.   He was subjected to
inconceivable obloquy, not alone in the Legislatures, but in
society.   Nothing but illustrious services or great moral courage secured decent toleration to such an offender.   The Southern leaders were models of politeness till their peculiar institution was touched.   Then the mask was dropped, and arrogance
expelled all courtesy.   Nobody who did not agree with them
was invited to their houses, and, as they controlled the Administration, of whatever party, the few anti-slavery men had to live
among themselves.   Now all is changed.   Men meet together
and discuss politics like philosophers.   Go to one of Fernando
Wood's great parties, and you find people of all opinions.   Look
in upon one of Charles Sumner's unequaled dinners, and you

see him surrounded with Democrats like Thurman, of Ohio, and
Casserly, of California.   Call on brave Ben Butler at one of his
receptions, and note among his guests many whom he has most
steadily antagonized.   When Thaddeus Stevens lived, his most
intimate companion at whist and euchre was the venerable
John Law, the distinguished Democrat from the Indianapolis
district.   But in nothing is the change more marked than in the
manners of the two houses.   First is the evident absence of
public dissipation—that fruitful source of evil during the old
slave *régime.*   You do not see men inflamed by bad whisky
seeking quarrels with their associates.   The night is no longer
made hideous by personal altercations.   The bowie-knife, the
pistol, the bludgeon, lie buried in the grave with secession and
State rights.   There are lively disputes, of course ; Butler and
Sunset Cox indulge in an occasional passage ; Schurz and Car-
penter exchange repartee ; and now and then Mr. Vorhees flies
his eagles with angry and fervid declamation ; but there are no
hostile messages, no clandestine consultations, no summonses
to Bladensburg or Canada.   The shots that are fired are harmless; the swords are air-drawn ; the fierce charges explode in
fruitless investigations.   A colored member is listened to by
respectful houses, and silent if not responsive auditors ; and the
extremest Democrat, even from the South, yields a hearing and
a reply to a man like Benjamin Sterling Turner, the Representative in Congress from Selma, Alabama, who was born a slave
and is now a freeman.   How wonderful is the decay of prejudices that seemed to be eternal !   Is this the Capitol in
which Sumner fell under the blows of Brooks ?   From which
John Quincy Adams was sought to be expelled for words spoken
in debate ?   In which Toombs thundered, Keitt lightninged, and
Wigfall threatened ?

And as I turn from this profound lesson, and look over the
fair city as it stretches before me from the west windows of the
Congressional Library—in which I notice colored men and

women reading in the quiet alcoves — I find other and even better manners. Cars traversing streets as clean as those of Paris in her best days, and carrying both races without protest, even from the delicate ex-rebel ladies who are coming back to us on their silken wings, ready to sell guns or carry claims, as opportunity offers; the same schools for the education of black and white; colleges for the education of the freedmen; a great savings bank, in which the millions of former slaves are hoarded and increased; and, above all, a free press, that prints words and distributes thoughts which three years ago would have raised a mob and swung the writer to the lamp-post in front of his burning dwelling. And this social, political, and intellectual revolution is vindicated by results, which, like the glorious works of nature, give joy to all and real sorrow to none. The flowers and verdure of early spring, that bloom and grow all around us, are not more truly the proofs of the providence of God than all these changed manners at the nation's capital.

[April 28, 1872.]

LXIX.

A NATIONAL Convention of delegates representing one of the great political parties of a Republic like ours, called to nominate a candidate for President, is always interesting. No other country presents such a spectacle. The best ability is assembled. The sages and statesmen and the young men of the party take part in the deliberations, which are frequently interrupted by high excitement, and made historical by electrical displays of oratory. The vindication by Judge Holt, of Kentucky, of the character of Richard M. Johnson in the National Convention at Baltimore, thirty-six years ago, was a magnificent burst of eloquence. I read it in Greeley's *New-Yorker*, of that day, which spoke of it as a gem of finished rhetoric.   The white-haired statesman who rides along Pennsylvania Avenue every morning, on his way to the office of the Judge Advocate-General, is the same Joseph Holt whose youthful appearance and splendid argument thrilled the people in 1836.   W. L. Yancey, of Alabama, was another of the bright lights of the Democratic National Convention, and was a captivating speaker, and, like most of the school of extreme Southerners, exceedingly courteous and refined.   Never shall I forget the debate between Benjamin F. Butler, Mr. Van Buren's ex-Attorney-General, and Robert J. Walker, Senator in Congress from Mississippi, in the convention of 1844, on the two-thirds rule.   Van Buren, defeated in 1840 by Harrison, was again a candidate for the nomination, but he had faltered on the annexation of Texas, and, though he had a clear majority of the delegates, the adoption of the two-thirds rule ruined his prospects.   Butler was no match for the keen little Senatorial Saladin; and when he rose to reply the House had already been conquered by the logic of his adversary.   That convention was James Buchanan's first appearance as an aspirant for President, and had he remained in the field he would assuredly have been the candidate against Mr. Clay.   Polk was an accidental selection, and was never dreamed of till the conflict made a compromise necessary.   In 1848 Van Buren's men took ample revenge by running him as a volunteer candidate for President, and so defeating Cass and electing Taylor.   Buchanan's adherents were on the ground, but he had contrived to lose the friendship of many of the leading men of Pennsylvania, and was coldly jostled off the track.   In that convention Preston King was the Van Buren leader, backed by David Wilmot, and when New York seceded the doom of the party was sounded.   Daniel S. Dickinson headed the New York Hunkers, and took strong ground against the Little Magician, as Van Buren was called.   King was cool, calm, and resolved, Dickinson witty and sarcastic, Wilmot aggressive and defiant.

In 1852 Mr. Buchanan was again presented and defeated, Frank Pierce, another Accident, winning the prize. That year sounded the death-knell of the old Whig party. Rufus Choate was present in the Whig National Convention as the champion of Daniel Webster, and made a speech of marvelous force and beauty in his support, but in vain. The politicians wanted an Availability, and got him in General Scott, who was overthrown in November by the Democrats. On the fourth trial, in 1856, Mr. Buchanan was successful at Cincinnati, because of his supposed identity with the sentiment in favor of making Kansas a free State. That event lost Judge Douglas his chance. He was taken to Charleston, S. C., in 1860, and there defrauded, in advance of his more deliberate slaughter at the adjourned convention in Baltimore. Young Breckinridge was the candidate of the extremists of that year, a curious sequel in a life which opened in 1851 in Congress in avowed sympathy with the anti-slavery idea.

Henry A. Wise, in his late work on John Tyler, reveals a picture of the disappointed ambition of Henry Clay, when in 1840 he failed of the Whig nomination, and when he could easily have defeated Van Buren. Alas! his fate had been the fate of many. Crawford, Calhoun, Cass, Douglas, all felt the same sharp sting before they were called away, and even some of those who won the golden bauble lived to find it a barren sceptre. A candidate for President soon realizes the value of political fealty, and I have often thought that in the nervous struggle for that high honor even the best man loses faith in others, and forgets his own obligations in his distrust of his supporters. The vast patronage of the office, and the vexations and heart-burnings of those who seek place, open a wide avenue to intrigue and deception. And yet, as a general thing, the conventions of the past have not been disgraced by corruption. Douglas was undoubtedly juggled in 1860, but there was no direct use of money. He was simply overborne by the South.

Lincoln was fairly chosen by the Republicans that year, but not until Mr. Seward had come to grief by having been compelled to drink of the bitter cup drained before by Cass, Webster, and Clay.

As population increases and the Government grows more and more imperial, these quadrennial National Conventions become intensely important. It is no longer a question that they are the best methods for choosing Presidential candidates, and the fierce struggle for the control of the Government is itself one of the strong points in our system. That which adjourned in Cincinnati on Friday was more like a great town meeting than a National Convention ; but its work will be felt far and near. Among the characters most talked about in that body is Colonel A. K. McClure, of Pennsylvania. He is in the prime of life, about forty-three, of herculean frame, at least six feet two, winning address, and great powers of endurance. His career has been full of incident. Beginning life poor, as a country printer, he afterward studied law, and soon became a Whig leader. He is a consummate newspaper writer, and a fine speaker. Bold, dashing, resolute, and full of resources, he is a valuable friend and a dangerous foe. Among all the diversified elements of the Cincinnati gathering there was no one man, not even Carl Schurz, who has a better knowledge of public men and manners than McClure. I say all this the more freely because I think he has committed an irreparable mistake in opposing President Grant's re-election ; but as he owns himself, I presume he best knows what he is about.

[May 5, 1872.]

LXX.

A PRESIDENTIAL election always has its comic side, and if some of our book-makers would study the newspapers of the time, a mass of genuine wit and humor could be collected. The songs of the period, the jokes, the travesties, the satire, would fill volumes. Franklin would have made a splendid campaigner, with his keen sarcasm and his homely phrases, but he died before the close of Washington's first term (April, 1790), and before he could realize the passions and prejudices that afterward entered into these quadrennial struggles. The libels of Freneau, the fierce invectives of Cobbett, the short paragraphs of John Binns, all of them first appearing in Philadelphia, would interest the country if they could be reproduced to-day. George Dennison Prentice was, however, the prince of this style of writing. Beginning as the editor of the *Louisville Journal*, in 1831, he soon became a host in the opposition to Jackson, Van Buren, Polk, and other Democratic Presidents, and his epigrams, bright and sharp, often bordering on the severest personality, were far more effective than the heavy columns of his editorial foes, Duff Green, Shad Penn, Francis P. Blair, and Thomas Ritchie. And yet, while he could sting like a hornet, he could sing like a nightingale. It is not often that one who distilled such venom into his paragraphs, could exhale so much sweet fragrance from his poems. We had a rougher wit in William B. Conway, the editor of a little Democratic paper called *The Mountaineer*, printed in Cambria County, Pennsylvania, who threw off some of the finest party songs and repartees of his time.

To Mr. Greeley, however, must be assigned the post of honor in making this sort of literature an effective weapon in Presidential elections. He started *The Log Cabin*, in 1840, to aid in the election of Harrison and Tyler, and threw such force and variety into it that it soon ran into an immense circulation, and became the basis of *The Tribune*, established in 1841. A file of *The Log Cabin* would be choice reading, now that Mr. Greeley is himself a candidate for the highest office in the nation, and might be a model and guide to those who desire to make merry at the Philosopher's expense. From this example grew an army of imitators on both sides. Greeley's followers sung themselves hoarse for

"Tippecanoe, and Tyler, too!"

and the Van Burenites roared for their favorite in the famous ditty beginning—

"When this old hat was new
Van Buren was the man."

Living men who saw those days will not forget the monster parades of the Whigs after the Maine election in 1840, when they chorused the popular refrain, opening and ending with

"Oh! have you heard the news from Maine, Maine, Maine?"

a lesson not lost upon the Democrats four years after, when they took up the same song and thundered it back upon the Whigs, who lost Maine in the fall elections, and the Presidency in the November following. Tammany Hall came forth in a tumultuous delirium, making night hideous with exulting iteration.

The elections of 1840 and 1844 were far more exciting than any of previous years, excepting always that of General Jackson in 1832, and the amount of speaking and writing was prodigious. All the best talent of those talking times was out: William Allen, Thomas H. Benton, Silas A. Wright, Andrew Stevenson, Robert J. Walker, James Buchanan, Daniel S. Dickinson, C. C. Cambreling, George W. Barton, for the Democrats; Webster, Choate, W. C. Preston, S. S. Prentiss, Thomas F. Marshall, for the Whigs, called out fearful crowds, whose glees and shouts rang from Maine to Georgia in response to the humor and invective of their orators and organs. Thomas F. Marshall's celebrated speech at Nashville, in 1844, against Polk, contained an allusion to Old Hickory, then at the Hermitage, and even at his great age inspiring his hosts of friends, which ought not to be lost. I quote from memory. It is a little irreverent, but there is a spice in it that shows how freely we treated our idols a generation ago :

"What a career has been that of Andrew Jackson! A career of success by brutal self-will. No impediment stood in his way. If he saw and fancied a pretty woman, even though she was another man's wife, he took possession of her. If he entered a horse at a race, he frightened or jockeyed his competitor. If he was opposed by an independent man, he crushed him. He saw the country prosperous under the Bank of the United States, and shattered it from turret to foundation stone. His rule has been ruin to this people, his counsel full of calamity. And now, when he is approaching his last hours, when good men are praying that he may be punished for his many misdeeds, *he turns Presbyterian and cheats the devil himself.*"

The war called out a flood of witty songs and speeches, and much fine poetry and prose in both sections, only a portion of which has formed several volumes of Frank Moore's invaluable "Rebellion Record;" but peace has made us less sentimental. Our satire now takes the shape of caricature. The photograph and the printed picture supplant the paragraph and the palinode. *Harper* and *Frank Leslie* laugh at their adversaries through grotesque illustrations, and millions are satisfied or irritated by sarcasm that needs no prose to strengthen, and no poetry to intensify.

[May 12, 1872.]

LXXI.

ONE of the sweetest poets of any age was last Tuesday, May 14, 1872, laid away among the oaks and flowers and monuments of Laurel Hill Cemetery, Philadelphia. Thomas Buchanan Read, in his fifty-first year, left Rome a little more than a month ago on a brief visit to his native country, and on his arrival at New York sent me his card, now before me, with these words: "Shall see you soon. *Am coming home!*" Poor fellow! He is now at home—his last home. Rarely have so many gifts been found in one man. Painter, sculptor, poet; susceptible, high-strung, loving his country and his friends, his soul was too intense for his body, and, like the fabled sword, literally consumed its scabbard. The war brought us close to each other. Our sympathies were in common. His genial nature, his genius, his brilliant conversation, his tenacious memory, made him a delightful companion. Now he is gone, I love to cherish his memory. I wish I could describe his wit, eloquence, and imagery. The rebellion touched his every chord, and roused him to superhuman efforts. His loyalty was an ecstasy, his pictures and his poems were effusions of purest inspiration. Who will forget, that ever heard it, the manner in which Murdoch recited the great ode known as "The Patriot's Oath?" I serve a double purpose in reproducing it, while my friend's grave is still covered with the freshest and loveliest flowers of May, and while the enemies of the nation are organized to repossess themselves of the government. The circumstances under which this wonderful lyric was composed deserve preservation. The news of the brutal murder of General Robert McCook by guerrillas, while he was traveling in Kentucky during the war, reached Cincinnati when Mr. Read happened to be in that city, and aroused universal indignation and horror. Mr. Read participated in this sentiment, and applied the oath of the ghost in Hamlet with thrilling effect.   Shortly after, Mr. Murdoch was the guest of a Kentucky loyalist, at his residence in Danville, in that State.   While partaking of his hospitalities, in company with a number of the leading men of the neighborhood, the question of allegiance to the General Government was warmly discussed.   Mr. Murdoch's host remarked that many of his friends, although patriotic, were not so clear on the subject of putting down the rebellion as he could wish them to be; upon which Murdoch said he did not desire a controversy, but if he were permitted he would appeal to their sympathies by an invocation to their duty and their principles. They gladly assented.   He stood in the centre of the drawing-room with the gentlemen around him, and there recited this magnificent appeal.   Intense silence pervaded the assemblage. At the close the entire group was spell-bound.   Tears were streaming down the cheeks of many, while others, with the solemnity which marked the absorbing interest awakened by the poet, grasped the hands of their neighbors.   The host turned to the sideboard in silence, and as each guest raised his glass to his lips there was a pause which seemed to render audible the words "We Swear."

> "*Hamlet.* Swear on my sword.
> *Ghost* (below). Swear!"—SHAKESPEARE.

> " Ye freemen, how long will ye stifle
>   The vengeance that justice inspires?
> With treason how long will ye trifle,
>   And shame the proud name of your sires?
> Out! out with the sword and the rifle,
>   In defense of your homes and your fires!
> The flag of the old Revolution
>   Swear firmly to serve and uphold,
> That no treasonous breath of pollution
>   Shall tarnish one star on its fold.
>   Swear!
> And hark! the deep voices replying,
> From graves where your fathers are lying—
>   'Swear! oh, swear!'

"In this moment, who hesitates barters
    The rights which his forefathers won;
He forfeits all claim to the charters
    Transmitted from sire to son.
Kneel, kneel at the graves of our martyrs,
    And swear on your sword and your gun;
Lay up your great oath on an altar
    As huge and as strong as Stonehenge,
And then, with sword, fire, and halter,
    Sweep down the field of revenge.
            Swear !
And hark ! the deep voices replying,
From graves where your fathers are lying—
            'Swear ! oh, swear !'

"By the tombs of your sires and brothers,
    The host which the traitors have slain;
By the tears of your sisters and mothers,
    In secret concealing their pain;
The grief which the heroine smothers,
    Consuming the heart and the brain;
By the sigh of the penniless widow,
    By the sob of our orphans' despair,
Where they sit in their sorrowful shadow,
    Kneel, kneel, every freeman, and swear !
            Swear !
And hark ! the deep voices replying,
From graves where your fathers are lying—
            'Swear ! oh, swear !'

"On mounds which are wet with the weeping,
    Where a nation has bow'd to the sod,
Where the noblest of martyrs are sleeping,
    Let the wind bear your vengeance abroad;
And your firm oaths be held in the keeping
    Of your patriot hearts and your God;
Over Ellsworth, for whom the first tear rose,
    While to Baker and Lyon you look,
By Winthrop, a star among heroes,
    By the blood of our murder'd McCook,
            Swear !

> And hark ! the deep voices replying,
> From graves where your fathers are lying—
>   'Swear ! oh, swear !' "

To add to the solemnity of the occasion, General Robert
McCook's brother, George, was present, and was much affected
by the unexpected mention of his murdered brother's name.
"The Oath," rehearsed by Murdoch, is a drama in itself. Those
present when, at the request of the lamented Lincoln, he repeated it in the House of Representatives during the war, can
vividly recall its effect. I have on more than one occasion
witnessed the involuntary answer of thousands to this electric
invocation. It is easy to imagine how it must have been received by the soldiers in the field when the enthusiastic *histrion*
visited their camps. Identified with the war, he was particularly attached to Mr. Lincoln and Mr. Lincoln to him, so it
happened that many of his productions had reference to the
Martyr. One of the most prophetic of these were the allusions
in "The New Pastoral," a poem written by Buchanan Read in
1850, which Murdoch read for the first time in the Hall of the
House of Representatives, 1864, at a benefit for the sick and
wounded soldiers. Just as he uttered the following prophecy
concerning the future, Lincoln entered the chamber and took
a seat on the right of the Speaker's stand :

> "Let Contemplation view the future scene :
> Afar the woods before the vision fly,
> Swift as the shadow o'er the meadow grass
> Chased by the sunshine, and a realm of farms
> O'erspread the country wide, where many a spire
> Springs in the valleys, and on distant hills,
> The watch-towers of the land. Here quiet herds
> Shall crop the ample pasture, and on slopes
> Doze through the summer noon ; while every beast
> Which prowls a terror to the frontier fold,
> Shall only live in some remembered tale,
> Told by tradition in the lighted hall,
> Where the red grate usurps the wooded hearth.

Here shall the city spread its noisy streets,
And groaning steamers chafe along the wharves;
While hourly o'er the plain, with streaming plume,
Like a swift herald bringing news of peace,
The rattling train shall fly; and from the east—
E'en from the Atlantic to the new-found shores
Where far Pacific rolls in storm or rest,
Washing his sands of gold—the arrowy track
Shall stretch its iron band through all the land.
Then these interior plains shall be as they
Which hear the ocean roar; and Northern lakes
Shall bear their produce, and return them wealth,
And Mississippi, father of the floods,
Perform their errands to Mexico Gulf,
And send them back the tropic bales and fruits.
Then shall the generation musing here
Dream of the troublous days before their time,
And antiquaries point the very spot
Where rose the first rude cabin, and the space
Where stood the forest chapel with its graves,
And where the earliest marriage rites were said.
Here, in the middle of the nation's arms,
Perchance the mightiest inland mart shall spring;
Here the great statesman from the ranks of toil
May rise, with judgment clear, as strong, as wise,
And, with a well-directed, patriot blow,
Reclinch the rivets in our Union bands
Which tinkering knaves have striven to set ajar!
Here shall, perchance, the mighty bard be born,
With voice to sweep and thrill the nation's heart,
Like his own hand upon the corded harp.
His songs shall be as precious girths of gold,
Reaching through all the quarters of the land,
Inlaid so deep within the country's weal
That they shall hold when heavier bands shall fail,
Eaten by rust or broke by traitor blows.
Heaven speed his coming! He is needed now!
O thou my country! may the future see
Thy shape majestic stand supreme as now,
And every stain which mars thy starry robe
In the white sun of truth be bleach'd away!

Hold thy grand posture with unswerving mien,
Firm as a statue proud of its bright form,
Whose purity would daunt the vandal hand
In fury raised to shatter !   From thine eye
Let the clear light of freedom still dispread
The broad, unclouded, stationary noon !
Still with thy right hand on the fasces lean,
And with the other point the living source
Whence all thy glory comes ; and where, unseen,
But still all-seeing, the great patriot souls
Whose swords and wisdom left us thus enrich'd,
Look down and note how we fulfill our trust !
Still hold beneath thy fixed and sandaled foot
The broken sceptre and the tyrant's gyves,
And let thy stature shine above the world,
A form of terror and of loveliness !"

Lincoln was not observed at first.   Gradually his presence
was felt and applauded, which quickly became general, as the
application to him of the poet's language was made apparent.
This poem, written eleven years before the rebellion, was remarkable.   Recalling it as a portrait of the coming man, Read
wrote during the war the following, on the occasion of the presentation to Mr. Lincoln of three ancient relics, consisting of a
piece of Penn's Treaty Elm, of the old frigate *Alliance*, and
of the halyards of the sloop-of-war *Cumberland*, nobly apostro-
phized by Boker in his great poem :

"THE APOSTROPHE.

" Great ruler, these are simple gifts to bring thee—
    Thee, doubly great, the land's embodied will ;
    And simpler still the song I fain would sing thee ;
    In higher towers let greater poets ring thee
        Heroic chimes on Fame's immortal hill.

" A decade of the years its flight has taken,
    Since I beheld and pictured with my pen
How yet the land on ruin's brink might waken
To find her temples rudely seized and shaken
    By traitorous demons in the forms of men.

" And I foresaw thy coming—even pointed
   The region where the day would find its man
To reconstruct what treason had disjointed.
I saw thy brow by Honesty anointed,
   While Wisdom taught thee all her noblest plan.

" Thy natal stars, by angels' hands suspended,
   A holy trine, were Faith and Hope and Love—
By these celestial guides art thou attended,
Shedding perpetual lustre, calm and splendid,
   Around thy path, wherever thou dost move.

" No earthly lore of any art or science
   Can fill the places of these heavenly three;
Faith gives thy soul serene and fixed reliance,
Hope to the darkest trial bids defiance,
   Love tempers all with her sublime decree.

" 'Tis fitting, then, these relics full of story,
   Telling ancestral tales of land and sea—
Each fragment a sublime *memento mori*
Of heroes mantled in immortal glory—
   Should be consigned, great patriot, unto thee."

I could fill a volume with reminiscences of Thomas Buchanan Read.   One of the giants of American literature said, "His poetry is the embodiment of nature's fanciful creation, of the exquisitely bright and the delicately beautiful, as expressed in the loves of the fairies and the poetry of the stars, in maiden purity and youthful heroism.   His pictures are poems, and his poems are pictures."

[May 19, 1872.]

LXXII.

MORE than fifty colored delegates in the Republican National Convention at Philadelphia, June 5, 1872 !   Shades of John C. Calhoun, Barnwell Rhett, Dixon H. Lewis, John Slidell, and

W. L. Yancey, is this to be permitted? Little did the lords of slavery twenty years ago think that such an offense would ever be dared. When I recall Dawson, of Louisiana, with his curls and jewels and gold-headed cane; Ashe, of North Carolina, with his jolly yet imperious style; John S. Barbour, of Virginia, with his plantation manners; Governor Manning, of South Carolina, as handsome as Mrs. Stowe's best picture of the old Southern school in "Uncle Tom's Cabin;" Pierre Soulé, with his handsome, haughty face, true types and apostles of the peculiar institution, I wonder how they would feel to see the South represented in a National Convention by their former slaves. A little more than ten years have sufficed to disprove all the predictions against the colored race, but in nothing so much as in the intelligence of their representative leaders, and in their own general improvement. If you were to compare the chiefs of the freedmen with the chief slaveholders, knowing them as I knew them, you would soon realize that John M. Langston, professor of the Law Department of the Howard University, is as thorough a lawyer as Pierre Soulé in his best days; that Robert Brown Elliott is a better scholar and speaker than Laurence M. Keitt, who, having helped to create the rebellion, died in fighting for it; and that Benjamin Sterling Turner, of Selma, Alabama, a self-educated slave, and now a freedman in Congress, is as practical a business man as John Forsyth or George S. Houston.

Frederick Douglass was famous as an orator before the war. With the fall of slavery, however, he rose to the highest position. His eloquence is formed on the best models. Captivating, persuasive, and often profound, he wields an increasing influence in both races.

But among the colored delegates in the Republican National Convention none will attract more attention than Robert Purvis, of Philadelphia. I hope some day to relate the romance of his life. Born in Columbia, South Carolina, he left it fifty-three years ago, when he was about seven years old. A few weeks since he returned to his native city, and was eagerly welcomed by his own people, and by many of the old citizens, who favorably remembered his father and mother, and had watched his own career with friendly eyes. The changes wrought in this more than half a century were more than revolutionary. The stone rejected by the builders had become the head of the column. The magnates had disappeared, and those who made them so had taken their places. It was a bewildering dream; yet the retributive fact stood prominent.

The descendants of Calhoun, Rhett, M'Queen, Hayne, and Brooks no longer ruled like their fathers. New influences and new ideas prevailed. Mr. Purvis stood among his kindred like another Rip Van Winkle, with the difference that he was not forgotten; and as he walked the streets of Columbia and received the ovation of his friends in Charleston, he saw and felt that, although slavery was dead and the old slave-lords deposed, the sun shone, the grass grew, the flowers bloomed, the birds caroled, and the waters run, as when the magnates lived on the labor of others as good as themselves, and often died confessing that their bad work must come to a bitter end.

Robert Purvis is one of the best proofs of the influence of education, travel, good associations, and natural self-respect. Few would distinguish him to be what he often proudly calls himself, "a negro." His complexion is not darker than that of Soulé or Manning. His manners are quiet and courtly. His general knowledge is large, and his conversation easy and intellectual. Educated at some of the best of our Philadelphia schools before there was any prejudice against the reputable man or woman of color, and when colored votes were thrown at all the elections, he has reached sixty, universally esteemed. His family is among the most refined in the aristocratic country neighborhood where he lives, and he commands respect of others by the courage with which he and his children respect themselves.

Yet while he walks erect in all circles, and yields to none in the graces of manhood, and in the observances of what we call society, he is the ardent friend of his people, determined that they shall eventually secure all their civil, as they have now their political, rights. No more useful or influential man will sit among the delegates to the Philadelphia National Convention, Wednesday, the 5th of June, 1872.

As these colored colleagues of Robert Purvis from the South gather around their friend and teacher, how many a story they could relate of their individual lives! Each has had his romance of hard reality. Their struggles as slaves—their experience as freedmen—their "hair-breadth 'scapes by flood and field "—their restoration to family and friends—the fate of their old "masters"—what material for the poet, the novelist, the historian, and the philanthropist!

[May 26, 1872.]

LXXIII.

PHILADELPHIA was honored by a national convention in the shape of the Colonial Congress, which, ninety-six years ago, next 4th of July, proclaimed American independence. The body which is to assemble at the Academy of Music, Wednesday, June 5, will be one of the only three that gave practical expression to the ideas of the Declaration. While slavery existed, no national convention of any party could consistently plead for freedom. And as the years rolled on, the fetters of the bondmen were more closely riveted, and the chains of the political leader made heavier. Now all is in harmony with the protest and prophecy of Thomas Jefferson and his compatriots. Thousands will be present who never saw Philadelphia; and if they will trace the growth of their country in the growth

of the City of Brotherly Love, they will study American history
on the spot where American liberty was born.   They will walk
the streets trod by Washington.   They will see the places described by Franklin in his incomparable autobiography.   They
will be taken to the spot where he was buried.   They will realize where John Hancock, Samuel Adams, John Adams, Roger
Sherman, Alexander Hamilton, Robert Morris, Andrew Jackson, Delegates or Senators in Congress, Cabinet Ministers,
financiers, etc., lived in those trying times ; and as they follow
up the progress of events from their source they will better understand why President Grant is to-day the strongest public
man in America.   Discounted by the accidents, and, if you
please, by the errors of all men in his position, you find the
great fact remaining, that he is the only man who ever had the
full opportunity, and seized that opportunity boldly, to prove
his devotion to the principles of the Declaration of Independence.   Without any thing like a party record, and without the
slightest pretension, he has grasped the whole situation, with all
its obligations, and has been as true to advanced Republican
doctrines, as these have been crystallized by experience, as if
he had made that species of philosophy a study.   The danger
has always been that those earliest in defending great truths
become hypercritical as they grow old.   Grant's rare merit is
that he accepts a fact proved by trial, and incorporates it into
his administration.   In this respect he resembles George Washington.   Washington never was a political experimenter.   He
never reveled in theories.   He was not carried away by visionary hopes of human perfectibility.   He wrote little and spoke
less.   And yet, as President, he executed the laws, kept the
peace between Hamilton and Jefferson, bore with the eccentricities of John Adams, and never lost his temper when Thomas
Paine and Philip Francis Freneau hurled their bitterest shafts
against his private character.   I need not elaborate the parallel.   You have Grant before you, and can do it without my aid.

Twenty-four hundred years of human effort, revolution, and ambition may be studied in the remains of ancient and the triumphs of modern Rome. With the torch of our new intelligence we light up and restore the memories of those almost forgotten centuries. "A railroad to Pompeii!" says that fascinating writer, George S. Hillard, of Boston, in his charming book, "Six Months in Italy"—"it seemed appropriate to be transported from the living and smiling present to the heart of the dead past by the swiftest and most powerful wings that modern invention has furnished." Our one century of government discloses wonders and trophies of another kind. The world has gone forward with the speed of magic, and as we turn back for a moment to contemplate what has been done in that cycle, what better aid could we have to illuminate our path than the living lessons of the city of Philadelphia, as taught by the men of the Revolution, whose posterity can even yet recall their features, and rejoice with us among the magnificent harvest of the seed which they planted ninety-six years ago?

[June 2, 1872.]

LXXIV.

HENRY WILSON, our candidate for Vice-President, is a fine example of the effect of free institutions upon the struggling youth of America, and also a proof of the practical consistency of the Republican party. I have known him well for over seventeen years. Twelve months younger than Mr. Sumner, he has always been his friend, even when compelled to differ with him. Wilson is one of the men who wear well. Time and trial improve and ripen them. No day passes that they do not learn something. I met him while I was presiding over the House of Representatives in the stormy session of 1855–56, and had a chance to study his character. He saw that the time was coming when Democrats like myself would be compelled to choose between liberty and slavery, and his anxiety to secure such a reinforcement to his party was shown in his kindness to and confidence in that brave and earnest body of men. And when the storm broke, in 1858, and Buchanan sought to force the Lecompton Constitution upon Kansas, Henry Wilson threw himself with especial fervor among the revolting Democrats. He consulted with us and encouraged us; he traveled far and near to effect co-operation and organization; and when my name was presented for Clerk of the House in 1859, he insisted that I should be elected without pledges. These had been demanded by some of the more violent Republicans, and sternly refused. I did not ask for the place, and would not have touched it if it had interfered with my independence as editor of *The Press*. Wilson declared that I was right, and with the aid of Charles Francis Adams, John Hickman, John B. Haskin, and John Schwartz, we organized the House, and soon after the anti-Lecompton Democrats constituted a resistless Republican reserve. Henry Wilson is a superb organizer. His temperate life and high principles, his fine health and strong convictions, his knowledge of the prejudices and wants of men, made him a great power against the rebellion, as well in the army as at the head of the Committee on Military Affairs. The amount of work performed was prodigious. He was a real break-of-day man—a sleepless, untiring, and unmurmuring patriot. A little too impulsive, perhaps, his is one of the truest of hearts, warm, generous, and forgiving. His frugal habits accord with his strict integrity. He is inexpensive in his tastes and desires, and lives among his books and his friends. He visits a great deal, and reads much. Active and quick, regular in his seat in the Senate, he is often seen on the Avenue and in society, though he never touches wine or cigars. He is a thorough common-sense man, and a natural medium between

quarreling friends.   His blows are for the enemy; his forgiveness for his associates.   He hates corruption as he hated slavery, and he will go far to punish a faithless trustee.   Such is
our candidate for Vice-President.   Is he not an argument in
himself?   Especially so when we reflect that this man worked
for the lowest wages as a boy on a farm, and began to learn
shoemaking when he was twenty-one years of age!

[June 9, 1872.]

LXXV.

I WAS a boy in a Lancaster printing-office when the Jackson
party swallowed the old Federalists, and when the Democracy
took a fresh start under the banner of Old Hickory.   There
had been no trenchant Democratic organization till that day,
when the Iron President rallied and crystallized it.   In 1824
every aspirant for President was a Democrat—Clay, J. Q. Adams, Crawford, Calhoun, and, of course, Jackson; but there
was no vigorous antagonism till the Whigs rose out of Mr.
Clay's aspirations, and died with their decline.   James Buchanan was an early Federalist, and sat in the Pennsylvania Legislature from Lancaster as a Federalist, and afterward in Congress as a representative of the same party; and when he joined the Democrats, under the Jackson standard, about 1828–30,
he had to endure many bitter sneers from his old associates.
They charged him with having gone over for a selfish purpose.
They alleged that he ought to have been, in the logic of events,
a good Whig; but he pointed to the fact that the Jackson party
contained thousands of Federalists as active as himself, and
that many of the Whig leaders were once Democrats like Clay.
This was the Democracy forty years ago.   It has passed
through many changes since, and survived many storms.   It

killed the Whigs in 1844, the Native Americans in 1845, the Taylorites in 1849–50, the Websterites in 1852, and the Know-Nothings in 1854. At last, however, it undertook a job bigger than itself. It entered into partnership with the rebellion, was bankrupted by the investment, and finally died in the arms of its ablest enemy, Horace Greeley. So history repeats as it runs! Old Hickory made the modern Democracy, and Horace Greeley unmakes it! The one presided at its marriage with the Federals in 1828–30, the other follows it to its grave in 1872. The real Democracy of our times is the Republican party, of which President Grant is the leader; but from this hour, whatever may be the issue of next November's contest, there will be as earnest a rivalry to prove which is the better Republican as, forty years ago, there was to prove which was the better Democrat. Most of the politicians in those early days were anxious to show their devotion to the Democracy, and now John C. Breckinridge, Horatio Seymour, W. W. Corcoran, Charles R. Buckalew, and even Jefferson Davis, are anxious to show their devotion to the Republicans. Thus we gather a great lesson over a grave. Under Jackson the old Federalists were buried in a Democratic sepulchre. Under Greeley the Democrats are buried in a Republican one. And now that the Republicans have fairly absorbed the Democrats, how long will the new departure last?

[July 21, 1872.]

LXXVI.

MASSACHUSETTS, and, indeed, most of the New England States —but Massachusetts above all—presents the very best modern ideal of a thorough Republic, not alone in her productive capacities, nor yet in her scientific excellences, nor even in her high collegiate establishments, but in the primary elements of general education, public lectures, town halls, large libraries, and local historians. The opportunities for universal information are most general, and almost perfect. The fundamental principle of republican government is typified in the frequent popular meetings, wherein are discussed all municipal necessities, in spacious buildings, which can also be utilized for other purposes, and which are, in every case, I think, connected with libraries open to every class and condition. The result is an insatiate appetite for learning. The whole social frame-work is permeated by healthy competition. No ordinary or superficial lecturer or book satisfies the public. Accustomed to read the best authors, they will tolerate none but the best of speakers. Agassiz, Emerson, and Dr. Holmes are preferred to feebly forcible wits and glittering declaimers. These are the influences which produce so fine and wholesome a literature in New England—which open so many doors to Massachusetts scholars—which place Longfellow, Whittier, Bancroft, Motley, Hillard, Prescott, Dana, Lowell, Ticknor, and Sprague at the head of the American schools of learning—which send forth to States and Territories intelligent young men and women qualified to lead in art and in industry—whether these relate to the labor of the hands or to the labor of the brain. When Mr. Sumner returned from his last tour through Pennsylvania, after having repeated in many of our prominent places his great lectures on "Caste," "Lafayette," and "The Franco-Prussian War," he spoke in raptures of the extraordinary variety and fertility of our soil and our productions, especially of the wonderful mineral and agricultural developments in such counties as Lebanon, Schuylkill, and Wyoming, and along the region of the Alleghany Valley. "But," he remarked, "that which pained me, in the midst of all this affluence, was the absence in your most populous interior cities of libraries and town halls, such as we have in New England; and I beg of you," he said to me, "to employ your pen in calling the attention of the people of the Middle States to the vital importance of securing such institutions wherever the population warrants them." As these thoughts occurred to me, I recalled an unpretending and humble scholar—the most active and accurate, if not the most elegant and polished of our local historians—whose life in itself is an example to our youth, and whose efforts, extending through now nearly half a century, might have been fittingly imitated by men of loftier pretensions and more numerous acquirements. I deplore the fact that, whereas Massachusetts has at least one or two first-class historians and biographers in every county, Pennsylvania has yet to find a perfectly qualified mind to prepare or to compile such a book for the State itself as would do justice to our past and our present, and fit us for the future, and at the same time stimulate others to follow in the lead of the subject of this notice—I. Daniel Rupp, Esq. He was born near Harrisburg in 1803, and is now living, in his seventieth year, at West Philadelphia. This quiet yet laborious man has produced a variety of works of all kinds—most of them devoted to the early records of Pennsylvania. Allibone's "Dictionary of Authors" speaks of him as an industrious historian, translator, and agricultural writer. Without enumerating his productions on other subjects, the Pennsylvania reader will be surprised to see how much of his time has been given to that State, as proved by the following list: History of Lancaster County; History of the Counties of Berks, Lebanon, York, Northampton, Lehigh, Monroe, Carbon, Schuylkill, Dauphin, Cumberland, Franklin, Bedford, Adams, and Perry; History of Western Pennsylvania and the West, from 1754 to 1833; History and Biography of Northumberland, Huntingdon, Mifflin, Centre, Union, Cambria, Juniata, and Clinton Counties, and a Collection of Thirty Thousand Names of German, Swiss, Dutch, French, Portuguese, and other Immigrants to Pennsylvania, originally covering a period from 1727 to 1776—an invaluable book to all persons anxious to ascertain the names of their ancestors—now, I fear, almost out of print—published at Harrisburg on the 25th of January, 1856.   He has also ready for the press a monograph of the Hessian mercenaries in the British service during the Revolution, from 1775 to 1783, and has been engaged since 1827 in collecting materials for an original history of the German, Swiss, and Huguenot emigrants to Pennsylvania.

Owing to lack of means, this really useful work has not yet been published.   Under New England influences it would long since have been given to the world.   It must not be understood as depreciating my native State ; but is it not true that, with the exception of Breckinridge's Western Pennsylvania ; Watson's Annals; the works of Chas. Minor ; Rupp's contributions above named, and a few excellent but incomplete memoirs, we are sadly deficient in literature inspired by our early struggles and present pre-eminence ?   A history of Pennsylvania adapted to the times has yet to be written.   Mr. Sypher's book for schools has decided merits ; but we wait for a work equal to the traditions, the facts, the men, and the manners of past days brought down to the present time.   When will that historian appear?

[July 28, 1872.]

LXXVII.

No problem of modern civilization is so vexed as that of municipal government, or the difficulty of securing good rulers for great cities, of regulating taxation, and preserving the public credit.   Paris became the dazzling metropolis of the Continent under the irresponsible rule of Louis Napoleon, whose chief agent, Baron Haussman, executed his master's commands without much regard for private rights, but certainly produced matchless results. The money spent and squandered upon the French capital under Haussman reached a fabulous sum, but the comforts and luxuries secured to strangers were equally unusual. London is controlled by a number of corporate bodies, and many complaints are heard against their profligacy. Berlin and Vienna are magically improved in every direction. Brussels is a miniature Paris, and the Dutch cities, The Hague, Amsterdam, and Rotterdam, are famous for their institutions of art and learning, and the comparative comfort of their overtaxed population. But these, like Edinburgh and Dublin, are governed rather by the monarch than by the people. It is when we come to apply popular rule to municipalities that the worst difficulties are encountered. The rapid growth of our American cities, the necessity for heavy expenditures in paved streets, public buildings, water, light, and the preservation of property, open the door to endless speculation. Boston is unquestionably the best-managed city in America, mainly because there is very little politics in its administration, a severe system of finance, a police extending over the State, and a rigid attendance at the primary elections by prominent men. He who visits Washington to-day, after an absence of twenty years, will be amazed at its progress and its promises. We may prefigure its future by its contrast with the past. As we remember its dusty streets in summer and its muddy streets in winter, its poor hotels and boarding-houses, its miserable police, its disorganized finances, in the light of its increasing miles of broad and beautiful drives, its new temples of education and learning, its gallery of art, its splendid public edifices, with the superb Capitol crowning the whole, unsurpassed in the world, we may easily anticipate the day when Washington will be the favorite and the loveliest city on our side of the sea. President Grant struck the key-note when he appointed Henry D. Cooke Governor of the District of Columbia under the Congressional act of reorganization, which made the popular branch of the local Legislature elective, and gave the people a Delegate in Congress. Mr. Cooke is one of the many proofs of the wisdom of our Chief Magistrate. He is just forty-seven, and when he accepted the post had accumulated a handsome fortune, which placed him beyond temptation. Whatever may be said of the propriety of opening public positions to every condition, experience has proved that the mayor of a great city should be beyond pecuniary want. Undoubtedly the choice of such a man as William M. Tweed at the head of perhaps the most important department in the city of New York opened the way to that series of speculations and corruptions which tottered to its fall, amid the congratulations of the people, in the autumn of 1871. In olden times, the mayors (for instance) of Philadelphia were men who had acquired independence by long years of industry and frugality, and our people proudly recall the days when worthy citizens like Wharton, Scott, and Page acted in that capacity. It is true, Philadelphia during that time was not what it is to-day, with its increasing population and necessities. Perhaps, if they were now in command, they would not escape the censure so fiercely passed upon their successors. Governor Cooke, at the head of the government of the District of Columbia, has come in for his full share of criticism, but his vindication closely follows the proofs of the justice and the sagacity of his administration. His career is an example of his fitness to preside over the destinies of a great cosmopolitan centre. Born in Ohio, educated at Meadville, Pennsylvania, bred to the law, then a school-teacher and a newspaper editor in Philadelphia, where he formed the acquaintance of literary lights like Joseph R. Chandler, Joseph C. Neal, and Robert T. Conrad, then Vice-Consul at one of the South American ports under his connection, Consul-General William G. Moorhead, more than twenty-five years ago, and finally finding fortune in acquiring a knowledge of banking under Jay Cooke, in Philadelphia, his removal to Washington, at the beginning of Mr. Lincoln's administration, and his connection afterward with the great banking-house with which he is still identified, he has gathered enough knowledge of men to qualify him for the arduous services which have made Washington City what it is. Fine manners, princely hospitality, warm and ardent sympathies with the new citizens and the cause of universal education, make him acceptable to every class. Never a politician in the vulgar interpretation of that word, although a sincere and consistent Republican, and rich enough, as I have said, to escape suspicion, his intercourse with the Representatives and Senators in Congress of every shade is agreeable to himself and profitable to his constituents. The generous bounty of Congress to the District at the last session, inspired by the explicit recommendations of General Grant in his annual message, is to be attributed to the confidence reposed in Governor Cooke; and when our law-makers meet in December they will be surprised at the enormous amount of work done under the auspices of Governor Cooke and the energetic Board of Public Works appointed by the President, with Alexander R. Shepherd at their head.

In five years from to-day the District of Columbia will be the choice winter resort of the country, and will be to the people of wealth and intelligence—to inventors, our men of science, and to foreigners, an irresistible attraction. Directly connected, North and South, by new railroads, and offering extraordinary inducements to persons of moderate means who desire to live in a healthy climate and to enjoy the best society, it will be sought by men from every State, whether as visitors or residents. And when that day comes, no name will be more affectionately remembered and honored than that of Governor Henry D. Cooke.

[August 4, 1872.]

LXXVIII.

" OUR future leaders—where are they to come from?" was
the question of a friend, a short time ago, after an interesting
discussion on the necessity of securing the best material in the
management of government, society, and business. We were
looking out of the window of my editorial room in Philadelphia.
I answered, pointing to the newsboys and bootblacks congregated at the corner of Seventh and Chestnut Streets, "There
are your future leaders. That little fellow with the curly hair
is an embryo merchant; that one with torn trowsers is the sap-
ling of a sturdy politician; that black-eyed lad is saving his
money to pay for a collegiate education." And has it not been
so of most of the strong men of our times? On the Pacific
coast many of the great houses grew from just such seeds.
Sargent, the United States Senator elect, visited Philadelphia
twenty-five years ago to get work as a journeyman printer, and
failed; Latham, the millionaire, who has been in both houses
of Congress and Governor of the State, began life very poor;
Broderick was in New York a Bowery boy in 1847; and the
railroad kings, most of them, began life as low down as the little Bohemians at our corner. The sons of the rich, the educated darlings of the great families, are nowhere. All their
gifts were so many fatal temptations, and they themselves are
forgotten, like bad copies of good pictures. "It is the rough
brake that virtue must go through."

A recent writer insists that a grandfather is no longer a social institution. Men do not live in the past. They rarely
look back. "Forward!" is the universal cry. Perhaps our
reverence for our ancestors suffers, but such a thing as a great
family in this country helps nobody. Even the Adamses of the
present day make little out of their former generations of greatness. Thomas Hughes struck the key-note when he said that

the absence of the laws of primogeniture and entail in this
country opened a wide door to poor young men, and compelled
the very rich to spend their money in good deeds to save it
from being wasted by their posterity, and thus great fortunes
change hands almost as rapidly as the changes of life.   But we
must not forget that many of the most useful and illustrious of
the English leaders are the growth of the long years of patient
study and careful rearing of their fathers.   One fault of our
system is the absence of this very experience, and the presence
of so much undisciplined intellect in our public places.   Yet,
with all these drawbacks, how easily the machinery of American
government moves on; how successfully it survives accident;
how providentially it seems to order and control itself!   And,
though we sometimes mourn for our great ones gone, there is
not a day that does not teach the wholesome lesson that nobody
is necessary or indispensable.   Every hour some new man
starts up to fill the vacancy made by the death of an old leader,
and in nearly every instance the new man is found equal to the
emergency.   Ours may be called the Age of Utility.   We are
not prolific of statesmen or orators, and politics has degenerated
into a poor strife between speculators and mediocrities.   But
for all this the country is safe.   One such man as Leland Stan-
ford, of the Central Pacific Railroad, or Dean Richmond, of the
New York Central, or Ben Holliday, Jr., of Oregon, or John Ed-
gar Thomson, or his vigorous vice-president, Thomas A. Scott,
may do more practical good, and has more real power, than a
Webster or Clay.   And when we consider that, like Webster
and Clay, they have all risen from small beginnings, is it going
too far to say that they may purify and elevate our politics even
as they extend their great enterprises and enrich themselves?
He who inherits wealth without mind is always sure to under-
rate mind, but he who by sheer hard knocks works his own way
through the rock of adversity into affluence, is sure to set a
high price upon intellect.   And thus it stands that many of

those who have grown to great riches by their own exertions have taken every opportunity, like Asa Packer, Pardee, Cornell, A. T. Stewart, George Peabody, and George W. Childs, to give liberally to the education of the masses from whom they sprang.

[September 15, 1872.]

LXXIX.

I HAVE been enjoying, for the first time, William H. Seward's "Life of John Quincy Adams," published in 1849, and I pronounce it among the best biographies I ever read. It is the tribute of one great man to another. I do not compare Mr. Seward to John Quincy Adams, but if any writer in his forty-ninth year—the age when Seward wrote his life of Adams—would now undertake the same work for Seward, he would produce a book of uncommon interest. Mr. Adams was over eighty when he died in the Capitol of the country he had served so well. Mr. Seward is now in his seventy-second year, and his experience, though not marked by the austere lines of that of Adams, is one of the eventful examples of our day. He "still lives" at Auburn, New York, in a body wrecked by accident and the assassin's dagger; but his intellect shines through the shattered casket like light through a ruined castle. He will be fortunate if the historian of his varied and somewhat grotesque career—a combination as it was of curious evolutions, daring experiments, and very great abilities—is as careful and thoughtful a delineator of human nature as the biographer of John Quincy Adams.

But I did not intend to compliment Mr. Seward, nor to draw a parallel between him and John Quincy Adams, in nothing more striking than the fact that both are supposed to have kept a close and graphic detail or diary of their political and official relations. The volume before me, chiefly the product of his brain, has been so long forgotten, and contains so many new suggestions, at least to the present generation, that a glance through its pages may be pleasant and profitable to the reader of these Anecdotes.

The American progenitor of the Adams family was Henry Adams, who fled in 1639 from ecclesiastical oppression in England, and was a member of the first Christian Church at Mount Wollaston, the present town of Quincy, Massachusetts, and died on the 8th of October, 1646. His memory is preserved by a plain granite monument in the burial-ground of Quincy, upon which John Adams, second President of the United States, caused the following inscription to be carved :

"In Memory of

Henry Adams,

"Who took his flight from the dragon Persecution in Devonshire, in England, and alighted, with eight sons, near Mount Wollaston. One of the sons returned to England, and, after taking time to explore the country, four removed to Medfield and the neighboring towns, two to Chelmsford.

"One only, Joseph, who lies here at his left hand, remained here, who was an original proprietor in the Township of Braintree, incorporated in the year 1639.

"This stone and several others have been placed in this yard, by a great-great-grandson, from a veneration of the piety, humility, simplicity, prudence, patience, temperance, frugality, industry, and perseverance of his ancestors, in hope of recommending an imitation of their virtues to their posterity."

If we trace the descendants of Henry Adams we shall realize how faithfully the ideas carved on the stony monument of their great ancestor have been cherished. Three generations have attested their devotion to these valuable precepts. I recollect no American family that can point to so many great minds, all formed, as it were, upon one model. The sons of the living Charles Francis Adams, himself the son of John Quincy, are far above the common standard, John Quincy Adams, Jr., being a political leader of acknowledged power, and a writer of uncommon gifts. But none of the name, not even the second President, have made such a mark upon his age as the successor of James Monroe.

Mr. Seward shows how carefully John Quincy Adams was trained for the battle of life. At a period when our American youth are too apt to neglect their precious and surpassing opportunities, it may be useful to recall the boyhood of that remarkable man. Born at Quincy, May 11, 1767, he was literally cradled in the Revolution, and almost baptized in its blood. His great grandfather, Quincy, on his mother's side, was dying, and his daughter, grandmother of young John Quincy, was present at the birth of the latter, and insisted that he might receive the name of Quincy; and in one of his letters the incident is thus referred to : " The fact, recorded by my father at the time, has connected with portions of my name a charm of mingled sensibility and devotion. It was filial tenderness that gave the name. It was the name of one passing from earth to immortality. These have been among the strongest links of my attachment to the name of Quincy, *and have been, through life, a perpetual admonition to do nothing unworthy of it.*" Fortified by the example of his ancestors on both sides, and by the care of a cultivated father and a careful mother, he was so studious and manly that Edward Everett, in his eulogy, said : " There seemed to be in his life no such stage as that of boyhood." When only nine years old he wrote as follows to his father :

" BRAINTREE, June 2, 1777.

" DEAR SIR,—I love to receive letters very well, much better than I love to write them. My head is much too fickle. My thoughts are running after birds' eggs, play, and trifles, till I am vexed with myself. Mamma has a troublesome task to keep me studying. I own I am ashamed of myself. I have but just entered the third volume of Rollin's History, but designed to have got half through it by this time. I am determined this week to be more diligent. Mr. Thaxter [his teacher] is absent at court. I have set myself a task this week—to read the third volume half out. If I can keep my

resolution, I may again at the end of the week give a better account of myself. I wish, sir, you would give me in writing some instructions with regard to the use of my time, and advise me how to proportion my reading and
play, and I will keep them by me and endeavor to follow them. With the
present determination of growing better, I am, dear sir, your son,

"JOHN QUINCY ADAMS.

"P. S.—SIR,—If you will be so good as to favor me with a blank book, I
will transcribe the most remarkable passages I meet with in my reading,
which will serve to fix them upon my mind."

Here we see the beginning of that extraordinary diary which
was continued down to the period of his death in the Speaker's
room of the House of Representatives, on the 23d of February,
1848. That great work has not yet seen the light, but is in
process of preparation for publication by his son, Charles Francis Adams, and will be issued at an early day by the great house
of J. B. Lippincott & Co., Philadelphia. The value of such a
diary is proved by Mr. Seward's biography. It is in most cases
infallible, and whenever Mr. Adams allowed a reference to be
made to its pages, the evidence was decisive. Accurate and
painstaking in every thing, living by rule, he stated a fact exactly as it occurred, and at the exact time, and from his authority there could be no appeal. Mr. Seward himself seems to
have adopted John Quincy Adams as his model, at least in his
later years. His late travels round the world, his steady refusal
to intermix with passing politics, and his entire independence in
the expression of his opinions, taken in connection with the
general belief that he is busy preparing his own memoirs, show
that, unlike most retired statesmen, he is not insensible of the
world's judgment, and that in his old age he is still keenly alive
to the progress of his country. But he can leave no memento
that will do him more credit than his "Life of John Quincy
Adams," published in 1849.

[September 22, 1872.]

LXXX.

Now that the Territories have assumed a significance, not to say grandeur, unknown in the days of Jackson and Polk, we may better appreciate Thomas H. Benton's stereotyped advice whenever a young man called on him in Washington to ask his influence for a clerkship in one of the Departments: "Go to the Territories, sir; or to one of the new States. Go to Iowa or Missouri; go to Wisconsin or Illinois. If you are a lawyer, hang out your shingle and show that you are deserving; if a farmer, buy a quarter-section of land and cultivate it; if a mechanic, open your shop and work; but don't stay here to burn yourself out with rum, or to rust with idleness. Do any thing but serve as a slave in one of these wretched bureaus." Good advice thirty, forty, even fifty years ago, and better to-day. The men who went forth into the Territories in Benton's time, when he left Tennessee for Missouri, or when Sam Houston left Tennessee for Texas, or when John C. Breckinridge tried his young fortunes by removing from Kentucky to Iowa, after the Mexican war; like the early pioneers to other regions, when the West was bounded by the Missouri River—these men had a hard time of it. They had to meet not only a primitive people, but to traverse a primitive country, with few or no conveniences, either of food or of shelter, and to give weeks and months of valuable time before they reached their destination. How different to-day! We go West in palace cars, swift "as the sightless couriers of the air," to find even in the heart of the Rocky Mountains, and in the defiles of the Sierras, the best luxuries of life, and the choicest temptations to business enterprise or professional ambition. These modern inducements take off much of the superior material of the older States, and we need not be surprised if the West and the Pacific slope furnish, hereafter, the strongest minds in public affairs. Perhaps the mani-

fest depreciation of the lawyers of the old States is to be attributed to the exodus to the more attractive fields of our young
men.   Brains have not long to wait for employment in the Territories; they are in constant demand, and always at a premium.   Money goes a great way, but it can not forever buy mediocrity into office.   There are too many competitors for the
prizes, and in fact too much capital in the hands of able men
to give an inferior man a superior chance.   No doubt money
decides many a contest, but the winner is nearly always fit to
fill the place he secures.   As the opportunities for wealth increase with the chances for preferment, you may prepare for a
new rush to the Territories without parallel.   We are, in fact,
in the mere infancy of development.   Marvelous as the contrast is between the present and the past, it is as nothing to the
contrast between the present and the near future.   Our progress has many opulent worlds to redeem and some to conquer
from our neighbors.   Men like Senators Nye and Stewart, of
Nevada, Governor Evans, of Colorado, Governor McCormick,
of Arizona, Ben Holliday, of Oregon, and W. C. Rallston, of
California, fortunate and honored as they are, will be succeeded by intellects as marked, and by success as brilliant; and
most of us will live to see it for ourselves, and to realize that,
however heavy the reinforcements, there is room enough and
reward enough for all.

[October 6, 1872.]

LXXXI.

Now we add to the catalogue of the suddenly called the
name of the beloved William Prescott Smith, of Baltimore, who
died last Tuesday evening, October 1, in his forty-eighth year.
It seems only yesterday that I rode with him to Philadelphia,

the time passing swiftly under the influence of his pathos and humor. I can recall no character that filled a larger space with brighter gifts. He was in every respect an original man, a combination and a form indeed of most diversified qualities. For many years identified with the Baltimore and Ohio Railroad, and lately recalled to an important position in its management, he was as accurate in his business aptitudes as he was genial in social and literary circles. Successful alike in his dealings with the stern chiefs of great enterprises, he was beloved by all his associates and subordinates, and when he turned from work, to rest from his official duties, to books and the fine arts, he was a companion for scholars and statesmen. Nature had endowed him with a rarely handsome form and features. His manners were unusually fascinating ; his tastes were cultivated and refined ; his memory acute and tenacious ; his knowledge of men most thorough. Modest and retiring, he bore himself like a prince in every presence. His ambition seemed to be to make others happy. In society always a universal favorite, and invited every where, his wit shone and sparkled, but never stung. He had no enmities and few enemies, never mixed in politics, and conciliated the affection and confidence of most antagonistic elements. His genius was as marked in the hard attritions of railroad competition as in the skill with which he invented the means of intellectual enjoyment. To soften asperities, to smooth the pathway of life, to befriend the distressed, and to help forward poor young men, these were his chosen ambitions. His mind was instinctively elevated, and when he threw off his daily cares it was surprising to note the variety and purity of his comic talent. Who that ever witnessed his imitations and his burlesques can recall one that approached vulgarity ? I remember our voyage across the Atlantic, our rambles through England, and our experiences in France ; how fresh and ever-renewing his fun ; how vivid his perceptions ; how full and ripe his knowledge as he reviewed it in the famous historical places ;

and how, when he longed for home, he would brighten the gloom with some fitting story, or mimic one of the many odd foreigners around us. He was naturally considerate and unselfish, and his deafness made me always anxious to amuse him by that which pleased his eye; but he would anticipate me by taking tickets for the theatre or the lecture-room, and, though he could scarcely hear a word, would appear to enjoy himself like others. He had a habit of ridiculing politicians by making speeches in which he would travestie their manners and make them express thoughts exactly opposite to their own. No comedy ever surpassed these capital scenes, and when he had his friends around him at his own house, he delighted to surprise them by some entertainment, always novel and yet always pointed with a moral. Who can ever forget his Washington's Farewell Address in the Revolutionary costume of the Father of his Country? It was a composition worthy of Boucicault or Dickens. These and his books were the pleasures of his leisure hours. And now our friend, so full of health and hope only a few days ago, is laid away among his fathers. Lost to us his beaming smile, his splendid form, his grace, his courtesy, his flowing humor, his gentleness, and his generosity; every thing gone but their memory, which will live long in the hearts of thousands who were made happy by his own happy nature, and better by a native toleration and affection at once impartial and sincere.

[October 6, 1872.]

LXXXII.

PRESIDENTIAL elections are proverbially uncertain until the October contests are decided, and many conflicting hopes are entertained by rival parties. The exultation of the victors and the disappointment of the vanquished are naturally extreme. Never shall I forget the exciting struggle in 1844, when James K. Polk defeated Henry Clay. The rejoicing of the Democrats and the agony of the Whigs of Philadelphia were literally terrific. Francis R. Shunk had been elected Governor of Pennsylvania in the previous October by a small majority, and the struggle in November was intense. Immense sums were hazarded by the betting men ; but when the October fiat was pronounced in Pennsylvania, the verdict in November was decided. It also practically decided the fate of the Whigs as a party. Mr. Clay was regarded as so far superior to Mr. Polk that the triumph of the latter was accepted as the recognition of a mere politician and the degradation of a great statesman. The Kentuckian never recovered from it. His real chance was lost in 1840, when Harrison was elected over Van Buren, and I was not surprised at his violence after his party had preferred a military availability, so graphically described by Henry A. Wise in his biography of John Tyler, just published by J. B. Lippincott. There was no actual contest in 1848, for the Democrats were divided between Cass and Van Buren, and General Taylor had an easy time of it. In 1852 the Whigs made their last stand as a party. Having set Mr. Clay aside in 1844, they ignored Webster for Scott in 1852, and broke the heart of the great New-Englander. Pierce literally walked over the course, aided by hosts of angry Whigs. But in 1856 the old fires were relighted. The Republicans came on the stage that year in great force, openly flying the banner of anti-slavery, and they would have won but for the pledges of the Democratic candidate of justice to Kansas. The October fight in 1856 in Pennsylvania decided the Presidency. The Democratic majority was small, but it did the work in November. In 1860 there was again not much of a struggle, for there was a hopeless division among the Democrats, who from that time began to grow weaker and weaker, until their folly ripened into the rebellion.

That overthrown, the drama was soon ended. Their single hope of recovery, after General Grant's inevitable re-election, is to accept Republican ideas in full, and to earn the confidence of the country by long and honest devotion to them.

Equanimity in defeat is as pleasant, and yet as difficult to exercise, as magnanimity in victory. A good story is told of the veteran Major Noah, of New York, who, after having been several times chosen to a valuable local office, lost renomination and ran as a stump candidate, and was badly beaten. His negro man, not realizing the event, and not understanding that the groans of the nocturnal visitors to the Major's mansion were any different from their cheers of former times when they came to congratulate him on his triumph, rushed to his master's study, exclaiming, "The boys are at the door, and want to see you." "Give them my respects, Sam," was the good-natured reply, "and tell them they have left the Democratic party." Mr. Clay once sarcastically announced to Van Buren, while the latter was Vice-President, a great Whig triumph, upon which Van Buren left the chair, and, walking to the Kentucky Senator's seat, took a pinch of snuff out of his box, and then drew himself up directly in front of him and heard him through. I saw Judge Douglas in the House of Representatives in February of 1861, while the electoral votes were being counted, announcing his defeat and Lincoln's election, and could not sufficiently admire his *bonhomie* and wit. It was a period of painful suspense. Breckinridge, as Vice-President, was president of the convention of the two houses, and had himself been defeated for the first office in the nation. Many of the Southern Senators and members had left their seats in advance of the formal act of secession, and some of those who remained were glowering over the constitutional act of recording the vote of the people in favor of the abolitionist, Abraham Lincoln. They had a special hatred of Douglas, whose refusal to yield to Breckinridge had given the election to Lincoln ; but how well he bore himself, how jovially, how easily, none but those who saw him can conceive. Hate and distrust around him—the hate of the Democrats and the distrust of the Republicans ; but through all he bore himself like the truly great man he was. In six months he was in his grave.

[October-14, 1872.]

LXXXIII.

DURING the exciting contest led by the *Philadelphia Press* against James Buchanan's Administration, I was invited on the evening of October 28, 1858, to speak in the beautiful city of Camden, New Jersey. My audience was large, and my reception cordial. *The Press* had attained a considerable circulation in Camden, and a great majority of all parties sympathized with me in my somewhat hazardous and independent stand.

The following passage from my speech I take from *The Press* the next day, October 29, 1858 :

"Now, gentlemen, I have a most melancholy announcement to make. It is that the newspaper *The Press* is stopped—my *Press* is stopped. [Sensation.] I did not expect, in coming here, to be compelled to make this sorrowful announcement, but it is nevertheless the fact. *The Press* is stopped, not the establishment, but the single copy which the President of the United States takes—it is stopped. [Long-continued shouts of laughter.] I suppose I shall survive it. [Renewed laughter.] I have no doubt I shall survive it. But it was a terrible blow. I do not think ever two cents created so much havoc before. But we shall recover ; we shall get over it. And now for the bright part of the story: I shall receive in a few days almost the only dollar that I have ever received from the Federal Administration—which will be about $7 50 in payment of

The Press. [Laughter.] We see that this proscription runs
from great to small.   It attacks a popular tribune, and it strikes
down a newspaper.   It turns out a postmaster, and it refuses to
pay two cents to an independent journal.

" 'To such base uses must we come at last.'

" Thus we see the Administration of the Federal Government,
presiding over thirty millions of people, with all its vast patronage, with all its great power, forgetting all its duties and all its
pledges, and becoming a party to the petty proscriptions which
village politicians would despise, and which honorable men
would laugh at.   [Applause.]

" When this Administration policy was first announced, I said,
in *The Press,* that the effect would be to disgrace the party, unless the party should repudiate it ; and, in the next place, to defeat hundreds of men who would be put upon Democratic tickets, not having had any thing to do with the betrayal.   Such
has been the result.   Many and many a glorious Democrat,
placed upon the Democratic ticket, has been sent to obscurity
because the opposition party has risen against the mistakes of
the Federal Administration, and because the Democratic party,
through the conventions of its office-holders, has been committed
to these mistakes and pledged to support them as a portion of
the party duty.

" You have seen how this petty proscription has extended
itself to citizens of your own vicinity.   I need not mention
names ; they are all familiar to you.   But it is well that it is
so ; it is better that it is so—it is a great deal better.   We have
had a trial that has done us all good.   It has taught all parties
that the day for betraying public opinion and for violating solemn pledges has gone.   You will have no more traitors.   The
men who go to Congress now, if they desire to live and to die
respected, will stand by the pledges which they make."

This transaction proved not so much the prejudice of my old
friend, Buchanan, as it did his littleness ; and now, in the new

and difficult path I am treading, I quote the example of 1858 to show how history repeats itself in 1872. That remarkable man, remarkable in almost every sense, the lamented William M. Swain, one of the proprietors and founders of the *Public Ledger*, always liked to relate the incident from which I took the idea that excited the risibilities of my Camden audience. The story is so much better told by my friend J. D. Stockton, of the *Philadelphia Morning Post*, that I use his words :

" By his course in regard to some public matter he had offended a number of his readers, one of whom met him on Chestnut Street, and thus accosted him :

" ' Mr. Swain, I've stopped *The Ledger.*'

" ' What is that, sir ?'

" ' I've stopped *The Ledger*,' was the stern reply.

" ' Great heavens !' said Mr. Swain ; ' my dear sir, that won't do. Come with me to the office. This must be looked into.' And taking the man with him, he entered the office at Third and Chestnut Streets. There they found the clerks busy at their desks ; then they ascended to the editorial-rooms and the composing-rooms, where all was as usual ; finally, they descended to the press-rooms, where the engineers were at work.

" ' I thought you told me you had stopped *The Ledger*,' said Mr. Swain.

" ' So I have,' said the offended subscriber.

" ' I don't see the stoppage. *The Ledger* seems to be going on.''

" ' Oh ! I mean to say—that is, that *I*—ah—had stopped *taking* it.'

" ' Is that all !' exclaimed Mr. Swain. ' Why, my dear sir, you don't know how you alarmed me. As for your individual subscription, I care very little. Good-day, sir, and never make such rash assertions again.' "

LXXXIV

HENRY WIKOFF, better known as "the Chevalier," was born
in Philadelphia, where he studied law and was admitted to
the bar. He must now be over sixty, though his adventures
would indicate him to be a much older man. He is living in
London at present, and is still a devoted adherent of Louis
Napoleon, who has retired with Eugene and the Prince Imperial to Chiselhurst, some twelve miles from that great metropolis. Chevalier Wikoff is one of his constant attendants and
friends. His devotion to Louis Napoleon began more than a
quarter of a century ago. He visited him when he was a prisoner at the Castle of Ham, in 1845, three years before he was
made President of France, and wrote a "biography and personal recollections" of him in 1849. Very near him when he
became Emperor, he enjoyed large advantages during the brilliant era between the *coup d'état* of 1851 and the flight after the
fall of Sedan, in 1870. Once more an exile, Louis Napoleon
has no more devoted supporter than Wikoff. A characteristic
of this citizen of the world is his attachment to celebrated people. His early relations with Fanny Elssler, marked by a bitter quarrel with James Gordon Bennett, of the *New York Herald*, closed in the warmest friendship with the veteran journalist,
which remained unbroken down to his death.

You might travel a long way before meeting a more pleasant
companion than the cosmopolite Wikoff. He has seen more
of the world than most men, has mingled with society of every
shade and grade, has tasted of poverty and affluence, talks several languages fluently, is skilled in etiquette, art, and literature,
and, without proclaimed convictions, is a shrewd politician, who
understands the motives and opinions of others. He has written several books in addition to the biography of his idol, Louis
Napoleon, including his strange experience with Miss Gamble,

entitled "My Courtship and its Consequences," "The Adventures of a Roving Diplomatist," "A New-Yorker in the Foreign
Office, and his Adventures in Paris." Here we have the photographs of his life. From these we realize how such a character
would entertain an editor like Bennett, a statesman like Buchanan, a monarch like Louis Napoleon. Ranging through all society, he can talk of love, law, literature, and war ; can describe the
rulers and thinkers of his time, can gossip of courts and cabinets, of the *boudoir* and the *salon*, of commerce and the Church,
of the peer and the pauper, of Dickens and Thackeray, of Victor Hugo and Louis Blanc, of Lamartine and Laboulaye, of
Garibaldi and the Pope, of Lincoln and Stanton, of Buchanan
and Pierce, of the North and the South, of the opera and the
theatre, of General Sickles and Tammany Hall, and of the inner
life of almost any capital in the world. With such gifts, aided
by an air *distingué*, a fine address and a manner after the English model, Wikoff has the *entrée* in many circles which higher
intellect and deservings can never penetrate.

Wikoff's diplomacy was never better illustrated than in making James Gordon Bennett and James Buchanan friends. Bennett had taken great dislike to Buchanan, and opposed his
election in 1856 with unsparing severity. Never was *The Herald* more sarcastic. Every paragraph told ; every sentence
touched the sensitive nerve ; and when the fight was over, and
Mr. Buchanan was successful, the rejoicing was not less general
because it was supposed that Bennett had been annihilated.
But now Wikoff began to operate. He knew how much Buchanan feared a great newspaper, especially an independent
one like *The Herald*, and he soon convinced Buchanan that it
would be fortunate if he could secure *The Herald* as a supporter
of his Administration. I do not think any consideration was
named, for, whatever may be said of Mr. Bennett, he accepted
no office while he was a journalist, though it is known that more
than once high position was tendered to him. At all events,

The Herald changed tack promptly and gracefully, and Wikoff was ever after a welcome visitor at the White House. The Presidential mind was set at ease, until the Kansas war broke out, when *The Herald* faithfully represented public opinion, and warned the Administration of the folly of its course.

Count d'Orsay was evidently Wikoff's ideal, and the two men were much alike. It was d'Orsay that effected the interview between Louis Napoleon and Wikoff in 1845. The following extract from the opening pages of Wikoff's book, describing this visit, is interesting, as it is a fair specimen of the style of the Chevalier, and a fair portrait of the titled exquisite he tries to imitate. This passage is not less curious because Wikoff is just now the courteous intermediary between Louis Napoleon, ex-Emperor, and such Americans as desire to pay him their respects in his retreat at Chiselhurst :

"In passing from Philadelphia to New York, in the summer of 1845, just previous to my departure for Europe, I stopped at the princely residence of the late Joseph Bonaparte (near Bordentown), ex-King of Spain, to make *mes adieux* to its present owner, the young Prince de Musignano, who, having inherited this, along with other valuable property in this country, from his grandfather, had just arrived from Italy to take possession.

"The few brief hours to which I was limited sped rapidly in the gay society of my affable host and his intelligent companion, M. Maillard, and we had barely time to glance at the numberless and splendid objects of art and curiosity which embellished this luxurious mansion, when a servant announced the approach of the New York train.

"As I was hurrying away the Prince remarked, 'You are going to France ; why not make an effort to see my unfortunate cousin, Prince Louis?   He will be glad, I am sure, to meet an old acquaintance, and I should be delighted, on your return, to receive personal tidings of his health, which, I am distressed to learn, is sadly deranged by his imprisonment.   If you should

succeed, tell him * * * And say, also, that my best wishes
are with him.'

"I relate this simple circumstance because it explains in a
word why I formed a resolution on the instant to get an interior
view of the Citadel of Ham, if such an enterprise should prove
at all compatible with the very rigid notions of political seclu-
sion entertained by Louis Philippe and his Ministers. During
my stay in London I mentioned my project to several friends
of Prince Louis, who thought the idea rather quixotic, as the
Government suffered no relations of any sort to be kept up with
the lone captive of Ham. The late well-known refusal to allow one of his family, sojourning by permission for a few days
at Paris, to visit him, was suggested as a proof of the impracti-
cability, if not absurdity, of my hopes. There was one individual, however, whose views were more sanguine, and I was naturally more inclined to coincide with him. But there were better reasons still to rely on, whatever advice he gave. I am
speaking of the far-famed Count Alfred d'Orsay, whose reputation is spread over the fashionable world of Europe and America, but whose real merits soar much beyond the frivolous accomplishments which have given him such wide celebrity. To
be celebrated at all, no matter by what means, be they high or
low, elevated or vulgar, talent I consider is indispensable; and
to obtain the social position held at one epoch by a Beau Brum-
mel, and, at a later, by a Count d'Orsay, nothing short of mental superiority of a high cast is requisite. This idea is fully supported, at all events, in the present instance, for I have seldom,
in any rank of life, or among the higher grades of employment,
encountered intellectual qualities of rarer excellence than those
which distinguish a man chiefly known in the light of a vain
'carpet knight.' An elegant and fascinating man of the world
he undoubtedly is. An adept in dress, easy in manners, accomplished in the conventions of the drawing-room—a science
apart, made up of the dictates of good-breeding and the require-

ments of etiquette—fertile in conversation, and of brilliant wit, the Count d'Orsay is certainly well-qualified to realize our visionary ideas of that paragon of whom the poet dscribes as 'the glass of fashion and the mould of form.' Those, however, are rather the endowments which would secure him pre-eminence in the land of his birth; for France is *par excellence* the land of society, and to succeed there, grace of manner and charms of mind are indispensable. But in England the case is very different; and Count d'Orsay, with all his *savoir faire*, would never have reached the position he has held for so many years unrivaled, without an equal skill and proficiency in those ruder but still manly accomplishments which constitute the basis of his English popularity. The best rider, the most daring sportsman, the skillful bettor, the inimitable shot, the unrivaled sparrer, these are the merits towering in English eyes, and which have made his name in England so long familiar as a household word. Of later years, abandoning these grosser occupations, he has, with that well-poised effort which never falls short of its mark, and which explains his marvelous success in all he has undertaken, given himself wholly up to art, and his productions in painting and statuary have already thrown the world of taste in commotion, and are building him a reputation which, if less sounding than that he has hitherto enjoyed, is infinitely more enviable. But to me the attractive feature of Count d'Orsay's character has always been what the promiscuous world he lives in knows nothing about, and that is, his cultivated and aspiring intellect, which, in depth and keenness, is adequate to the comprehension of the grandest questions, and capable of estimating them accurately in their nicest details. His knowledge of men and things is extensive and rare, and his criticisms overflow with point and *finesse.* It is little imagined by the giddy crowd around him, whose dullness is enlivened by his wit, that the showy man of fashion is a studious thinker and a careful writer, and that the moments of leisure, stolen from the gay dissipations of the London world, have been devoted to the record of his impressions on life, numbering some seven volumes of manuscript. Their merit may be inferred from the glowing praise bestowed by Lord Byron on his traveling journal, written when only twenty years of age. In a word, Count d'Orsay may be esteemed beyond comparison the Admirable Crichton of the day, and I have cheerfully allowed myself to run into this digression concerning this remarkable person, as so enviable a chance may never offer to give the result of many years' observation of a character variously interpreted and little understood.'"

Men have different tastes. Some aspire to wealth, some to high office, some to scientific fame, and others to excellence in works of charity; but Wikoff is only happy in the society of the cultivated and the powerful. He is the Boswell of our day, who prefers to bask in the fame of others rather than in the milder radiance of his own. He must not be called mercenary. Unlike the favorites that were sunned and ripened in the smiles of Louis Napoleon, he sticks to the unfortunate Emperor. He clung to General Sickles in his darkest hour, and though he sturdily stood by James Gordon Bennett, the rich man, he was also one of his most industrious correspondents. But he never quarrels with power if he can get on peacefully. Politics make no difference with him. He was just as friendly with Lincoln as with Buchanan, and did Mr. Seward's work as faithfully as that of Louis Napoleon. One of his mottoes is never to adopt the enmities of others, but to make life pleasant, and to cultivate kindly relations with "all the world and the rest of mankind," as President Taylor said with awkward benevolence in his first and last message to Congress.

[October 27, 1872.]

LXXXV.

WHAT a mine of incident is such a life as that of William H. Seward! He dies at a time when at least one of his theories is practicalized. He has been pleading for reconciliation for a long time, and he dies in the midst of reconciliation. The advanced anti-slavery leader, he has always been one of the most moderate and conciliatory of men. In 1860–61, after Mr. Lincoln's election, Mr. Seward was distinguished for his efforts to keep the peace between the sections. The Southern men were violent. Wigfall thundered his anathemas; Slidell was satirical; Toombs was threatening; Mason was dictatorial—but, obedient to Mr. Seward's counsel, the Republicans, having won the administration of the Government, were generally silent. Andrew Johnson, a Democrat, broke the bonds in December of 1860, and again in February of 1861, and bold Ben Wade, of Ohio, answered the South in the fiercest rhetoric. Mr. Lincoln surprised every body by a visit to the Hall of Congress on the 23d or 24th of February, 1861, in company with Mr. Seward, then known to be his Secretary of State, and the exceeding mildness of his inaugural address—the succeeding inauguration speech of March 4—was undoubtedly inspired by Mr. Seward's counsel. He knew at an early date that Mr. Lincoln's life was threatened; he had a full foretaste of the conspiracy which, four years after, in April of 1865, killed Mr. Lincoln and came near killing himself; and his effort was to ward off the blow that finally and fatally fell. It is a curious comment on the times that the most generous and magnanimous men of the first real Republican administration of the Government should have been the first official victims of the pro-slavery fanatics. Had Lincoln lived, the whole current of legislation would have been different. I am disposed to believe that his death did not force more vigorous measures, though Andrew

Johnson was a sad supplement in himself. He offered much, and lost all, to the South, and he made a rigid reconstruction so necessary that even the men who complain of it most no longer deny that it was justified.

I heard an anecdote of Mr. Seward's patient temperament a few days ago that deserves mention. In June of 1856, after Preston S. Brooks committed his brutal assault on Charles Sumner, Mrs. Seward was exceedingly anxious for the safety of her husband, and advised him to protect himself. "Well, my dear," was the answer, "what shall I do? I am a man of peace; I never reply to personal attacks; how am I to defend myself? Shall I go to the Senate with a musket or rifle on my shoulder? If I use pistols, I am sure you will not ask me to shoot anybody without notice. You say no. Well, then, it will be my duty, if I carry revolvers, to lay them on my Senatorial desk, so that all men may see that I am ready to kill anybody at a moment's notice. I think this is my best weapon," he said, as he closed the interview, and picked up the whip he carried as a sort of metaphorical help to the old horse that carried him to the Capitol.

He goes hence to the mysterious world, while Thurlow Weed, his devoted chief, is dying, and while the house of Horace Greeley, his early advocate, is stricken with unspeakable woe. So the "human ocean" moves on. Like the eternal sea itself, its current is perpetual, though millions live on its bosom and perish in its depths.

[November 3, 1872.]

LXXXVI.

I MET, a few days ago, one of the members of the House of Representatives of the Thirty-fourth Congress, and together we talked over the exciting session during which, as Clerk of the old House, I officiated as presiding officer when the new body was preparing to organize. It was a long and angry struggle, and from December 2, 1855, to February 2, 1856, I played Speaker to the best of my ability, receiving, when the contest closed, the unanimous thanks of the House, and double the Speaker's pay. My friend Horace Greeley was the chief correspondent of the *New York Tribune,* and at first severely criticised me because he thought I was a prejudiced partisan ; but, as the fight progressed, he discarded his suspicions and stood by me to the end, going so far, in 1857, as to ask President Buchanan, in an editorial article, to put me in his Cabinet —a compliment, by the way, which I had the honor to reciprocate four years after, in 1860, when Mr. Lincoln wrote me a letter of thanks for my opposition to the Buchanan Administration, in reply to which I suggested Horace Greeley for his Postmaster-General. Mr. Lincoln had already selected Mr. Seward for the State Department. In his answer to my recommendation he paid Mr. Greeley as high a compliment as one great man could pay to another. Many of those who figured in that trying period in Congress have gone to their rest, while the survivors have met strange vicissitudes. Sixteen years have wrought curious results. Howell Cobb, of Georgia ; Anson Burlingame, of Massachusetts ; Henry Winter Davis, of Maryland ; Henry M. Fuller, of Pennsylvania, are in their graves. They were men of mark, far above the common level, and were early called. Governor Cobb was worn out by the rebellion, in which he took an active part ; Burlingame died in the midst of an extraordinary diplomatic career ; Davis, the most incisive and brilliant orator of his time, passed off in the zenith of his fame; and Fuller left a mourning family and a host of devoted friends at a time when the future seemed bright before him. Of the living, the most distinguished are John Hickman, of Pennsylvania ; Alexander H. Stephens, of Georgia ; N. P. Banks, of Massachusetts; James L. Orr, of South Carolina; E. B. Washburne, of Illinois (now American Minister to France); Schuyler Colfax, of Indiana (Vice-President); John Sherman, now Senator in Congress from Ohio; and Francis E. Spinner, of New York, present United States Treasurer. The whole time from December to February was consumed in ineffectual ballotings to elect a Speaker, and in discursive debate, involving the issues of the day and every conceivable subject. Parties were closely balanced, the Know-Nothings or Americans holding the balance of power; but, as they were not united, no decision could be reached until Congress and the country were fairly worn out by the weary conflict. Finally Hon. Samuel A. Smith, a Democrat, from Tennessee, on Saturday, the 2d of February, offered the following resolution, which was adopted by a vote of 113 to 104:

"*Resolved,* That this House will proceed immediately to the election of a Speaker, *viva voce.* If, after the roll shall have been called three times, no member shall have received a majority of all the votes cast, the roll shall again be called, and the member who shall then receive the largest vote, provided it be a majority of a quorum, shall be declared duly elected Speaker of the House of Representatives of the Thirty-fourth Congress."

This brought the protracted struggle to a close. Several efforts were made to repeal it. Hon. Percy Walker, of Alabama, one of the Know-Nothing leaders, saw that Mr. Smith's resolution looked to the election of a Republican Speaker, and made every effort to rescind it. As we were not acting under any rules, and a good deal of the work before the House had to depend on the common-sense of the Chair, I decided that his motion to rescind the resolution was in order, rather to let him see that I was impartial than to show my tenacity in adherence to Parliamentary law. An appeal was taken, and, as I expected, my decision was overruled. Then came the vote on the resolution itself, and on the 133d ballot, after a two months' fight, N. P.

Banks was chosen Speaker on a plurality. The practice in former years had been for the House to adopt a resolution declaring the Speaker who had received a majority of the votes to be elected; but I saw that such action would reopen the question, and would force the House to another vote, perhaps into a revolution, and, by consulting the tellers, who represented both parties, we determined to declare Banks elected, without any reference to the House. A scene of the wildest confusion ensued. I was denounced in unsparing terms, and Mr. A. K. Marshall, of Kentucky, took the ground that I had transcended precedent. I quote the following from the official proceedings in *The Globe*:

Mr. Marshall, of Kentucky. "I ask now, in connection with the remarks which I have made, whether the gentleman who now acts as Clerk of this House [Mr. Forney], and who has presided with so much fairness and so much dignity, and without having assumed the exercise of any right which was not clearly and legitimately his, who has refused on questions of order to give any decision — I ask that gentleman if he will now, on this great and vital question, dare — ah! that is the word — whether he will dare, in the absence of all official power, to induct into that chair a man who has not received a majority of the votes of this body? If he does, I will, for one, have to change much of the high opinion which I have and still hold for that honorable gentleman."

The Clerk (Mr. Forney). "The gentleman from Ohio will permit the Clerk to make a few words of explanation. The House adopted a resolution to-day providing in terms that at a certain stage a plurality vote should govern. The Clerk will say to the gentleman from Kentucky that if he has any feeling in this canvass it is not certainly in favor of the gentleman from Massachusetts. The course was pursued according to the terms of the resolution, which it was thought was the proper one. The Clerk was actuated by no motives but those of a desire to continue to be impartial. He consulted with the officers of the House, who are older and better acquainted with the duties of this station than himself. He also consulted with the gentlemen who are tellers, and who represent the two great parties respectively. The consultation resulted in this conclusion. If there is error in the matter he throws himself on the indulgence of the House, trusting that the gentlemen who have sustained him thus far will carry him through the question which is now about to be settled."

Mr. Campbell, of Ohio. "Mr. Clerk, from the beginning I have held that a Speaker ought to be elected by a majority vote, and I now submit it to the honor of those gentlemen who voted for the plurality rule, whether it does not become them now to carry out that rule and end the struggle that has been disgraceful to us and the country. I have heard a great deal about the danger of a dissolution of the Union. What! Has it come to this, that the election of any man can dissolve this glorious Union? [Applause.] I do not care what may be the sentiments of the gentleman who is to preside over our deliberations; I shall be found one of the foremost in assailing him if he dares to do any thing that would separate the Union of these States.

"It would seem that the gentleman from Kentucky has taken the Union under his particular charge. Sir, I think that there are those of us in the free States who will be found to the last for the union of these States. I am an American. I am for the Constitution of my country as the highest law which is to control our political action, and for the union of these States under any circumstances that may surround us. If I thought that my heart was capable of cherishing a sentiment that would tend to a disruption of this Union, I would, if I could, tear it out and cast it to the dogs."

Mr. Clingman. "I have the floor now to say a few words. I was endeavoring to get it when the gentleman from Ohio rose, and as soon as the point of order was raised. I anticipated something of this early in the session; and when I spoke of going for the plurality rule, the question was frequently put to me by gentlemen upon the other side, whether, if that rule was adopted, I would then vote for such a resolution as was adopted in 1849. I replied that I regarded no such resolution as necessary, because the previous resolution was sufficient—that it was the act of a majority of the House. That was the opinion I then entertained, and hold the same opinion now. The resolution declares that the person who receives the highest number of votes shall be Speaker. The tellers merely announce who has that vote, and I entertain the opinion that the gentleman from Massachusetts can take his seat under the resolution; that was and is now my opinion. But I saw that if the plurality rule were resorted to, whether or not you could pass a resolution declaring the gentleman who received the highest number of votes for Speaker would depend upon its phraseology. I say now to the gentleman from Ohio, and to others, that if a resolution shall be offered declaring that the gentleman from Massachusetts has been elected Speaker by virtue of that plurality resolution, if they think it necessary, I will vote for it."

MR. COBB, of Georgia. "Allusion has been made to what occurred here at the time that I was elected Speaker of this House; and as I differ with some of my friends with reference to their construction of what was done then, and what is necessary to be done now, and as I may be called upon to vote upon some resolution connected with this matter, I desire to place myself right before the House, and to give the reasons for the vote which I shall give. In 1849, when it was determined to adopt the plurality rule, it was assailed as violative of the Constitution. In order to avoid any difficulty upon that subject it was, by general consent among those who were in favor of it, agreed that a resolution should be offered affirming the election, and that was done. At the time, occupying the position that I did, I was asked the question, 'Whether, in my opinion, it was necessary that this should be done?' I gave the same opinion then that I entertain now, and that I have repeatedly given when asked the question during this canvass; and I feel it due to candor now to state it. I hold that it is necessary for a majority of this House to elect a Speaker; but I hold, at the same time, that a majority of this House adopting the plurality rule, where a plurality vote is cast for any member, he is elected by virtue of the resolution originally adopted by a majority of the House. [Applause.]

"When, sir, it was thought there was a probability that the gentleman for whom I voted would be elected, I gave that opinion then. I also gave it to those on the other side of the House who thought proper to ask my opinion upon the subject. I entertain no doubt in reference to it. Therefore I can not agree with either of my friends from Kentucky that it is incumbent upon those who voted for the plurality rule to perfect the election of Mr. Banks by a resolution. I think Mr. Banks has already been elected. My friends upon this floor know that I have appealed to them from the commencement of this struggle."

MR. WHEELER. "I offer the following resolution:

"'*Resolved*, That the Hon. Wm. Aiken, of South Carolina; the Hon. Henry M. Fuller, of Pennsylvania; and the Hon. Lewis D. Campbell, of Ohio, be appointed a committee to wait upon the Hon. Nathaniel P. Banks, Jr., of Massachusetts, the Speaker elect, and conduct him to the chair.'"

MR. GIDDINGS. "I hope that resolution will not be adopted. It is an innovation on the whole past practice of the House. The Clerk always appoints a committee to conduct the Speaker to the chair."

MR. WHEELER. "I withdraw the resolution."

"The Clerk then requested Messrs. Fuller, of Pennsylvania, Aiken, of South Carolina, and Campbell, of Ohio, to conduct the Speaker elect to the chair.

"The gentlemen designated proceeded to discharge this duty, and Mr. Banks was thereupon conducted to the chair, and took his seat.

"After a moment's pause the Speaker rose and addressed the House as follows :

"GENTLEMEN OF THE HOUSE OF REPRESENTATIVES : Before I proceed to complete my acceptance of the office to which I am elected, I avail myself of your indulgence to express my acknowledgments for the honor conferred upon me. It would afford me far greater pleasure in taking the chair of the House were I supported even by the self-assurance that I could bring to the discharge of its duties, always arduous and delicate, and now environed with unusual difficulties, any capacity commensurate with their responsibility and dignity. I can only say that, in so far as I am able, I shall discharge my duty with fidelity to the Constitution, and with impartiality as it regards the rights of members. I have no personal objects to accomplish. I am animated by the single desire that I may in some degree aid in maintaining the well-established principles of our Government in their original and American signification ; in developing the material interests of that portion of the continent we occupy, so far as we may do within the limited and legitimate powers conferred upon us ; in enlarging and swelling the capacity of our Government for beneficent influences at home and abroad ; and, above all, in preserving intact and in perpetuity the priceless privileges transmitted to us. I am, of course, aware that I can not hope of my own strength to be equal to the perfect execution of the duties I now assume. I am, therefore, as every man must be who stands in such presence, a suppliant for your co-operation and indulgence ; and, accepting your honors with this declaration, I again offer you my thanks."

MR. STANTON (Dem.). "I have a resolution that I desire to offer, which I know will meet with the unanimous approbation of the House, and it would spoil by delay. It is as follows :

"'*Resolved*, That the thanks of this House are eminently due and are hereby tendered to John W. Forney, Esq., for the distinguished ability, fidelity, and impartiality with which he has presided over the deliberations of the House of Representatives during the arduous and protracted contest for Speaker which has just closed.'"

MR. CAMPBELL, of Ohio (Whig). "I sought the floor to offer a similar resolution, and I hope that it will be unanimously adopted."

"The question was taken, and the resolution was unanimously adopted.

MR. WHEELER (Rep.). "I offer the following resolution, and upon it demand the previous question :

"'*Resolved*, That there be paid out of the contingent fund of the House to John W. Forney, late Clerk, in addition to the salary allowed him by law, eight dollars per diem for the additional services performed by him from the 3d day of December, 1855, to the 4th day of February, 1856.'"

"The previous question was then seconded, and the main question was ordered to be now put.

MR. JONES, of Tennessee (Dem.). "I object to that resolution, and I think it is not in order to introduce it."

THE SPEAKER. "The Chair understands the House to have ordered the main question to be put."

"The question was then taken on the resolution, and it was agreed to."

I will be pardoned for quoting the personal resolutions which closed this extraordinary struggle, because they develop the characteristics of the leaders of opposing parties, and also because they show how even ordinary integrity and decision are certain of ultimate compensation. General Banks has just been defeated for Congress in Massachusetts, after a long career, but I can not forget the manner in which he pronounced his inaugural address as Speaker of the House sixteen years ago.

His deportment during the succeeding session, his impartiality, his courtesy, and his uniform integrity, proved him to be an unrivaled statesman, and I am not without hope that we shall hear of him honorably in the future. Quitman, Barksdale, Rust, Keitt, Eustis, and other Southern fire-eaters have gone to their last account. They were men of varied and distinguished abilities, and yet not one of them, if he could speak from his grave, but would say that Nathaniel P. Banks was a just and honest presiding officer.

[November 10, 1872.]

LXXXVII.

WASHINGTON CITY has been a vast newspaper sepulchre. It has witnessed the rise and fall of more dailies and weeklies than any other city of equal size and pretensions in the world; and if they could be catalogued and accompanied by a sketch of the hopes that tempted and the disappointments that killed them, a very interesting *morceau* would be added to the curiosities of literature. The closing of the Democratic organ at the national capital, *The Patriot*, last Monday, revives the recollection of the long procession that have passed away. *The Patriot* was conducted with signal ability, counting in its corps some of the best talent of the country, including W. B. Reed, James E. Harvey, Henry Adams, and the finest Democratic minds in Congress. Undoubtedly President Grant's re-election hastened its overthrow, but in the long run, at least in these later days, a national Administration can not of itself sustain a Washington newspaper. It must have a specialty of its own, and be noted for fine writing and unusual spirit to keep it afloat. Dr. Bayley's weekly, *The Era*, flourished, and for a while most profitably, chiefly on account of that marvelous romance, "Uncle

Tom's Cabin," Mrs. Stowe's great work, of which Mr. Parton, in one of his "Topics of the Times," speaks so justly and so graphically. *The Daily Chronicle*, which I established in 1862, made money for several years because it had for a constituency a reading army. But we did not know our advantages, and were never prepared for the hosts who clamored for it. It was no uncommon thing for us to print thirty thousand a day, a circulation that could have been trebled if we had possessed the material to do the work. But few persons had any confidence, or, indeed, any desire, that the war would be so long protracted. We looked for the collapse of the rebellion every day, and were not surprised, after the troops had gone home, and the camps were broken up, and the hospitals turned into school-houses and dwellings, at the vast difference in our income. But what a change the war has made in the Washington newspapers. *The Sunday Chronicle*, which was the first of its class ever seen at the capital, established in March, of 1861, gave more news and telegrams in one number than all the old-time dailies did, I was going to say, in a week; and now there are no less than four other Sunday journals. Then compare *The Star, Daily Chronicle*, and *Republican* with the old *Globe, Union*, and *Intelligencer*. I know all about the two eras, for I worked in both. Twenty-five years ago a telegraphic dispatch or regular local department was a rarity. We were literally drenched with eternal politics. Our editorials were all about the party. Our news was heavy, and our ways were the ways of leisure. The world moved slow, and the newspapers were slower. We generally went to press about 10 P. M., and our matter was always early in hand. Expenses were light, except the salaries, which were always liberal. The profits of the proprietors, especially if they happened to own the organs, were enormous, large enough, in fact, to enable these same proprietors to retire upon handsome fortunes. The last was Mr. Buchanan's champion, General George W. Bowman, the well-known editor of *The Bed-*

ford (Pennsylvania) *Gazette*, now living, I think, in Cumberland County, in that State, the possessor of a competency earned in Washington. Organship died with the rebellion. The public printing wholly ceased to be a job under Mr. Lincoln, and those who came to make newspapers in Washington have had to do it by hard work, by heavy outlays for news and telegraphs, and by a constant hand-to-hand struggle with a busy competition. The old correspondents, " Potomac," " The Spy in Washington," " Observer," of *The Ledger ;* " X," of *The Baltimore Sun ;* " Independent," of *The North American ;* and later than these, "Occasional," of *The Press,* gave way to the new guild, the alerts of Fourteenth Street, with their ravenous pens, their insatiate greed for news, their sparkling repartees, their genius, wit, and dash. Supplementing these came the modern plan of " interviewing," which no public man, if he values his soul, can shirk without ridicule. Following this new fashion came the fluttering swarm of lady correspondents, with their delicious gossip, their bright sentences, their pictures of great people, and their unequaled photographs of receptions and parties. Only Annie Royall represented the gentler sex thirty years ago, and she had the ill-luck to be a terror rather than a temptation, for she wore a man's hat and carried an umbrella as large as that of " Paul Pry."

Yet, with all these advantages over the past, few fortunes are made by the hard-working men in the business of journalism in Washington, excepting, perhaps, *The Evening Star,* the popular publication of the city, with its large circulation and its comparatively small force of writers. And I perceive that *The Star* is being steadily pushed by a new rival, called *The Daily Critic,* which has achieved an immense circulation almost without cost. The expense is too heavy, and the reading public too limited. Government advertising, however liberal, is not sufficient. There must be a community of producers, and Washington is still a city of consumers, men and women in the Departments,

who get their daily literature gratis, and devour it in the easy
intervals of their routine work.   When factories become as frequent as fashionables, and when commerce is as active as politics, and when the nation's capital is belted by brilliant country
towns like Chester, Norristown, Germantown, Media, West
Chester, Manayunk, Frankford, and Camden (New Jersey),
near old Philadelphia, a daily newspaper will be a pleasing and
profitable investment.

[November 17, 1872.]

LXXXVIII.

FROM his high place as President of the new Convention to
reform the Constitution of Pennsylvania, William M. Meredith
can overlook the eventful past, in which for half a century he
has been a commanding figure.   As he aids to smooth the
path of the future he will be largely aided by the light of his
long experience.   Mr. Meredith is now in his seventy-fourth
year.   He has, therefore, reached the philosophic age, and like
the traveler who, at the close of a protracted journey, reaches
the crest of a mountain, and surveys all he has seen, he may
rest in supreme content upon the retrospect.   In the very hall
in which Mr. Meredith now presides, he was, thirty-five years
ago, a member of a similar convention from the city of Philadelphia.   He was then about thirty-seven, one of the youngest
of the delegates, and also one of the most distinguished.   The
stately character of his ripened age is the fulfillment of his early
manhood.   None of the old men of the Convention of 1837
surpassed Mr. Meredith in mental gifts and solid judgment, and
there were some far advanced in the vale of years at that time.
Thaddeus Stevens was a delegate from the County of Adams,
and was in his forty-fourth year.   Ritner was Governor of Penn-

sylvania, and Stevens was the acknowledged leader of the anti-
Masonic party—in fact, the controller of the State administration.   John Sergeant, of Philadelphia, was president of the
convention, the *beau ideal* of a gentleman, jurist, and citizen.   I
can recall him, when, as a boy, I sat in the galleries and watched his courteous manners and impartial rulings.   Of medium
height, there was that in his sad and saturnine face, in the
glance of his eye, and the tones of his voice, which gave unspeakable dignity to the Chair.   Parties were in no pleasant mood.   No such era of good feeling pervaded the people as at the present day, when other delegates are called to
amend our fundamental law, surrounded by every inducement
to avoid a prejudiced and partial course.   The Democrats had
lost the State by the Wolf and Muhlenberg quarrel in 1835–36,
and were rapidly reuniting to regain it in 1838.   Mr. Stevens
carried things with a high hand.   He boldly wielded the patronage of the State administration to strengthen Governor Ritner; he attacked the Masonic Order, and had some of the most
eminent of its members summoned before his Committee of Investigation.   He assumed the leadership of his party in the
Reform Convention.   Yet in despite of his dogmatism there
was an indescribable charm about Thaddeus Stevens.   If he
was a violent partisan, he was a generous friend and a chivalric foe.   If he struck hard with his clenched hand, he gave and
forgave freely with his open one ; and though often intolerant
and illogical in his war upon secret societies—as he afterward
proved in 1854, when he joined the Know-Nothings—his splendid championship of universal education and his support of
universal emancipation, made men forget his sharp sayings, and
compelled admiration if they did not arouse affection.

    Young Meredith was not disposed to follow the imperious
New-Englander, and there was an early conflict between them.
The attack upon the Masons was particularly distasteful to
Meredith, and he revolted from the attempt to introduce politics

into the convention. At last the storm broke. On the 5th of June, 1837, Mr. Meredith paid his respects to Mr. Stevens in a remarkable speech, of which the following is a specimen :

"Mr. President, when the home of my birth and affections was causelessly assailed, I defended her. What man would have done less? I defended her with warmth. Who would have wished me to do it coldly? It is said that I used strong language, and yet, sir, I used the feeblest of all the words that were rushing from my heart to my lips. This is the very head of my offense. For this I am thrown, like a captive Christian, naked into the arena, where the Great Unchained of Adams is baying at my throat, while my vulpine friend from Franklin eats smoothly into my vitals ; and, like the Spartan fool, I hug him to my bosom. Alas, sir ! what a spectacle do we here exhibit ! What monuments of weakness are we leaving for posterity ! How far is our position below the true and just standard of a body charged with functions such as these we are appointed to fulfill. In all the other States discussions on the framing of their constitutions have been temperate and deliberate. Even the hot-blooded South can consider its organic laws calmly, coolly, and dispassionately. Here alone, here in Pennsylvania, we seem resolved to prove to the world that if we can not determine every thing according to the dictates of absolute wisdom, we can at least debate with indecent heat, and degrade the assembled majesty of the people by party strife and personal bitterness. In all that I have said, sir, I have been actuated by a desire merely to discharge my duty by defending my constituents and myself. I entertain no hostility to the gentleman from Adams. Indeed, why should I? On the contrary, no man admires more than I do his great abilities. I avow that he displays talents which, within their proper sphere, are, in my experience, unsurpassed, if not unrivaled. In party tactics and small manœuvres I have never seen his equal, and do not expect to meet his superior. Who can forget the mingled sar-

casm, eloquence, and pathos of his harangue on the assistant
doorkeeper? Or who was not delighted with the precision, accuracy, and effect of our evolutions under his drill through the
election of officers? The gentleman is an honor to his halberd.
How close was his formation of our column! How rapidly did
he deploy us into line! How skillfully was our front dressed!
How rigorously were the deserters shot! Never did a more
accomplished orderly report a company 'formed' on a parade
ground. It is very true, I fear, that while he was putting us
through the manual exercise in the court-yard, the enemy were
climbing in at the back windows, for I observe that we have six
secretaries, whereas I do not remember to have voted for more
than two. However, this is but the fortune of war, and detracts
nothing from his merit. Has he not glory enough? The gentleman has other duties to perform. To him it belongs to superintend the executive administration. The Masons, we know,
are ordered for punishment, and when the day arrives when they
are to be had up at the triangle, we shall doubtless see him in
the fervent fulfillment of his employment, with his ready instrument well prepared, and we shall hear

'The long resounding line and frequent lash.'

"Do not all these occupations furnish sufficient scope for the
ambition or activity of the gentleman's character? Why will
he grasp at more? What has he to do with the basis of repre-
sentation? Within the limits of his appropriate functions, he
commands from us a respect not unmingled with a certain awe.
But instead of confining himself within those limits, he seems
occasionally to run beyond himself, mistakes his yellow cotton
shoulder-knots for golden epaulettes, and his halberd for a lead-
ing-staff, mounts a ragged hobby, and when we are perhaps in
the midst of an important affair, in the face and under the fire
of the enemy, down gallops our mad sergeant along the line,
and insists on our suspending all other operations that we may
be instantly put through some unknown *posé*, or some new

movement to the shoulder of his own devising, and which none of us ever heard of before. And then, upon the least demur at compliance with his odd demands, he rides furiously into our ranks, breaking his halberd over the head of one, lending a horse's kick to another, covering a third from head to foot with mud, throwing our battalion into inextricable confusion, and exposing us to inevitable defeat. And all these misfortunes are to be suffered because one gentleman has not learned to discriminate between yellow cotton and gold lace! No, sir! they can not be much longer suffered. We would not touch a hair of our eccentric's head, nor even of the tail of his hobby. At present I merely beg to remonstrate kindly and gently with him, as I have been doing, against his persistence in these ludicrous yet injurious assaults upon those who, however feebly and humbly, are endeavoring to discharge their duty."

The rejoinder of Mr. Stevens was very severe and even personal. Reading it over, now when the Great Commoner is in his grave, it seems a loud report over a very small matter, and stands in curious contrast with his immortal utterances in the great struggle for the life and liberty of a nation. The protest of Mr. Meredith against party politics in a Constitutional Convention is more pertinent, and may be profitably studied by the delegates to the body now in session.

[November 28, 1872.]

LXXXIX.

WE shall have many interesting historical developments during our preparations for the great Centennial. The men and measures of the Revolution will reappear in a new light, and the contrast between the past and present will be drawn in radiant colors. In reading over a few of the periodicals of the

last quarter of the last century I found some incidents and
passages in the lives of Washington, Jefferson, and Franklin,
that may have been forgotten by the very old and have certainly never been read by the very young.   One of these is
the following original letter of General Washington to the distinguished Matthew Carey, whose no less distinguished son,
Henry C. Carey, is still living in Philadelphia, at an advanced
age, the centre of a circle of loving friends:

"MOUNT VERNON, July 21, 1788.

"SIR,—If I had more leisure I should most willingly give you any such
communications (that might be within my reach) as would serve to keep up
the reputation of your *Museum*.   At present, occupied as I am with agriculture and correspondence, I can promise little.   Perhaps some gentlemen
connected with me may make some selections from my repositories ; and I
beg you will be persuaded *that I can have no reluctance to permit any thing
to be communicated that might tend to establish truth, extend knowledge, excite
virtue, and promote happiness among mankind.*

" With best wishes for success, I am, sir, your most ob't h'ble serv't,

"GO. WASHINGTON.

"MR. MATTHEW CAREY, Editor of the *American Museum*."

Here are the qualities that make the modern philosopher and
journalist.   Matthew Carey was anxious to preserve for posterity the treasures that George Washington had collected in his
illustrious career, and Washington responds gracefully to the
request.   The closing sentence in italics is Washington's ideal
of the creed of a patriot, and a fine index of his own character.
Jefferson's tribute to Washington is very beautiful :

" I own," he says, " I regard it, though but a single view of
the character of Washington, as one of transcendent importance, that the commencement of the Revolution found him already prepared and mature for the work, and that on the day
which his commission was signed by John Hancock—the immortal seventeenth of June, 1775—a day on which Providence
kept an even balance with the cause, and while it took from us
a Warren, gave us a Washington—he was just as consummate

a leader for peace as for war, as when, eight years after, he resigned that commission at Annapolis."

But he did not hesitate to counsel and even to criticise his chief, as the following will show :

"PARIS, May 2, 1788.

"*To General Washington :*

"I had intended to have written a word to your Excellency on the subject of the new Constitution, but I have already spun out my letter to an immoderate length. I will just observe, therefore, that, according to my ideas, there is a great deal of good in it. There are two things, however, which I dislike strongly :

"*First.* The want of a declaration of rights.

"I am in hopes the opposition in Virginia will remedy this, and produce such a declaration.

"*Second.* The perpetual re-eligibility of the President.

"This, I fear, will make that an office for life, first, and then hereditary. I was such an enemy to monarchies before I came to Europe, I am ten thousand times more so since I have seen what they are. There is scarcely an evil known in these countries which may not be traced to their king as its source; nor a good which is not derived from the small fibres of republicanism existing among them. I can further say, with safety, that there is not a crowned head in Europe whose talents or merits could entitle him to be elected a vestryman by the people of any parish in America !"

What a picture he draws of the European sovereigns in 1789 :

"I often amuse myself with contemplating the characters of the then reigning sovereigns of Europe. Louis XVI. was a fool, of my own knowledge, and in despite of the answers made for him at his trial. The King of Spain was a fool, he of Naples the same. They passed their lives in hunting, and dispatched two couriers a week one thousand miles to let each other know what game they had killed the preceding days. The King of Sardinia was a fool. All these were Bourbons. The Queen of Portugal, a Braganza, was an idiot by nature, and so was the King of Denmark. Their sons, as regents, exercised the powers of government. The King of Prussia, successor to the great Frederick, was a mere hog in body as well as in mind. Gustavus, of Sweden, and Joseph, of Austria, were really crazy, and George, of England, you know was in a straight waistcoat. There remained, then, none but old Catharine, who had been too lately picked up to have lost her common-sense. In this state Bonaparte found Europe, and it was this state of its rulers which lost it with scarce a struggle."

Reluctant to undertake a public tour while President, he seems to have had pretty much the notion of Washington, in that respect, that our people have of Grant :

"WASHINGTON, June 19, 1807.

"*To Governor Sullivan:*

"With respect to the tour my friends to the North have proposed that I should make in that quarter, I have not made up my final opinion. The course of life which General Washington had run, civil and military, the services he had rendered, and the space he therefore occupied in the affections of his fellow-citizens, take from his examples the weight of precedents for others, because no others can arrogate to themselves the claims which he had on the public homage."

ON CIVIL SERVICE.

"WASHINGTON, July 17, 1807.

"I have never removed a man merely because he was a Federalist. I have never wished them to give a vote at an election but according to their own wishes. But, as no Government could discharge its duties to the best advantage of its citizens if its agents were in a regular course of thwarting instead of executing all its measures, and were employing the patronage and influences of their offices against the Government and its measures, I have only requested they would be quiet, and they should be safe."

GLAD TO GET RID OF THE PRESIDENCY.

"WASHINGTON, March 2, 1809.

"*To M. Dupont de Nemours:*

"Never did a prisoner, released from chains, feel such relief as I shall on shaking off the shackles of power. Nature intended me for the tranquil pursuits of science, by rendering them my supreme delight; but the enormities of the times in which I have lived have forced me to take a part in resisting them, and to commit myself on the boisterous ocean of political passions."

In his Memoirs he often sketches his associates and contemporaries. John Adams is "vain and irritable," but as "disinterested as the being who made him." Pendleton, of Virginia, "the ablest man in debate I have ever met," "without the poetic fancy of Mr. Patrick Henry, his sublime imagination, or his lofty and overwhelming diction." He was in love with James Madison, "who never wandered from his subject into

vain declamation, but pursuing it closely in language pure, classical, and copious, soothing always the feelings of his adversaries by civility and softness of expression, he rose to the eminent station which he held in the great National Convention
of 1787." George Wythe, also of Virginia, "was a man of the
first order of wisdom among those who acted on the theatre of
the Revolution." "Lafayette is a most valuable auxiliary to
me," Jefferson writes from Paris; "he has a great deal of
sound genius, is well remarked by the king, and rising in popularity."

But no character shines with a purer lustre than that of Benjamin Franklin, who, besides being a natural philosopher, was
also a politician and a statesman. Jefferson writes about him
from Paris, September 11, 1785, as follows:

"At a large table where I dined the other day, a gentleman
from Switzerland expressed his apprehensions for the fate of
Dr. Franklin, as he said he had been informed that he would
be received with stones by the people, who were generally dissatisfied with the Revolution, and incensed against all those
who had assisted in bringing it about. I told him his apprehensions were just, and that the people of America would probably salute Dr. Franklin *with the same stones that they had
thrown at the Marquis Lafayette.*"

Could I better conclude this letter of reminiscences than by
the following extract from Franklin's reply to Lord Howe, commander of the British forces, dated Philadelphia, July 30, 1776?

"It is impossible we should think of submission to a government that has, with the most wanton barbarity and cruelty,
burned our defenseless towns in the midst of winter, excited the
savages to massacre our peaceful farmers, and set our slaves
to murder their masters; and is even now sending foreign mercenaries to deluge our country with blood. These atrocious
injuries have extinguished every spark of affection for that
parent-country we once held so dear; but, were it possible for

us to forget and forgive them, it is not possible for you, I mean the British nation, to forgive the people you have so heavily injured."

[December 1, 1872.]

XC.

WHAT a delicious volume that famous man of the world, Sam Ward, who is every body's friend, from black John who drives his hack to the jolly Senator who eats his dinners and drinks his wine—from the lady who accepts his bouquet to the prattling child who hungers for his French candies—what a jewel of a book he could make of the good things he has heard at his thousand "noctes ambrosianæ!" He is again domesticated at John Welcker's, in Washington City, where, during the session, he will preside like a very prince of good fellows, attending to business and pleasure at the same time. Such men are treasures in many ways. They live to make themselves and others happy. They have seen so much of the world that they have ceased to quarrel with other men's ideas. They have lost their reverence for mere names, but not their love for genuine greatness. True cosmopolites, they are every where at home. Eager to know all that is going on, they will give you in return for your news or jokes hours full of gossip and stories. They know every body if every body does not know them, and, as they are always well-bred gentlemen, they never descend to vulgarity or slang. To sit at Ward's table, to see him manage a dinner, and to hear him call out his guests, not to speak of his mastership of the *cuisine*, including his science in wines, is to enjoy something more than the delicacies he spreads before you. He would have made a capital companion for Sheridan or Tom Moore, and doubtless spent many a joyous night with James T.

Brady and John T. Sullivan. I heard him relate how he helped
a friend with the present Emperor of Brazil, a few days ago,
and I question if ever Lever wrote a more amusing incident.
Sam Ward belongs to the old school, though he is full of the
progress of the new era. He looks very like the late David
Paul Brown, dresses with equal care and taste, and his heart is
as big as was the heart of that good man and grandiloquent
orator.

"Once on a time," many years ago, I saw Webster, Benton,
John M. Clayton, James Buchanan, Judge Douglas, and William
R. King at dinner. I was a sort of David Copperfield among
them—a minnow among Tritons. But I never shall forget their
conversation and their humor. Buchanan was a capital host.
He did not tell a good story, but he enjoyed one; and when
Webster was roused he kept a table in a roar. And "Colonel King," as they used to call the bachelor Senator from Alabama, was amusing in his dry way. Douglas was almost unrivaled. His repartee was a flash, and his courtesy as knightly
as if he had been born in the best society. But none of them
could surpass Sam Ward either in giving a good dinner or in
seasoning it with Attic wit and Chesterfieldian politeness.

Rough John C. Rives, of *The Globe*, was a different character.
His anecdotes always had a special flavor, and never a sting.
One day, when Douglas and a few of us were standing in "the
Hole in the Wall," a celebrated resort for Senators and members, Rives came in and joined us. It was in 1854, just after
Douglas had introduced his bill to repeal the Missouri Compromise Line. Rives, like his partner, Francis P. Blair, was opposed to it, and made no hesitation in saying so. Douglas
twitted him about getting out of the party lines, and tried to
convince him that his measure was right. "I don't like it,
Douglas, and never can like it. It is uncalled for. It reminds
me of the fellow who, having gone pretty nearly through all the
follies of life, took it into his head to hire a bully to do his fight-

ing. He made a contract with the stoutest bruiser he could find, and they started on their journey down the Mississippi. At every landing the quarrel was picked by the one and the battle fought by the other. It was tough work sometimes, but rather enjoyable. At last they reached New Orleans. On the levee they found a stout, brawny stevedore, and, after some chaffing, a row was started, and the two began to pummel each other. They were well matched, but, aided by his experience, the bully beat the stevedore. 'I say, boss,' said his fighting man, 'I give up this job; you is too much for me! *I don't see any reason in that ere last fight.*' " Of course, the laugh was against Judge Douglas, and none relished the hit more than himself.

But perhaps nobody at a dinner-table of the present day is so welcome as James W. Nye, Senator from Nevada. I wish I could congratulate him upon his certain re-election, though Mr. Jones, who will probably succeed him, is himself a character, and will make his mark. Governor Nye will always be a noted personage. His memory is prodigious, his wit electric. A face of singular fascination and a manner debonair, in his Senatorial seat he recalls the best ideals of the past. Social, genial, generous, he takes possession of a dinner-table at once. His magnetism seems to pervade the whole company, and when he tells a story, always relating to some incident familiar to the guests, and illustrated by quaint expressions, with a bright eye and musical voice, the gravest must bow to his irresistible influence. He dines with Sam Ward frequently, when it will be worth much to be present.

[December 8, 1872.]

XCI.

DEATH is busy among the brave and the gifted. William Prescott Smith, George Gordon Meade, Horace Greeley, have been called in the prime of life and usefulness. They faded suddenly from the ranks of men; and nothing remains save the memory of the exquisite humor and kindness of the one, the modest courage of the other, the various resources and ceaseless benevolence of the last. But none of the many that have been summoned will live so long in our hearts, not even William H. Seward, the venerable sage who led the way full of honors and of years, as the silver-haired philosopher of the *New York Tribune.* The incidents preceding his death, the manner of it, and the rare events that followed and crowned it, will supply material fifty years hence for a most touching drama. In one respect the tributes to his memory must always be unequaled. I mean the literary laurels laid upon his grave by his associates of the press. The eulogies upon Washington and Lincoln were more numerous, perhaps, but they were not so original, and certainly not more sincere. Differing from the worship of Lincoln, martyr as he was, what was said of Greeley came as warm from the impulses of his enemies as from the impulses of his friends. To employ Mr. Sumner's splendid figure : " Parties are always for the living; and now, standing at the open grave of Horace Greeley, we are admonished to forget the strife of party, and to remember only truth, country, and mankind, to which his honest life was devoted. In other days the horse and armor of the departed chieftain have been buried in the grave where he reposed. So, too, may we bury the animosities if not the badges of the past. Then, indeed, will there be victory for the dead which all will share." Every journalist who has written, and all have written, has, with some unforgotten exceptions, poured his warmest affections into the sobbing hearts of a sympathizing

people. Each has done his best, and many have surpassed
themselves. There has been an intellectual rivalry among these
masters of the pen. Who will not cherish the glorious effusion
of the *New York World* on Friday, December 1, 1872, the fervent eulogy of the *New York Herald*, and the splendid homage
of Theodore Tilton in the *Golden Age*, Sam Bowles in the *Springfield Republican*, William Cassidy in the *Albany Argus*, W. F.
Storey in the *Chicago Times*, and their contemporaries, North
and South, East and West? Preserved, as they will be, in one
or more volumes, they will be a monument to Horace Greeley
more enduring than the loftiest column of bronze or marble,
though covered with bass-reliefs, and gorgeous in compliments
carved by cunning hands.

The last time I saw Mr. Greeley was at the Continental Hotel
in Philadelphia, several weeks before the Cincinnati Convention.
The interview had been arranged by one of the gentlemen of
The Tribune at Mr. Greeley's request, and we had a long and
confidential talk. I am quite sure he did not then entertain
the remotest idea of his nomination against General Grant, and
though he was earnest in expressing the belief that the man
could be found to defeat Grant, he listened patiently to my
earnest appeal to him. I told him that both of us owed allegiance to the Republican mission, that General Grant deserved
re-election, that there was not the slightest prospect of defeating his renomination, and that I longed to see the great *Tribune*
in the lead of what would be an assured victory. He was unusually genial and kind, and I have always believed that, when
we parted, he was carefully reconsidering his course. He used
no harsh words in speaking of the President, and seemed to be
animated only by solicitude for the country, and never once referred to himself as a possible Presidential candidate.

As I sat, Wednesday, December 4, in the Church of the Divine Paternity, New York City, and noticed the multitude of
representative men—Thurlow Weed's aged form ; Chief Justice

Chase, with bare and bending head; William Evart's spare figure and mobile face; General Dix, the Governor elect of New York—among the pall-bearers; the President, his secretaries, and part of his Cabinet; the crowds of editors from all parts of the country—and heard the sacred music and the magnificent discourse of Dr. Chapin, I thought of the death and burial of the great Frenchman, Mirabeau, April, 1791. Very different were the two men, but their lives were equally eventful and their last hours equally dramatic. Mirabeau was exhausted by his frequent public speaking. Five great orations in one day finished him; and when brought to his final hour, he exclaimed, "To-day I shall die; envelop me in perfumes; crown me with flowers, and surround me with music, so that I may deliver myself peaceably to sleep." Our poor friend did not call for odors or roses or sweet strains; they came from the spontaneous love of his saddened friends. Like America with him, however, Mirabeau's death extinguished all the envies and enmities of the French. Party feuds dissolved in tears over his body, and he passed to his rest through an avenue of hundreds of thousands of former foes. Says the historian:

"The proceedings of the Assembly were immediately suspended, a general mourning ordered, and a magnificent funeral prepared. 'We will all attend!' exclaimed the whole Assembly. In the Church of Saint Geneviève a monument was erected to his memory, with the inscription:

'A GRATEFUL COUNTRY TO GREAT MEN.'

"It was situated next to that of Descartes. His funeral took place the day after his death. All the authorities, the departments, the municipalities, the popular societies, the Assembly, and the army accompanied the procession; and this orator obtained more honors than ever had been conferred on the pompous funerals which proceeded to Saint Denis. Thus terminated the career of this extraordinary man, who has been greatly

blamed, who effected much good and much evil, and whose
genius was equally adapted to both.   Having vanquished the
aristocracy, he turned upon those who contributed to his victory, arrested their course by his eloquence, and commanded
their admiration even while he provoked their hostility."

But how different the recollection of these two men!   Mirabeau is rarely recalled, and only as an impassioned tribune—a
man of sentiment rather than of action, with few fixed convictions.   Greeley will live as a marvelous aggregate, strong in
good works, his fame growing riper with the increasing fruits of
his gigantic labors for humanity.

[December 15, 1872.]

XCII.

I AM reading, with infinite zest, John Forster's second volume
of the Life of Charles Dickens.   Every page is a new pleasure,
every chapter a new revelation of the better side of the truest
friend of humanity in the literary world.   Neither Shakespeare,
nor Byron, nor Walter Scott, nor Tom Moore, nor Alfred Tennyson, deigned to show so honest a devotion to the poor and the
unfortunate as Charles Dickens.   He always seized the holidays, and especially Christmas, to extend his warnings to the
rich and his encouragement to the poor.   "Blessings on your
kind heart," wrote the great Jeffrey, of the *Edinburgh Review,*
in 1842, after he had read "The Christmas Carol;" "you should
be happy yourself, for you may be sure you have done more
good by this little publication, fostered more kindly feelings,
and prompted more positive acts of beneficence than can be
traced to all the pulpits and confessionals in Christendom."
"Who can listen," exclaimed Thackeray, "to objections regard-
ing such a book as this?   It seems to me a national benefit,

and to every man or woman who reads it a personal kindness."
"It told," says Forster, his biographer, "the selfish man to rid
himself of his selfishness; the just man to make himself generous; the good-natured man to enlarge the sphere of his good
nature. Dickens had identified himself with Christmas fancies.
Its life and spirit, its humor in riotous abundance, of right belonged to him. Its imaginations, as well as kindly thoughts,
were his; and its privilege to light up with some sort of comfort the squalidest places he had made his own." "With brave
and strong restraints, what is evil in ourselves was to be subdued; with warm and gentle sympathies, what is bad or unre-
claimed in others was to be redeemed. The Beauty was to
embrace the Beast, as in the divinest of all those fables; the
star was to rise out of the ashes, as in our much-loved Cinder-
ella; and we were to play the Valentine with our wilder brothers, and bring them back with brotherly care to civilization and
happiness."

After the "Christmas Carol" came "The Chimes," for the
holidays, in 1844. This beautiful story was written in Genoa,
Italy. The argument here, as in the first, was to induce the
rich to help the poor, and the poor to forget their miseries. It
is curious how he found the title of "The Chimes." He had
the subject, but not the name of his book, in his mind, and,
says Forster, "sitting down, one morning, resolute for work,
such a peal of 'chimes' arose from the city as he found to be
maddening. All Genoa lay beneath him, and up from it, with
some gust of wind, came in one fell sound, the clang and clash
of all its steeples, pouring into his ears, again and again, in a
tuneless, grating, discordant, jerking, hideous vibration, that
made his ideas spin round and round till they lost themselves
in a whirl of vexation and giddiness." "Only two days later
came a letter, in which not a single syllable was written but
'We have heard "The Chimes" at midnight, Master Shallow;'
then I knew he had discovered what he wanted." His one

great idea was always that the poor should be led out of their
poverty ; the vicious out of their vices ; the unfortunate out of
their misfortunes, and that Christmas was the season to enforce
the moral.   In Venice he said, " Ah ! when I saw those palaces, how I thought that to leave one's hand upon the time,
lastingly upon the time, with one tender touch for the mass of
toiling people that nothing could obliterate, would be to lift
one's self above the dust of all the Doges in their graves, and
stand upon the giant's staircase that Samson could not overthrow."

In 1845 he conceived that splendid Christmas ideal, " The
Cricket on the Hearth."   When he was deliberating it he wrote
to Forster that his new story should contain "*Carol* philosophy,
cheerful views, sharp anatomization of humbug, jolly good temper, and a view of glowing, hearty, generous, mirthful, beaming
reference in every thing to home and fireside ; and I would call
it, sir, ' The Cricket ; a Cheerful Creature that Chirrups on the
Hearth '—natural history."   " It would be a delicate and beautiful fancy for a Christmas book, making the cricket a little
household god—silent in the wrong and sorrow of the tale, and
loud again when all went well and happy."   Those of us who
recollect the wonderful charm of the " Cricket on the Hearth,"
with its weird and simple characters, will not need to be told
by Forster that " its sale at the outset doubled that of all its
predecessors."

Christmas always inspired him.   The holidays were his season of joyful thoughts and magnetic writing.   And now, as we
recall him in the glowing pages of his confidential biographer,
why should not we remember those who are so well and gratefully remembered during this immortal interval—the parenthe-
sis, so to speak, between the old year and the new—the pleasant porch in which we take leave of the one and enter upon the
other ?   A benefactor of his species, like William W. Corcoran,
of Washington, D. C., fortunate in his active life, and still more

fortunate in its closing days, because encompassed by the prayers of those he has aided by his liberality, and by the respect and honor of the great District he has beautified by his princely endowments—such a man ought to spend a most comfortable Christmas; and George W. Childs, of Philadelphia, whose royal bounties all the year round have so touching a crown in his holiday gifts to the needy, as if to show he does not forget how he broke the prison bars of poverty and escaped the "twin jailors of the daring heart;" and Jay Cooke, with his great heart full of the warmest impulses, and eager to help with uninquiring benevolence—the patron of every noble art and the helper of every stricken wanderer; and W. C. Rallston, of San Francisco, who, also risen from the ranks of toil, recollects that he should

and,
> "Give, as 'twas given, a blessing to thee;"
>
> "Gives, as 'twas given, a blessing to be;"

and bright Thomas A. Scott, a prototype of Rallston, who ever thinks of the unfortunate or the unlucky, and aids with equal modesty and profusion.

Thanks be to God! there are many more in the ranks of the living—more, many more, who prove that Humanity has yet earnest ministers in a world too often abused as cold and callous. Nor let us forget the graves of those who toiled to bestow their wealth upon the poor and the needy. There is an altar in Girard College where the orphans can spend Christmas in honor of the great Frenchman, who accumulated millions by hard work and close savings, that he might pour them down through the ages upon the fatherless and the motherless. There are palaces in London and colleges in the South where grateful thousands can recall every Christmas-day the New-Englander who was almost a miser in life, that, after death, he might approve himself a Midas in the distribution of his countless treasures for Charity and Education. And presently there will rise a temple to Art and to Benevolence, on the loveliest shore of the Delaware, in which the name of Edwin Forrest, never so honored as it will be on this coming Christmas, will be preserved as that of one who toiled through fifty years of successive penury, privation, triumph, envy, and admiration, that he might die the best friend of the unfortunate children of the English and American stage.

[December 22, 1872.]

XCIII.

JOSEPH HARRISON, JR., of Philadelphia, probably the richest man in that city to-day, was apprenticed in a machine-shop when he was fifteen. He was foreman in the same establishment when he was twenty, and at twenty-seven partner in one of the earliest locomotive manufactories in this country. Every life, however humble, is a lesson—sometimes an example, and sometimes a warning; but a lesson always. Joseph Harrison's experience is an example. Born in 1810, and now in his sixty-third year, it is interesting to follow his career, and to trace the effect of foreign travel, careful study, and business ambition upon a mind which had few or no advantages of early education. He was a worker in iron, and proud of his trade. Perhaps the words he used at a public dinner to Henry C. Carey, in 1859, may be cited as the ideal of his mission : " That glorious metal, Iron, must ever be the great agent for promoting the mechanic arts. Iron is the true precious metal, a metal so interwoven with the wants of life, and with our very enjoyments, that to do without it would be to relapse into barbarism. Take away gold and silver, and the whole range of baser metals, leaving us iron, and we would hardly miss them. Take away Iron, and we lose what is next to life, and that which sustains life, the greatest boon the Almighty has conferred upon man."

These words were spoken in 1859, and they are a more correct picture of the utilities and adaptations of iron in 1872. Covering most of the necessities of life, iron has become one of the essentials of art in its highest aspirations ; entering into the luxuries of our homes ; into the triumphs of our progress ; in fact, into most of the realms of science and imagination. And yet all the objects to which it may be applied are unknown. The iron production and development are in their infancy.

Mr. Harrison spent twelve years in Russia, building iron roads, locomotives, and bridges for the Emperor Nicholas, and receiving, with his partners, the costliest presents for the fidelity and efficiency of their work. In such society the mind of the young mechanic rapidly expanded. He saw a new civilization and entered upon a broader field. Intercourse with men of science gave him a deeper insight into the secrets of his own trade, and opened before him a future of boundless interest. He studied, not alone the practical, but the æsthetic side of the subject. He saw the finest specimens of art in the galleries of Europe, read the best books, and gathered information from his conversations with learned men, and when he came back to his native city he had grown in experience and in knowledge. But he had not forgotten that he was a worker in iron. He had not forgotten his humble origin, and if you could visit his magnificent mansion in Eighteenth Street, near Walnut, in Philadelphia, you would see in one of the panels in his gallery, among some of the finest triumphs of art, a picture called the "Iron-Worker and King Solomon," painted in 1865 for Mr. Harrison by the celebrated Christian Schuessele. The object is to show that iron is the chief agent in all the mechanic arts ; and a Hebrew legend is quoted, setting forth that when Solomon's Temple was about to be opened, the blacksmith, finding himself omitted from the list of invited guests, boldly marched into the Temple, fresh from the forge, and, taking the King's own seat, insisted that without him the splendid fane had never been con-

structed.   King Solomon heard the appeal, and the blacksmith
sat by his side at the royal feast.   And in a beautiful volume
of Mr. Harrison's writings, printed for private circulation, we
find the painting described in a very excellent poem, from his
own pen, dedicated to his "dear children and grandchildren,"
to impress upon their minds the value of what is too frequently
thought to be very humble labor.   Following the other pages
we find this idea elaborately presented by other hands, including addresses by Mr. Harrison on art and science before our
great institutions, and a proposition for the erection of a gallery of art in Fairmount Park, which is to be adorned by several
of the best pictures in his gallery, presented to the Park Commissioners.   There is also a series of careful essays on his
steam-boiler, an invention to prevent destructive explosions,
even when carelessly used.   The variety of the subjects discussed and the style of writing, the noble aim apparent throughout, show that Joseph Harrison's life has been a useful experience to himself, and a lesson and example to others.

[December 27, 1872.]

XCIV.

How to distribute large individual wealth is one of the prob-
lems of civilization.   Stephen Girard seems to have solved it,
if his great foundation, "The Girard College," is tested by its
marvelous and increasing success.   Its massive and harmonious
proportions, seen from afar, do not more recall and refresh his
memory than the occasional parades of the orphans through
the streets, or their decorum, subordination, and intelligence
within doors.   These youth make little noise in the world, but
they are felt, far and wide, as so many missionaries.   Their
gratitude to their benefactor is proved by the fact that there

are few failures among them. I know of many excellent men who have found the dead Frenchman a living father, and whose ability, integrity, and energy are the fruit of the seeds he planted. He survives in their ever-renewing gratitude; and if it were necessary, I could name lawyers, architects, physicians, manufacturers, bankers of eminence, who proudly look to Girard College as their *Alma Mater*. The orphan who goes in without a friend emerges with hundreds, and, what is better than all, with a self-respect that makes him richer than if he had been left the irresponsible heir of a fortune he could not count. The crop of boys is systematically replenished. They enter from six to ten, and are bound out, between the ages of fourteen and eighteen, to agriculture, navigation, arts, mechanical trades, or manufactures. No stigma attaches to their probation, and the name of Stephen Girard is enshrined among their sweetest memories.

As an illustration of the present position of the Girard College, of which so little is known to the outside world, it is only necessary to say that at the last annual meeting the reported number of pupils was 550! What a sight it would be if Girard himself could reappear upon the scene and study the harvest of his superb benevolence! He died on the 20th of December, 1831, in Water Street, above Market, Philadelphia, a little more than forty years ago. In this interval Philadelphia has grown into a vast metropolis, the nation into something more than an empire, and the world revolutionized by the agencies of science; but no wonder would so impress him as his own College and its matchless influence upon civilization. He would realize that his behests had not been disobeyed, and that his bounties had not been misspent. He at least sets a good example to other men of opulence.

I wish our American manufacturers and capitalists, whose colossal fortunes are no less the outgrowth of the industry of their workmen than of their own opportunities, could see the

town of Halifax (England), seventy miles from Liverpool, and
there study one of the most striking manifestations of individual
munificence in the world for the benefit of the laboring classes.
Sir Francis Crossley, lately deceased, lived at Halifax.   He
died leaving an immense sum for the use of his worthy opera-
tives.   He had no higher ambition than to promote the comfort
of those whose toil had made him opulent.   More than a thousand of them had taken advantage of his proffer and became
interested in his business, which is that of a manufacturer of
magnificent carpets.   His establishment is the largest in the
world, comprising eighteen and a half acres, using two thousand
horse-power in its steam machinery, giving employment to over
four thousand men, women, and children.   His patent looms
for the weaving of tapestry, velvet, and Brussels carpets, table-
covers, and hearth-rugs; his hand-looms for weaving Scotch
carpets; his facilities for preparing and weaving linen, cotton,
and woolen carpets, and for spinning, dyeing, and printing, are
all on the same premises.   These are not simply curious and
wonderful in themselves, but impressive evidences of human
ingenuity and skill.   I saw the thousands dismissed for and returning from their noon-day meal, and can never forget the
sight, especially as I turned to the beautiful town itself, a miniature metropolis, with long rows of elegant stores, comfortable
dwellings, a lordly town-hall, fine hotel, churches, and other
public buildings.   Every where you remarked evidences of the
wise generosity of Sir Francis Crossley and his family; every
where you saw how the enormous profits resulting from their
astonishing enterprises are shared with the industrious and the
deserving.   The beautiful park was the gift of the Crossleys
to the people.   The massive town-hall was built out of their
money, and an Orphanage for the education of the fatherless
children of their more emulous workmen.   The whole air of
the place, with its clean, stone-laid streets, the broad, level
roads in the environs, the well-dressed population, and the love-

ly valley in which it was set like a picture, comes back to me an instructive and pleasing memory. And when we reflect upon the incomes of many of our American manufacturers and capitalists, especially as we visit the busy centres in which they and their workmen live, we can not repress the prayer that the time may come, and come soon, when the contrast between the luxury of the employer and the poverty of the employed, in this country, may not be as startling as it is to-day. In other words, that while the riches of the one are almost incalculably increased, the comforts of the other should be as carefully considered and cultivated. The example of the great English manufacturer, Crossley, whose name, like that of Girard, the greatest of the benefactors of Philadelphia, will be remembered and revered as long as the town of Halifax stands, ought to be copied largely in the United States.

[January 5, 1873.]

XCV.

AH! if men of note could only realize how much their true fame depended on their biographies, written by themselves. Two late instances will suffice to prove the point. Had Charles Dickens and Edwin Forrest kept fair records of their experiences, what treasures they would have left to posterity! The French translator of Dickens's works once asked him for a few particulars of his life. He replied that he kept them for himself. I never met Forrest that I did not implore him to invite my faithful short-hand writer to report the story of his life, as he could only tell it himself; but the answer always was: "Not now; some time when we both have more leisure we will undertake it together." Alas! his light, like that of Dickens, was quenched in a second. Both these men were unrivaled talk-

ers, and they liked to talk among their friends. How full and
affluent their memories! how varied their trials! how unusual
their triumphs! One hour with Forrest, in private, when he was
in the vein, was better than an evening with him on the stage.
He was full of wit. Conversation brought him out ; and it was
wonderful how easily he unfolded his stores of information.
Foreign manners ; domestic customs ; the vicissitudes of his
early life ; his sketches of the public men he knew at home and
abroad ; his adventures in the old stage-coach, on steam-boats,
and cars ; his favorite books ; his pictures ; his statuary ; his
amazing *repertoire* of quotations and imitations ; even his prejudices—as these fell from his lips—would have made a volume
almost as interesting as " Boswell's Johnson." And this may
be said with even greater truth of Charles Dickens. Both died
suddenly, "in the twinkling of an eye," and the loss to the
world is beyond reparation. When we think how easy the art
of autobiography has been made by modern invention, it is painful to think how men, whose lives are crowded with knowledge
that should survive, postpone the pleasing task of recording
their recollections. What better materials for history than
these personal details ! Object as we may to the fashion of interviewing public characters, there is no reading like the reports
of their habits and ideas, and none more enduringly preserved.
Louis Napoleon is dead, and nothing that we have of him will
be more profitably recalled than Chevalier Wikoff's admirable
conversations with him after the fall of Sedan, in the *New York
Herald*. What a fine talker says in his social hours to a friend
is very different from what he writes. There is a sparkle in his
words, a flow in his sentiments, a freedom in his manner, that
can be photographed only by the quick skill of the short-hand
writer ; and once down, they last like the paintings of a great
master. A fair copy of Senator Nye's quaint sayings and odd
stories at one dinner-party would be a classic. The bright *bon
mots* of William M. Evarts, if they could be recovered, would

shine like gems in the choicest magazine. A night with Oliver
Wendell Holmes would supply gossip more delightful to literature than any thing he has achieved in "The Autocrat of the
Breakfast Table." Henry C. Carey, of Philadelphia, much as
he has written, is never so happy as when he relates the incidents of other days at his "vespers." My cherished and lamented friend, William Prescott Smith, used to set the cars in a
roar with his matchless skill in satire and in story. Nothing is
more eagerly read and re-read than a pleasant autobiography
or diary, whether it be Pepy's, Benjamin Franklin's, Boswell's
Johnson, Coleridge's Conversations, Crabbe Robinson's, the
recollections of the actor Young, by his son, or the works of the
elder Mathews. And if John Forster could have added a volume of Charles Dickens's own experiences, as these fell from
his lips, to the two he has already published, his book would be
without a rival in modern biography. The difference between
autobiography and biography is thus quaintly drawn by the
French author, H. A. Taine, in his late work on "The History
of English Literature :"

"On the day after the burial of a celebrated man his friends
and enemies apply themselves to the work : his school-fellows
relate in the newspapers his boyish pranks ; another recalls exactly, and word for word, the conversations he had with him a
score of years ago. The lawyer who manages the affairs of the
deceased draws up a list of the different offices he has filled,
his titles, dates, and figures, and reveals to the matter-of-fact
readers how the money left has been invested, and how the fortune has been made ; the grandnephews and second cousins
publish an account of his acts of humanity, and the catalogue
of his domestic virtues. If there is no literary genius in the
family, they select an Oxford man, conscientious, learned, who
treats the dead like a Greek author, amasses endless docu-
ments, involves them in endless comments, crowns the whole
with endless discussion, and comes ten years later, some Christ-

mas morning, with his white tie and placid smile, to present to
the assembled family three quartos of 800 pages, the easy style
of which would send a German from Berlin to sleep. He is
embraced by them with tears in their eyes ; they make him sit
down ; he is the chief ornament of the festivities ; and his work
is sent to the *Edinburgh Review.* The latter groans at the sight
of the enormous present, and tells off a young and intrepid
member of the staff to concoct some kind of a biography from
the table of contents. Another advantage of posthumous biography is that the dead man is no longer there to refute either
biographer or man of learning."

[January 12, 1873.]

XCVI.

WILLIAM HAZLITT, in his delightful " Table Talk," describes
an " Indian juggler," and makes his theme the occasion of
some humorous and sensible reflections. Meeting Signor Antonio Blitz at a last New-year's reception, in his sixty-third year,
I was reminded of that curious essay, and of the Signor's claims
to favorable recollection. His face is fresh, though not unwrink-
led ; his hair and beard are white ; his eyes bright ; his step
quick ; his vivacity fairly contagious. *Here* is a character who
has grown rich as a proficient in legerdemain, yet has outlived
criticism, and by the practice of a genuine philanthropy, and
the observance of his duties as a citizen, made himself an honorable name. For fifty years he has contributed to the innocent enjoyment of old and young. His peculiar talents, early
shown, induced his father to send him out upon the world when
he was a little over thirteen, making his first appearance at Ham-
burg, playing in succession at Lubeck, Potsdam, and the principal cities of Northern Europe, every where exciting wonder

as "The Mysterious Boy." After two years of adventure, the youngster returned home, in time to be folded in his mother's arms and to see her die. He was fifteen when he appeared in England, and had rare success, but did not venture upon the London boards till he was eighteen. Good fortune welcomed him from the first, and would have waited on him to the last had he not been cheated by his managers. His Irish and Scotch tours were full of incident and anecdote. In 1834, in his twenty-fifth year, he landed in America, and performed at Niblo's Garden, where he met Norton, the great cornet-player, so well known in Philadelphia, and witnessed the long contest between him and his rival on the same instrument, Signor Gambati, and played some of his best tricks on Hamblin and Price, the distinguished theatrical managers. After a tour of New England and the West, he appeared in Philadelphia under the patronage of Maelzel, the proprietor of the celebrated Automaton Chess Player, the Burning of Moscow, the Automaton Trumpeter, and the wonderful Rope Dancer, and made his bow at the northeast corner of Eighth and Chestnut Streets in that city. What scenes of our childhood come back to us at the mere mention of these names! He next journeyed through the South, the British Provinces, the West Indies, beginning at Barbadoes and ending at Havana. After his return to the United States he settled in Philadelphia, where he has ever since resided, to use his own words, "In my own house, with ample means for all the necessaries and comforts of life, surrounded by a host of near and dear friends, whose warm hearts and smiling faces always greet and cheer me." It was in Philadelphia that he spent most of his time, not relaxing his work, and giving pleasure to thousands of all conditions in life, in public and in private. No social party in the winter is complete without his cheering presence and amusing deceptions.

I have read the autobiography of Signor Blitz, published in 1872, not so much because it is the story of a successful necromancer, as to show how invariably he turned his talent to good account, and how often a ventriloquist and a "magician" may accomplish what defies the physician, the lawyer, and the philosopher. Some of these experiences will show that the good Signor has not labored as a mere juggler, but has left a broad white mark in history showing that he had a higher aspiration than the tricks of his trade.

His landlady in London was so alarmed by his skill, which she regarded as superhuman, that she begged him to leave her house. "Do go away sir, do; and, there, let me give you this, and perhaps you will not be tempted again;" and she handed him a Bible. He accepted it; but, on opening it, found and handed her a five-pound note from between the leaves, placed there quietly by himself, and then she felt that he was not in league with Satan. This same landlady had a son, who was the pride of her heart, but secretly an inveterate gambler, who played away all his earnings, and finally used his employers' money. The Signor resolved to save him if the young man would agree to his conditions. He gladly consented, and the Signor was duly introduced to the gambling-saloon, and began to play cards. At first he lost, but gradually won until he had secured one hundred and fifty pounds, when, with his friend, he left the place. But let Mr. Blitz tell the sequel:

"After I had gained the street, and was a considerable way from the house, where my visit had not been a very agreeable one to some, who wished me to remain longer, I turned and said: 'There, Harry, you see what I have done. This fortune, as you gamblers call it, is a cheat, and the money which I have taken from those scoundrels who robbed you, was done in accordance with their own principles. Here are the cards I played with,' and beneath the light of a street-lamp I showed him a pack of cards, so arranged that I could always hold the game in my hands. Besides, I designated marks by which I could tell the character of every card in the hands of my opponents.

'There,' said I, 'in those and similar ways lies the art of gambling. You have been duped, but I know that you will not be so again.

"'I see it all—but now it is too late!' exclaimed the poor fellow. 'Now I see my disgrace.'

"'Not yet; promise me but one thing and you shall be saved.'

"'What is it? I will do—aye, be any thing, only for my poor mother's sake.'

"'Give me your word of honor, then, that you will never again touch card or dice-box, and there is the money which I have won. Take it; pay back the sum which you have taken from your employers, make what honest and true account you can to your mother, and remember as long as you live the night of the 10th of March, 1829.'

"The young man promised, and I never had occasion to doubt but that he kept his word."

He not only puzzled and amused the ignorant, but the educated and the scientific, among the latter the celebrated Dr. Crampton, of Dublin, forty years ago, who fled with his students from his dissecting-room, when the Signor, who was present, threw his voice into the body of a female subject, and protested against the sacrifice. At Limerick, one of the female servants stole some jewelry from one of the ladies, and the Signor was called on to point out the culprit. He called all the servants of the hotel together, told them of the theft, and said he knew the guilty one was in the room; but, to avoid all exposure, he would wait a few hours, to give a chance for the return of the property. At midnight the poor girl came to his room, gave back the jewelry, and on her knees begged forgiveness, and prayed she might not be exposed, as it was her first offense. He promised, kept his faith to her, and restored the trinkets to their owner. The incident added vastly to his fame. A rascally tax-collector was seen carrying off one of his rabbits, and the Signor proceeded to his house and demanded it. The

scamp denied his crime, and a dispute ensued, when the rabbit
broke from its concealment, exclaiming, in a gruff tone, "You
are a scamp, and the Lord have mercy on your soul." "Who
dares call me a scamp?" screamed the thief. "I do!" the
rabbit answered. "You never paid a ha'penny for me, Ryan.
Did you not bring me here last night from the hall? To-night
I will call my imps from below, and take you to the deepest
regions of fire." The scoundrel took fright, and restored the
rabbit as one "bewitched." The whole community were relieved at the detection of the dishonest official. One day he
frightened an exorbitant landlord into decency by making a
parrot echo his own denunciation of the tyrant. He was introduced to ex-President Van Buren (often called "the Little Magician") in New York, and exchanged compliments, which
closed by Mr. Van Buren saying, "I have often seen our names
coupled, as wielding the magic wand; but I resign to you the
superiority. You, Signor, please and delight all ages and sexes,
while my jugglery is for political purposes." O'Connell, the
Duke of Wellington, and many of the nobility visited his rooms,
just as Van Buren, Clay, and Webster patronized him in this
country. Once he saved his life by imitating a conversation
with different persons in different voices, and mingling all with
the barking of two dogs. This was when he lived near the
New York Croton Works, while they were in course of construction, and when Fifty-third Street was beset by ruffians. His
jokes were never cruel, as, for instance, his taking a bottle of
whisky out of the hat of Governor Briggs, of Massachusetts, a
noted temperance man, or his asking the Boston philanthropist,
Josiah Bradley, to lend him his coat for one of his tricks, which
the good old man did, to the infinite amusement of Daniel Webster, who sat in the audience. He was welcome at Harvard
University, and played for the *alumni* and the *acolytes*. The
great and graceful Justice Story came often to his exhibitions,
and would take a seat among the boys on the front bench, en-

joying himself to the full, " where he would laugh away dull
care," and, returning home refreshed, " would write till morning ; for nothing so restores the brain as a good hearty laugh."
He met Millard Fillmore on a canal-boat in the West, and years
after saw him in Washington, when Mr. Fillmore said, " Little
did I expect, Signor, when traveling with you on the canal, I
should ever become President of the United States." His description of the great Automaton Chess Player, and of the two
players—Maelzel, the inventor, outside, and Schlomberg within
the figure—both masters of that scientific game, is full of interest. " Maelzel and Schlomberg were, in their time, the great
living representatives of chess ; their hearts and feelings were
so identified with the game that they dreamed of it by night
and practiced it by day. At every meal and in all intervals a
portable chess-board was before them. They ate, drank, and
played, while not a word escaped their lips. It was a quiet,
earnest, mental combat, and the anxiety of every pause and
move was defined in each countenance, their features revealing
what the tongue could not express." Schlomberg died of a
fever, and poor Maelzel expired on his way from Havana to
Philadelphia, and was buried in the ocean. The Automaton
Chess Player was destroyed by fire with the Chinese Museum,
and the Automaton Trumpeter is now the property of Mr. E.
N. Scherr, the retired piano-maker of Philadelphia. He relates
a pleasing incident of the illustrious John Bannister Gibson,
Chief Justice of Pennsylvania, one of his best friends, who was
surprised to find the Signor's wallet in his pocket, though he
sat at a distance from him. His interviews with Webster and
Clay, during John Tyler's administration, proved the respect
they had for him. " Give me," he said to Webster, " one hundred thousand Treasury notes to count, and watch closely, and
you will find only seventy-five thousand when I return them."
" Signor," responded Webster, with lively animation, " there is
no chance ; there are better magicians here than you ; there

would not be fifty thousand left after their counting." Henry
Clay asked him to visit the Senate Chamber and throw his voice
among his Democratic friends, so that they might vote for the
measures they had opposed, and added, " It would cause a glorious excitement among the Democracy." He met John Quincy
Adams in Canada, and was much impressed by his conversation.   In his tour to the West Indies he had a fine field in the
superstitions of the people.   They regarded him as something
more than mortal, and called on him to work impossibilities.
The sick, the lame, the blind, the unfortunate, hailed him as the
good physician. He told them he was no dealer in miracles,
no spiritualist, no astrologer, nothing but an artist traveling to
make a living for himself by giving innocent pleasure to others,
and at the same time to show by his own progress the progress
of science.   Yet, with these qualities, he did what many an ancient necromancer would have failed in.   He reconciled hostile
parents to the marriage of faithful lovers ; frightened the drunk-
ard into temperance ; infused courage into a ship's crew during
a storm at sea, and once compelled the restoration of her fortune to a poor girl by making the portrait of the dead brother
of the dishonest guardian speak in stern rebuke of his guilt.
But no part of this curious character is so agreeable as his constant attendance upon the insane.   With his birds, his rabbits,
his ventriloquy, he is greeted with joy by the poor creatures,
whose minds, " like sweet bells jangled out of tune," are made
briefly happy by his kindness and his skill.   During the war he
was omnipresent in the hospitals, performing gratuitously to the
maimed and broken, filling the hours of convalescence with joy,
and smoothing the pillows of the weary.   He gave one hundred
and thirty-two entertainments before sixty-three thousand soldiers, and three weeks, every afternoon and evening, at the
" Great Sanitary Fair," in Logan Square, Philadelphia.   All
this work was gratuitous.   I quote from his autobiography his
own idea of his mission :

" Such witless sighing and croaking oddly contrast with the full free bursts of glee which break forth from the merry troops of children we meet on every hand, or the loud and joyous songs of the bright birds, to whose pure notes the streams and winds join their full chorus.

" It was a laugh which gave birth to Eden's first echo, and why not let it still live on ?

" He who gives us one hour's pure pleasure is a far greater philanthropist than he who prates of charity and heaven, which can only be obtained, so says his creed, by passing through lives of sighing, fasting, and continued slavish fear of Him who would have us in all things free, living for the beautiful and good alone."

This is my ninety-sixth anecdote ; and yet, among the numerous characters I have attempted to describe, no one has done more to promote the happiness of his fellow-beings than Antonio Blitz.

[January 19, 1873.]

XCVII.

FOR many years before the war the northwest corner of Seventh and Chestnut Streets, Philadelphia, was a popular resort of public men of all sides. The head of the house was Harry Connelly, one of the handsomest men I ever knew, and full of excellent traits. You would not have taken him for the proprietor, with his exquisite dress, ruffled shirt, and easy manner. He was like one of his guests, and left his business to a bright mulatto called " Lew," who was the *factotum* of the concern, and relieved his employer from a world of care. Both master and man are gone, and the old dingy building has given way to a stately structure, in part of which Colonel Greene's *Sunday*

Transcript is printed and published; but the men who gathered in the ancient back room every day for years still live in many memories. They met involuntarily, and spent many happy hours. Harry Connelly saw much of society of all kinds, and was an especial favorite with the Southerners. He was the intimate of many of the great horsemen of Kentucky, and he had been present at more than one desperate personal encounter. Naturally most amiable, he believed in the *code of honor*, and was a party to more than one "affair." A prince in expenditures, and a gentleman in manners, his rooms were sought by his friends far and near. " Harry Connelly's " was the scene of many important discussions and business operations. It was a rendezvous for people of diverse views and objects— a sort of neutral ground, where every body uttered his own ideas, and where every gentleman was tolerated. And it was pleasant to note that those who gathered at Connelly's were always careful in their treatment of each other. Henry Clay liked Harry as one of his original supporters, and frequently dropped in with his friend, ex-Mayor John Swift; Daniel Webster, who stopped at Hartwell's (now Bolton's) Washington House, two doors off, liked to take one of the rickety armchairs and talk to the pleasant host, and John J. Crittenden would stay for hours to gossip over the times. I have met in this dark back room, with its low, cobwebbed ceiling, most of the public characters between 1845 and 1860. Robert T. Conrad, author of " Jack Cade," and Robert M. Bird, author of the "Gladiator;" David Wilmot and Henry M. Fuller ; John C. Breckinridge and Jesse D. Bright; James Buchanan and John Slidell ; Josiah Randall (father of the present Representative from the First Congressional District, Pennsylvania), and James Watson Webb ; George W. Barton and Ovid F. Johnson; James A. Bayard, who was a Senator in Congress, and George Gordon ; Stephen A. Douglas and W. A. Richardson ; John R. Thompson, of New Jersey, and George Law, of New York ; the

Pennsylvania Governors, D. R. Porter, W. F. Packer, W. F.
Johnston, and Andrew G. Curtin ; George Ashmun and Charles
F. Train, of Massachusetts ; Thaddeus Stevens, Jack Ogle, Dr.
William Elder, Justice Thompson, Henry S. Magraw, Aristides
Welch, D. K. Jackman, A. K. McClure, Charles Wister, of Pennsylvania, were among the visitors.   You met there the kings of
finance, of the stage, of the turf, and of politics.   It was altogether a novelty, a spontaneous growth.   I look over the long catalogue of those who made " Harry Connelly's " their head-quarters, and discover that while most of them are dead, none who
survive can fail to realize that when our generous friend was
himself called away we lost one of the few who was never half
so happy as when he was making others happy.

[January 24, 1873.]

XCVIII.

THE art of caligraphy, or fair handwriting, is one of the most
useful of accomplishments, and the manner in which a man
puts down his thoughts is often taken as an index to his character.   But it is a great mistake to suppose that all our statesmen, old and new, did not or do not write plainly, and that the
habit of rapid composition and heavy correspondence leads to
carelessness.   Washington's State papers, his letters, and his
accounts, are models of order and cleanliness, rather set off by
his antique spelling.   James Madison wrote a small, beautiful
hand, in keeping with his chaste and classic oratory.   General
Jackson wrote with the direct boldness of his nature, though
somewhat indifferent to his orthography.   James Buchanan
prided himself upon his cautious style, his careful spelling, his
exact punctuation, and the absence of interlineations.   Henry
Clay wrote plainly, like an outspoken and intrepid soul.   Web-

ster's hand, without being ornate, was strong.   George M. Dallas was a master of the art.   Nothing could be more exquisite or more graceful, in manner and matter, than his notes and letters. John Van Buren was not nearly so exact as his great father. Albert Gallatin wrote like copper-plate.   I hold in my hand a letter of his, dated New York, April, 1843, in which, referring to Thomas Jefferson, he says: " As the testimony of the only surviving member of Jefferson's Cabinet—as one entirely acquainted with him, who enjoyed his entire confidence—I can bear witness to the purity of his character, and to his sincere conviction of the truth of those political tenets which he constantly and openly avowed and promulgated.   I do also aver, with a thorough knowledge of the facts, that for his elevation Thomas Jefferson was solely in debt to the sense entertained of his public services, and of his well-known political opinions, and that he was, altogether, the spontaneous choice of the people—not promoted by any intrigue, nor ever nominated by any assembly or convention, but without any preconcerted action, and yet without competitor, selected unanimously in every quarter as their candidate by the majority which elected him."   No lady in the land could surpass this fine autograph.   Martin Van Buren's tribute to Jefferson is written in a rather large hand, and in a flowing style.   He says, " With the single exception of General Washington, no man ever lived whose claims upon the gratitude of mankind for public services were greater than those of Jefferson."   How beautifully the lamented William Wilkins, of Pittsburgh, whose venerable widow is now living in elegant retirement in Philadelphia, spoke on the same theme in the same year : "Why is it," he asks, in a most satisfactory handwriting, "that time, so fatal to ordinary reputations, only serves to brighten the fame of him we delight to honor?   The cause is not to be found in any or all the great actions of his life, however illustrious ; it is due to that of which all these were but the outward manifestation, of the earnest and deep-seated confidence of the people. He loved and trusted his species—he has taught us this great secret of his confidence." And here before me are two letters, one from each of the rival candidates for Governor of Pennsylvania thirty years ago—Henry E. Muhlenberg and Francis R. Shunk—both accurate and intelligible, and that of Shunk unusually bold and large. Thomas Ritchie wrote a hand not quite so difficult to make out as that of Mr. Greeley, but in the same style. His editorials were dashed off in great haste, sometimes on long slips, sometimes on small ones, and he composed with extraordinary facility. General Cass, who wrote much, and always like a scholar, had an editorial hand; while Andrew Stevenson, of Virginia, father of the present Senator from Kentucky, could have set copies for a country school, and yet in the ardor of composition he would make himself very difficult to decipher. Senator Sumner's writing is characteristically large and distinct; short sentences, carefully pointed, good ink, and excellent stationery—somewhat after the Parliamentary fashion. He is a prodigious worker, and, I fear, even in his prostration, can not keep his hand from pen and pencil. Caleb Cushing writes very rapidly, and it requires one familiar with his manuscript to interpret it. Of all men, however, none was harder to understand than Thaddeus Stevens. I have some notes of his which would puzzle an expert. John Lothrop Motley, the historian, is singularly precise. Thackeray seemed to rejoice in small feminine characters, and took great delight, in his letters to his friends, in decorating the border with all manner of curious caricatures. Robert T. Conrad, the poet, was a most delicate and *dilettante* writer. Some of his poems were not less models of literary beauty than of mechanical taste. William B. Reed, so well known in politics and in literature, writes a hand much like the venerable Henry C. Carey—fair to look upon, but sometimes hard to decipher. Stephen A. Douglas dashed off his letters without much regard to appearance. He seemed to be always under a high pressure, and what he wrote was written with intense feeling.   John C. Fremont signs his name boldly, a little after the Dickens style. William H. Seward was excessively particular in the preparation of his speeches, and composed with deliberation.   I heard an old stenographer say that after he had taken down Mr. Seward, literally, in one of his greatest efforts, and presented him the full report, the statesman recast the whole discourse, and sent it to the printers in his own hand.   Senator Morton writes in bold, round characters.   Thurlow Weed's is significantly editorial—anybody who sees it can tell that he has reeled off multitudinous leaders.   McMichael, of the *North American*, writes nervously, in straight lines, frequently hard to solve.   He would be a fortune to any newspaper if he would allow a short-hand reporter to take down the words as they fall from his lips.   We have no better debater nor conversationalist.   Boker, the poet, prides himself upon his cool and dainty chirography.   Rufus Choate was a dreadful affliction to the printers when they got hold of his legal papers, and the man who most resembled him, in his time, George W. Barton, of Pennsylvania, was almost as prolific in his oratory as in his handwriting, and it was far easier to enjoy his magnificent rhetoric than his written sentences. Fillmore's style was methodical and slow; Pierce's quick, bold, and legible; Lincoln's small, careful, and rather labored; Grant's unpretending, and easily read.   Perhaps I can not better terminate this desultory anecdote than by giving you the following copy of an autograph letter, now before me, written by Edwin Forrest in 1856, when he sent a subscription of two hundred dollars to the treasurer of the Democratic Committee of Pennsylvania to defray the expenses of electing James Buchanan.   It is very carefully composed, and indicates the business exactitude which marked him throughout life.   The verse of poetry which he inclosed with his check seemed to have been cut from a country newspaper, and was pinned to his signature :

"Boston, November 29, 1856.

"My Dear Sir,—You must excuse me for not replying sooner to your letter of the 21st inst., but an unusual press of business, and other matters, prevented me from doing so at an earlier period.

"I herein inclose you a check for two hundred dollars, which you will apply to the liquidation of the debt incurred by the Democratic Committee during the late political canvass.   Truly yours,

"Edwin Forrest.

> "'When Fremont raised a flag so high,
>   On Rocky Mountain's peak,
> One little busy bee did fly,
>   And light upon his cheek;
> But when November's ides arrive,
>   To greet the Colonel's sight,
> Straight from the Democratic hive
>   *Two* B's will on him light—
>   Buck and Breck.'"

[February 9, 1873.]

XCIX.

A republic in Spain, bloodless as yet, and therefore full of promise of permanence, is indisputably the significant event of the times. As a peaceful revolution, it is a menace more formidable than armies to the absolute powers. As a result of free opinion and fearless discussion, it marks the education of nations and their upward growth to good government. Exactly how it will progress, or where it will end, save that it is one of those advances that know "no retiring ebb," it is not necessary to debate. The formal and almost unanimous proclamation of the Spanish Republic, and the abdication of the foreign Italian King, remind me of an anecdote which may now be related as an instance of prophecy fulfilled. Edwin M. Stanton was always friendly to Daniel E. Sickles, and when the latter was most bitterly assailed he had a stanch champion in the

great lawyer, before and after he was a member of Lincoln's
Cabinet. He believed the talents of Sickles were too signal not
to be made use of during the war, and when the war was ended and Grant was President, he strongly urged that the accomplished New-Yorker should be called into the diplomatic service.   When, therefore, General Sickles was appointed American Minister to Spain, in 1869, Mr. Stanton was much gratified.
The ex-Secretary was at home at his residence, on K Street,
Washington, D. C., when General Sickles and myself called on
him.   He was reclining on his bed as we entered his chamber,
but he rose and greeted us heartily.   It was evident that he
was doomed.   Worn out in one of the severest struggles that
ever taxed human energy, and wasted in the weary conflict with
Andrew Johnson, all that was left was the clear and magnetic
brain.   Walter Scott in his magnificent "Talisman" describes
Richard of the Lion Heart sick in his tent among the Crusad-
ers, and that splendid portraiture might have been applied to
the invalid Secretary, with his feeble frame, and eager, nervous
interest in passing events.   Nothing escaped him.   He was *en
rapport* with the whole machinery of affairs, full of solicitude
for Grant, and earnest for exact justice to all sections.   "I
wanted to see you both," he said ; "you, General, as the new
Minister to Spain, and you, Forney, as my steady newspaper
friend. We must make no mistake about Spain.   She is one
of our oldest and ablest allies, and behaved splendidly to us
during the rebellion, refusing to open her ports to the Confederate cruisers, and never plotting through her Minister here,
like England, against our cause.   The Spaniards are a proud,
peculiar race, and we can not do any good for liberty in Cuba
by hasty action.   Their prejudices must be respected ; their interests must not be invaded ; their traditions must be remembered.   Things are moving in the right way at Madrid.   I know
this, gentlemen.   There is a new Spain, and you will both live
to see a solid Spanish Republic there if we can only restrain

our politicians about Cuba. That pear is ripening, and will fall as soon as the days of the kings are ended in Spain." There was much more, equally emphatic and pointed. The wise, cautious, yet fearless conduct of General Sickles at the Spanish court greatly aided the Republican cause, and contributed much to the preservation of peaceful relations with the United States, and I have no doubt that this sagacious and prophetic counsel of Mr. Stanton was always present in the memory of the American Minister at Madrid.

[February 16, 1873.]

C.

ON January 15, 1871, the first of these anecdotes, of which this is the last, appeared in the *Washington Sunday Morning Chronicle*. Written to rescue some of my experiences of men and things, they grew upon my hands until I found myself pledged to extend them to a hundred. As I review the curious medley, they resemble a picture-gallery crowded with familiar faces, many of them, in fact most of them, dead; and, alas! not a few within the little more than two years during which these hasty sketches have appeared.

Following out the plan of delineating the best traits of my subjects, just as the painter conceals the blemishes even as he achieves a faithful portrait, I have also attempted to discover the objective point of every life, especially if this could be set out as an example to the young. What better theme could I desire, then, than George W. Childs, the proprietor of *The Public Ledger*, who will not be forty-four till May 12, 1873? He has accomplished as much in the last quarter of a century, and has done as much for his fellow-beings, as any character within my recollection. In his fifteenth year he came to Philadelphia, like

Benjamin Franklin, without a friend or a dollar. His only wealth was industry, perseverance, and a stout heart, and with these resistless weapons he fought his way through inconceivable obstacles, until he has become the living illustration of that noble characteristic, so rare among men of affluence—*the accumulation of riches, not for himself alone, but to make others happy during and after his life.* I take it that a man who utilizes such a theory can afford to be criticised, as Mr. Childs has been, by a few of those who never see a good action without seeking a selfish motive for it. But a fine example is its own best eulogy. It lives and it lasts. It bears fruit before our eyes and refutes censure by practical results. Instances like this are infrequent. Wealth too often breeds avarice and suspicion. Too many hoard money for a graceless posterity, and in blind selfishness make themselves miserable while they live, that they may leave fortunes to spendthrift children. The career of this young man, Childs, teaches so different a lesson, that a friendly reference may perhaps stimulate others to an earnest imitation of it. And when we read this career in the light of the story of *The Public Ledger,* and how he got possession of it, and how he has improved and enhanced it, it sounds very like a romance.

The first number of *The Ledger* appeared March 25, 1836. The proprietors were three journeymen printers—W. M. Swain, Arunah S. Abell, and A. H. Simmons. It was published at six cents a week, and rapidly rose into a great circulation, not alone because its proprietors were energetic, but because they were bold and independent. Wisely employing the powerful pen of Russell Jarvis, they took the right side of every question, and especially the right of the people to assemble in public meeting and discuss all matters of principle or policy. *The Ledger* did not hesitate to criticise courts and juries, and to expose oppression, and was soon involved in a libel suit, which it met with a pluck that excited universal applause. Jarvis was a writer of vast ability, a little too personal and trenchant, but possessing a style of rare force and fascination. He grappled with every question. He chastised the rowdyism of the students of the two great medical colleges, who had long terrorized the city; he denounced, with terrible invective, the burning of Pennsylvania Hall on the 17th of May, 1838, by a mob of madmen, resolved that no speeches against human slavery should be delivered in Philadelphia; and when that infamous cowardice was followed by attempts on the two succeeding days to destroy the asylum for colored children on Thirteenth Street, above Callowhill, and the African Church in Lombard Street, near Sixth, the mob made several demonstrations against *The Ledger* office; but as it was known that Mr. Swain was in hearty sympathy with his brave editor, and was prepared to defend his property at every hazard, the ruffians were cowed. Not less fierce were *The Ledger's* denunciations of the Native American riots in 1844. Such newspaper courage was uncommon in Philadelphia, and for a time *The Ledger* suffered severely, but it gradually recovered its prestige, and grew into enormous influence. It was after these events that George W. Childs, a lad of eighteen, who had worked as an errand boy in a bookstore three years before, hired a little room in *The Ledger* building. Here he waited his opportunity. Sixteen years after, December 3, 1864, he startled the town by the announcement that he had purchased the great paper.

The example set by the original proprietors was not forgotten. There is at least equal enterprise, the same independence, tempered by a less personal tone, and the same vigilance over the interests of Philadelphia and the State. But a new element pervades the establishment—an element characteristic of Mr. Childs in his first successful business venture—that of helping others out of his own fortune. A few instances will show how steadily he has worked to this end. Before he was twenty-one he was in the firm of Childs & Peterson, book publishers. A

work compiled by Mr. Peterson, entitled "Familiar Science,"
young Childs pushed into a circulation of two hundred thousand
copies.   Dr. Kane's " Arctic Expedition " he put forth in splendid style, and paid a profit to the author of $70,000.   He en-
gineered Senator Brownlow's book in the same way, and paid
over to the eccentric Tennesseean a premium of $15,000.   More
than any other influence he deserves the credit of the great
success of that massive work, "Allibone's Dictionary of Authors."
The following tribute on one of the initial pages of that book—
perhaps the most indispensable in every library—is more enduring than any title of nobility :

"To George W. Childs, the original publisher of this volume, who has
greatly furthered my labors by his enterprise, and zealous and intelligent interest, I dedicate the fruits of many years of anxious research and conscientious toil.   S. AUSTIN ALLIBONE."

George W. Childs never fails a friend.   His brother publisher, George P. Putnam, of New York, prints a letter in which he
gratefully acknowledges the prompt and cheerful manner in
which Childs gave him his name as security for $100,000 in his
hour of adversity.   After referring to this act of substantial
friendship, Mr. Putnam speaks of Mr. Childs as publisher of *The
Ledger :* " Such an enterprise as would positively frighten most
of us timid and slow-moving old fogies, you in your shrewd energy and wide-awake sagacity enter upon as a positive.   You
wave your magic wand, and, lo ! palaces rise, and the genii of
steam and lightning send forth from their subterranean cells
and lofty attics thousands of daily messages over the continent ;
and fortune follows deservedly, because you regulate all these
powers on liberal principles of justice and truth."

There are three hundred and nine employés in *The Ledger*
establishment, exclusive of the newsboys.   At a Fourth of July
dinner given to them by Mr. Childs in 1867, the accomplished
general manager, the leading editorial writer, W. V. McKean,
made some interesting statements.   These workingmen, he

said, represent a large amount of individual capital, not less than half a million. "The carriers, although they do not make the highest wages, have been among the thriftiest of the employés, and the aggregate value of their *Ledger* routes would sell at the Merchants' Exchange, as readily as Government securities, for a sum not less than two hundred and fifty thousand dollars." At the same time, Mr. Mucklé, who has charge of the cash department, "referred to what he considered the great feature of the day—the assemblage of one hundred and ten newsboys, where all was joy and happiness. Here again was another evidence of Mr. Childs's kindness ; and, as another striking proof of his kind disposition, he would state that during the two years of the present proprietorship he had dispensed for him more money in charity than was given during all his twenty-three years' connection with the establishment."

These three hundred and nine employés sent to Mr. Childs a testimonial, in which they called him their honored and esteemed employer, and expressed their heartfelt thanks for his great kindness and consideration for all of them, continued without intermission since he had been proprietor of *The Public Ledger;*

"For your innumerable acts of generosity and courtesy, of which all of them have been the frequent and gratified recipients ;

"For your goodness of heart, your benevolence, your enterprise, and your cardinal virtues, which not only honor you, but reflect honor upon those who labor for you ;

"For the uniform justice with which you have ruled *The Public Ledger* office—a justice always tempered with mercy—a mercy always anxious to pardon ;

"And, above all, honored sir, your employés desire to thank you :

"For having built a palace for them to work in ; a printing-house which is unparalleled in the world ; a printing-office which, in all its departments, is the most healthy, comfortable, and spacious on the American continent.

"For all this, and more than this, that you have done for them, your employés desire, though it be in insufficient words, to convey to you their most sincere thanks."

What this gratitude means was told by the lamented Ellis Lewis, former Chief Justice of Pennsylvania, at the dedication of the Printers' Cemetery, a gift of Mr. Childs to the Philadelphia Typographical Society. I was present on that occasion, and can never forget the effect produced by the following words of the venerable man, now in his grave:

"Some men pursue military glory, and expend their time and energies in the subjugation of nations; Cæsar and Napoleon I. may be named as types of this character. But the blood and tears which follow violence and wrong maculate the pages of history on which their glory is recorded. Others erect splendid palaces for kingly residences, and costly temples and edifices for the promotion of education and religion, in accordance with their particular views. But views of education and religion change, buildings waste away, and whole cities, like Herculaneum and Pompeii, are buried in the earth. Others, again, win public regard by the construction of means of communication for the furtherance of commerce. The canals, railroads, and telegraphs are glorious specimens of their useful exertions for the public good. But the marts of commerce change. Tyre and Sidon and Venice are no longer commercial centres. The shores of the Pacific are even now starting in a race against the great commercial emporium of our continent. But Mr. Childs has planted himself in the human heart, and he will have his habitation there while man shall live upon earth. He has laid the foundation of his monument upon universal benevolence. Its superstructure is composed of good and noble deeds. Its spire is the love of God, which ascends to heaven. Such a monument is indeed

> "'A pyramid so wide and high,
> That Cheops stands in envy by.'

"I have not enumerated the numerous private charities of Mr. Childs. The magnificent building which he erected for *The Ledger* at a cost of half a million dollars, as a newspaper establishment, is unparalleled in the world; and he could not erect this building without providing that the press-room, composing-room, and reporters' room, and every other room where his employés are engaged, should be carefully warmed, ventilated, and lighted, so that they should be comfortable in their employment, and enjoy good health in their industry. Even the outside corners of his splendid building could not be constructed without bringing to the large heart of Mr. Childs the wants of the weary wayfarer on a hot summer day. Therefore it was that each corner is provided with a marble fountain to furnish a cup of cold water to every one who is thirsty. Mr. Childs provides for the health of his employés during life. He has introduced bath-rooms into various parts of the building for the use of the workingmen, who avail themselves freely of the privilege afforded them. He secures an insurance on their lives for the benefit of their families after death, and even then he does not desert them—he provides this beautiful and magnificent burial-lot for the repose of their lifeless bodies. Such a man surely deserves the love and gratitude of his fellow-creatures on earth, and the blessings of his Creator in the world to come."

No charity appeals to Childs in vain; no object of patriotism; no great enterprise; no sufferer from misfortune, whether the ex-Confederate or the stricken foreigner. He enjoys the confidence of President Grant, and yet was among the first to send a splendid subscription to the monument to Greeley. He, more than any other, pushed the subscription of over $100,000 for the family of the dead hero, George G. Meade, and yet Alexander H. Stephens, of Georgia, has no firmer friend. His list of unpublished and unknown benevolences would give the lie to

the poor story that he craves notoriety.   When I carried letters
from him to Europe in 1867, his name was a talisman, and it
was pleasant to see how noblemen like the Duke of Bucking-
ham honored the indorsement of an American who, thirty years
ago, walked the streets of Philadelphia without a friend or a
dollar.   He made his money himself, not by speculation or
office, and got none by inheritance.   He coins fortune like a
magician, and spends it like a man of heart.   He likes society,
and lives like a gentleman.   He is as temperate as Horace
Greeley ever was, and yet he never denies his friends a generous
glass of wine.   His habits are as simple as Abraham Lincoln's,
yet his residence is a gem bright with exquisite decoration, and
rich in every variety of art.   He gives a Christmas dinner
to newsboys and bootblacks, and dines traveling dukes and
earls with equal ease and familiarity.   He never seems to be
at work, goes every where, sees every body, helps every body,
and yet his great machine moves like a clock under his constant supervision.

In a sketch like this I have no space to do more than allude
to *The Ledger* under the management of Mr. Childs ; to the palace, which cost, with the ground, over $500,000, in which he
prints and publishes it, and to his circulation, running at times
to 95,000 copies a day.   But there is one aspect that must not
be omitted as I close these anecdotes.   I mean the perfect independence of the paper in regard to local and general corruptions.   It does not hesitate.   It strikes out bold and quick.   Its
rhetoric is not so trenchant as that of Russell Jarvis, when he
took "the bull by the horns" twenty and twenty-five years ago,
and when he stirred the sensibilities of the medical students and
the pro-slavery mobs ; but it is more effective, because more
moderate.   George W. Childs, an intimate friend of President
Grant, does not fail to tell him in his *Public Ledger*, as he does,
I hope, in his private talk, that among those who affect to support Grant in Philadelphia, there are creatures who do not care

three continental farthings for him, except as they can use him. It is something to feel that there is at least one man in Philadelphia who has money enough not to want any more, and who can afford to tell General Grant the truth without being accused of a longing for his favor.

INDEX.

Davis, Jefferson, as a speaker, 58.
  Walter, of Maryland, 57.
Dawson, John L., his "Buried Joe Sanders" story, 274.
Decoration Day in Washington, 91.
Democracy, course and death of, 344.
Democrats in Convention in 1844, 117.
Diaries : of John Quincy Adams, 14 ; of James Buchanan, 14.
Dickens, Charles, 294 ; his extensive humanity, 400 ; his Christmas feelings, 401.
Dimitry, Alexander, description of, 279.
D'Orsay, Count, and Louis Napoleon, 368 ; his character, 370.
Dougherty, Daniel, his lecture on Oratory, 56.
Douglas, Stephen A., compared with Washington, 18 ; anecdote of, 19 ; monument to, 20 ; great extent and variety of general information, 21 ; supports annexation of Texas, 51 ; retained friends, 146 ; at the outbreak of the Civil War, 225 ; his western tour, 225 ; dies at Chicago, 226 ; overborne by the South, 325 ; a defeated Presidential candidate, 362 ; his sons, 226.
  Mrs. Stephen A., 307.
Douglass, Frederick, on the Decoration Day, 92 ; a great orator, 337.

Elder, Dr., anecdote told by, 16.
Ellet, Mrs. Mary, a nonogenarian, 221.
European cities, how governed, 348.
Evening Star, of Washington, 385.
Ewing, George W., Indian Agent, a letter from, revealing the Slocum romance, 208.
Executive Session of the United States Senate, 72.

Fairmount Park, Philadelphia, proposed statues of Pennsylvania worthies in, 218 ; Art Gallery in, 406.
Faulkner, Charles James, of Virginia, 57.
Felton, Samuel M., his narrative of Mr. Lincoln's escape from assassination, 248.
Fiction, truth in, 293.
Fillmore, Millard, and Signor Blitz, 417.
Fitzgerald, Thomas, his pictures, 98.

Forrest, Edwin, Clay's apology to, 10 ; at the Astor House, 70 ; Sympathy with the Union, 76 ; at the Mills House, 77 ; letter from, 425.
Forrest Letter, use made of, 13 ; statement relating to, 35.
Forney, John W., elected Clerk of the House, 32 ; "Mazeppa" speech by, 33 ; letter from, at opening of the Thirty-fourth Congress, 109 ; edits *Washington Union*, 110 ; retires from, 194 ; solid compliment to, as Clerk of the House, 381.
Franklin, Dr., his indignant reply to Lord Howe, 393.
Frederick the Great and Lord Bristol, 265.
Freedman's Savings Bank, in Washington, 234.
Fremont, John C., explores California, 314 ; opposed by T. B. Benton, 22.
Freneau, Philip, extract from his satirical verses, 239.

Gales & Seaton, of the *National Intelligencer*, 109.
Geary, John W., anti-slavery Governor of Kansas, 32.
Gibson, Chief Justice, 214 ; and Signor Blitz, 417 ; on D. P. Brown, 214.
Girard, Francis J., a versatile journalist, 108.
  College, 407.
Globe, The Congressional, 105.
Grant, General U. S., letter to, from Secretary Stanton, on the capture of Richmond, 186 ; story of his first nomination for President, 287 ; his disinclination, 288 ; his character resembles Washington's, 340.
  Mrs. U. S., in the White House, 312.
Greeley, Horace, 69 ; his *Log Cabin* and *Tribune*, 328 ; his solid friendship, 374 ; Sumner's tribute to, 397 ; last interview with, 398.
Guy, John, of Baltimore, and General Lewis Cass, anecdote of, 165.
Gwin, Senator W. M., of California, 314.

Hall, Dr. J. C., of Washington, his anecdote of President Jackson, 189.
Handwriting of public men, 421.
Harper's Weekly, pictorial satire in, 329.

444   INDEX.

THE END,